How to be a
Successful
Frauditor

A Practical Guide to Investigating
Fraud in the Workplace for
Internal Auditors and Managers

PETER TICKNER

A John Wiley and Sons, Ltd, Publication

ISBN 978-0-470-68185-5

A catalogue record for this book is available from the British Library.

Project Management by OPS Ltd, Gt Yarmouth, Norfolk
Typeset in 10/13pt Photina and Univers Light
Printed in Great Britain by TJ International Ltd, Padstow, Cornwall

Contents

Foreword

I first became aware of Peter Tickner when the Metropolitan Police Authority was created in June 2000 to take over responsibility from the Home Office for the budget, scrutiny and oversight of London's Metropolitan Police. I was elected as the first Chair of the MPA and soon found that we had a robust and tenacious chief internal auditor with a somewhat fearsome reputation as Scotland Yard's very own rottweiler. What is more, this attack dog was quick off the mark with a (gleeful) warning to the incoming Authority that the Metropolitan Police didn't have a system for telling whether it had paid a bill more than once and that we should get on with sorting this out.

Peter had already made his mark as Director of Internal Audit at the Metropolitan Police since 1995 where he had been involved in successfully investigating fraud and financial waste by, among others, works and maintenance contractors, IT consultants and police employees. Following the GLA elections in 2004, I stood down as Chair of the MPA, but was reappointed to the Authority as the Home Secretary's representative. It was then that I joined the Corporate Governance Committee, to which Peter regularly reported. I took over as Chair in 2006 and with that found myself responsible during the next three years for trying to exercise a degree of control over Peter's activities as Director of Internal Audit. As anyone who knows Peter will appreciate, this was no mean task and, perhaps surprisingly for a relatively dry subject, Corporate Governance meetings were often lively. This was in no small degree due to the occasions where Peter would draw attention to matters of financial probity or fraud that had crossed his path since the Committee had last met.

I soon realised, as did fellow members of the Committee, that although Peter was a thorough audit professional he had a particular interest in the frauds and financial waste that came to light in his work. It was therefore no surprise when he announced that on his retirement he would be writing a book about how to investigate staff and contractor fraud.

I am delighted to be asked to write the foreword to this, Peter's first book—and one that focuses on his favourite area of business activity.

Right up until his retirement from the MPA in September 2009 I met regularly with Peter in private session to discuss, inevitably, some of his more sensitive investigations as well as progress with the audit programme. Some of these internal inquiries were very high profile and often ended up featured in national newspapers, with the inevitable pressure that the spotlight brought to bear on progress with his investigations.

I am sure that you will find Peter's professionalism and knowledge of the subject matter will shine through in this book. He has also written it in his own inimitable style—a style that I can confirm he also brought to the Committee table, although sadly the official minutes cannot reflect the wry sense of humour and the enthusiastic presentations when we strayed onto Peter's two-minute 'Mastermind' topic of fraud.

Lord Toby Harris

Preface

've written this book for anyone who's either found themselves asked to investigate a fraud or has wanted to get involved with a fraud investigation at work but doesn't feel they know enough to go about it successfully. Whether you are an internal or external auditor, trainee investigator or line manager who finds they need to conduct a fraud investigation on behalf of your employer, or indeed just an employee or academic with an interest in the subject matter thinking of taking it further, then this book is intended for you.

The story of my own journey from auditor to 'frauditor' started in December 1971, when I was appointed as a trainee executive officer in the Department of Health's National Health Service Audit Branch.[1] In those days you started working life in NHS Audit straight into 'the field', reporting in my case for a first-day's duties to the Audit Room at a large psychiatric hospital in Kent. We had no permanent office, desk or telephone, as only the appointed Auditor for each NHS region had such luxuries. We were expected to be provided with temporary accommodation at each hospital group where the audit was taking place. Because of this nomadic lifestyle we were inevitably forced to get out and about in the NHS and see what went on in reality—and as such it was an excellent grounding for any auditor or would-be frauditor. We travelled from hospital group to hospital group conducting their external and operational audits, borrowing

---

[1] Technically the DHSS but Health and Social Security remained entirely separate, each with their own personnel, finance and audit departments, despite the years they were merged together.

working accommodation and office supplies at each unit where we were auditing.

The first week into the new job, as a 19-year-old and still wet-behind-the-ears trainee NHS auditor, I was sent out with a more experienced colleague to observe the routine weekly 'pocket money' cash payments to the long-stay psychiatric patients at a large hospital in the southeast. I overheard one of the patients, after collecting his weekly cash, turn to the Charge Nurse and say 'Here's your cut, Bill.' The Charge Nurse turned bright red and said to the patient 'For Christ's sake not now, the auditors are here!' I was shocked, genuinely shocked. My more experienced colleague was not. He looked me up and down calmly, only the tiniest hint of sadness mixed with the cynicism borne of the 20 years more of life's twists and turns etched into his face. 'Peter, just think of anything in this world that a human being can do—and they will do it!'[2] These were wise words indeed and stayed with me throughout my career.

A few weeks after stumbling across the patient's money scam, at our next audit I was sent out with one of the other experienced auditors on the team to conduct a surprise visit and cash-up at the hospital offices. He wasn't so keen to have an inexperienced junior sent out with him and was very clear to me about it on the way to find the hospital cashier's office. 'Do as I say, don't touch anything, don't question anything I say and keep your ******* mouth shut until we have finished. Is that clear?' It certainly was and, considerably affronted, for once in my life I did exactly as I was told, even when behind my colleague's back I noticed the cashier slip a roll of notes into his back pocket before they had been counted. I had been told to keep my '******* mouth shut' so I was absolutely determined that it would stay shut while we were there.

Later, as we were driving away from the hospital in his two-seater sports car, I meekly asked if I could speak now. 'Of course,' came the somewhat irritated reply. I put on my most anxious-to-learn expression. 'Is it normal for the cashier to take a roll of notes out of the safe and put it in their back pocket before we have counted it?' He very nearly swerved off the road and then sharply pulled the car up to an immediate halt. 'What?' he screamed at me, 'why by all the thundering gods didn't you say anything back there about it?' I paused as innocently as I could. 'But you told me to keep my mouth shut until we had finished.' After the frisson that followed,

---

[2] Bernard Mensa Boateng, colleague, friend and 'personal tutor' during my 'field' years in NHS Audit, 1971–1978.

" GOODBYE. THANKS FOR THE AUDIT ! "

I was, thankfully, given back to the cynical and worldly-wise Bernard to learn the ropes from then on!

What my NHS Audit experience did teach me over the years was that there was a lot of fraud going on out there and most of the bosses I worked for either couldn't see it or our lords and masters were less keen to pursue it than we were. The frauds and scams Bernard and I found being perpetrated on the NHS in the 1970s, long before the NHS Counter-Fraud Service came into being, are still around in modern variants today. It was very much where I cut my teeth, both learning from the experienced and cynical auditor alongside me and also learning by my mistakes, one of the best and most practical ways of becoming a successful frauditor.

After 12 years in NHS Audit I had a five-year spell teaching auditors from all parts of central government before I became Head of Internal Audit at Her Majesty's Treasury. While I was there I managed to keep up my track record by unearthing a few scandals, including sending an undersecretary who'd been in charge of a government agency to prison for fraud.

My track record and lucky timing (they had just had a major fraud!) got me the job that I did for the last 14 years of my career as the Director of

Internal Audit for the Metropolitan Police in London. I had only been there a few weeks when thanks to my usual luck I found myself on the trail of an armed robber who'd slipped under the radar and managed to get his company a works and maintenance contract with the police. Within a year I had so many fraud investigations on the go that my then bosses gave in and let me set up an internal fraud investigation team, headed by a retired detective superintendent who'd done several tours at various ranks in the Fraud Squad. His experience proved invaluable and filled in the blanks in my investigative education.

Eventually the investigative side of my work expanded to a branch headed by an experienced ex-head of internal investigations from HM Customs, nine investigators, a fraud prevention manager and two analysts in support. Over the years we were able to save Scotland Yard and the tax-payer millions of pounds as well as remove fraudulent contractors and staff from the organisation. We were also able to clear innocent people wrongly suspected of wrongdoing (an often forgotten benefit of doing an investigation thoroughly).

In this book I'm trying to pass on to you the accumulated experience of 38 years as an auditor and investigator—a frauditor—covering from the very basics of how you find and deal with cash frauds, through to investigative techniques, dealing with the police, the law, taking civil action, types of fraud that you're likely to come across and understanding the risks of fraud for your organisation. My style is conversational and wherever possible I've tried to give you real cases from my own experience as examples of what can go both right and wrong during fraud investigations and the ways in which you can ensure that you have the best chance of being a successful frauditor.

Do have fun reading this book, that way I can assure you that you will learn much more from it. All the case studies are from real life and there isn't anything in the book that hasn't actually happened.

Writing this book over the months that it has inevitably taken has brought back many fond memories for me of past cases and investigations, as well as painful reminders of times when I got it wrong, experiences that I hope will enable you to learn from my mistakes without finding the need to repeat them yourself, whether you are working on your own, as part of a small unit or as part of a larger team when the call comes to investigate a fraud at work.

Acknowledgements

F irst, I have to thank Elaine, my wife, who has had to put up with me at home far more frequently than she was expecting, following my decision to retire early and have a change of career. Since then I've written away obsessively, occasionally surfacing from the study to exclaim about some fraud I've remembered—or to give a few well-chosen expletives when a computer failure has just prevented me saving the latest version of the chapter I've been working on.

I must give a special mention to Spencer Pickett, who convinced me that I could and should write this book and then showed me how to get the project off the ground. Also my special thanks to Barrie Cull, former colleague and friend who has kindly provided the excellent cartoons that you will find in this book. And a thank you to Mike Comer, who to my mind wrote the seminal book on fraud investigation and who was generous enough both to encourage me that I could also write a book about fraud and to let me refer to one of his earlier cases.

I am grateful for advice and assistance from former colleagues and friends: in particular, Ken Gort, Assistant Director (Forensic Audit) at the Metropolitan Police Authority, without whose help I'd never have sorted out the structure and some of the investigative content of this book; ex-Detective Chief Superintendent Phil Flower, whose invaluable knowledge of both the law and the police were of great help; retired Fraud Squad Detective Superintendent Russ Allen, for friendship, encouragement and reality checks in equal quantities; Alan Wright, retired police intelligence officer, for his helpful views on the use of analysts and intelligence; Neville Dyckoff OBE, former Head of Catering at the Metropolitan Police, for letting me take further advantage of his hospitality in using one of his cases from an earlier career; and Catherine Crawford, MPA Chief Executive, for kind comments on my early draft chapters.

I am also grateful for the comments and advice I have had from: Head of the Governance and Counter Fraud Practice Derek Elliot; Alan Bryce and staff in the Counter Fraud Practice of the Audit Commission; Greg Marks and his colleagues at CIPFA; Professor Alan Doig for forbearance and support (I will get back to the PhD one day Alan!); Richard Kusnierz of IDM Ltd—who reviewed the early draft of Chapter 7 and made some helpful suggestions; Alan McDonagh and Caroline Waddicor of Hibis Europe for their support and encouragement; and the Metropolitan Police Authority for permission to reproduce an extract from its 2009 *Fraud Risk Analysis*.

I am bound to have forgotten someone, but others who deserve thanks for their kindness and support when I first started on the journey that led to this book include: Joe Mensah for sticking by me when it really mattered; Steve Hutton for his cheery enjoyment of my bizarre sense of humour; Paul Randall for his friendship, remarkable intelligence and equally remarkable indifference; Julie Norgrove who cleared up behind me at the MPA and seamlessly took over as I approached retirement; Satya Minhas for a decade of loyalty and friendship; Pam Brar for more loyalty and for longer than anyone deserves; likewise Andy Dimon; Irene Lloyd for quiet yet effective support; Colin and Emma Durnford for their friendship and support; Mike S. Robinson for friendship and cynicism in equal measure; Frank Hailstones for sharing the passion; Linda Duncan for her advice and encouragement; Jim Scully and Gareth Oakland for sharing some of the frustrations in one of my longest and toughest investigations.

Last and not least I must thank Minnie, our 12-year-old tabby cat, who has spent many hours beside me when I've been busy on the book, occasionally waving a paw at the keyboard or indicating that she's concerned about what I've just written, but generally sitting patiently by my side and keeping me calm in my more excitable moments.

Part PART ONE **I**

Understanding fraud

CHAPTER ONE

Fraud overview

Falsehood and fraud shoot up in every soil—the product of all climes

Joseph Addison (1672–1719)

CHAPTER**SUMMARY**

What do we mean by fraud? An up-to-date definition—and an old one as well. The Fraud Act 2006. Drawing a distinction between fraud and corruption. Getting to grips with understanding and recognising fraud. The guiding principles at the start of a fraud enquiry. Simple cash frauds and their recognition and detection.

WHAT DO WE MEAN BY FRAUD?

This isn't as straightforward to define as you might at first imagine. At a glance it is simply a deceitful act perpetrated by one person on another. A sham, a lie. But lies and deceit can occur without fraud, so how best can we define the specific characteristics of fraud?

Fraud as a concept has been understood ever since human society became organised. More than one ancient Greek or Roman author has commented on fraud in state affairs or business. Closer to home the Saxon and Danish kings in England understood fraud but it took William the Conqueror to set out the first English administrative system designed to prevent and detect fraud. He made his barons and sheriffs 'account' annually for their business affairs and had his most trusted aides hold 'audit' courts to hear what the barons had to say against the previous year's records. It was these arrangements, designed both to maximise tax revenues and to set out an ordered feudal system, that eventually led to the idea of accountants, auditors, controls and segregation of duties (i.e., the basics of modern business controls in the public and private sectors).

Although there have been legal maxims around fraud enshrined in codifications of English and UK law that developed during the Middle Ages, these references do not define what is meant by fraud. Instead they set out its impact on the legal system in coming to a judgement about a matter affected by the fraudulent behaviour of one or other of the parties in court. For instance, it is a legal maxim that 'fraud is odious' and that a fraudster shall not profit by their own fraud in a judgement by the courts. However, until 2006 there was no criminal offence of 'fraud' in UK law and, apart from Scotland, no common law offence either. All that changed with the Fraud Act 2006, enacted in UK law from 15 January 2007.[1]

Many bodies had attempted to give an all-embracing definition of fraud before that, particularly the major accountancy and auditing bodies. Most of these definitions either were incoherent, too detailed and therefore lacking clarity, or too oriented towards the accountancy profession and not user-friendly for would-be investigators. For UK police and those conducting criminal investigations, prior to the Fraud Act they generally placed their reliance on the Theft Act to define whether an offence was likely to have been committed by a fraud reported to them.

Perhaps the snappiest older definition came from a Scotland Yard Fraud Squad detective sergeant at the National Police Detective Training School, who in the 1980s defined fraud simply as *a sophisticated sort of thieving* to each new generation of would-be detectives. In many ways that description has to have been the most accurate of all until the 2006 Fraud Act came into being.

The 2006 Fraud Act describes and defines three key types of fraud that are the most relevant to organisations, their employees and their contractors.

- Section 2: Fraud by false representation
- Section 3: Fraud by failing to disclose information
- Section 4: Fraud by abuse of position

Having given these new offences some thought, my then Head of Forensic Internal Audit[2] and I came up between us with the following new definition of fraud in 2008:

> Fraud is an offence resulting from dishonest behaviour that intentionally allows the fraudster or a third party to gain, *or* cause a loss to another. This can occur through false representation, failure to disclose information or abuse of position.

If in doubt, then fall back on the definition of that old (and wise) detective sergeant. The one aspect that his broader definition covers and that is not covered by most others, including the accountancy and audit bodies, is the modern world where fraud can be a paperless crime.

The sad truth is that most professional bodies—and the professional members of those bodies do not want to be seen to be responsible for detecting fraud—and I include police officers among that number.[3] No one minds a straightforward theft, where it is clear what has been stolen and who has lost it, even if you don't immediately know who took the cash, asset or other item that has been stolen. Fraud is usually much more complex and most people would prefer it to be someone else's problem.

DRAWING A DISTINCTION BETWEEN FRAUD AND CORRUPTION

Corruption, effectively collusion between two or more individuals in order to commit fraud or other serious crimes, is generally far more difficult to get to grips with than fraud. Except, oddly, inside organisations such as the police—where much research and effort in the last 30 years has gone into the means of detecting corrupt police officers dealing with the public and bringing them to account for their behaviour.

Corruption can take many forms and its defining characteristic is that the colluding parties conspire together to enable the intended event to occur, which might be a fraud, or could be as simple as the enhancement of an individual's career through corrupt influence. Fraud may or may not involve others and individuals can commit frauds on other parties without the need to involve other fraudsters, but corruption can only take place between two or more individuals.

As a general principle, you should *try to avoid having to prove corruption when looking at potentially fraudulent activity*. The only exception to this is when two or more conspirators are either caught in the act with irrefutable proof (e.g., reliably recorded on camera and sound—and preferably a suitably upright citizen as a witness as well) or all the parties to the corruption are prepared to confess on paper and when interviewed. It doesn't usually help the investigator with a case if only one party admits the corruption, although it can be useful intelligence that may help find a fraud further down the line.

For a classic example of the difficulties in pursuing corruption with its roots at the top end of an organisation, the case of Gordon Foxley is worthy of study, even just from the details available through the likes of Wikipedia. Foxley was the Head of Defence Procurement at the Ministry of Defence (MoD) between 1981 and 1984. Prior to that he was Director of Ammunition procurement for a number of years and during that time had developed cosy and corrupt relationships with a number of major suppliers of ordnance to the MoD. The MoD is one of the few organisations in the UK that has its own private police force, including a fraud squad, and it was to them that the responsibility for investigating Foxley's activities finally fell. They estimated that Foxley had received millions in bribes. The case took many years and cost an inordinate amount to the taxpayer to bring home. Eventually Foxley was convicted in 1996 on £1.3m of bribes and sentenced to four years. He was due to serve a further sentence if he did not hand over assets purchased with bribe money. Foxley never did and the Crown Prosecution Service 'forgot' to pursue him about it. After serving two years, mainly in an open prison, Foxley was a free man with most of his ill-gotten gains still in his possession. As a result of one of his corrupt deals the Royal Ordnance Factories were closed with the loss of thousands of employees' jobs.

The investigation into Foxley was also a classic example of the difficulty in dealing with fraud and corruption cases once they become a criminal investigation, more of which will be covered in later chapters.

There is a great tendency in my line of business to see every fraud as a conspiracy and indeed on occasion frauds can involve a large number of employees or contractors. However, history clearly shows that hard as it is to bring home a fraud case, it is 10 times harder to prove corruption, whether in civil or criminal proceedings. It is far simpler and safer to look for the evidence that you need to prove what each individual has done. Then, as soon as you have sufficient information, you can act. Prevarication, waiting for the 'Mr Big' or over-elaborate and complex investigations to get to the root of everything have an inverse proportional relationship between the complexity and length of the investigation and the likelihood of a successful outcome.

Short and sharp works, long and complex doesn't. For an object lesson in long and complex leading to inevitable and ultimate failure, just take the case of Her Majesty's Customs and Excise, an organisation prone in its latter years to run overly elaborate investigations to find 'Mr Big'. The end result of this approach? They deliberately let millions in unpaid duty escape them, never caught the ring-leaders, compromised themselves with their own informants and in the end paid the ultimate price—when the department lost its independence and most of its investigative responsibilities in the merger with Inland Revenue to create HMRC, the hiving off of its ports business to the UK Border Agency and the residue of its investigators to the Serious Organised Crime Agency (SOCA).

I think that I know the difference between fraud and corruption, but how do I know whether I've found a fraud?

I'm tempted to give the trite answer here—that only experience ever answers this question—but one of my driving reasons for writing this book is in the hope of helping others learn from my early mistakes and experiences—to equip the reader better to answer this very question and then learn how best to determine what to do next.

For any organisation, discovering fraudulent activity by employees, contractors or outside organisations can come about by a wide range of circumstances. Usually it is readily apparent that something has gone or is going wrong and as a consequence the organisation is losing cash or other assets to fraudulent activity.

So the starting point is the ability to spot whether something is going wrong—and whether that is causing a loss to your organisation. For those who are internal auditors or middle managers reading this book, then you are already well equipped to spot a potential fraud. You will know your organisation and what you expect to happen. The art is to get to the bottom of why the expected hasn't happened—and learning when to persevere and persist until you can answer that question.

There is a basic truism inherent in every fraud ever committed on any organisation. The fraudster intends one of two outcomes. Either (1) to steal cash or assets from your organisation or (2) divert cash or assets intended for your organisation to themselves or a third party. So, *the guiding principle for the investigator is, wherever possible, to follow 'the money'*. Ultimately its trail will lead you to the fraudster.

The fraudster's motive is always greed, wanting something to which they are not entitled, although they will often intellectualise the reason for committing the fraud and may deny (as some have) to their dying day that they did it for anything other than the noblest of reasons. It is this self-justification and rationalisation—particularly prevalent among managers who commit fraud against their own organisation—that allows an otherwise apparently moral and socially responsible individual to continue their fraud. Don't be fooled or feel soft-hearted. Fraudsters are greedy, they want something that isn't theirs and they are prepared to alter records and lie and cheat in order to get it. They are not pink and fluffy—or innocent victims—however convincing their tale of woe may seem when caught.

Understanding your way to finding a fraud

For those of you who have had training as auditors or managers, you will have probably spent some time, whether overtly or by more subtle means, looking at the behavioural aspects of your fellow human beings. Much is made about the need to adopt a more participative approach to tackle some of the negative images associated in the mind's eyes of employees when an auditor calls. Equally, managers are usually taught to understand their staff and how their own actions and behaviour can be perceived by their employees. The techniques taught in these areas can be used to advantage in trying to track down potential frauds, by enabling you to understand how the behaviour of others is being perceived within their offices and enabling you to recognise mismatches between body language and words used.

Many years ago I spent some time training internal auditors for government bodies. I used to emphasise to them that in any part of an organisation *there are always three systems—the prescribed, the alleged and the actual*. The 'prescribed' is the system laid down in the manuals or set out in practice notes and the like. The 'alleged' system is the one that management will be keen to tell you is the way that it is done. It will inevitably usually meet most, if not all, of the expected controls to prevent fraud in a particular business area. But the 'actual' system will be the one that managers and employees are applying in practice on the ground. Until you can be sure that you have found the actual system, you won't know for sure what is happening in that part of the business.

The same applies when looking for signs of potential fraud. You need to be able to find out what has been going on in practice, as opposed to the idealised view that everyone is so keen to impart when asked. It is a natural human trait to look for short cuts or to become blasé about routine tests and controls, particularly if they have developed a working or social relationship with any of the individuals to whom they are supposed to apply the controls.

Almost all frauds have relied at some point on either the manager that turns a blind eye, over-familiarity by checking staff who don't bother to check thoroughly or a relaxed attitude by work colleagues to supposed controls as they all know each other and they don't believe that anyone they know that well will do anything wrong at work.

 ## CASH, CASH, CASH

Stop thief!

The simplest frauds are those that involve the straightforward removal of cash (or other portable assets) and its concealment by altering or suppressing the records.

Taking the cash or assets without altering the records is just plain and simple theft. If an auditor or manager (or indeed a colleague) discovers that a member of staff or a contractor has been stealing from the organisation in such a direct way it should be relatively easy for the line manager to institute disciplinary or other formal action immediately. In all decent organisations theft is grounds for swift dismissal as an act of gross misconduct by a member of staff and instant removal from the premises for a contractor. As with any fraud, you need to establish the scale of the loss to the organisation as quickly as possible and then decide how best to recover any lost cash or other assets.

I will return to this point later but *the guiding first principle with cash or asset losses is to stop any on-going loss as soon as you can.* Don't worry about getting in the way of a later criminal enquiry. If you have reason to believe that significant cash or assets are being lost in real time then your priority is to stop the haemorrhage as soon as you can, before your organisation runs out of its lifeblood.

The investigative decisions for the organisation on any scale of theft above low-value opportunist theft are little different from those outlined in this book for pursuing fraud and can read across to the same decision-making points described in Chapters 3 and 4.

This section covers some of the commonest cash frauds and ways in which they can be detected.

With cash, the highest risk is the point at which an organisation receives it, the next highest is the place where it is kept before it gets banked and entered into the accounting system.

At first glance, the records of cash receipts at an organisation may look complete. But the trouble with cash and cheque income is that you can only ever know the totality of what you have received and recorded, not what the organisation should have received. Modern analytical techniques can help here (see Chapters 6, 7 and 9) but even they won't always tell you about something that you've never had. The same also applies to cash floats or imprests,[4] you can only be sure about that for which the records are complete.

Surprise, surprise!

Never, ever underestimate the value of surprise.

One simple—and often under-used—way of finding out if all the cash is where it should be is the surprise cash check, although it is important to do your research thoroughly before embarking on such a course of action.

I had an early experience that taught me two vital lessons about surprise cash checks. First, do your homework before a visit to any outlying part of the business and, second, keep your wits about you. When you are out there at the organisation's coal-face, you will come across frauds and fraudsters, whether or not you recognise them.

Real case: Example 1

As a young health service external auditor in the 1970s, I often found myself with a colleague conducting cash checks, starting with the main cashier of a hospital group. On this occasion, we turned up as planned—but unannounced—to do a surprise cash count at the cashier's office of a large psychiatric hospital in Kent. As usual, we made the cashier open his large, walk-in safe, with books and records as well as cash within it. We started to count the money and then hit our first problem. The cashier's records showed transactions between his cash account and another account at the same hospital—a second cashier in another building. We hadn't known about this—although if we had done our homework properly we would have realised that it was not unusual for a large psychiatric hospital to have a 'patients' bank' as well as the main hospital cashier.

As it was, there were only two of us and we couldn't cash up both safes at the same time, since we needed one to record and the other to count, also to act as witnesses for each other in case we found any money was missing. I took an executive decision to continue the main cash count and leave the other one until we had reconciled the records where we were. Needless to say, the records would not reconcile to the cash. We worked out that the cashier was short of £200—shown on a scrap of paper in the cashier's handwriting as a 'loan' to the other cashier who ran the patients' bank.

As we couldn't agree the reconciliation with the first cashier I couldn't leave him alone while we went to cash up the other safe, but I had no other auditors available to help me. In the end I left my less experienced colleague with the first cashier and went to check the second cashier on my own. When I counted the cash, he too was short of £200—but had a note in his cash drawer saying that he had loaned it to the main cashier (who had also signed the note). I went back to the main cash office, now looking for £400, not £200 as I had first thought. The first cashier had disappeared. I was not a happy bunny and I told my colleague as much. 'I thought I told you to stay with him until I got back.' I snapped. 'I tried,' he replied, 'but he insisted he had to go to lunch and just walked past me, I haven't seen him since.'

We sat down contemplating what to do next. At that moment, to our surprise, the cash office door opened and the cashier appeared from within and beckoned us to come inside. I looked meaningfully at my colleague. 'Peter, honestly, he didn't come back past me and this is the only door.' As we walked in, I noticed that the window to his ground floor office was wide open. The cashier's invisible return was at least no longer a mystery. The cashier was beaming. 'Think I've solved your problem lads, I forgot about that envelope with £400 I'd put to one side to sort out the patients' bank.' He then took us into the walk-in safe and reached for a white envelope clearly sticking out between two books. He opened it and, hey presto, there was £400 in new, shiny £10 notes. Just like magic. Very tight-lipped I thanked him, noted our records and withdrew with my colleague. My less experienced companion seemed happy. 'Well, that's a relief then, Peter.' 'No it ******* isn't' I growled, 'I searched all those books earlier while you were checking the contents of the cash drawer. There was no envelope there then!' 'Ah.'

A lesson learned the hard way. We couldn't prove anything because we had compromised our own cash-up, first through poor preparation—not realising that there were two safes and two cashiers—and then by allowing the first cashier to leave before we had completed our checks and got him to sign up to the cash deficit. But I knew what had happened and now I knew that the first cashier was dishonest and capable of committing theft. I had a quiet word with the treasurer about it. He caught him trying the same trick a few months later and fired him on the spot.

THE BASIC AND BASIS OF ALL CASH-HANDLING FRAUDS—TEEMING AND LADING

So—I have a question for you before we get into this troublesome area of morality. Is it fraud or theft to borrow money from the petty cash of an organisation overnight, if the individual intends to replace it the next day? Of course you will have answered 'yes'. But a surprising number of people I've met over the years don't think that it is. And although the answer is indeed yes, it is unlikely that anyone would ever get charged or convicted criminally for a small amount, returned the following day in a one-off instance. But if they've done it and got away with it once, why stop there? It is only one short step from 'just borrowing it—I'll put it back when I go to the bank tomorrow' to a full-blown fraud.

Although anyone who is capable of 'borrowing' from the official cash of an organisation is, in my view, a future fraudster as well as a current thief, sometimes a bit of over-exuberant claiming or one-off dodgy-looking expenses voucher is just that, over-enthusiasm egged on by a colleague or ignorance about what is right, rather than a premeditated attempt to defraud. The investigator has to learn to tell the difference between the two. For instance, in most of central government, one could claim a meal allowance if more than five miles away from the office for at least five hours and *actually* and *necessarily* incurring expense. I have known otherwise upright internal auditors absolutely insist that it is their right to claim the allowance, because they were more than five miles away for more than five hours, even though they were eating lunch in a subsidised work canteen no different from their normal lunchtime arrangements. They had conveniently 'forgotten' the actual and necessary part of the right to make that expenses claim. *So, another 'rule of thumb' principle when looking for fraud: Don't get obsessed by the one-off incident. Everyone makes mistakes.* However, if you see more than one such incident (preferably at least five if you want to guarantee to nail the fraudster) then, as with the fictional Holmes, the game is afoot!

If you know how teeming and lading works—and how to spot it—you can happily skip to the 'General Principles' at the end of this chapter. If not, then read on and I'll explain.

Teeming-and-lading study: Fictional example

Freddie Fraudulent banks cash and cheques received by his company every weekday. On Monday morning he opens the post and finds £1,000 in cash and £3,500 in cheques. Monday lunchtime he banks the previous Friday's takings, £4,300 in total. On Tuesday morning he opens the post and finds £750 in cash and £3,000 in cheques. Tuesday lunchtime he banks £4,500, the total of Monday's takings. On Wednesday morning he opens the post and finds £1,500 in cash and £2,600 in cheques. Wednesday lunchtime he banks £3,750, the total of Tuesday's takings. Thursday morning Freddie opens the post and finds £1,200 in cash and £4,000 in cheques. Then Freddie makes up a bag to go to the bank with £4,100, the total of Wednesday's takings.

Just before Freddie is about to go to the bank on Thursday the internal auditor, Arthur Sleep, arrives to carry out a surprise cash check. Freddie points out a little crossly that he has just put the previous day's takings together to go to the bank and hasn't yet had time to write up today's takings. Arthur doesn't want to offend him and agrees just to check the takings prepared for the bank. They do indeed tally up to the total of the previous day's takings, but Arthur is a little puzzled, as the split of amount received between cash and cheques doesn't seem to be the same as shown in the post-opening book records for the previous day. Freddie explains that he cashed some personal cheques for staff and that altered the split of money. Arthur reminds him that it is company policy not to do this and makes a note.

Arthur is about to leave it at this when he notices something odd about the cheques making up the total of Wednesday's takings to be banked. Two of the cheques are definitely not from staff but are also not in the post-opening records for Wednesday either. He checks to see if they were accidentally missed off from Tuesday's post-opening records but they weren't and, as they both have Tuesday's date, it seems unlikely that they were received any earlier than that and left off from the subsequent banking.

Before going any further I suggest that you make a note of what you think has happened here. In particular:

- ▪ Has Freddie simply made an error with these two cheques and failed to record them on Wednesday or has he sneakily stolen some money?
- ▪ If you think Freddie has stolen some money how has he done it?
- ▪ And what could he have taken, since his bankings each day add up to the right amount of money?

■ What conclusion should Arthur draw from the facts that he has been able to establish?

■ Is there something he can do to confirm whether he is right?

Now read on!

Arthur realises that it cannot be possible to have the right total ready for banking, unless Freddie has put in some of the cheques from Thursday morning to cover cash that should be there and isn't. He confronts Freddie about this and after looking initially very uncomfortable Freddie then says he may have made a mistake in totalling up Wednesday's cheques.

Arthur looks him in the eye and asks Freddie again. 'Are you sure that you want me to write down that you think you may have made a mistake recording these two cheques, before I examine the rest of the bankings this week to confirm your explanation?' Freddie looks even more uncomfortable and tries to persuade Arthur that there is no need to check back, it was a one-off mistake. Arthur is now getting a little irritated with Freddie. What was meant to be a routine surprise check is turning into a problem that will delay lunch for both of them.

He asks Freddie to explain why the 'one-off mistake' means he doesn't have to go back over the earlier records. Freddie then finally admits that he was 'a little short last night' and had temporarily borrowed £500, intending to repay it as soon as he had been to the bank today. If Arthur hadn't arrived to do a surprise cash-up no one would have been any the wiser. He assures Arthur that he'll put it right at lunchtime when he gets to the bank, provided Arthur can see his way clear not to make a hasty note now, before Freddie has had a chance to replace the missing money.

1. What should Arthur do next?
2. What should Arthur have done once he found the cheques substituted in Wednesday's banking?
3. Why is it good practice not to allow the cashing of personal cheques by staff?

(*My illustrative answers are at the end of this chapter, see if you can do as well or better by noting down your answers now, before reading on.*)

The above example is an illustration of how teeming and lading works in practice. In essence the fraudster is able to 'borrow' cash without being obliged to return it (i.e., steal!) provided sufficient money comes in to substitute for the stolen cash from future takings before they have to account for their earlier takings. It is often 'phase one' before a more serious and sustained fraud takes place. By its nature, the amount that the fraudster can borrow in a 'teeming-and-lading' fraud is limited by the amount that comes in for the subsequent banking before having to bank the previous receipts. It only takes one bad day and the fraudster will have insufficient new receipts to cover the money stolen from the old receipts due to be banked. At that point, unless they are able to borrow from someone else, they will be forced either to confess or to commit a fraud and falsify or suppress the records to cover the theft. It may come as a surprise, but in my experience very few people in this position choose to pick the 'confession' option!

Variants can be found on the basic cash teeming-and-lading fraud (which our US cousins prefer to call a 'lapping' fraud.) Anyone responsible for the receipt of funds from customers can operate such a fraud if they are never subject to surprise checks or proper segregation of duties and independent reconciliations.

Perhaps the most unlikely teeming-and-lading fraud I have ever come across, was in the crime property store of a large police station in London. When prisoners are arrested, any cash or other goods in their possession, from drugs through to possible stolen property and weapons, are taken from the prisoner. Some may go off for forensic examination but all will be placed in tamper-proof evidence bags or secured in locked cupboards in the crime property store. When any forensic examination is complete the property will generally be returned to the property store to keep until the court case or other disposal (e.g., returned to the original owner or confiscated and destroyed or sold off, depending on the nature of the item).

Only the police officer handling the case should have access to the relevant property bags once in the crime property store, as they may need to confront a suspect or show them to a witness in order to gather evidence for possible prosecution. Also they will often need to produce the evidence at court hearings and any eventual trial. They will often take the bag out in such circumstances, returning it still intact after they have finished with it.

This was 1998 and early in my career at Scotland Yard, when I had just a small section to assist with internal investigations. One of my three investigators got a phone call from the local chief inspector asking for our help with tracking the potential theft of crime property from the store at this large police station. During a check of police officers' personal lockers, the officer conducting the check had found a crime property bag for a case in a detective's locker. That should simply never happen and it aroused his suspicions. The detective in question was confronted and asked for an explanation. His reply took the officer by surprise. 'I wasn't going to give that bag back to the crime property officer, he's a thief. I don't want this case compromised by tainted evidence in court.' The officer was puzzled. 'How do you know he's a thief?' The detective explained: 'I was running with a 1996 burglary involving cash and cigarettes, but thanks to a number of delays we took two years to get to court. When I went to get the evidence bag out of property, the property officer couldn't locate it on the system. Later he came up to me in the canteen and handed over a brand new bag, saying that the original one had got accidentally damaged, which is why he couldn't find it earlier.' 'Well, that might have happened.' 'Yes, but when I emptied the contents out ready for court I found a 1997 pound coin in the new bag for my 1996 case! I knew then that he must have stolen and then replaced the cash. I wasn't going to let him tamper with any more of my evidence.' 'Why didn't you report him immediately?' 'What? And lose the chance to get my scroat banged up. Are you mad? By the time you'd have sorted out the paperwork my case would have been well and truly down the toilet!'

We joined forces with the local CID to conduct the investigation into that crime property store and the property officer. We searched his office desk with the police present and found all the evidence we needed there. He had been identifying cases that he thought would never come to court and stealing anything of value in the associated evidence bags. However, just in case, as with the instance that had come to light, he had kept a record of what he had stolen in a desk drawer notebook, cross-referenced to the original evidence bag. He had also kept all the tags identifying the evidence bags that had been tampered with and contents stolen in his desk drawer. This was a new variant on teeming and lading to us. He then had one 'super' evidence bag, in which he kept a float of cash and other items that he might have to re-constitute, hence his error in including a 1997 coin in a 1996 evidence bag.

When confronted by the investigating CID officer, with one of my team alongside at the interview, the property officer confessed immediately. My investigator had also noted nearly 200 small cash donations to the Police Widows' and Orphans' Fund in the front-desk records, but no sign of the money being paid in to the fund. When asked what had happened to this money, he just looked up and said quietly 'Yes, I stole all of those as well.' It was one of the shortest and quickest confessions ever witnessed by my investigator, who had 30 years' experience as a detective before he had retired and been re-employed by me to conduct audit investigations.

The crime property officer was dismissed following a disciplinary hearing and eventually pleaded guilty in court to the theft of some £16,000 in cash from property and donations, as well as a considerable quantity of stolen cigarettes that had been re-stolen by the property officer.

Teeming-and-lading study: Answers

1. *What should Arthur do next?*

   If possible, simultaneously secure the evidence and get a note down about what Freddie has just said to him. If at all possible get Freddie to sign the note as an accurate record of what he has just told Arthur he has done. Then Arthur should immediately contact a senior line manager with cash responsibility and report what he has discovered. It is poor practice to carry out a surprise cash check single-handed and once a problem is identified it will be hard to prove what was said and done at any hearing later.

2. *What should Arthur have done once he found the cheques substituted in Wednesday's banking?*

   Apart from not turning up on his own (any cash-ups, surprise or otherwise, should always be carried out by a minimum of two people other than the person holding the cash), Arthur should be checking previous days' entries against the split of cash and cheques shown in the bank paying-in records.

3. *Why is it good practice not to allow the cashing of personal cheques by staff?*

   Two main reasons. It avoids any difficulty if a staff cheque subsequently 'bounces' and it also stops anyone hiding a teeming-and-lading fraud.

General principles and axioms**from Chapter 1**

■ Be cynical. In the words of my first mentor from NHS Audit, think of anything that a human being can do—and they will do it!

■ Look for fraud rather than corruption. Fraud is easier to prove.

■ Short and sharp works, long and complex doesn't. The more complex and detailed an investigation becomes, the more likely it is to fail.

■ Wherever possible, follow 'the money'. Ultimately it will lead to the fraudster.

■ There are always three systems—the prescribed, the alleged and the actual. Until you know the actual, you won't know what is really happening.

■ Try to stop any significant on-going cash or asset losses as the first priority for the investigation.

■ Don't get obsessed by the one-off dodgy-looking item. But if it occurs again or repeatedly, hone in on those involved.

CHAPTER TWO

Fraud basics

CHAPTER**SUMMARY**

Noticing and recognising the pointers to potential frauds. Basic income frauds. Basic expenditure frauds. Common procurement frauds.

THINK FRAUD FIRST!

In his seminal 1976 book on computer crime, the US information technology specialist and author Donn Parker quotes Professor Polya's[1] advice to would-be research scientists: *Believe nothing, but question only that which is worth questioning.* That quote has been my guiding principle for more years than I care to remember. It has a resonance to the founding father of the Greek sceptic movement, Pyrrho of Elis,[2] who travelled with Alexander the Great on his conquest of Asia in 327–325 BC. He was so taken by the philosophical views that he found there that he returned to Greece to live a simple and austere life, believing nothing yet remaining in a state of perpetual curiosity and indifference to the world around him.

One rather curious fact about Pyrrho, who in every other way I would recommend as the model for a would-be investigator, is that he never wrote anything down. We only know of his life from his contemporaries.

The biggest stumbling block to anyone finding fraud is the way most of us want to see the world. There is a tendency to assume the best until something comes to light suggesting otherwise. Even then a desire for the status quo and peer pressure will influence, many will then find a way to fit the unexpected behaviour into an 'accepted' pattern rather than challenge it. While I am not advocating assuming the worst as a way of life for everyone, my starting position is that without information to indicate good or bad I remain sceptical and assume nothing, a truly Pyrrhonian position. As a former teaching colleague used to say to me during the five years I spent as an audit lecturer at the Civil Service College, 'Peter, no news is,—no news!' Indeed. I don't assume, but I do start with a healthy propensity to be suspicious of anything that is unusual or unexpected.

So, are there any specific signs that might suggest someone is a fraudster? There are many pointers to peculation, once you know what to spot. I have set out those that you are most likely to come across in the following paragraphs.

Contrary to perceived wisdom there is no personal profile that would identify a fraudster beyond doubt. The classic view is that serious and serial fraudsters tend largely to be male middle and senior managers. However, more recent scientific studies suggest that this is a hangover from the first three-quarters of the last century, throughout most of which a high proportion of all management positions were held by men. Now there is a more even spread, the evidence from such studies in the US indicates that fraud is happening in proportion to the sexes and that if there is any emerging profile, it is that those at different positions and experience in life and organisations tend to commit frauds commensurate with their knowledge and work experience. 'Blue-collar' staff at the bottom end of organisations are more likely to be involved in warehousing, stock and theft of asset frauds. 'White-collar' staff in junior and middle management are likely to commit procurement frauds or setting up of bogus companies, false invoice payments and expenses frauds. Senior and top management are more likely to commit ongoing 'false-accounting' frauds of the type that bring the whole organisation crashing down, if not stopped or unearthed.

PETER'S POINTERS TO PECULATION (I.E., FRAUD)

Fraud pointers fall into a number of categories. Those that are most common can be grouped as follows: lifestyle, behaviour of individual at work, business performance data, financial patterns and organisational signs. *An individual pointer means little on its own, but when two or more are present then their cumulative weight is greater than the sum of the individual items.*

Lifestyle

Often information about lifestyle comes from gossip, rumour or an allegation. On its own it is particularly unreliable and not to be trusted without some evidence through pointers in other categories. Obvious indicators of concern are if the individual is known as a regular gambler or drinker. Also if there are any sudden changes in an individual's personal circumstances, particularly if they have recently separated from a long-standing partner or are known to have a complicated personal life. The 'classical' male boss who leaves a wife of many years and runs off with a much younger woman who works under him is an example of this. Have they suddenly started buying expensive things? Are they always jetting off on expensive holidays that others around them don't seem to be able to afford? Are there rumours of County Court judgements or attachment of earnings orders against them? Do they seem to borrow excessively on credit cards? The company the potential fraudster keeps in their social life is another pointer, especially if that company is known or believed to be 'dodgy' or criminally minded.

Behaviour at work

The classic pointer for the 'white-collar' fraudster is the failure to take accrued leave and/or a willingness to come into the office at odd times (e.g., the weekend or working late every night). It is also, of course, potentially the sign of a very hard-working and conscientious employee who is under pressure. So, how can you tell the difference? If there is nothing obvious in their work that would give them the opportunity to commit fraud then without any other pointers I might reluctantly conclude that they were just hard-working—but before I did, I would check that there were no 'hidden' opportunities and want to know whether they were in receipt of significant bonuses or overtime payments. I would also take an interest in their line management and how well they are supervised.

The reverse pointer is someone who always goes missing at the same time on the same day of the week. Are they secretly signing on for state benefits under another identity? Other pointers include signs of stress, smelling of alcohol in the morning, a reluctance to leave their desk/work-station unattended, keeping an obsessive eye on their work effects, especially papers and any briefcase or bag that they take to or from work, secretive behaviour and unexplained phone or mobile calls.

A couple of real-life examples here may help.

Real cases: Example 2

In my early days as a health service auditor I missed a classic income fraud because I misread the reasons for the behaviour of a hospital cashier. We were conducting a surprise cash-up and it was obvious from the start that the cashier was extremely nervous. He was sweating profusely and constantly having difficulty in speaking without stuttering and shaking nervously. Our suspicions aroused, we went through his safe with a fine toothcomb. We found absolutely nothing of note. There was a minor discrepancy on the cash, due to a transposition error—but we quickly found that and everything else was apparently as it should be. The cashier remained nervous and I remained suspicious. We checked all the records that we could think of that passed through his hands, still nothing. The following day the cashier went off sick. I asked my team leader if we could stay longer at the hospital but was told that without any paperwork to go on I'd just have to give up on it and move on to our next hospital audit. I was unhappy but for once did as I was told.

As it later transpired, I was rightly suspicious with the nervous cashier who then went off sick, but not for the obvious reason. He was not the one committing the fraud. However, he knew who was committing it—his boss! What we missed (and part of the reason why we missed it also taught me a valuable lesson about audit tests) was the income that wasn't there.

This was a hospital that had a very limited amount of income from five private patient beds, a tiny amount of their total bed availability. Our tests of three months' transactions prior to our audit didn't detect any private patient income, so we weren't expecting to find any in the cashier's records. We were told by the hospital administrator that the beds had been largely unoccupied in recent months because of maintenance work in that part of the hospital. However, unknown to us, but known to the hospital cashier, there were also a number of 'special' private patients from overseas. This was a well-known London 'teaching' hospital and embassies from outside the European Union would make arrangements with the hospital's world-famous consultants for seriously ill but rich patients to be treated privately and looked after at the hospital, where they had to pay for every aspect of their health care. Most of these patients were used to paying in cash and would hand over thousands of pounds in advance to pay the consultants for their treatment. The consultants used the hospital administrator to collect the cash on their behalf. As a result these transactions never passed through the main hospital books. However, the patients still had to pay for occupying a NHS bed, even though it wasn't necessarily one of the designated private beds for UK patients.

The cashier had given the administrator, who was also his boss, a receipt book for collecting the income due to the hospital off these 'special' private patients and then paying it over to the cashier to bank with the other hospital income. At first that was what had happened, but on one occasion the cash turned into a cheque from the administrator's personal account. When the cashier saw what had happened, he realised from the dates in the administrator's receipt book that the administrator had 'borrowed' the cash for several weeks and had then repaid it. He was too afraid of the administrator to tackle him about it but also worried about his own position, so he photocopied the cheque from the administrator and put it in his desk drawer. If he had put it in the safe we might have found it. If we had checked the previous year's income we'd have realised that such monies normally came in via the administrator. If we had been allowed more time for the audit, who knows what we might have found? If only!

When we were finally called in I was sent back to the hospital to work out how much had been stolen. At the time I was very much embarrassed by the missed fraud and how easily we'd been fooled by the administrator, largely because we were convinced the cashier was the problem. The administrator had been confident and calm while the cashier had been nervous and unsteady. I found that £45,000, a serious sum of money in the 1970s, had been stolen in the eight months since the administrator had paid in the cheque for the money that he'd first 'borrowed'. We never did discover how much of the consultants' money he'd also helped himself to in that time.

The fraud was finally discovered by a retired hospital treasurer who had looked at the books to help prepare their annual accounts and realised that much of the overseas income was missing. After the administrator had got away with the personal cheque he had starting issuing top copies of the receipts to patients for the right amount but making sure that the carbon copies were later creations for less money, helping himself to the difference. (In one instance a patient had paid £3,000 and he created the carbon copy for £300, duly handed on to the cashier.) Later on, during the period when we were conducting our surprise check, he had started stealing all the income and not submitting any receipt, hence why we had not found anything to check in the cashier's recent records. It also turned out that he had been cheekily charging the hospital consultants a 'handling fee' for collecting the cash for them from overseas patients!

▨ Lesson 1—body language matters but don't jump to conclusions without the evidence!

▥   Lesson 2—check a sufficiently wide period of time to know whether anything has changed! (If you don't have time to check many transactions, then consider appropriate sampling techniques to cover a wider time period.)

Real cases: Example 3

A junior member of staff in the Human Resources Department in London's Metropolitan Police used to behave very oddly in the office. He was an administrative officer employed to check personnel records that were being converted from a manual to a computer system. He would arrive each day with a battered briefcase which he'd insist on keeping either on his desk or with him at all times. He was very secretive and would often receive private phone calls. His boss didn't challenge this strange behaviour or make any enquiries to see if there was anything wrong or stressing the individual.

In an apparently unrelated incident, two Drugs Squad detectives arrested a man on suspicion of driving while under the influence of drugs or alcohol. On searching his vehicle, to their surprise and astonishment, they found Metropolitan Police documents and a link to the man with the battered briefcase in the Met's own Human Resources Department. Following the link back they arrested the 'battered briefcase' man at work, seizing his briefcase. It turned out to be a treasure trove. Inside the briefcase were the bank account details of police staff that he'd copied while reviewing personnel files at work, a company stamp for the company that had given his reference for the job with the police—and an application form for a 'friend' to join the Metropolitan Police as an administrator, giving the same company reference and phone number. Also—and perhaps more seriously—he had a 'fake' ID for a police officer with his photo on it. Three more such 'fake' IDs were found in his possession. (We discovered later that he had previously been an administrator in a local police station, where one of his jobs was the collection of police warrants from police officers when they retired or resigned. Instead of arranging for the destruction of the old warrants, he had stolen them, removed the original photos and substituted his co-conspirators and himself in the photographs.)

The company reference and phone number found in his briefcase traced back to his former home address, where his ex-wife still lived. Had anyone checked the address for his reference when he was first appointed they would have discovered that the company address he had given was also at that time his home address. As it was, they had simply phoned the number given for the company, whereupon his wife had obligingly answered the phone and confirmed his employment history with them!

He was discovered almost by accident—and yet there were sufficient signs in his behaviour at work to arouse suspicion, both in his HR role and in his earlier posting at a police station, from where he had been moved to the HR role for 'disciplinary' reasons, but nobody liked to say too much, as he could get aggressive when challenged.

When the police looked into his real employment history there was another surprise in store. He had already worked for two government organisations, one of which had sacked him after he disappeared while off sick—and the other had taken him on without checking the gap in his employment history where he had decided not to mention his employment with the organisation that had sacked him. And one of those two organisations? The Ministry of Defence!

The fraudster here represents a particularly dangerous type, who often gets underneath the radar in larger organisations.[3] They are generally part of an organised gang, rarely working on their own. They will quite deliberately target low-level clerical and administrative jobs in organisations with a high profile or reputation, particularly in the public service. They are intelligent and resourceful and often have little difficulty in beating off competition to get a junior post. Once they are on the 'inside', they steal anything that will help them, whether information or documents from the organisation (or indeed any cash or assets that they can lay their hands on). All are then passed on to the outside accomplices.

Business performance data

A manager, who is rewarded for their performance, whether directly in bonus or salary or indirectly in career enhancement, will be tempted to manipulate data in their favour. Pointers can include a continually improving performance curve, month on month. Also the manager who always meets their targets and is spot on with the budget would arouse my suspicions, no one is that perfect. Sales frauds often occur where bonuses or even business success are at stake. If sales are increasing, is that reflected in the incoming cashflow to the organisation?

Laundering the laundry manager

The earliest fraud of this type that I came across was in the National Health Service in the 1970s. Hospitals often had their own in-house laundries in those days and the laundry manager and staff would be paid a performance bonus based on the throughput of items in the laundry. One laundry manager became particularly friendly with a clerk in the finance department responsible for processing the results measured from the counters on the laundry machinery. As their 'friendship' blossomed, so his performance—and pay—increased, until the day it was noticed during a routine maintenance check that the results processed by the clerk bore no resemblance to the numbers actually shown on the counters in the laundry itself!

Insuring the uninsurable

One of the worst frauds ever committed by the senior management of an insurance company involved them sitting down to make up false clients whose policies were then sold on to other insurance companies as genuine. They dodged audit queries by diverting calls to check the existence of clients to themselves and pretending to be the client. As the fraud grew, more and more senior managers got drawn into it to help 'validate' the non-existent clients. Fake customers were given a special '99' computer prefix on the company's systems, echoed curiously 30 years later by Nick Leeson with his 88888 account at Barings. The company expanded almost exponentially on its apparently inexhaustible customer base to the point where, shortly before its collapse, they were able to launch take-over bids for some of the largest corporations in the United States. As the fraud had grown in size, one glaringly obvious pointer to the fake customer base had been missed by auditors and regulators alike. The company's share of the market was so large that on paper its total number of customers exceeded the available insurable population![4]

Financial/Accounting patterns

If sales are always increasing in the financial records, look at asset and stock records. Is their value or quantity moving in tandem the opposite way? Is someone manipulating stock levels or journal entries between different parts of the ledgers (e.g., between cash and payroll expenditure)? Who earns the most overtime? Are there part-time employees earning far more than full-time equivalents—if so, why?

If your organisation has regular income or outgoings from known sources, then there should be records stretching back over time that show the volume and value of receipts and payments in each of these areas. Any significant change of pattern, increasing or decreasing, is worthy of closer attention to find out why things have changed. If it is a significant area of business or if the reasons given don't feel right then it is time to test the explanation by pulling some records and checking out the actual transactions. In my experience, except where the sums involved are very small, *the more managers tell you that you are wasting your time pursuing an explanation then the more likely it is that something is being covered up, whether fraud or just waste and incompetence.*

There are many ways in today's world in which financial records can be electronically examined and the results processed to identify potentially fraudulent activity. However, I have a word or two of caution here. There are some types of analysis that are particularly valuable and useful, others are less so. If you are confident that you know what you are doing and whoever has done the analysis for you can interpret the results meaningfully then this can be a very fruitful way to identify pointers to potential frauds.[5]

A useful and relatively simple statistical tool that can be applied to any financial population (and which works particularly well with a review of invoice payments) is the application of Benford's Law, a principle that has been known about for more than a century. Benford built his model on an original discovery by US astronomer and polymath Simon Newcomb, who noticed in 1881 that his students' logarithm books tended to have greater wear and tear in the early pages. In 1938 Benford, an engineer and mathematician, presented a probability model from this for the likelihood of the value of the first digit in any numerical population, regardless of the unit of measurement.

Since the first digit in financial populations can only hold the values 1 to 9, natural logic would lead most of us to assume that the likelihood of the first digit being any of those numbers is a '1-in-9' chance (i.e., the first digit has a 11.1% chance of being 1, 11.1% chance of being 2, 11.1% chance of being 3, etc.). With any large population of different numbers, such as invoices, data analysis shows that this simply isn't the case—there is in fact a diminishing chance of each successive number appearing.

Benford's law gives the following percentage chances of the first digit being that number:

Digit	Likelihood
1	30.1%
2	17.6%
3	12.5%
4	9.7%
5	7.9%
6	6.7%
7	5.8%
8	5.1%
9	4.6%

It is particularly useful for comparisons of financial numbers in accounting systems although you can also apply the principle to anything else that might be counted or measured. But it is important to remember that this is a rule about the first digit only, it must not be applied to second and subsequent digits in a number.

Deviations from the above may be due to some entirely naturally occurring event in your organisation's line of business but any significant deviation is worthy of close attention. Also if similar activities in different parts of the business can be measured they should show a similar pattern to each other, the odd one out then should earn the right to have much closer attention paid!

Organisational signs

These are pointers that can suggest a contractor or sub-contractor is up to no good. As with any other indicators, it is the accumulation of pointers that exponentially increases the risk of fraud, waste and losses occurring.

The procurement process while the contractor is coming on to the books is the first area where some obvious pointers can easily be detected. Classics to watch out for at this stage include

Business addresses

Does the business address you've got match the one for the same company at Companies House? What about the main directors' addresses? I have known directors hide their home addresses by using a co-conspirator's address as their home address. I've also seen a company based at a business unit that was non-existent, to hide the fact that they were running the business from their private address.

Company registration number and name

It is not uncommon for businesses to set up a special purpose company for a particular contract either to join forces with a fellow bidder or to minimise their risks should anything go wrong. However, the more unscrupulous organisations will neglect to tell you any of this and even go as far as using the same invoices and letter heads for entirely different entities. Commonly on this type of fraudulent activity you will appoint R Fiddling Ltd with Companies House registration number XXX but you will be invoiced by a company whose invoices look identical to R Fiddling and until you look at the small print no one notices that their registration number is YYY not XXX. That is an entirely different company in law. It may—or indeed may not—be connected with the company to whom you thought you had awarded the contract. The end consequence is that any financial guarantees or sign-up to ethical conditions or company policies are now meaningless and probably unenforceable.

Off-shore ownership

Personally I wouldn't go there but many do. The company bidding for the work may appear to be UK-based, but who are the beneficial owners of the business? If the parent company or the major shareholders are based in well-known off-shore tax havens it tells you two important things immediately. First, parent company guarantees are going to be worthless and, second, the owners are keen to avoid EU regulation and UK tax laws where they can. It might not be a significant risk to buy products or services from such companies in some circumstances, but if anything goes wrong there will often be no recourse and any money paid over will be lost.

(This is also a risk that can creep up later on with service providers. You may have outsourced an activity to a legitimate UK-based company but if subsequently it is taken over by another organisation with off-shore tax haven credentials then unless the handover and contract novation is handled appropriately your organisation could be put at serious risk further down the line.)

Case study: Example of 'Peter's pointers to peculation'

A senior employee Anthony Williams, the so-called Laird of Tomintoul, defrauded Scotland Yard of more than £5m over a six-year period between 1988 and 1994. When he was finally caught it became apparent that he had given a number of classic pointers but no one had collectively put them all together and realised what was going on.

1. He had divorced his first wife and married his secretary. Monthly maintenance payments to his first wife took more than half his take-home pay and he had set up home with a second wife who had three children from an earlier marriage all still needing to live at home.
2. He 'accidentally' paid several thousand pounds due to the Police Welfare Fund, where he was the treasurer, into his own account instead of the fund account. When it was discovered he claimed an accounting error and repaid it. No action was taken and it was less than two years later that he started on the major fraud.

3. Once the major fraud was under way, he became the senior manager who was never in and people got in the habit of bypassing him when they needed to get decisions.
4. He started to dress in expensive clothes and have expensive habits. This was noted but he explained it away as an inheritance from a rich uncle.
5. He accidentally showed a cheque book in the office in which he was shown as 'Lord Williams' but no one thought it odd enough to report.

Any one of these individual pointers was explainable, although pointer 2 should have been enough to stop his future fraudulent career. Collectively they should have raised serious doubts.

There was also a second set of hidden pointers, known to only a few senior managers, that had they been put together with the more generally known pointers should have led to an immediate investigation into his affairs. These pointers were hidden because he stole from a secret 'covert account' set up to run a counter-terrorism operation. Had it been a less sensitive area, some financial pointers would have been visible and may have prevented or cut short the fraud. Also back in 1988 no one had considered the need for financial vetting of senior officers on sensitive duties. Any such check would have exposed that it was not possible to meet his financial commitments from his salary at the time.

Pointers that might otherwise have aroused suspicions included changing the covert account set-up so that he did not require a second signatory to draw the money and blocking any attempts at audit of the transactions of the accounts by either external or internal auditors on the grounds that they were too secret for any auditor to see them. Any review of the system would have shown that there was no segregation of duties in the key part of the process, no supervision of Williams and a complete segregation of knowledge between those using the covert funds and those providing the covert funds to Williams to pass on to the covert operation. Had his busy line manager taken the time to examine the transactions, he would have seen that the amount drawn down from the covert account by the counter-terrorism operation was far less than that claimed by Williams to replenish the covert account.

When the fraud came to light in 1994 it became obvious that Williams must have been planning to commit a fraud on the covert account before it was set up. Internal correspondence found in his possession when he was arrested showed that he had 'doctored' a note from a senior officer to ensure that the suggested checks and balances in the note were not considered when the papers were passed to those setting up the account.[6] While the senior officer had agreed that the funding for the operation should be set up along the lines that Williams proposed, he had also recognised that there were risks to the organisation if it was done as outlined by Williams. Sadly—but fortunately for Williams—the senior officer, who was already terminally ill, died not long after he wrote the note. Williams took the opportunity to make sure that no one else ever saw the full note.

 ## SOME BASIC FRAUDS AGAINST ORGANISATIONS

For the purposes of this book I've tried to avoid being too obsessed with the classification of frauds. There are many different ways of classifying and grouping types of fraud, some more useful than others. Joseph T. Wells, the founder and owner of the Association of Certified Fraud Examiners, came up with the most comprehensive and logical classification system that I've seen to date. If you need to pick a system, it is as good as any, albeit there is a need to translate some of the US terminology into UK English.

I try to keep the classification of fraud at a broader level, seeing the basic ones as (1) income, (2) cash or other asset, (3) procurement or expenditure. Some are more likely to be committed by contractors, others by staff and some by senior or top management. Clearly other types of fraudulent activity can occur within an organisation (e.g., manipulation of financial statements) and certain types of fraudster will commit more than one type of fraud at the same time. It is for these reasons that I don't get too hung up on the classification of types of fraud, as I am far more interested in identifying the fraud, stopping it and then finding the fraudster. Having said that, it is useful, when understanding frauds, to appreciate the different characteristics of income frauds over cash/asset frauds and how both differ from procurement/expenditure frauds.

Typical income frauds

Income frauds are often the hardest to find—and also the hardest to track down and secure the evidence. It is for that reason that in any risk analysis I always rate each £1 of income as five times more vulnerable than each £1 of expenditure. By its very nature you often don't know what has not arrived and income is usually stolen on its way in and the records either altered to conceal the fraud or never completed in the first place.

Income frauds are generally only detected where there are excellent internal controls, including random checks of those responsible for income collection and receipt, or by chance events outside the control of the fraudster, provided someone is alert enough to recognise what has happened.

Typical income frauds include

1. Suppressing cash and cheque receipts—either by running a private receipt book alongside the real one or, simply, by not entering the receipt in the organisations records and pocketing the money.

Real case: Stealing from the NHS

The NHS charges for a range of appliances from wigs through to artificial limbs that patients might need. These are usually fitted at a separate day clinic where the patient will have to pay the charge in order to collect their appliance and have it fitted. At a south-coast hospital group no one had noticed that for several years the income had been steadily falling from one of their clinics, although it was dealing with a similar volume of cases. By chance, the cashier who collected the income died suddenly. Nothing came to light immediately but a few months after his death his landlady sent in several books of hospital receipts that she had found among his effects and that she assumed the hospital would want back. There was only one slight problem. These were his own 'hospital' receipt books that he had made up and none of the collected charges recorded in them had ever been paid in to the hospital! Over many years he had stolen cash income paid over by outpatients and day patients, but had kept his level of theft steady and low enough not to draw attention to the fraud.

Real case: After dark in the museum

At one point a well-known London museum charged a cash entry fee for all visitors. On the surface this was well controlled, with daily cash-up and banking arrangements, CCTV coverage of the payment areas and intrusive management supervision. Also, since most of the cash was in the form of £1 and £2 coins, it seemed unlikely that any substantial income fraud could be committed. Unfortunately, the senior supervisor had a serious personal problem—he had a cocaine habit. Such habits are expensive and he needed to feed it with cash. So, he started manipulating the banking records and stealing cash before they banked it. In the meantime some of the staff collecting the cash realised that their supervisor wasn't up to it and that he paid little attention to proper reconciliation of their takings. They too started helping themselves to the cash until eventually the museum's management noticed that they were suffering a significant drop in income. CCTV checks failed to identify the problem but did show that certain staff seemed to leave with quite heavy clothing, even in the height of summer. A surprise raid and cash-up after closing time but before the staff had left for the night caught the chief culprit and a search of lockers and jackets identified those who had been filling their pockets with coins before they left each night. When they protested their innocence they were shown the CCTV footage of them leaving with bulging pockets. Confessions and instant dismissal followed in quick succession.

Real case: A magician at work

In my early days dealing with Scotland Yard we had a call from a police officer who was convinced that the cashier at his local police canteen was on the fiddle. He'd bought lunch in the canteen and noticed that she had only rung up a subtotal when charging for his meal. This is one of the classic signs of a till fraudster. We looked at the income for the canteen and noted that it seemed down by about £1,000 a week compared with similar sized units elsewhere in the Met. We then spoke to the local catering manager and he agreed that we could put a camera in above the till. We ran it for three days when this cashier was on duty and then one of my investigators had the laborious task of going though many hours of recorded evidence.

The cashier was so quick over the till keys and in her actions when giving out change and collecting money that at first we could see nothing wrong. On slowing down the recording on each transaction we then spotted that she wasn't always pressing the right keys on the till. As the police officer had noticed, whenever someone bought a small value item or meal she was carrying forward subtotals and only entering in to the till the difference necessary to make it add up to the right total for the next customer. We ran the till rolls against our observations and also noticed that she had a very high proportion of 'no sale' items, where it looked like she had rung up the correct amount but had cancelled the transaction once she had taken the money from the previous customer and before serving the next customer.

But how was she getting her hands on the excess cash that she had generated out of the till drawer? The tills were always totalled and the cash drawers taken away to be cashed up as soon as the canteen was shut. When we slowed down the recording even further we were able to work it out, she was a master of sleight of hand, worthy of any member of the Magic Circle. She kept a vase-like clay pot near the till. Every time she had made around £10 from her subtotalling trick or the bogus 'no sales' she would scoop up an extra £10 note from the cash drawer as she went to give out change to the next customer. On the way to hand over their change she would pass her hand over the pot and drop the £10 note into it while seamlessly handing over the correct change to the customer. When the canteen closed and the cash was being counted, she simply emptied the contents of the clay pot into her handbag when no one was looking. We were mightily impressed—but we still had her 'nicked' by the local CID the next time she stepped out of the building with her handbag stuffed with cash.[7] She was charged with theft and pleaded guilty in court. In all she had got away with some £90,000 before we had caught up with her, thanks to that alert customer.

2. Running a private till. This is one that any restaurant, shop or bar area can fall victim to if supervision is either inadequate or the local supervisor is the fraudster. The catering manager at a large organisation was puzzled by the drop in takings at one of his evening bars. The local supervisor could offer no explanation so one night the manager dropped in unannounced and sat in the bar having a few drinks. It all seemed very busy as usual and all the tills were regularly ringing up money. The following day he asked for the analysis of each till. All three tills showed the expected turnover in their records. He was mulling this over when the truth suddenly dawned—when he was sitting at the bar he'd counted four tills in operation, not three. The cheeky fraudster (the local supervisor) had put in an identical till and was keeping all the takings from it!

3. Teeming and lading (see the example in Chapter 1).

Common cash and asset frauds

Cash and asset frauds occur when the segregation between those responsible for the records and those who are holding the asset breaks down. Where segregation simply isn't possible, as with a cashier or a small business area, then the organisation will always be vulnerable to a potential fraudster. This is where independent reconciliations and surprise cash and stock checks can play a valuable part in ensuring that all is well.

The classic stock fraud is either to understate deliveries or to overstate issues of stock, in both instances the fraudster will have found a means to remove the stock that is now in excess of that shown in the records. In my experience stock frauds are often among the easiest to detect and to pursue the guilty. There is usually a good paper or electronic trail and surprise checks can be very rewarding. It is also an area where there is often an element of collusion, either between individuals working in the area where the stock is stored before usage, or between whoever receives the deliveries and those delivering the goods. Unless it is a complete mess you should be able to establish what came in and what the records say went out and reconcile that to the stock held. A small trick here, only check the items of most intrinsic or usable value, don't get tempted to do a full stock check of everything, or you'll never see the light of day.

Doctoring the suits at the hospital

Patients in long-stay hospitals who don't have any personal assets will often be entitled to clothing provided by the hospital. In larger units they would hold a stock of standard suits for men and dresses for women. In one instance we received a tip-off that suits were being sold on Saturday morning at a pub just round the corner from the hospital. My boss checked this out and, sure enough, the storekeeper was flogging suits to pub customers. The following Monday we pounced on the hospital stores and checked the stock on the shelves which, unsurprisingly, agreed with the bin card totals entered by the storekeeper for each item. An important lesson here. *Never, ever, rely on bin cards as an accurate record for stock.* They are only an accurate record of what the storekeeper has determined is the stock. If the storekeeper is honest it's no problem—but if they are not . . . beware! We didn't trust the bin cards in this instance and went through the receipts and issues of suits and found the evidence we needed, he had been doctoring the issues records after they had been signed for but before they got to the ledger. If the issue sheet showed one suit, he'd make it ten by adding a nought, if it showed five suits, he'd make it fifteen by adding a one and so on. Wherever he could crudely adjust the numbers he did. No one had checked the issues against the requisitions from wards for patients, so they hadn't noticed that on paper he was issuing far more suits than anyone had ordered.

Basic procurement and expenditure frauds

The fundamental point about expenditure frauds is that there will always be some evidence to find that will tell you that cash has been diverted. By their nature, money will have been spent and with spending comes an audit trail, unless the organisation is really in a hopeless and unrecoverable financial mess. In the public sector and in medium to large organisations in the private sector that is highly unlikely and therefore you should always be able to find some useful evidence about the fraud and where the money has gone.

Often these can be the most damaging frauds to hit an organisation, only top-management manipulation of the data in published accounts is likely to cause more damage. Everything from fake invoices, bogus companies or unfulfilled service contracts can potentially cost many millions if not detected in time. At the lesser end of the business false expenses claims by employees also feature here. While individual expenses frauds may be relatively small, the more senior those involved the more likely that the scandal will have a significant impact upon the organisation.

Typical expenditure frauds

1. The bogus company—This is probably the second most common internally committed fraud after employee expenses fiddles. If at any point there is a weakness in the system for the creation of new business or creditor accounts, sooner or later a rogue employee will find it. Two examples here, one from some time ago and the other much more recent

Pharmacutical suppliers turn out to be a bitter pill to swallow ...

A long time ago, in a galaxy far away ... no ... hold it! In a hospital in a major city before the advent of on-line ordering and e-procurement they had a supplier ordering system for the pharmacy that on the face of it seemed relatively well controlled. The pharmacy clerk would complete the serially numbered triplicate order form, the pharmacist would check it for quantities and the right supplier, he'd then sign to authorise the order and it would go directly from his office to the mail room to be despatched to the company, with a copy of the order going to the finance department to enter the information into the accounting system. When the goods were delivered, a delivery note would be completed by the storekeeper for the pharmacy store and passed to the pharmacy clerk who had prepared the order for the pharmacist. The clerk would check against the order docket, certify that it was correct and pass both to the finance department to generate payment to the supplier.

How could such a simple system go wrong? Well, the pharmacy clerk had a bit of a problem. He wanted more money to live off than he could earn as a pharmacy clerk but he hadn't got the patience or inclination to train to be a pharmacist—and he didn't want to do any other line of work. So, he worked out that he could get an extra batch of serially numbered order forms from the finance department. He just upped the apparent usage of them and they duly obliged by sending through order pads to him more frequently. But the usage was entirely bogus. He set up a number of dummy companies, wrote out orders to them himself and then forged the pharmacist's signature. All of the dummy companies were linked to the same answering machine at a separate line in his home, just in case anyone should happen to ring up with a query about the order or invoice for one of the bogus companies. No one of course ever received the goods, but he managed to obtain a supply of goods-received pads as well, saying he was collecting them on behalf of the storekeeper, then he'd complete fake entries against the orders, then put the fake order and fake goods-received note through the internal mail to get paid by the finance department.

All went swimmingly well with the fraud and he wasn't too greedy as the years went by. It was a large busy hospital and his level of fraud never stood out enough to show up either as a massive or unexpected spending on a particular supplier or on the overall pharmacy budget. Pharmacists came and went and finance staff and auditors were now used to the regular low-level use of his bogus suppliers turning up in the records. With each new pharmacist he practised their signature until he could fake it convincingly enough. But time went by and he had to retire. So now he faced the prospect of not only having to give up his fraud but also living off half his real salary and not the lucrative earnings to which he had grown so accustomed. Had he just retired he may well have got away with the fraud and no one would have ever known about it. But greed is a strong motivator ...

When he left he took with him as large a stock of blank order forms and goods-received pads that he could smuggle out of the hospital without detection. He then continued to complete them for the fake companies, sealing them up in the envelopes used in the internal mail to send items to the Finance Department. Every few weeks he would pay a visit to the hospital and engage the porter on the main gate in conversation. At a convenient point when the porter was distracted by another visitor or a delivery arriving he would quickly slip his completed envelopes into the internal mail tray in the porter's office. In due course the payments went rolling out as before to his bank accounts for the bogus companies. But two things then conspired to expose him. First, the accounting system changed and a new ordering system was put in place, as he didn't know this he continued to submit the now defunct orders, which were noticed by finance, who sent a strongly worded note to the new pharmacy clerk reminding him to use the right forms. Not unnaturally he was surprised and asked to be sent back copies of the orders in question. At the same time there was an efficiency drive and the pharmacist was asked why he was continuing to spend at the same levels on certain companies but had reduced his spending on others, per the current hospital edict. When the pharmacist, clerk and finance staff all compared notes they realised that the pharmacist had never heard of these companies and the clerk didn't have any details either—but when they went back through the records they found not only notes from the retired clerk about these companies but also some scraps of paper where he'd been practising the last pharmacist's signature. The game was up and the investigation eventually discovered that the fraud had carried on for at least 10 years, including a further two years after the fraudster had retired!

A resourceful resources manager

In my latter years as Director of Internal Audit at the Metropolitan Police, I was sitting in the audience at a public meeting of the police authority when my Executive Assistant appeared and passed a note along the row to me. It simply asked if I could contact the Head of Finance urgently. I dashed out of the meeting and gave him a call. "What's the problem?" "Well Peter, this is a little embarrassing. We think one of our finance and resource managers has had some bogus invoices paid to him for a non-existent company." I sounded suitably curious and concerned. He cleared his throat. "Ah, yes. Well ... yes. He was loaned from our own finance team to the police business group concerned and he seems to have used his knowledge of the system to set up a false vendor.[8]'' ''How much has he got away with?'' ''We're not sure'', he replied, ''We think there are only five bogus transactions—but they come to about £200k''. ''How did you discover this and what are you doing—apart from contacting me?'' ''It's all right, Peter, all under control, we just need one of your people to come over and confirm what we've got. I've got my own people right now pulling out all the dodgy material and looking at it.'' My heart sank for a moment.

''Well, would you mind just telling them to hold fire until I can get one of my professionals down there, *please*!'' ''I think we know what we are doing financially, Peter, you needn't worry.'' I paused for a second or two while I considered how to put this politely. ''I hadn't realised your people were fraud experts, I thought their expertise was in the financial system itself. I know they are financially trained but there are rules of evidence and being a police organisation we can't be seen to get them wrong or the judicial system will jump all over us in any future criminal case or employment tribunal.'' There was a significant pause before he replied.

''Well ... hmm ... that's why I was ringing you, Peter. We need your people's help to sort out the evidence once we've got it all.'' My heart sank further. ''Look. Whatever your team think they are doing please stop them immediately. I will send down my best available professional investigators and they will be with you in less than 30 minutes and will take charge on the ground. Please tell everyone just to sit tight until they get there. Whatever they do, they are not to detach, move or deface in any way the documents that they are searching through. My people will secure them properly when they arrive.'' I could tell that the last point had finally sunk home.

''But ... but ... but,'' he stammered, ''We had to pull the documents out and look at them before we rang him to ask why he had done these transactions.'' ''You did *what*?'' I was stunned. ''What on earth did you think you would discover by doing *that* at this stage? Do any of you have any training or experience in fraud investigations? Have you any idea?'' I took a deep breath and counted to 10 before I spoke again, trying to be as calm and matte of fact as I could. ''Did anyone actually get to speak to him on the phone—and what did he have to say?'' At that point the Head of Finance realised that I had to have the full story in its proper sequence.

''Look, Peter, this is not quite as it might seem from what we've discussed so far. Let me give you the full sequence of events here. It all started when we had a phone call from a female member of the public. She was in the process of starting up a retail business in a previously empty shop in the approach road to the station in Addusawl. When she opened up the premises she found the usual pile of junk mail dating back several weeks, which had been pushed through the letter box. But in amongst the junk she found two envelopes from the Metropolitan Police to a company at that address. She immediately checked with her landlord who assured her that there had been no tenant there for several months—and certainly no company or shop with the name on the two envelopes. She then opened the envelopes and found they both contained remittance advices to a company at that address from the Metropolitan Police for £50k. Both were dated only two days earlier in the week. She then panicked and became worried that the police would think that she had taken the money in question, so had rung up our Finance Department to tell us that the company address had to be wrong and to make it clear that she had not had a penny of the money."

"She spoke to Manjid in the office here. He was immediately concerned and took down the full details on the two remittances. He then checked on the accounting system and saw that we had made five payments to a company at this address in the last two weeks. The company had only been put on the system shortly before the first payment. This new creditor had been personally authorised by the Resources Manager at XXX Police Command Unit. Thinking that this had to be an error, Manjid then rang the Resources Manager and asked him to check the paperwork on these five payments to see if the addresses had got mixed up. The Resources Manager had been very vague and had told Manjid that he was suffering a migraine and would need to ring him back when he felt better."

"Manjid had waited two days and when he hadn't heard had rung up again, only to be told by the Resources Manager's assistant that he had gone sick two days ago and hadn't been seen since. Manjid reported this to me and—rightly or wrongly—I told him to pull out the invoices and look at them. We saw that they had all been authorised for payment by a temporary assistant in the Resources Manager's office. Manjid then rang the assistant up and they said that the Resources Manager had told them to authorise the invoices. They had no idea what they were for or why. The assistant had simply done as she was told. I was concerned by this and asked the Resources Manager's line manager to contact him at home and find out when he was going to return. When the Head of Unit rung him, he claimed that he had deliberately paid several invoices to himself as the budget was significantly underspent and he couldn't see any other way of the Unit holding on to the money without the Finance Department taking it back at the year end. He said that he had no intention of benefitting from it personally and he was coming in to the office to explain more fully to his boss today—but he hasn't turned up—and that is why I am now asking for Internal Audit's help."

Although I now understood, I had little sympathy. "Right. Do nothing further, please. My staff will be with you shortly. If the Resources Manager turns up, call me at once. Have you told the police yet?" "We rang up Chief Supt. XXX and he advised us to dig out the paperwork and keep on trying to contact the Resources Manager." "Well this is not his field of expertise, so do not do either of those things until my staff can deal with this and they will make the liaison arrangements with the appropriate police unit."

Despite the well-meaning but misguided efforts up to that point we were still able to rescue the investigation and facilitate an effective result for all concerned. A glance at the paperwork coupled with the reports from finance staff suggested an open-and-shut case of straightforward fraud. We rang the Economic Crime Unit (Fraud Squad as they are better known to the world at large) and explained that they had a chance for an easy collar in a £200k internal fraud and that we were babysitting the evidence for them. They nearly bit our hands off in their haste to seize the evidence and call round at the home address of the Resources Manager.

They arrested him on his own doorstep and a quick search of his home computer found the fake invoices from the company that he had set up to get the money, as well as the evidence that it had all gone into his personal bank account. My staff then got him to sign a piece of paper assigning the money back to us. The following day we called round at the bank, collected the £200k from his account and paid it back into police funds.

The Resources Manager was charged and in due course pleaded guilty. It turned out that he had noticed an empty shop on his way home from work and it had occurred to him that if he used that as the address for his fake company the remittance advices would be sent out to this dead letter drop and no one would realise that he had paid the money to himself. It was his bad luck that a shop that had been vacant for a year got a new tenant the very week he started his fraud.

The most disappointing aspect of this case was that my audit staff had spotted the very weakness exploited by the Resources Manager a whole year before this, while we were reviewing the creditor payment system. The MPS had agreed to fix it, but had delayed implementing the change while they were waiting for an upgrade to the software that ran our accounting system. While they had prevaricated, the weakness that we identified in our audit report had been exploited.

General principles and axioms**from Chapter 2**

- The biggest stumbling block to anyone finding fraud is the way most of us want to see the world. There is a tendency to assume the best until something comes to light suggesting otherwise.

- Contrary to perceived wisdom there is no personal profile that would identify a fraudster beyond doubt.

- An individual pointer to fraud means little on its own, but when two or more are present then their cumulative weight is greater than the sum of the individual items.

- Body language matters but don't jump to conclusions without the evidence.

- When checking for signs of fraud check a sufficiently wide period of time to know whether anything has changed.

- A manager, who is rewarded for their performance, whether directly in bonus or salary or indirectly in career enhancement, will be tempted to manipulate data in their favour.

- The more managers or employees tell you that you are wasting your time pursuing an explanation then the more likely it is that something is being covered up, whether fraud or just waste and incompetence.

- Benford's Law is a useful tool in the fight to find frauds, but it is important to remember that this is a rule about the first digit only—it must not be applied to second and subsequent digits in a number.

- Income frauds are often the hardest to find—and also the hardest to track down and secure the evidence.

- Cash and asset frauds occur when the segregation between those responsible for the records and those who are holding the asset breaks down.

Part II

PART TWO

Planning and managing

CHAPTER THREE

Planning a fraud investigation

CHAPTER**SUMMARY**

S etting a strategy for a fraud investigation. Key parties in the organisation and the roles they should play. Beginning with the end in mind. The basic principles that apply to any fraud investigation. How best to deal with corruption involving senior or middle management. Case study: The role that basic expenses checks can play in nailing a corrupt fraudster.

■ SETTING THE STRATEGY FOR THE FRAUD INVESTIGATION

Whether you are the internal auditor or the line manager concerned, when a potential fraud comes to light you will need to get together with the key parties as a matter of urgency and plan your strategy to deal with the fraud.

Some golden rules apply here—and before I start I apologise for any offence I'm about to cause if you are either a lawyer or a forensic accountant (or indeed if you happen to be that rare animal, a police officer who has successfully investigated significant frauds). I am not criticising the legal profession, forensic accountancy or the police. It is simply that the best-run investigations are supported by experts, rather than controlled by them.

▨ Golden rule 1: *do not* put a lawyer in charge of your internal investigation.

A lawyer is concerned with the ins and outs of the legal system and, by and large, will investigate to the law. What you need in an investigation is early establishment of the facts, regardless of where the law might then take you. I speak with many years' practical experience when I tell you that, generally, lawyers are not best placed or inclined to see the world in that light.

▨ Golden rule 2: *do not* put a forensic accountant in charge of your internal investigation.

Forensic accountants should support investigations, not run them. By and large their day comes when you need to prepare evidence for court. If you are not likely to go to court you shouldn't need them. And they are far more expensive than doing it yourself. It is far better to use them to advise and assist, or, if you have the in-house skills and time, do the investigation yourself.

Some readers may already think that I've taken leave of my senses, especially as I'm about to give the next and probably most contentious golden rule for successful fraud investigation.

▨ Golden rule 3: *do not* call the police and ask them to investigate.

(At least, not just yet!) And I am speaking after many years' experience of working with and for the police!

If you have a friend in the police who knows about fraud and in whom you trust, by all means speak to them. But otherwise, don't waste your breath—or the police's time—until you know exactly what you've got and what you need to do with it.

" YOU WANT US TO INVESTIGATE A FRAUD ? "

" I'M SORRY. WE DON'T HAVE ANYBODY AVAILABLE. "

You have to remember that the police are used to pursuing criminals when a crime has already been committed and identified or is happening as they watch. Fraud is not a specific target for the police and few detectives specialise in it. It is not the same thing at all as getting back the proceeds of crime or dealing with money laundering, two areas well understood by police officers who specialise in the financial side of crime.

In the early days of a fraud investigation you often won't know the scale of the problem or indeed if a crime has actually been committed, or by whom. None of these positions will endear you to the local CID, who'd much rather be out feeling a villain's collar, raiding a crack house or travelling to somewhere nice in the Caribbean to find a witness to a dodgy drug deal or a shooting. Ploughing through your paperwork when they've got enough of their own already simply isn't anywhere on their list of things to do today, next week or indeed next month.

So if you shouldn't do any of the above, what should you do?

First, if there is a senior manager with the bigger picture or a chief internal auditor then they are probably best placed to oversee the preliminary investigation. If you are lucky enough to have an internal investigative department already set up, then they can do the initial work, provided it is reported to and overseen by a team chaired or led by the senior manager or chief internal auditor. The initial work may include securing or locating any potential evidence, although special circumstances may apply here (see Chapters 8 and 9).

By the initial work I mean the establishment of the basic facts of the matter under investigation. If an allegation has come in via a third party, then the initial work will include trying to contact the witness or person that first made the allegation and getting their story in their own words. This is not the actual investigation itself, although properly gathered evidence at this stage will eventually form part of the investigation material and may be used either in court or at disciplinary hearings later. Where, as in my last organisation, there are well-established processes for these matters, it is quite normal for the initial fact-finding enquiries on 'routine' internal and contractor frauds to take place without any involvement of senior managers or specialist advisers outside those within the internal investigations department. However, for a significant matter, or where there is no routine activity and internal department to conduct it, then the model below should apply.

If internal fraud is suspected then other key players will include someone senior from human resources and the organisation's solicitor. For external fraud you may need your senior procurement adviser. You need to get the key management players together urgently and agree and record how you will proceed to conduct the initial investigation. That may seem strange but trust me on this one for now. You need to agree and note the key decisions taken—and a little about why you've taken them. It can all unravel horribly later on if you don't take these simple precautions at the beginning.

Likely key players—and their role—at this stage may include a selection of or all the following, whether your organisation is in the public or private sector:

(A) The 'source' of the allegation (by this I mean either the individual to whom the allegation has first been reported or the line manager, staff or auditor who has discovered the suspected fraud).

The source needs to explain why they suspect fraud and what they have done so far to the assembled senior team. Unless they will be actively involved in the investigation or potentially taking disciplinary action later their role will be limited to providing a suitably detailed account of what is known to date and making themselves available to answer questions to whoever will be running the initial fact-finding enquiries.

(B) The senior responsible officer. Usually a top manager or, if such a role exists, the deputy chief executive, who will determine the overall strategy and appoint the person who will be charged with conducting the initial fact-finding enquiries.[1] They should receive regular updates from the investigator and keep the board (or for a lesser matter the appropriate senior management) in the picture.

(C) The chief internal auditor/chief investigator (where such roles exist; may be one and the same or two separate individuals). If such individuals are not in post or the function is outsourced then it will be whoever is appointed to lead the investigation. Their role is to oversee the arrangements for the investigation and to act as the senior liaison and point of contact with others involved in conducting or advising the investigation.

(D) The specialist investigator/auditor. They will be the lead individual conducting the preliminary enquiries before the actual investigation, either on their own or with a team. Depending on what happens next after the initial facts have been established, they may also end up leading the actual investigation that follows.

(E) The organisation's HR adviser on disciplinary matters. Particularly necessary where internal fraud is suspected, to ensure that the line between fact-finding and disciplinary process is understood and to make other parties aware of the legislation and organisational rules that may impact on the way in which the investigation can be conducted.

(F) The organisation's legal adviser. They have a dual role in protecting the organisation's wider interests and in acting as the first port of call to obtain any specialist legal advice or potentially counsel's opinion on evidence that comes to light.

"RING, RING"

"OF COURSE. WE'D BE DELIGHTED TO INVESTIGATE YOUR FRAUD!"

Once the source has provided the necessary background to the suspected fraud the initial meeting can be quite brief, merely getting the senior responsible officer's approval for the preliminary enquiries and agreeing urgency, reporting arrangements and when next the parties concerned will meet to consider progress.

PLANNING THE INITIAL INVESTIGATION

This next rule may sound as tricky as the first time you had scientific sampling explained to you, but for any fraud investigation to have a chance of success you need to *begin with the end in mind*. It is no good setting off to investigate to the nth degree with a vast army of forensic accountants, auditors and lawyers trailing behind you trawling through every possible avenue. The investigation will quickly lose focus, almost as quickly as the costs will mount and the likelihood of a successful outcome will diminish. Whatever other ends you have in mind the first one, except in the rare case of a one-off fraud, will be to stop the fraud as quickly as you can!

It is wasteful, time-consuming and almost certainly pointless to send off an auditor or investigator with orders to gather every available document about the matter and see where it leads. And yet many chief internal auditors have done just that (and I include myself among that number, before I learned better of it, through practice and experience). Often the end in mind can be far more efficiently achieved with a short, sharp and focused investigation.

This is best illustrated by an example. Let us suppose that at Company Z James Dodger, Deputy Head of Procurement is suspected of favouring Company A in return for some on-going bribe, as yet to be discovered. What does Company Z want to do about this? There are a range of options and each one requires a different investigative response to achieve your organisation's objectives in that scenario.

- Option 1: Pay lip service in case shareholders or an external reviewer notice the problem later. High-level investigation only, by a trusted senior manager or director who can be relied upon to come to the right conclusion, followed by the discreet resignation of the Deputy Head of Procurement if he admits anything.
- Option 2: Play it low-key, but establish whether there is any evidence that should be given to the line manager for disciplinary

action. You will keep the investigation internal and in the hands of a trusted employee with no staff or specialist assistance.

■ Option 3: Assume the worst but because of the current political climate you want to keep a low profile as an organisation. You will keep it internal but put your best available team on the job.

■ Option 4: You are deeply concerned and want a full investigation as a matter of urgency. Integrity is ultimately more important to the long-term survival of the business than any short-term adverse publicity. You will work on the assumption that if you find evidence of his guilt, you will throw the proverbial book at him. This will involve the best available team and appropriate external professional support.

In other words, if the organisation's policy is to get rid of anyone suspected of a corrupt relationship, then your 'end in mind' is to establish as soon as you can whether there is sufficient information to sack the individual and, if not, whether you can find sufficient evidence to exonerate or not. If your organisation's policy is to keep a low profile unless there is a burden of proof, then time and outside support becomes a secondary planning issue.

Senior management will be looking for advice around the risks and potential outcomes associated with each course of action before deciding how best to proceed. This is where you need to have a clear view of your own responsibility and influence over any input into the decision. Experience shows that some outcomes can be predicted with a higher degree of certainty and likelihood than others.

The rough guide below may help clarify thoughts at this stage. Options for the end in mind deliberately do not include 'find the fraud' as finding a fraud is simply a useful stage along the journey to resolve the problem the fraud is likely to be causing to your organisation. It is not, of itself, an end in mind—although data-mining[2] specialists often seem to think that it is! The ends in mind are not mutually exclusive and it is acceptable to wish to pursue more than one of them with equal vigour. Possible ends in mind include

1. Prevent further losses to a fraud and recover as much as you can of the losses already sustained.
2. Be rid of a suspected lone fraudulent employee.
3. Be rid of a small group of suspected fraudulent employees.

4. Stop suspected fraud where no employees are clearly identifiable as the fraudsters.
5. Be rid of a fraudulent contactor.
6. Stop a fraud where no one contractor is identifiable as responsible.
7. Stop suspected collusion between a contractor and a member of staff to commit fraud.

End in mind 1 above usually goes hand in glove with one or more of ends in mind 2 to 7.

As a general rule, the early efforts of an investigation need to concentrate on how quickly and successfully further losses can be prevented, closely followed by an assessment of how difficult it will be to recover monies already lost to the fraud.

Once you know precisely how the fraud has occurred, audit staff can be tasked separately with working out whether any system changes would have prevented the fraud. I'll return to this subject in later chapters but the usual immediate 'gut' reaction of line management is to impose draconian levels of checks and controls that can tie the organisation in knots or slow down legitimate business, with the risk of creating more damage to the organisation than that caused by the fraud in the first place.

FIRST STEPS, STOPPING THE LOSSES AND STARTING THE INITIAL FACT-FINDING

This section concentrates on end in mind 1 in combination with 2. You suspect an individual is committing fraud, your management want to prevent further losses and recover already lost funds and they want to get rid of the individual concerned as quickly as they can.

The first and most obvious step is to remove the individual's means of committing the suspected fraud, so that you can immediately prevent any further losses. How far you can go with this depends on how much has come to light from the initial allegation or discovery.

The classic 'not to do' step at this stage—and I have seen otherwise sane and logical senior managers do it—is to call the suspected individual in, late on a Friday afternoon, confront them with the allegation and then ask for an explanation.

I make no apologies for reiterating this. *Do not, unless it is absolutely unavoidable, call in and confront any suspected internal fraudster in the office late in the day on a Friday.* First, if they do confess you may well find it impossible to take any action until the following week, especially if you need to speak to others in Finance and HR but they've already left—or are in a nearby hostelry for the remarkably popular Friday night office drink before going home. Second, the suspect will now have the weekend to cover their tracks while your hands are tied. Third, if they are under extreme stress and/or covering for someone else they may collapse or self-harm over the weekend while mulling over your accusation and their own actions. Finally, if they brazen it out or accuse someone else, what are you going to be able to do about it late on a Friday afternoon that will have any effect?

One such manager, accused late on Friday afternoon, immediately offered his resignation, which was accepted. Over the weekend he persuaded the security guard to let him into the office (after all, no one had yet had time to tell the office that he'd resigned with immediate effect) and proceeded to destroy incriminating documents as well as help himself to spare keys, cash and stock, all loaded into a hired van with the helpful security guard's assistance!

Generally, it is a bad idea to confront a suspect with an allegation or rumour before you have conducted any background checks to establish the substance or otherwise of the allegation. It is a practical fact that many line managers will do this before the need for an investigation is realised. At worst a potentially successful investigation may be compromised and the fraudster now alerted to the fact that they are under suspicion and the net is closing in. At best it will muddy the waters and any unexpected admission of guilt will need a well-prepared and experienced line manager if it is not to lead to chaos and confusion. This is where appropriate fraud awareness training across the organisation can help reduce the likelihood of this scenario arising (see Chapter 17).

If a line manager does get into contact to say that they have confronted an individual who has admitted their part in a fraud before an investigation has been launched then you need to ensure that, as a minimum, the following steps have been taken:

1. The line manager has made a record of the salient points, either during the interview or immediately afterwards.
2. The line manager has applied any relevant HR policy with immediate effect, including suspension/removal from the premises of the individual concerned.
3. The line manager has taken steps to prevent the individual's access to

the organisation without supervision, including removal of physical and electronic passes and closing off their access to work IT systems.

4. The line manager has secured any relevant documentation or other media immediately available, preferably in a way that does not compromise any future evidential trail. [3]

It is not necessarily the end of the world if none of this has occurred but it will make it much harder both to investigate and to bring any criminal or disciplinary proceedings against the suspect. While retrospective action may miss the boat or leave the organisation at risk in the courts, it is still arguably far better than failing to take any steps to deal with the problem.

If, on the other hand, a line manager approaches you first with an allegation about a member of their staff (or indeed it comes to you via a third party and no one has confronted the suspect) then there is a chance to plan properly and get any subsequent investigation off to the best possible chance of success.

Common possible scenarios for the suspected fraudster at this initial stage include that

a. They work in a finance or accounts department and are suspected of diverting funds though false invoices paid to a bogus company or an account under their control.

Initial action to take—either arrange their immediate suspension or, if possible, check the validity of suspicion by making a Companies House search or identifying an invoice unrelated to the organisation's business and then suspend once that evidence is found.

b. They are a cashier or deal with accounts receivable and are suspected of diverting or suppressing income.

Initial action to take—undertake a surprise cash-up or check at the point they are processing funds. If anything at all suspicious is found then suspend immediately. If not, get the appropriate line manager to suspend as discreetly as possible, with a replacement cashier lined up to take temporary charge.

c. They work in the warehousing part of the business and are suspected of diverting or stealing significant amounts of supplies.

Initial action to take—undertake a stock check of 'at risk' items and if discrepancies are found that link to the individual then suspend immediately. If not, get the appropriate line manager to suspend the individual more discreetly and use accurate information from the check to work back and identify whether significant amounts of stock are missing. If a stock check isn't possible then consider searches of all staff on leaving the premises or alternatively whether delivery and issue information can be checked remotely.

    d. They work in the procurement part of the business and are suspected of bending the procurement process in favour of an existing or potential supplier.

Initial action to take—recover any relevant procurement files/ doumentation that can be picked up without alerting the suspect. Usually any completed supply process will be capable of acquisition or electronic access without alerting others to your interest. This area is always difficult to prove so be prepared to consider other options. For instance, do they claim any expenses or have a company car? Often fraudsters will turn their hand to any cash or asset that they can abuse and it is a lot simpler to nail them on expenses than prove a corrupt relationship.

    If this isn't possible could a bit of covert surveillance or even *agent provocateur* action get them to 'show out'? Both these are high-risk, potentially expensive strategies and should only be considered if the other options are unlikely to get a result (see Chapter 8).

    e. They are a senior manager and are suspected of falsifying performance or accounting data to make their business look profitable or to hide losses.

Initial action to take—gather any of the performance/accounting data that can be checked independently of the senior manager under suspicion. This is one area where you are unlikely to get the individual suspended without absolutely cast iron evidence or 100% chief executive support. It is also a high-risk investigation as any mistakes could have dire consequences all round for the organisation.

With scenarios 'a' to 'd', where it would be impractical or dangerous to try to catch the individual in the act, wherever possible arrange for the line manager to suspend the individual as soon as the initial suspicion can be linked to any factual material that supports it.[4] It is an act that protects the organisation as a precautionary measure without accusing the individual at this stage. It is far better—at worst—to have to undo the suspension with suitable apologies all round later than to leave a potential fraudster in place while you search out the extent of the fraud.

Scenario 'e' requires a slightly different but realistic approach. In theory you don't treat any employee differently, however senior or near the top of the organisation. That is fine once the fact-finding has produced incontrovertible evidence, but in my experience when the facts are still being sought top-management's reluctance to act increases in direct proportion to the seniority of the suspect. So, concentrate your effort on the most likely item for a quick result. Again, if the area concerned is complicated to prove, look around for an easier option for quick evidence (e.g., their expenses claims). As internal fraudsters are usually after money it is almost a racing certainty that they won't pass up on the chance to fiddle their expenses.

 ## EXPENSES—THE SHORT-CUT ROUTE TO SUCCESS

In order to understand the basics of fraud investigation, it is important to understand the dynamics of investigating in real time, as opposed to an after-the-event review. When suspected fraud first comes to light, it is often unclear and you can frequently be unsure how hard to press matters at that stage, particularly if the prime suspect is either a very senior manager or someone who is known to be aggressive or belligerent if anyone dares to challenge them.

Dealing with a senior manager: fraud case study (fictional example)

Case study: Part 1

This case study, although fictional, draws on a combination of facts and actions taken from a genuine case that crossed my path a few years ago. There is nothing described in it that has not happened in reality, either in that case or similar ones that cropped up later on.

Read the scenario set out below and then, where indicated, pause and consider what you think might be wrong and what course of action you would take at this point in time. If possible, do not read on until you have decided what should be done and have noted your initial thoughts.

Scenario background information

For the purposes of this exercise imagine that you are the internal audit team leader responsible for the audit of Research X, a government agency based in London that researches information technology and advises other government bodies. Research X is overseen by another government body, the Funding Agency for Research Organisations Using Technology (FAROUT). You are part of a consortia audit service which provides the internal audit both to FAROUT and to Research X. You report to the Chief Executive of FAROUT.

Research X spends about £50m a year, including £30m on IS consultancy and product purchases. It raises £25m a year in revenues by charging other government bodies for IS consultants and software licence fees. The rest of its funding comes from a government grant through FAROUT.

Research X has a director, Dr Sidney Smarmcharm, appointed a year ago on a three-year contract. Dr Smarmcharm brought with him a business manager, Miss Loyal, also on a three-year contract. Shortly after his appointment he also brought in a business consultant, on free loan from Haadyew, a global consultancy organisation not previously used by Research X. Popular rumour, passed on to you by the Finance Director at Research X, an old golfing partner, is that there is a very cosy relationship between Miss Loyal and the apparently 'happily married' Dr Smarmcharm.

Research X's Finance Director has also muttered about the number of times that Dr Smarmcharm has demanded some improvement to his office. Only last week he had a huge captain's desk delivered, even bigger than the desk of the Chair of FAROUT. Despite his mutterings, the Finance Director has continued to pay for the office improvements.

Monday 10th February, Research X: payments audit

Your team has started a routine payments audit at Research X. You have asked your one and only team member, an experienced but suitably cynical (and grumpy) internal auditor, to take a sample of payments and test them to see if appropriate controls have been correctly applied. He sets out to grab the nearest bunch of vouchers for testing, but you are wise to this and send him back again to get a proper scientific random sample. He sets off muttering about the 'waste of time' as 'nothing ever comes out of this anyway, what a ...' You miss the last word as he disappears out of sight on his way back to the Finance Office.

One of the items now properly selected for the sample is a claim for reimbursement by Dr Smarmcharm for a restaurant meal involving four consultants from Haadyew and four Research X staff, including Dr Smarmcharm and Miss Loyal. There is no restaurant bill to support his claim but there is the top copy of the personal Visa slip which shows £450 for a meal, although the line on it noting 'meal for X persons' seems to have the 'X' smudged out so that the number of persons can't be read. Dr Smarmcharm has noted that the electronic card reader was broken, hence the copy Visa slip.

Your cynical team member is suspicious of this item. He knows that under Research X's hospitality rules staff meals can only be reimbursed if there is at least as many outside consultants as internal staff. It seems odd that this item has been inked out on the Visa slip and there is no attached bill from the restaurant. Even if the card reader was broken, wouldn't they have provided a separate bill anyway? He holds the Visa slip up to the light and notices that it reads '7' in the bit that has been smudged out.

Now please write down your answer to the following questions before reading on further:

1. Is your cynical but experienced auditor right to be suspicious of this item?

   Yes / No / Don't know

2. What course of action would you take next?

   2.1 No action?

   2.2 Look for further items of expenses claimed by Dr Smarmcharm?

   2.3 Go to the Director's office and ask Dr Smarmcharm for an explanation.

   2.4 Speak to Miss Loyal or Dr Smarmcharm's secretary about it?

   2.5 Check the expenditure on budgets and accounts controlled by Dr Smarmcharm?

   2.6 Combination of the above?

   2.7 Other action? (please specify).

Case study: Part 2—Tuesday 11 February–Wednesday 12 February

You decide to check any recent payments for expenses to Dr Smarmcharm. A quick comparison shows that he has spent far more in the last 12 months than his predecessor did in the previous three years.

Expenditure	Dr Sidney Smarmcharm	Sir Titus Thriftpenny
Meals/entertainment	£3,760	£27
UK travelling/hotels	£2,566	£158
Overseas travel/hotels	£9,570	£505
Taxi fares	£1,320	None
Lodgings near office	£8,440	£4,753

The spend for Dr Smarmcharm's support unit includes £85,000 on 'office refurbishment' of which £15,000 appears to have been spent on a leather-topped desk for Dr Smarmcharm and a further £127,000 on two extra staff, Miss Loyal and an assistant for Miss Loyal.

A quick comparison of Miss Loyal's expenses claims show that she has claimed a similar amount to Dr Smarmcharm in overseas travel and hotel costs, but only £250 for hotel expenditure in the UK and no travel, taxis or lodging claims.

Wednesday 12 February

In an unexpected moment of enthusiasm your team member calls a member of personnel he knows and asks them to let him have a look at Dr Smarmcharm and Miss Loyal's personal files, on the pretext that they may have been given the wrong start date on the payroll. In examining the files he notices two significant points. (1) Dr Smarmcharm only lives 20 miles from the office, although his predecessor lived over 100 miles away and needed occasional overnight lodging during the week. (2) Miss Loyal appears to have no previous experience as a business manager, as in her last job she was a junior official in a government computer procurement unit, of which Dr Smarmcharm was then the Deputy Head.

Now try the following questions:

3. Was your team member right to view the personnel files in this way?
4. Could the way the personnel files have been examined affect any later case against the Director or court proceedings?
5. How should you go about finding relevant personal information?
6. Now you have seen the patterns of expenditure should you seek to recover the original expenses claims, where they exist?
7. Should the recovery of expenses claims include Miss Loyal as well?
8. What other steps might you take at this stage?
9. Would you speak to anybody else about what has come to light so far?

Case study: Part 3—Monday 17 February–Wednesday 19 February

You and your team member have recovered a number of expenses claims from Finance for both Dr Smarmcharm and Miss Loyal. On examining and comparing them on UK travel and hotels you notice that Miss Loyal claimed a night's hotel costs in Birmingham for a computer conference. On her claim she has put that she travelled as a passenger in Dr Smarmcharm's officially provided car each way and that he picked her up and dropped her back at her flat in Little Horney, North London. Examination of Dr Smarmcharm's claim for the same period shows that he claimed for two nights in the Birmingham hotel and the car mileage with Miss Loyal shown as his passenger both ways. He has also put in an expenses voucher for a meal at £137, claiming that he dined out with the Managing Director of Haadyew, who was at the conference, as they could not go to the pre-booked hotel dinner because of the risk of being overheard by others at the same conference.

Thursday 20 February—11 a.m.

Your cynical team member has a bright idea. He rings up Miss Loyal, telling her he is calling from the Finance Department (this is technically true, although he neglects to mention that he is an auditor and not a finance clerk). He asks her over the phone if she stayed one or two nights in Birmingham. Miss Loyal is surprised by the question but adamant that she only stayed one night. Apparently Dr Smarmcharm had to be back in London by 2 p.m. the following day for a meeting. They had both stayed at the same hotel, the Exclusive, a five-star hotel that Dr Smarmcharm said was essential to their credibility. She recalled that they had dined there that night with the MD of Haadyew, dinner was included in the hotel price.

He then asks Miss Loyal if she can confirm the date claimed by Dr Smarmcharm for the meal with four Haadyew consultants and four staff from the original suspicious voucher. Miss Loyal checks her diary and says that there must be some mistake with the date on the claim. That day they had finished a major strategy review and as a reward Dr Smarmcharm had taken the six-strong team (including Miss Loyal) out for a slap-up meal. He had made a point of telling them he was paying for it himself as he knew the rules of Research X would not allow an official claim. They had all thought what a good egg he was.

Question time:

10. What risk has your member of staff run by making this telephone enquiry?
11. Is it valid to gather evidence in this way?
12. Can the evidence gathered be used in any subsequent criminal or disciplinary case?

Friday 21 February

On further examination of Dr Smarmcharm's claims, you realise that he has claimed full lodging allowances in a week last September when he was at a hotel in Amsterdam and not at his lodgings, a flat only a short walk from the office. The rules only allow for a reduced rate of claim when the lodgings are not being occupied. Looking back over his lodging allowance claims it is clear that he has regularly been claiming the full rate for staying there an average of three to four days a week, although his claims have reduced to one or two days a week since the Christmas break. You have a word with your old friend, Research X's Finance Director, about this. He is surprised—the lodging claims don't come through his office and he hadn't noticed the size or frequency of them. What particularly puzzles him is that he is pretty sure Dr Smarmcharm comes to work by officially provided car most days, it would be unlikely that he had driven such a short distance—although he did have a row recently with Dr Smarmcharm when he tried to get the Finance Director to pay for his and Miss

Loyal's parking fines for a night when they had both been illegally parked outside the flat.

Monday 24 February

In view of your mounting suspicions and the evidence gathered so far, you seek an urgent meeting with the Chief Executive of FAROUT to get his authority for a full and immediate investigation into all of Dr Smarmcharm's and Miss Loyal's expenses claims.

The Chief Executive of FAROUT, Sir Walter Underbridger, is very concerned and makes it plain that there are a number of wider issues to bear in mind here. Not least, they were just due to confirm Dr Smarmcharm in office and about to announce that he would be leading Research X into a new era as a fully commercial organisation, separated from FAROUT and the rest of government. The Prime Minister is due to make an announcement about it in the House just before the Easter recess.

Sir Walter is also a little personally concerned on the lodgings matter. He points out to you that he authorised the lodging arrangement himself and countersigns Dr Smarmcharm's lodgings claims before they are paid. He had already picked up the excessive use of lodgings and had told Dr Smarmcharm to reduce his number of days a week at the lodgings, which Dr Smarmcharm had now done. If, apart from that, the only concern was around errors in dates over a stay in Birmingham or a one-off clash between a week in Amsterdam and the lodgings claim, he couldn't see the justification for a potentially embarrassing investigation at a politically difficult time. Couldn't Finance simply adjust the overpayment and leave it at that? He could always have a quiet word with Dr Smarmcharm and remind him to take more care in submitting expenses claims in future. After all, in at most a year's time this would be no longer the business of FAROUT anyway.

At this point in a real case I needed to be at my most persuasive. The more senior an individual, the more important it is that they are above suspicion. For public office holders taxpayers have a right to expect officials to be both impartial and selfless in their duties and prudent with the public purse. Dr Smarmcharm has been far more costly than his predecessor. Although Sir Walter approved the lodging arrangement himself, it would be hard to justify it to any external scrutiny. Dr Smarmcharm lives 20 miles away, close to a main-line station where trains could bring him to London in 15 to 20 minutes. It is only a further 10-minute walk to the office from the London terminus. At the times when he claims to drive back and forth in the official car there would be relatively light traffic, again making it odd to see why an overnight stay would be necessary. He would have to be working very late to need to stay at the flat.

Looking at the matters that triggered the initial investigation, all the 'errors' have worked in Dr Smarmcharm's favour. There is also the clear alteration of the VISA slip. And Dr Smarmcharm seems to have a worryingly close relationship with the senior management of Haadyew. Miss Loyal does not appear to be appropriately qualified for the post that she holds and there is a strong suspicion that there is a personal relationship between her and Dr Smarmcharm that could potentially be very damaging to the organisation.

It would be difficult to find any information to form a view about the appropriateness of the relationships either with Miss Loyal or Haadyew, but it would be a relatively simple matter to conduct a more detailed examination of the various claims for expenses made by Dr Smarmcharm and Miss Loyal. That would at least identify any further errors or causes for concern and provide either the grounds for exonerating Dr Smarmcharm and Miss Loyal or sufficient evidence for any disciplinary or criminal investigation.

Reluctantly Sir Walter agrees that these matters need examining in more detail. However, the work must be completed before the Prime Minister is due to make the announcement about the future of Research X. You have exactly one week to find sufficient evidence one way or the other.

Sir Walter also makes it plain that he doesn't want anything to get out about the investigation until you have established beyond all reasonable doubt whether the points you have identified on expenses are just the result of careless errors by a busy senior official or a deliberate attempt to defraud FAROUT and Research X.

Further questions to consider:

13. What steps would you take next?
14. How would you ensure that sufficient evidence has been examined in the time available?
15. What can be done without word of the fact-finding investigation spreading?

Case study: Part 4—Monday 24 February–Thursday 27 February

You and your cynical sidekick work flat out to examine all the financial records held by the system that relate to Dr Smarmcharm and Miss Loyal in the last 12 months, including expenses claims for travel and subsistence, petty cash claims for taxi reimbursements, expenditure on petrol for the official car and lodging claims. All are cross-mapped to see any unexpected results. In summary you find the following:

1. There are eight separate occasions where, according to Dr Smarmcharm, he and Miss Loyal travelled together in his car to conferences and stayed for either two or three nights and returned. In every instance Miss Loyal has claimed for being away one day less than is shown in Dr Smarmcharm's claim.
2. There are 15 instances where Dr Smarmcharm has claimed a taxi reimbursement on his expenses claim but his secretary had already claimed the money for him out of the petty cash.
3. There are two instances where Dr Smarmcharm has claimed petrol mileage for his official car to Heathrow and back, when flying out to conferences abroad. In

both cases he has also put in and been paid for the taxi fares to Heathrow and back.

4. There is one instance where Dr Smarmcharm appears to have claimed for the same return journey to Heathrow on the same days three times over. First, he has claimed full mileage rate while using a hire car, including diverting via Miss Loyal's home to collect her and drop her back home on the return journey. Second, he has claimed first-class rail fares from his home to Heathrow (and return) and finally he has also claimed taxi fares to and from Heathrow out of petty cash for the same two days.

5. When you check the invoice for the hire car, the paperwork shows that it was provided for two months as a replacement for a pool car 'loaned' to Dr Smarmcharm during his first six months in post, before he was provided with an official car. The pool car came complete with its own petrol card for getting it fuelled up. Looking at the fleet petrol card withdrawals during the period when Dr Smarmcharm did have the pool car, there are numerous occasions when the amount of petrol used to fill up the pool car exceeds its fuel tank capacity. You know from his expenses claims that when Dr Smarmcharm has used his own car from home to a conference and claimed the mileage he has a large vehicle with sufficient fuel tank capacity for that amount of fuel.

Friday 28 February—7 a.m.

You come into the office very early on Friday morning to write up your findings ready for taking them to the Chief Executive at 3 p.m. on Friday afternoon, as planned.

Friday 28 February—7:45 a.m.

To your surprise, the phone rings. The Chief Executive's secretary informs you that Sir Walter wants to see you in his office immediately. She indicates that he isn't very pleased about something and your name is mud.

When you arrive, Sir Walter tells you that Dr Smarmcharm has demanded an urgent meeting with him at 10 a.m. today. He doesn't know why, because Smarmcharm refused to tell him over the phone, but he can only assume that somehow Smarmcharm has found out about your investigation and he wants to know what he is supposed to do when Smarmcharm gets there. He makes it plain that you will be held responsible if Dr Smarcharm takes out any kind of claim against FAROUT over this. He also demands that you find out before 10 a.m. how this information could have leaked out. Your investigation findings can wait until later, to avoid clouding his judgement when seeing Dr Smarmcharm.

As you are being ushered out of the office you can hear Sir Walter muttering, while shaking his head, 'I should never have allowed myself to be persuaded than an investigation was necessary, how am I going to explain this cock-up to the Prime Minister ... Why oh why didn't we appoint that other fellow, he wouldn't have been demanding investigations at the drop of a hat.'

You spend a miserable two hours thinking it all through but the explanation for the leak is obvious. It must have been that risky phone call to Miss Loyal. She has clearly spoken to Dr Smarmcharm about it. There is no other explanation that seems even remotely possible.

Friday 28 February—10 a.m.

Eventually you ring up Sir Walter's secretary to pass on the explanation. She seems surprisingly disinterested. 'Don't worry. The boss had another phone call from old smarmypants just after you left. He admitted he wants to see him about a job he's been offered in the private sector on far more money than we give him as the head of Research X—nothing to do with your investigation after all!'

Friday 28 February—3 p.m.

You turn up, armed with your report and supporting documents, to show Sir Walter what you have found to date. In the room, as well as Sir Walter, is FAROUT's head of HR and your old golfing pal from Research X, their Finance Director. Everyone listens attentively and it is clear that they all understand your findings and conclusions. They agree that Dr Smarmcharm has some serious explaining to do and, inexplicable as it seems for a man in his senior position, it looks like he has committed a number of petty frauds.

The head of HR explains that Dr Smarmcharm told Sir Walter at the 10 a.m. meeting that he is accepting the job he has been offered in the private sector and will be handing in his resignation to the Chair early next week. He has also indicated that he will be taking Miss Loyal with him. The Head of HR is firmly of the view that it would be best to forget this had ever happened and just let Dr Smarmcharm slide off into the private sector, never to darken Research X's doors again. Research X's Finance Director isn't so sure and is worried what else might come to light later. Sir Walter looks at you. 'Well, what is your view?'

The final question:

16. So what would you advise the organisation to do now?
    a. For the sake of the organisation let Dr Smarmcharm go and forget about it.
    b. Refuse to accept his resignation and suspend him while a full internal investigation is conducted.
    c. Call the police and ask them to investigate?

d. Sack him immediately?
e. Call him in and seek an explanation and then decide whether to accept his resignation or suspend him?
f. None of the above? (please write down what you would advise instead)
g. Some of the above? (please write down which options you would choose)

In a parallel real case the organisation in question refused to accept the resignation, suspended the senior officer and his business manager, called in the police and worked alongside them to complete the investigations. They discovered further discrepancies, including expenses claims made when technology companies had laid on and paid for everything, including flights and entertainment. Hotel rooms had been claimed by both of them when in fact he and his 'business manager' had shared a room. Even the costs of attending his interviews for the new job had been claimed off both organisations. The organisation that had offered the job withdrew their offer and when the police had completed their enquiries the senior officer was charged with a number of counts of theft (it was long before the Fraud Act). On being found guilty he was sent to prison, because, as the judge put it, he held a position of considerable trust that he had abused.

The business manager was allowed to resign and was never prosecuted. She had the defence that he had told her to make the hotel claims abroad and it was obvious from her expenses that apart from those occasions she had only claimed for her actual expenses, unlike her boss.

Some interesting patterns were apparent from the real case and have been reflected in the case study above. Signs were there for the more alert and naturally suspicious months before he came to Internal Audit's attention during the routine payments audit.

Had anyone looked properly at the lodging allowance request they would have noted not only the absurdity when he lived so close by and had two different ways of getting to and from work easily, but also that he had 'lifted' the body of his arguments for a lodging allowance from the letter written by his predecessor, who did live a significant distance away from the office.

The appointment of his business manager, who was patently under-qualified for the job, should have been challenged. Everyone in the office knew that she was really his mistress, but no one liked to speak up about it. In fact, when he was being vetted for his job, HR realised that he had a long history of sexual liaisons with women at work or women from consultancy firms vying for government business, but it was decided that this wasn't any concern or risk to the day job, since he was clearly so self-interested.

The self-aggrandising spends on the office and captain's desk—and insistence on having an official car as well as a pool car were also signs of someone with little regard for the rules—or the public purse. Any examination of his budget would have shown a spiralling spend on matters connected with his own office and immediate staff.

His 'free' consultant. There is an old saying in business that there is no such thing as a free lunch. The same applies to consultants. A check of hospitality records would have shown that he had been entertained by the Managing Director of this consultancy on many occasions in a relatively short space of time.

It was normal for senior officers to have their expenses claims compiled by their secretaries and then just sign them. Instead he insisted on completing his own. Within weeks of making his first claims, he became embroiled in correspondence with the Finance Department, demanding that they pay for or reinstate items that they tried to adjust. Often the sums being argued over were unbelievably petty. All this pointed to someone who was overly obsessed with money and likely to commit fraud.

CASE STUDY: ANSWERS

As in real life, not all the answers are clear-cut—you will have to use your judgement!

1. Is your cynical but experienced auditor right to be suspicious of this item?

   Yes!

2. What course of action would you take next?

   Gather the available background information to decide whether you need to investigate. Don't 'do nothing' and don't confront the suspect!

3. Was your team member right to view the personnel files in this way?

   No. It was unnecessary subterfuge. You should have a right to check supporting financial data to transactions. If necessary HR could ensure that you don't see any personal or medical information that is irrelevant to your search. Fishing expeditions are looked on very dimly by both criminal and civil courts!

4. Could the way the personnel files have been examined affect any later case against the director or court proceedings?

   Yes, adversely, if it comes to light.

5. How should you go about finding relevant personal information?

   By asking the holder of the information to provide you with access to the information that relates to your enquiry.

6. Now you have seen the patterns of expenditure should you seek to recover the original expenses claims, where they exist?

   Yes, as quickly and quietly as you can.

7. Should the recovery of expenses claims include Miss Loyal as well?

   Yes—and anyone else whose claims might cross-refer.

8. What other steps might you take at this stage?

   This one depends. I'd concentrate on expenses where he has to put in a claim of some sort to get them.

9. Would you speak to anybody else about what has come to light so far?

   I'd be inclined to give the boss an early heads-up, in view of the seniority of the individual in whom I'm taking an interest. I certainly wouldn't be asking others or calling the police at this stage.

10. What risk has your member of staff run by making this telephone enquiry?

    High risk of blowing out the case and alerting Dr Smarmcharm to the fact that you're on to him. Not recommended, although I have taken similar risks, but only when absolutely necessary.

11. Is it valid to gather evidence in this way?

    A moot point. You could easily undermine your own credibility and integrity, leading to challenges to the rest of your evidence.

12. Can the evidence gathered be used in any subsequent criminal or disciplinary case?

    Probably—but at court a stroppy judge or magistrate might just make you pay for it!

13. What steps would you take next?

    Plan who is going to do what—and make sure that you read every bit of evidence you gather, that way the bigger picture becomes clearer.

14. How would you ensure that sufficient evidence has been examined in the time available?

    Make sure that all claims for travel and subsistence are gathered and concentrate on 'errors' in them before checking other records.

15. What can be done without word of the fact-finding investigation spreading?

    Anything that just involves the 'normal' collection of financial records for audit examination. If you start interviewing or asking questions, then it will get out before you are ready.

16. So, what would you advise the organisation to do now?

    Tempting as it is for the organisation to let him go, you are a putative frauditor—we don't let them off the hook! Often senior management will automatically go for the quietest and easiest option. It is up to us to make them think very carefully about what is right and fair in such circumstances. Also, if a top dog gets away with it, the cultural damage down the organisation can be far more catastrophic than any publicity over pursuing a senior official for expenses fraud.

General principles and axioms**from Chapter 3**

The best-run investigations are supported by experts, rather than controlled by them.

Golden rule 1: *do not* put a lawyer in charge of your internal investigation

A lawyer will investigate to the law. What you need in an investigation is early establishment of the facts, regardless of where the law might take you.

Golden rule 2: *do not* put a forensic accountant in charge of your internal investigation

Forensic accountants should support investigations, not run them.

Golden Rule 3: *do not* call the police and ask them to investigate

▪ If you have a friend in the police who knows about fraud and in whom you trust, by all means speak to them. But otherwise, don't waste your breath—or the police's time—until you know exactly what you've got and what you need to do with it.

▪ Fraud is not a specific target for the police and few detectives specialise in it.

▪ At the start of the investigation you need to get the key management players together urgently and agree and record how you will proceed to conduct the initial investigation.

▪ For any fraud investigation to have a chance of success you need to *begin with the end in mind*.

▪ Often the end in mind can be far more efficiently achieved with a short, sharp and focused investigation.

▪ The early efforts of an investigation need to concentrate on how quickly and successfully further losses can be prevented, closely followed by an assessment of how difficult it will be to recover monies already lost.

▪ *Do not, unless it is absolutely unavoidable, call in and confront any suspected internal fraudster in the office late in the day on a Friday.*

▪ Generally, it is a bad idea to confront a suspect with an allegation or rumour before you have conducted any background checks to establish the substance or otherwise of the allegation. It is a practical fact that many line managers will do this before the need for an investigation is realised.

▪ When the facts are still being sought, top-management's reluctance to act increases in direct proportion to the seniority of the suspect. Concentrate your effort on the most likely item for a quick result. If the area concerned is complicated to prove, look around for an easier option for quick evidence (e.g., expenses claims).

CHAPTER FOUR

Managing the investigation

No plan of operations extends with any certainty beyond the first contact with the main hostile force

Field Marshall Helmuth Carl Bernard Graf von Moltke[1] (1871)

CHAPTER**SUMMARY**

W hy effective managing is the next most important task. Getting the basics right. Tips and suggestions to help manage the team. Keeping a proper record. The benefits of using specialised investigation management software.

WHY EFFECTIVE MANAGING IS THE NEXT MOST IMPORTANT TASK AFTER PLANNING

This is a very hard chapter for me to write and that may be some consolation for those of you who have a similar issue to me. I have always been in the vanguard of the need for proper planning and, over the years, built a reputation as a hard but fair professional boss. But the one thing that I always knew about myself was that I was a far better leader than I was a manager. I could inspire people and get them to follow my vision but the day-to-day management of the task often left me cold and I had to rely on the strength of the senior team around me to organise and control the investigations and audits that mattered most to us.

The paragraph above may sound a strange place to start but the single most important lesson that history can teach us about effective management is that the manager who understands themselves can build an effective team, regardless of any shortcomings in management that they may have personally. I always felt at work that I had the qualities of Napoleon's 'lucky general'. I wasn't the best or the most organised but was always wholly committed, utterly tenacious and had a knack of getting it right when it really mattered. By happenstance or judgement the inner team around me could always complement my weaknesses and I theirs. And I never lost that nose for fraud throughout my career!

So, the first step to effective management is always to ensure that you know yourself. In the context of fraud investigation it is particularly important to keep accurate records of what you have done and why. It is even more important to know when you need to make a decision, to make the best available decision and then to make sure that someone is keeping an adequate record of what you have decided and why. If either the decision making or the proper recording doesn't come naturally to you then you need to find somebody to work with who can do this, or you will come spectacularly unstuck when it matters most.

It is a sad truism that it isn't what you do today that comes back to haunt you in the world of investigations, it is what you did two or more years earlier. If, for any reason, you find yourself in front of a judge trying to explain why you took what now looks to everyone an unfortunate decision in an investigation, if there is a clearly recorded reason why you made that judgement and it was sensible on what you knew at that time, then generally you will not be criticised for taking a decision that in hindsight was wrong. You are far more likely to find yourself in hot water if you should have taken a decision and there is no evidence that you ever did.

▪ GETTING THE BASICS RIGHT

If you have the two key attributes of knowing yourself and being able to keep adequate readable and reliable records, then you can probably manage an investigation on your own effectively, should that be the scenario that faces you. On most occasions you will either be part of someone else's team or running a small team set up just for the purpose of getting to the bottom of the suspected fraud that has triggered the investigation. There are some basic steps that can keep the management of the investigation on course. These are summarised below—and remember, even though I used to rely on others for most of them, I was always acutely aware that you ignore the basics at your peril.

The 10 basics of effective fraud investigation management

1. Select the right team for the investigation.
2. Make sure that they are all fully briefed and understand the task and the terms of reference.
3. Hold regular sessions with the team to check progress with lines of enquiry.
4. Keep adequate records of all investigative decisions, especially when and why they were taken.
5. Keep your management in the picture but don't let them interfere.
6. Keep properly indexed records of all intelligence, evidence and supporting documentation.
7. Keep on top of new information and evidence as it is uncovered by your team.
8. Have the courage to change tack if new evidence comes to light, but don't forget to keep the original end in mind.
9. Keep a tight rein on external costs and consumption of internal resources.
10. Use legal, forensic, accounting and HR experts sparingly and wisely— but don't be afraid to ask for their opinions or assistance.

Keeping in touch with the plan

Even though investigation plans will often get cast aside when the case gets going (per the quote at the start of this chapter), for any investigation of any complexity, particularly where there are a number of competing priorities to be investigated, it is a useful discipline to draw up an investigation plan and allocate task priorities according to it. I can honestly say that I never did this myself, but it was always a weakness of which I was conscious. Instead I recognised the wisdom of von Moltke's words and tended to rely on my speed of reaction to the events that unfolded during the investigation, but on the more complex cases, with hindsight, it would have helped me if I had set out the priorities in a plan and used that as the basis for allocating investigative resource.

If you are more personally organised than I was, or indeed are concerned about whether you have got your priorities right, then an investigation plan that is regularly reviewed will be of considerable help in managing the investigation. But, although it is recognised best practice, I have to tell you that if you are the sort of investigator/auditor that I was, you will find that very quickly the plan gets out of touch with the tactical aspects of the investigation on the ground and you have to think on your feet to get the case home.

How to be sure that you don't underestimate those at the top of the food chain

Most organisations will either have a small investigative resource or rely on setting up an ad hoc team to run the fraud investigation when the need arises. This next section is particularly intended for your benefit if you fall into that category. On the other hand, if you have an established and budgeted investigative team, permanently set up and with an ongoing caseload then you are half-way towards ensuring that when the big case comes along you'll be able to manage the investigation. Hopefully you'll have an agreed strategy and resources available to meet it and there will be appropriate anti-fraud policies in place to back up your work (see Chapter 17: 'Fraud risk, awareness and whistle-blowing'). I'll return to that as there are still pitfalls when that mega-case arrives but for now I'd like to consider the management issues that are likely to beset either a one-off or a small team that has to tackle a potentially large investigation.

The title at the top of this section is a reminder that you will need to keep with you at all stages of managing the investigation, as you will also need to manage the expectations of the senior and top management in your organisation. When the initial fraud comes to light and the organisation is in fire-fighting mode it is all hands to the pump. After the first flurry of activity you now have to manage the investigation going forward. Your plans have by now been tacitly approved and you are gathering your resources and planning the work for the investigative team. It is not uncommon at this stage to find a very supportive top management anxious that you should get to the bottom of the matter and resolve things as soon as you can. To that end you may be told that this is a priority and resources won't be an issue. But beware—this honeymoon period won't last long.

However bullish your management might seem at first, unless the investigation comes to a remarkably rapid conclusion, they will start to wonder if they've given you too free a hand quite early on. As the weeks drag by without the quick 'kill' that they are expecting the more dove-like members of management will be whispering in the boss's ear and asking awkward questions about budgets and costs. No one ever expects an investigation to cost as much as it does, hence why you will need to keep your controllable costs on as tight a rein as you can, but top management will generally soon lose focus on the priority awarded the investigation once the next crisis hits their desk.

It is therefore particularly important that you don't only begin with the end in mind but you also manage the expectations of top management. Be absolutely clear about the risks if the investigation goes off half-cocked. Make sure they understand why you must complete your enquiries. Equally make sure that you have something in writing giving their expectations of your investigation, that initial terms of reference under which you are operating is all-important here.

Sometimes, however they sound in public, top management actually don't want you to find out the truth—either for political reasons or because you'll end up hitting too close to home for their comfort. It is important to read between the lines at an early stage and take a view. How do you feel about the case, are they really just giving you a token team and don't want a result? If it looks that way get a private meeting with the boss ASAP and get it from the horse's mouth. You can then decide whether you are going to obey orders or not.

If you're like me you'll probably press ahead anyway, but be prepared to take a mental battering if you do. On more than one occasion I've been ordered to pull an investigator off a case, or stop asking awkward questions or to use my investigative resource elsewhere. On one extreme occasion I was told I needed a 'rest' as I was clearly 'under stress' with a particular investigation. That was immediately after I was asked to pull my most experienced investigator off the case and I had refused! I was quite clear, I worked for the state and I was paid to do a certain job to protect the organisation and the tax-payer. If sometimes finding the truth in an investigation was too uncomfortable for my bosses but clearly in the interests of truth and justice—or indeed the tax-payer—then I would take on board their views but continue my enquiries.

Most of the time a lukewarm or hostile management response has simply strengthened my resolve to find out what it is that everyone is so anxious to avoid seeing the light of day. However, if the pressure is too much or you have to consider feeding your family then you'll have to make your own judgement, weighing up moral values against social needs. I was lucky that I didn't have to make my first career-threatening judgement call until I was already experienced and had a number of successful investigations under my belt. Even then I had days when self-doubt—both about whether I was right and whether I'd be employable again—would surface.

If it is a matter of integrity to get to the truth and the suspected fraud is a significant matter then if you find you are unable to gainsay the bosses, my personal advice in such circumstances would be to start looking around for another job ASAP. Otherwise once you know the integrity of your investigation has been compromised you know they cannot be trusted to support you when it really matters.

Overconfidence and doubt—their part in clouding the strategy from view

One more issue here. This is very much a personal view, but if you don't ever doubt that you're right I would be very concerned that you're either not seeing the whole picture or have convinced yourself that you are infallible. I was constantly re-evaluating and checking, recognising that it is normal to have got something wrong somewhere. During a fraud investigation there are always moments when you wonder if you've gone down the wrong line of enquiry or misread a key witness. If you feel that way at times, take comfort in it. There is nothing worse than the complacent investigator who sees every pattern fitting the case they see before them. It is almost the worst sin of commission that there is, for an investigator to have rigidly made their mind up before they have gathered all the relevant facts.

The real investigator's art is to take a broader view and while prepared to adapt if necessary, equally to think calmly and logically about the story you are unveiling by the facts being discovered during your investigation. During periods of self-doubt pause for a while and analyse what has actually happened. See it at a strategic level and all becomes clear. Then you will know whether it was just a moment of doubt or you genuinely need to adjust the flow of the investigation.

I can remember a very early experience that reinforced this for me. A particularly confident and experienced colleague had me in tow when

I was learning the ropes in NHS Audit in the 1970s. We were reviewing a hospital catering department that was massively overspent. All the signs were that it was out of control and we could see from the financial records that middle management (the Head Chef and his deputies) were getting paid incredible amounts of overtime when the junior cooks and support staff were largely earning the basic wage. My confident colleague told me that there could be no explanation other than fraud and incompetence for what was happening. We extracted all the relevant cost and management information that we could lay our hands on and set off to interview the Catering Manageress in the hope that we could get to the bottom of what had been going on. The last thing that he said to me before we went in to the interview was that there was nothing she could say to him that would change his view of what had gone wrong.

To give her credit, the Catering Manageress was very convincing. I was just the note-taker that day but every concern my colleague raised had an answer that on the surface seemed to see him off. As the interview went on, I began to anticipate her replies from the body language before me. It was all fascinating stuff and I felt I was getting a real lesson in how we did our work. It became clearer and clearer that no matter how convincing she sounded on each point, the whole story simply did not hang together.

We left the interview and were walking back to my confident colleague's car to go back to our base, some five miles away. He looked at me and asked what I thought. I wanted to look balanced so I just said. 'Those were some very interesting explanations.' He nodded, but not, as I soon realised, in agreement. 'Well, yes, I have to say. I think that explains everything. We don't need to do any more enquiries on this one.' I was stunned. How could he have fallen for that nonsense? I reminded him of what he had said before we went in. It seemed that now he was as confident of his view after interviewing her as he had been of the opposite point of view before the interview.

We got back to the office and my colleague told our boss that all was well and we should move on. I have never been that good at hiding my own body language and the boss sensed that I was a little agitated. He called me in to have a private word later. I explained that no matter what had been said, it simply did not explain what was happening on the ground, which had all the hallmarks of some organised fraud or abuse.

The boss believed me and gave me the investigation to do on my own. My colleague was furious and I was effectively ostracised by half the audit team for months. To cap it all, through inexperience and poor report-writing skills I didn't bring the investigation home, instead the chief culprit was commended by the hospital management for their hard work. (In part of my report I had pointed out that according to his clock cards, which were only punched in but always just a manual entry when he left, he had worked 91 days in succession from 6 a.m. to 9 p.m. I had assumed everyone would realise that the entries were a lie, but I didn't express it that way and they deliberately chose to take it the other way. It was a valuable lesson in the need to be clear and unambiguous in a report.)

Several years later the true extent of the frauds and abuse were revealed, when the culprit's two main sidekicks got caught running a commercial business with hospital equipment and supplies. That led straight back and the head cook and his four assistant head cooks were finally sacked. I was on a different team by then but the team that were there when it all came to light contacted me so that I knew what had happened. They had seen in the previous files that I was a lone voice saying there was fraud here and no one had supported me once I'd produced the results of my first investigation. They wanted me to know that I had been vindicated at long last.

Sensing the structure of the fraud

Always make sure that you can feel how the investigation is going. The best way to do this and keep on top of my top-10 tips for effective fraud investigation management is to keep an informal dialogue going with your key people on the investigation. In my mind's eye I'm constantly adjusting my radar and seeing further into the case with every team and individual update on the investigation. If you have a team doing the groundwork for you it isn't your job then to manage the day-to-day tactics on the ground but you should be thinking strategically about the bigger picture, keeping yourself and the team focused while at the same time seeing how every new discovery feeds into the emerging picture.

 ## TIPS AND SUGGESTIONS TO HELP MANAGE THE INVESTIGATION

The role of an independent 'mentor'

If the investigation lasts any length of time beyond a week it is worth having a weekly reflection for your own benefit on progress to date, in addition to any formal sessions you have arranged with the team to check progress with lines of enquiry. For ongoing weekly reflections in long or difficult cases it is helpful if you can identify a trusted individual who is not involved in the investigation to act as your 'sounding board' and also to point out the obvious.

When you are wrapped up in the intricacies of an investigation it is often very hard to see the bigger picture or even to think logically and calmly about any decisions that need to be taken. I always found it helpful to discuss cases in complete confidence with an old trusted friend, a Cambridge mathematician who could see logic and pattern where I couldn't. He always brought a wholly different perspective to our enquiries and made me think hard about whether I was on the right track or in danger of failing to see the wood for the trees. Even when I couldn't agree with him, it was worth the debate and discussion outside of the team just to clear my head and get the grey cells thinking clearly about how I was going to nail my fraudster.

For lengthy or complex cases it is a good idea to find a mentor who is recognised as an expert in the type of fraud that you have under investigation. Keep a record of your meetings and the key points discussed, so that when you are having case meetings with your team or debriefing senior management you can compare where you are planning to go with the independent view of the case to date. It may prove a godsend to be able to produce a formal record of your handling of the case if it is challenged later, either by management or the courts.

Keep as much of the ongoing case passing across your desk as you can

You mustn't slow down the work of the investigative team but it is important to read as much of the material coming out of the investigation as you practically can, not only to give a flavour of how the investigators are doing but also to make sure that you have a clear overview of how the case is developing and which leads look the most fruitful.

If you are the senior investigating officer for the case then you must read *all* new evidence as it comes in—it is the only way you are going to be able to make necessary tactical adjustments to the investigation. If the senior investigator is reporting to you then you need to make sure that they are reading and examining all evidence as it comes to light.

Use a recognised case management system to support the work of the team

In my last job we used a system common in many local authority investigation units. It enabled us to track the mechanics of the case to a suitable standard for any potential court proceedings, criminal or civil—and could be used as a secure database to extract independent information about when we had taken and recorded certain actions on a particular enquiry. It also had the advantage of matching the fraud investigation standards expected by the Audit Commission for local authorities. Such systems are essential if you have a number of cases running in parallel or a permanent team set up to investigate fraud.

Systems such as Civica's 'Fraud Detection' software provide automated case management for investigations, allowing both individual investigators to track their cases appropriately and line management to be able to see where investigators have—or haven't—got to with each of the cases that they are working on.

It is just about possible to use a standard audit management tool in this way as well, such as Teammate or Pentana, but their disadvantage is that they are not designed with the investigator in mind and as a consequence will not flag up the points where an investigator must ensure that they have an adequate record of what they have done. We looked long and hard at putting our investigators on the same system as our internal auditors but in the end concluded that the audit software was too rigidly aimed towards auditors to use effectively for investigative case management, even though the technical aspects of both software systems were very similar.

Check, check and check again!

As the case moves forward, the accuracy of the evidence and the facts gathered becomes crucial. There are always two stock errors built in to any investigation: (1) errors committed by those providing the evidence, either through exuberance, ignorance or mendaciousness and (2) errors committed by the investigator, either through a momentary lack of diligence or misinterpretation of the evidence. The only way to eliminate errors is to go through and double-check the evidence at every possible opportunity—and wherever you can to get the detailed facts checked by staff not involved in the compilation of the original evidence.

An entire investigation can be put into jeopardy by a single simple error of fact. If won't matter how good the rest of your case may be, if the opposition can unstitch just one matter and show doubt about a single fact presented in your case, then doubt will have been thrown on the accuracy of every other matter that you are presenting in that case. Hence I cannot emphasise enough that you must constantly check your facts and double-check, triple-check any evidence that is to be relied upon for the case.

Gather the facts and let the law worry about itself

The key to a successful investigation is to gather and produce the relevant evidence. Therefore, in managing your investigation, your priority is to ensure that you are gathering and properly documenting the evidence that you will need to prove the case. Facts are evidence, opinion is not. Evidence can be relied upon and produced in court. Opinions, except from a relevant expert, are meaningless as evidence.

While I have emphasised in dealing with the law (Chapter 15) that the police will see criminal cases in terms of the ingredients necessary to support a criminal charge, that should not be the driving raison d'être behind your investigation. You must establish the facts, wherever they may take you. It is only then that you can look at the facts and see if you have the right ingredients for a particular outcome from the investigation.

Cases move at different speeds and you will need to adapt your working practices to match the case. For instance, if it is a particularly fast-moving case, with new developments each day, then hold a daily case management meeting with the team. For other cases a weekly meeting may be sufficient.

Communicating effectively when writing up the investigation report

This is probably the single most common area where otherwise good professional investigators can let themselves down time and time again.

While decisions, data records and case management information can be written up well, writing a coherent and focused report addressed to the target audience is something that seems to have evaded most investigators with whom I have ever met or worked. Part of the problem is that those investigators that are ex-police are very much used to the highly stylised way investigative reports are written up inside the police community. While these may be appropriate for investigations into other types of crime, they are unhelpful for almost every type of fraud case that an internal investigator will come across.

Other investigators suffer from what I tend to think of less than fondly as 'the anally retentive auditor's disease'. This involves writing up reams of irrelevant detail about how they came to do the investigation, liberal use of jargon that no one outside the audit community will ever understand and a grammatically incorrect series of clumsily written statements that draw no conclusion and leave the reader in the dark about what has been discovered and what it might mean.

Either you, or if you have one, your head of investigations, will need to be skilled in the basics of effective report writing if the reports from individual investigators are to be turned into a usable product outside of the investigative team.

Most of an investigator's initial write-up of material is adequate for the preparation of any witness statements that may be needed for an internal inquiry or discipline board and can be used as the basis for a witness statement for either police inquiries or civil cases, where the means by which they came to discover their evidence will be important. However, except in very rare instances, it will not be suitable to write up the case for management or as a permanent record of the investigation and its conclusion. Over the years I can only think of one field investigator that I worked with who was able consistently to produce reports that only needed a minor tweak before I could update management or take strategic decisions about where we were going with an investigation.

Key elements for an effective *progress report* on an investigation include:

Main report

1. A brief 'executive summary' of what has been covered and what has been discovered, written in terms that the report's intended audience can follow.
2. Recommendations for any further investigative work and estimated time needed to do it.
3. Recommendations for likely outcomes (e.g., suspension [if it hasn't already happened], discipline investigation, charges, civil action, no action).
4. A more detailed (but not too detailed!) report of the investigation so far, including who has conducted it, timeline of both the investigation and the alleged events, what they have found and whether it is indicative of fraud, etc.
5. Conclusions.

Appendices

6. The agreed terms of reference for the investigation.
7. Details of any written professional legal advice supporting the work to date.
8. A few key documents supporting the findings and conclusions so far. [2]
9. Information on resources consumed to date and estimated further resources needed to complete the investigation.

Key elements for a *final investigation report* are

Main report

1. A brief 'executive summary' of what has been covered and what has been discovered, written in terms that the report's intended audience can follow.
2. Recommendations for likely outcomes (e.g., discipline investigation, charges, civil action, no action).
3. Recommendations to fix any system/business weaknesses identified during the investigation.
4. A more detailed report of the investigation, including who has conducted it, timeline of investigation and the alleged events, what they have found and whether it is indicative of fraud, etc.
5. Conclusions
6. Name and official title of the report author, date of report.

Appendices

7. The agreed terms of reference for the investigation and any amendments made and agreed during the investigation.
8. Details of any written professional legal advice supporting the work.
9. A comprehensive list of witnesses interviewed or contacted for information during the investigation.
10. All key documents and evidence supporting the findings and conclusions, including, where appropriate, copies of witness statements.
11. Information on resources consumed and comparison with allocated budget.

These reports are not witness statements. They are the final products of your investigation and should be treated with the care that they deserve. Some worthy organisations would have such reports start with a lengthy diatribe about the investigator's background and skills, to justify why they have the expertise to write the report. Trust me on this, it isn't necessary. If you need to prove your bona fides then that will happen in the witness box and you can include it at the start of any witness statement that you have to make.

Communicating with the organisation and the media

Fraud cases can often attract a lot of internal interest and media attention. If it is a sufficiently high-profile case or you have had to call in outside help or report the case to the police, the chances are that the press will get to hear and start to take an interest in your organisation's affairs. It is best to try to pre-empt this state of affairs by having a pre-prepared briefing for internal staff and a media line or lines to be taken by your organisation's press office or equivalent function. As the case develops, don't forget to get those lines updated and if necessary cleared with the organisation's lawyer.

You will also need to adopt whatever policy your organisation has in such circumstances. If it doesn't have one, then that is something that you will have to agree at one of your very first management meetings on the case. You will also have to warn your own team about rumours and not communicating to others outside the official press release—or, prior to that, ensuring that your team refers all media contact to the press office and declines to speak directly to the press. If you have an official media contact then all press and other enquiries should be routed through them.

Sometimes rumours will be rife and there will be speculation in the press, as well as considerable peer pressure inside the organisation. In such circumstances it is best to lie as low as possible, preparing additional defensive briefing lines for the public faces of your organisation and the press office, should they need to use them. Your lawyers will advise you, but for many cases you run the risk of prejudicing your own chances of court success if you talk to the media or speculate about the evidence that you have found. Often a simple matter-of-fact note to all staff will dampen down rumour and speculation without risking prejudicing your case. But don't forget, if any staff have been suspended then you cannot comment until the case has been resolved, however galling it might feel while those in ignorance gossip around you.

In a worst-case scenario, such as a live television broadcast, try to keep matters as low-key and matter-of-fact as you can. With all my years of experience I still found myself boxed in when a BBC TV crew turned up to film a public authority meeting at which I was speaking about one of our major fraud scandals. For half an hour I was able to make it so low-key that they were losing interest but then an eagle-eyed member of the public authority asked me if it was fraud. I couldn't lie about it and the next thing my live reply was the main item on the London news that day, despite the 30 minutes that I had avoided saying anything even remotely controversial. We did, however, have pre-prepared press lines and with a quick bit of tweaking after the public meeting we got back into our 'low profile until the case is resolved' mode.

Once a case is resolved in court, subject to any confidentiality agreements for any settlement, then the gloves are off and you can—and should—publicise any successes.

General principles and axioms**from Chapter 4**

▣ The manager who truly understands themselves can build an effective team, regardless of any shortcomings in their own management abilities.

▣ It is particularly important to keep accurate records of what you have done and why.

▣ It is even more important to know when you need to make a decision, to make the best available decision and then to make sure that someone is keeping an adequate record of what you have decided and why.

▣ It isn't what you do today that comes back to haunt you in the world of investigations, it is what you did two or more years earlier.

▣ Generally you will not be criticised in a court for taking a decision that with the benefit of hindsight was wrong. You are far more likely to find yourself in hot water if you should have taken a decision and there is no evidence that you ever did.

▣ There are 10 basics for effective fraud case management.

1. Select the right team for the investigation.
2. Make sure that they are all fully briefed and understand the task.
3. Hold regular sessions with the team to check progress with lines of enquiry.
4. Keep adequate records of all investigative decisions, especially when and why they were taken.
5. Keep your management in the picture but don't let them interfere.
6. Keep properly indexed records of all intelligence, evidence and supporting documentation.
7. Keep on top of new information and evidence as it is uncovered by your team.
8. Have the courage to change tack if new evidence comes to light, but don't forget to keep the original end in mind.
9. Keep a tight rein on external costs and consumption of internal resources.
10. Use legal, forensic, accounting and HR experts sparingly and wisely— but don't be afraid to ask for their opinions or assistance.

▣ No one ever expects an investigation to cost as much as it does, you will need to keep your controllable costs on as tight a rein as you can.

▣ It is particularly important that you don't only begin with the end in mind but you also manage the expectations of top management.

▣ Make sure that you have the initial terms of reference in writing with management's expectations of your investigation set out.

- There is nothing worse than the complacent investigator who sees every pattern fitting the case they see before them.

- The real investigator's art is to take a broader view and while prepared to adapt if necessary, equally to think calmly and logically about the story you are unveiling by the facts being discovered during your investigation.

- Always make sure that you can feel how the investigation is going.

- If you are the senior investigating officer for the case then you must read *all* new evidence as it comes in.

- If the investigation lasts any length of time it is worth having a weekly reflection for your own benefit on progress to date with a trusted individual who is not involved in the investigation.

There are always two stock errors built in to any investigation, (1) errors committed by those providing the evidence and (2) errors committed by the investigator.

The only way to eliminate errors is to go through and double-check the evidence at every possible opportunity—and wherever you can to get the detailed facts checked by staff not involved in the compilation of the original evidence.

An entire investigation can be put into jeopardy by a single simple error of fact.

Facts are evidence, opinion is not. Evidence can be relied upon and produced in court. Opinions, except from a relevant expert, are meaningless as evidence.

Communicating effectively is probably the single most common area where otherwise good professional investigators can let themselves down time and time again.

Either you or the senior investigator will need to be skilled in the basics of effective report writing if the reports from individual investigators are to be turned into a usable product.

Fraud cases can often attract a lot of internal interest and media attention. It is best to try to pre-empt this state of affairs by having a pre-prepared briefing for internal staff and a media line or lines to be taken by your organisation's press office or equivalent function.

If your organisation doesn't have a media strategy, you will have to agree one at early management meetings on the case. You will also have to warn your own team about not communicating to others except through the nominated media contact.

Once a case is resolved in court, subject to any confidentiality agreements for any settlement, then the gloves are off and you can—and should – publicise any successes.

CHAPTER FIVE

Gathering and using intelligence and evidence

Be subtle! Be subtle! And use your spies for every kind of business.

Sun Tzu[1]

CHAPTER**SUMMARY**

U nderstanding the difference between intelligence and evidence. Classifying and using intelligence. Gathering evidence, how to secure, review and use evidence. Electronic evidence. Email—can it be evidence? Dealing with the demon of disclosure. Why having whistle-blowers is one thing, but using a CHIS (Covert Human Intelligence Source) is something quite different.

WHAT IS THE DIFFERENCE BETWEEN INTELLIGENCE AND EVIDENCE?

The initial allegation of a fraud is, in its rawest sense, intelligence that needs to be analysed and evaluated before any actions that follow. It is not in itself evidence, although the original source of the allegation may have witnessed or found something that can be used as evidence. It is important to understand the difference between information that is intelligence and information that is evidence—as this is the key to how that information can be used to ensure that you bring home a successful fraud investigation.

Evidence and intelligence can be interchangeable, to a degree, so how does one tell them apart? Information passed on to you about suspected fraudulent activity is intelligence and can be classified using a similar system to the police, who receive all sorts of intelligence from all sorts of sources on a regular basis. If the source is reliable and the information is first-hand intelligence then it gets the highest rating of A1. If the source is unknown and the intelligence sketchy, third-party or hard to credit, then it could have a bottom rating of D4.[2] Equally if several different sources come up with similar information it will get a higher rating than only one source, unless they are absolutely trusted and known to be reliable. If you classify all intelligence received in this simple, structured way it will help decide where to throw the weight of your investigative effort.

A simple grid for classifying intelligence received about fraud or corruption

	A (100% trust)	B (75% trust)	C (New source)	D (Anonymous)
1 (Top quality)				
2 (Good quality)				
3 (Unknown)				
4 (Unreliable)				

A Impeccable source, trusted and proven to be reliable
B Good source, generally reliable or as-yet untested but trusted
C Unknown but identified source, as-yet untested, trust unknown
D Anonymous or untrustworthy source

1. Credible and supported information, high quality and accurate
2. Credible information, good quality but no corroboration
3. Unknown information, quality not great and uncorroborated
4. Vague, malicious or improbable and contradictory information

Evidence gathered that shows potentially fraudulent behaviour can be deliberately treated as intelligence, either to set a trap or to avoid interference in an on-going investigation involving the same individual. But beware! If you take such a decision, it will have consequences later. You have effectively ruled out its use at a later date and, for instance, if the fraudster is later caught for exactly that fraud and your un-acted-upon fore-knowledge comes to light (quite possible under modern disclosure rules), you run the risk of finding any claim for civil recovery or criminal charges being blown out as your organisation has effectively condoned the fraudster's actions. Some well-known government agencies have managed to fall foul of this very point before now.

One area where evidence and intelligence can overlap is where fraudulent behaviour is observed in circumstances where you may not be able to use the evidence without ruining a wider enquiry into a more significant fraud. In such instances a decision has to be made about the greater need of the organisation in that circumstance. If you decide to preserve the integrity of the wider investigation, thereby passing up on the opportunity to use the evidence of the lesser fraud, you have effectively turned that evidence into intelligence about the individual or individuals concerned that may still be used to support a later investigation (e.g., by pointing an investigator to the areas to examine where evidence may be found of a current fraud at that later date).

Another area of evidence and intelligence overlap is where an investigator is operating outside of the requirements of Code 'C' of the Police and Criminal Evidence Act 1984 (PACE) finds themselves listening to a confession about a criminal act. Although PACE is widely assumed only to apply to police officers, it also applies to certain types of appointed investigators.[3] An experienced investigator who could be expected to know about the principles in PACE and did not parallel them or take heed of them when dealing with a fraud suspect could find their evidence ruled out by a judge in any subsequent criminal trial or discounted in any later court proceedings. In such circumstances the investigator may choose to continue to gather the intelligence outside PACE but with no intention to use it as evidence in any later criminal or civil proceedings.

Two cases in the criminal courts, one from 1990 and the other from 2007, illustrate the fine line that needs to be walked by non-police investigators.

In *R v Twaites* (1990) the police interviewed the suspect under caution (per PACE) but got no admission of guilt. Subsequently investigators appointed by Twaites' employers interviewed her without applying a PACE caution and obtained a confession of guilt, prior to an internal disciplinary hearing. At the initial criminal trial the police used Twaites' confession as part of the evidence. It was accepted without any consideration of its admissibility by the trial judge and Twaites was subsequently convicted. However, the conviction was overturned on appeal where the Court of Appeal ruled that the appointed investigators fell under the meaning of 'other investigators' in section 67(9) of PACE and they should have cautioned Twaites. Without a PACE caution the investigator's evidence was inadmissible in court.

The point to bear in mind here is that if the intended outcome of the internal investigation was to dismiss the guilty employee then that objective was achieved for their internal disciplinary procedure. However, by getting the admission that way, they could only give the information to the police as intelligence, but by using it as evidence the police ultimately caused the criminal prosecution to fail.

In *R v Welcher* (2007) Welcher was an engineering technician suspected of receiving £500k in corrupt gifts and benefits. The chief engineer of the company interviewed Welcher on a number of occasions about the corrupt gifts and did not caution him. The explanations that Welcher gave to the Chief Engineer contradicted his explanations later during PACE interviews with the police. In this instance the evidence obtained by the Chief Engineer was considered by the trial judge and then ruled admissible. After his conviction Welcher's lawyers appealed against the use in the criminal case of the Chief Engineer's evidence but in this instance the Court of Appeal agreed with the Judge at the criminal trial that the evidence obtained by the Chief Engineer was admissible, as '*a company employee determining whether the conduct of another should lead to dismissal was not governed by Code C.*' Additional weight was also given to the consideration that the criminal investigation had not commenced at the point when the Chief Engineer was conducting his interviews.[4]

On a cautionary note here, the more 'professional' that the investigator is known to be—and in Welcher's case there was no claim that the Chief Engineer was in any way a trained investigator—then the more likely that in any subsequent criminal or civil case the judge will consider that the principles of PACE should have been applied and any oral evidence obtained by the investigator from the suspect will be ruled inadmissible.

The way I would sum this up is as follows:

■ If a line manager or other employee obtains a confession from an employee without giving a caution, provided they have not obtained the confession under duress,[5] then the evidence will still be admissible for any criminal proceedings.

▪ If an internal auditor or internal investigator obtains a confession without giving a caution, its admissibility will be a matter of circumstance, but in all probability it will be allowable for any subsequent court proceedings.

▪ If an external expert investigator is brought in, or the internal investigator is a retired police officer or customs investigator, then they will be expected by the courts to understand Code C of PACE and, for instance, apply a caution where appropriate. If they don't, the evidence might still be allowed, but could equally easily be ruled inadmissible.

When I ran a separate internal fraud investigation team at Scotland Yard, I often employed retired detectives, either with a fraud squad background or similar experience. As they were fully cognisant with PACE Code C and any judge would expect them to know what to do, this had to be borne in mind when interviewing witnesses and potential suspects. I was quite clear that we were neither the prosecutor nor the appointed police investigating officer. Our role was to investigate and establish the facts of a suspected fraud. Once we had established those facts to the point where we knew that a fraud had been committed and who we suspected had committed it, we then contacted the appropriate police to consider the best way forward. All the time that we were fact-finding and our interviewing was mainly about witnesses then there was no need to concern ourselves with the need to issue a PACE caution. Equally where we were dealing with an internal disciplinary matter, PACE did not come into it.

 GATHERING THE EVIDENCE

Although the planned outcome of an investigation may not envisage any criminal proceedings it is always best to assume the worst and *gather your evidence in such a way that it would meet the necessary standards for a criminal case*. This may seem like overkill but it has two useful outcomes. First, if anything does go horribly wrong or later you do discover a criminal investigation cannot be avoided, you will have gathered and kept your evidence to the required standards and that will make life a lot easier for statements, handing over the evidence and any court appearances that follow. Second, should you face any legal challenges during the enquiry—say at a later employment tribunal or civil action—you will have followed an impeccable set of procedures that will make it hard for anyone to claim bias in the investigation or its consequences.

Once a suspected fraud comes to light or is drawn to your attention you will have tracked down the original source of the allegation and heard their explanation as to why they are concerned, whether the information has come from examination of documents, electronic records or observations of the behaviour of an individual. At this early stage of your enquiries there are two main concerns: first, to stop any continuing fraud and, second, to gather and secure any relevant evidence of the alleged fraud. So, what is— or isn't—relevant evidence? And how can it be secured?

Gathering relevant evidence

As a rule of thumb it is better to seize too much rather than too little, you can always return unwanted or irrelevant evidence later but if you haven't got it in the first place you may never see it again. A sin of commission in gathering evidence is actually less of a sin than the sin of omission—an exception to the general rule that sins of commission are more damaging than sins of omission.

A word of caution here: auditors (both internal and external) have a tendency to gather everything that they can lay their hands on when looking for evidence in a fraud or corruption case. While it is always helpful to have the wider picture you can also end up losing focus and not seeing the forest for the trees. It is back to the guiding principle that you should begin an investigation with the end in mind, if that clarity of thought is kept then you are less likely to gather irrelevant evidence about matters that you are never going to be able to pursue to any useful or meaningful conclusion.

Securing the evidence

The guiding principle is to maintain the integrity of any evidence that you gather. Put simply, you need to gather evidence such that you can prove it has been held intact and unaltered from the moment that it came under your control or in your possession until it needs to be used for any civil or criminal proceedings. This has to be an audit trail where at every stage the evidence was clearly under the control of an appropriate individual. (For many years this was a serious difficulty for any electronic records but nowadays most of these can be secured in a way deemed appropriate for court purposes.)

An important point to grasp here is that you do not always need to hold the original evidence. It is simplest and best if you can, but sometimes it is impractical or beyond your powers to secure the original documentation (e.g., if the relevant documentation belongs to a third party). In such circumstances you can take copies of physical documents or computer records but you must adhere to certain basic rules if they are to be used for evidential purposes instead of the originals.

With computer records a properly imaged copy of a hard disk can be used instead of the original, provided it is tamper-proof and has been obtained by a recognised professional forensic IT specialist. For physical documents you need to date and time-stamp the copies with a reference to the individual who has taken the copy. It is not good enough to let a third party send documents off to be copied for you. Whoever secures the evidence must take the copies themselves, or be present and certify each copy as it is taken. They must be able to show that they know the original was copied in its entirety and the copy unaltered before it came into their possession.

In circumstances where I have to rely on authorised copies I will also take at least one backup copy of the copy to use as my working copy for the purposes of the investigation, leaving the 'original' copy in secure storage under my control. A similar principle applies to original documents. By all means examine them but have them kept in such a way that any examination can be conducted without accidentally contaminating or damaging the originals. Where possible, do detailed work on copies. I have known instances where the originals have had incriminating fingerprints. (In one instance we found a convicted armed robber's fingerprint on an apparently innocent quotation for minor work—it later transpired the whole quotation was entirely bogus to ensure that the armed robber won the contract with his live-in partner's quotation, which was less than the cost of the bogus quotation.)

It is tempting to put original documents into those little clear plastic wallets to keep them safe from dust and contamination. Don't. I have made that mistake myself in the past. While it isn't usually an issue for certified copies or where the evidence only comes from copies of documents it can cause original documents to deteriorate and sweat while in storage. Plastic gives off fumes and can after time cause chemical damage to ink and printing on documents. Keep originals in nice, safe cardboard boxes or folders. You'll get less damage and less friction. If originals are in a sequence or a file already then leave them as they are and store in a box.

Where you have sequential documents or books it may well be necessary to examine them for indentation of handwriting from missing documents above the next in sequence. In instances where the indentations are hard to see, an ESDA[6] test can produce results. This is a specialised test using particles of graphite and a machine with an electrostatic charge. It works well on documents where it is hard to see written material or faint indentations. However, it is frustrated by too much handling of the original by the investigator or by using plastic wallets and the like to hold individual pages of documents.

Expenses vouchers and invoices will often have little receipts or other documentation stapled or attached to the main document. Try to avoid separating them, even when taking certified copies. It is far better and more convincing to have them all attached rather than re-staple thereby creating additional holes or marks in the documents. Also in some circumstances you might want to apply physical tests to the documents to see if they were originally in the order in which you find them. It is difficult to tell if a document has been carefully removed from paperwork, but there are ways to tell if a document has been inserted out of sequence or after the event. A very simple test, using a short fluorescent tube of the sort of ultra-violet light that makes white clothing glow in the dark (very popular at parties when I was younger—even though it also picked out dandruff equally clearly!) can show whether documents have been substituted in a sequence or file, as they will glow visually differently from the documents either side of them.

In my last job we would use police evidence bags, which can take a number of documents or files. They had the advantage of tamper-proof seals, although you had to break the seal to examine any evidence and then re-secure it in a new bag, making a note of when and why you had broken the seal on the previous bag. There are commercial alternatives that can be purchased for this purpose, should you need them.

If it is not possible to remove evidence physically then it should be secured where it has been found; for instance, if you find something that happens to be very heavy or bulky, just leave it where it is but secure the room or cabinets in which it is stored in such a way that no one can break in without tampering with any seals or locks that you have applied.

Once evidence has been secured, whether in situ or in your possession, you must ensure its integrity from then on. By all means examine originals carefully (see above) if you really must, rather than copies, but do make sure when it is put away only one person has access to it and there are no spare keys or combination records available to anyone else.

Gathering and securing electronic evidence

Increasingly nowadays, basic business and financial systems are relying on electronic records as part of the process and in some systems the entire transaction will be electronic. In fraud investigations this means that electronic evidence needs to be gathered in such a way that you can prove it is authentic and has not in any way been altered within the system. The approach to gathering the evidence depends on the nature of the evidence that you wish to gather. I have set out below some common scenarios and the key points to bear in mind to gather such evidence successfully.

1. Accounting records held in a database (e.g., invoices, stock ledger, creditor or debtor files)

   The good news about this is that you can get reports and copies of electronic files without interfering with the integrity of the data. The bad news is that proving the integrity of the data at a given point in time can be tricky. Provided it is an established system, such as SAP, getting any evidence extracted accepted should not be a problem. It will be harder with home-tailored systems and expert help will be needed there. If you have internal IT or computer specialists working with you they should be able to use normal forensic interrogation software, such as IDEA, ACL or i2, to interrogate the data and produce reports from it.

2. Part-electronic ordering and payments system

   Provided that you can demonstrate integrity around any data scanned into the system (e.g., supplier invoices) then it should be possible to use screen printouts and electronic copies as equivalent to original documentation for evidence, certainly for a civil case.

3. Fully electronic ordering and payments system

   You will need specialist help to prove the integrity of the evidence but similar points to those under SAP at 1 above apply. As a lot of the traffic on e-procurement is the equivalent of a slightly more secure email a technical specialist will need to look at the system to make sure the data you wish to extract is right and accurate.

4. User files held on a laptop or standalone computer

Oddly, this is the easiest of all to deal with, although it must be done by an appropriate forensic computing specialist—and not just someone from the IT department who thinks they know what they are doing. Clever fraudsters can set all sorts of traps for the unwary on a personal computer or laptop that isn't part of the main network. The generally accepted technique here is to take an image of the hard drive(s) before you begin. By carefully removing and copying the hard drive any hardware-and-system-related booby traps can be immobilised or by-passed, just leaving any software traps still functioning but they won't be triggered by a proper imaging process. The image, suitably copied onto a DVD or another laptop, is then used to crack any passwords and step past any intended software booby traps. There are a number of well-known commercial forensic computing companies who can do this work for you.

5. User files held on a server or centralised system

Here the internal IT specialists can usually do the work for you. Most office systems are networked nowadays with most of the processing, email transmission and user file storage done through linked servers at some central point. If what you need is very recent, you should be able to seize a backup tape or disk of the day's business. And I'll offer a word of caution here. If there is more than one server involved in processing the information that you will be relying on later as evidence, get a specialist just to check that all the server date and time clocks are consistent.

We had a case a few years ago in my last job where two servers were set several hours out from each other, with the result that the dates and times when actions appeared to have taken place did not match, even though we were looking at both ends of the same activity. This can be particularly important if you are trying to place an individual at a terminal at the point when someone committed a fraudulent act on the system. In our case, we had chance eyewitness confirmation from two members of the IT department who were upgrading the systems while our corrupt individual was using his terminal. Once we realised the times didn't match they were able to cross-check against the upgrade running times and found that one server was several hours out on its time and date functions.

A point also worth remembering here is that all centralised systems I have ever come across keep some—if not all—deleted files and deleted email traffic as well, often for months or years, depending on their usage of storage and backup. Much of this can be copied onto CDs, DVDs or external hard drives for remote examination later.

6. Electronic payroll and pension system

Depending on whether it is in-house or provided by an external supplier (more likely nowadays), you should have the ability to copy relevant material and again bring in a specialist to locate and confirm the integrity of the data that you need. Payroll and pension data will usually be held on one of a limited number of well-known databases. The payment system should again be a standard well-known application. Unless you have a very dodgy pay and pension contract it should allow you as the client to have audit and investigative access rights not only to the data but also the systems used by the provider to process and interact with your organisation's data.

7. BACS and CHAPS payments

These are the two main bill-paying and expenses-paying systems used by most organisations. CHAPS is generally for the high-end large-value financial transactions between organisations. The release interface is also electronic so that system needs to be secure within your organisation. I have known a CHAPS interface failure stopping our pay and pension provider making the monthly payment run and another occasion when the same BACS run was put through the system twice. If a one-off error or fraud happens here, it could be very costly. BACS and CHAPS people can be very proprietary about their system but can and should provide you with the independent means to examine the individual payments made by the system.

8. Personal files or records on mobile or hand-held device (e.g., BlackBerry)

Again, this is best dealt with by a forensic computing specialist, as similar techniques to those required for laptops are needed. With any device such as this, it is important that it doesn't get forgotten about. The fraudster may well be able to access it remotely and delete data on it. The sooner it is examined by an expert and its contents and links are explored, the better. And I have known an incident where the battery ran flat before the expert got to it and we couldn't kick it into life again!

▓ EMAIL: CAN IT BE EVIDENCE?

In a word, yes. Increasingly email has replaced and supplemented the phone for messages and communication. Psychologically many people, fraudsters included, feel that they can treat email traffic as personal communication and are as careless with it as they would be with a telephone or face-to-face communication. It can both be a valuable source of evidence and an area where the organisation can leave itself vulnerable.

On organisational vulnerability with internal email correspondence, this is a real-life example from my work when I was running Internal Audit for Scotland Yard. I had a team of ex-detectives who conducted internal fraud investigations for me. On one occasion we were on the trail of a fraud and due to interview an individual who worked in the area concerned. I sent a short email to my boss explaining that we were about to interview Mr X in the hope that they could throw some light on the matter under investigation. I got an unfortunate reply in which he clearly implied that we suspected the individual of committing the fraud. I replied pointing out that if we indeed suspected this individual of committing the fraud then we would have to caution him under PACE and if we did that we were unlikely to establish any facts in this matter once the caution had been issued. However, while at the moment we didn't know who had committed the fraud but were simply trying to establish the facts of the matter there was no need to administer any caution.

If, of course, we had no intention as an organisation of making the matter the subject of a criminal enquiry or we knew it was only ever internal discipline then even if the individual confessed to a fraud during the interview there would be no need to administer a caution or apply any other aspect of PACE Code C. However, as we were a police organisation and an ex-detective was assisting me in this particular interview, had the individual confessed to a fraud and we were intending criminal prosecution, then we'd have run a risk of finding the confession inadmissible if we didn't stop him and caution him at that point.

WITNESS EVIDENCE GATHERING

Witness evidence is best gathered by some formal means. For complex or significant cases I favour the use of multi-deck tape machines or digital recorders. That way every word can be transcribed afterwards and the witness can be given the chance to adjust or clarify any parts of their evidence before they sign up to it formally as a true record. Also if in a difficult case the witness claims that they were intimidated during the interview, you can play back the recording to a third party and they will hear how you asked your questions and behaved during the interview.

At the Metropolitan Police Authority we used to have our own sound-proofed room attached to the internal Audit Office with built-in microphones. This had two advantages: first, it was a quiet and discreet place where you could build up a relationship with the witness (or suspect) and, second, because the microphones were built-in witnesses in particular soon relaxed and forgot that they were being formally recorded.

I have never yet felt the urge to take a video or digital film as well, but as long as the equipment has been proved to be tamper-proof then it is also an option, if you have the kit and someone to control it.

For less complex cases, or where the evidence from the witness is relatively straightforward, there is no harm in writing it up as you go along and then asking the witness to sign up to it at the end. This is often the way that many police witness interviews are conducted.

Although I emphasised the need to gather your evidence to the appropriate standards for a criminal case, please do not get tempted to use the standard police investigation form for your witness statements, with its references to PACE and the like. It is possible to gather witness evidence to the required standard without using such documentation. You are expecting your interview information to be used as part of either an internal disciplinary case or potential civil action later, either against a contractor or former employee. Civil courts do not like to see witness statements in civil cases written out as if they were part of a formal police process and your counsel may well ask you to redo anything presented in that form. The way to get round this is to start each statement with an 'I will say . . .' opening comment, going on to note that they are making this statement to the best of their knowledge and belief. If in doubt, your solicitor should be able to advise you on an appropriate form of words for such a witness statement.

In some instances, particularly if the witness cannot be persuaded to be interviewed, you can write formally to them setting out clearly what you wish to know and seeking their answers. That is the least satisfactory process, as inevitably they will either misinterpret something or give an answer that begs a supplementary question, thereby prolonging the correspondence and slowing down the evidence-gathering process.

 ## CHIS OR INFORMANT? WHAT ARE THE DIFFERENCES—AND THE RISKS?

CHIS stands for the rather pompous sounding 'Covert Human Intelligence Source'. The fundamental difference between a CHIS and an informant is that a CHIS is an informant acting under instruction from or in a direct relationship with their handler. Various concerns about this kind of activity and potential conflict with the Human Rights Act led to legislative change in 2000, with the Regulation of Investigatory Powers Act (RIPA). It applies equally to the police, central government, wider government bodies, public authorities and local authorities.[7] Among other matters, RIPA codified and identified the role of a CHIS. Part II Section 8 notes:

(8) For the purposes of this Part a person is a covert human intelligence source if—
   (a) he establishes or maintains a personal or other relationship with a person for the covert purpose of facilitating the doing of anything falling within paragraph (b) or (c);
   (b) he covertly uses such a relationship to obtain information or to provide access to any information to another person; or
   (c) he covertly discloses information obtained by the use of such a relationship, or as a consequence of the existence of such a relationship.

In commenting on the application of RIPA to local authorities, the Office of Surveillance Commissioners notes that: 'the most obvious candidates [to use RIPA powers] are trading standards, housing benefit fraud, internal audit and environmental health.' I will say more about RIPA in Chapter 8 when I will take a closer look at the potential value of covert surveillance in a fraud or corruption investigation.

A one-off informant who volunteers information to you is not a CHIS and RIPA doesn't apply; they are simply a source of intelligence for your enquiries. However, if you then have a dialogue with them or ask them to find or do something that they haven't already done for you, then if you are an employee or contractor of the State (local or central) they become a CHIS and RIPA applies.

While the concept of legislation for a CHIS doesn't exist for private companies, if you end up in a criminal or a civil court with a fraud case where directed intelligence gathering provided part of your evidence, the procedures and standards that you applied to gather that evidence are likely to be considered in parallel to the expected standards for a public authority, as they have been designed to ensure that the suspect's human rights have not been breached.

So, if you decide to turn an informant about fraud or corruption into a CHIS, someone senior will have to understand the legal requirements and be authorised by the chief executive or a similar ranking official to grant the required RIPA Authority. Not only is this essential if their evidence is ever to be relied upon later in court, but also if you don't do this and are subsequently accused of breaching the suspect's human rights, you may find that you have unwittingly committed a criminal offence by using a CHIS. For most internal and contractor fraud this is a dangerous path to take and needs careful consideration of the potential risks to the organisation as well as potential physical risks to the CHIS. While a proactive CHIS may seem attractive, it is worth bearing in mind that, in general, informants are not all that they are cracked up to be.

The risks that informants bring ...

Outside the world of social security and bogus benefit claims, informants are rarely the keen-eyed and altruistic good citizens that you might imagine. Internal or contractor informants will have a range of possible motives, through the whole spectrum from wanting to do right to a desire to take revenge on someone. In the more extreme circumstances they may set out to put others in the frame for their own fraudulent activity or at least to mitigate the damage to them from their own involvement in the fraud.

One-off informants are always a concern, as it can be difficult to assess their integrity. Where the individual is a like-minded soul and you have known them for a number of years then the relationship is different and they can form part of a helpful network to give a good pre-warning when things are going awry.

One of the more entertaining informants that came across my path in my early days investigating frauds by police contractors was an individual who ran a cleaning company that provided services to the Met across south-east London. He wrote in complaining that his company had been deliberately dropped from a police contract because of a conspiracy between the police cleaning contract manager and a rival cleaning company. I took one of my staff with me and went to see this character in his office in South London. He was a down-to-earth self-made East-Ender and made no bones about either his motivation and behaviour or that of the rivals on whom he wanted to inform.

'Look, Mr Tickner, I admit we ain't exactly been squeaky clean ourselves. Might 'ave put in the odd duplicate or moody invoice—but that was only when I lorst me finance director and 'ad to do the bills meself for a couple of months. I'm 'appy ter own up to that and take it on the chin.' I gave him a suitably stern look, to which he responded with what, I imagine, was meant to be charm but came across as a crude attempt to bribe or compromise me. 'Do yer fancy meeting George Best? E's a good mate of mine.' I politely declined and we finally got down to business.

The tale that he told had a ring of truth about it. Although truth is never as crystal clear as you might have been led to believe, experience told me that the gist of what he wanted to tell me had to be true. He knew he was being conspired against because one of his own staff had overheard a conversation between the new works manager and the cleaning rival's boss in the police works office. The reason why a member of his staff had overheard all of the plotting for the conspiracy, which involved his company being asked to do a job that they could only fail? He was outside on a hot summer's day, cleaning the works manager's open windows as part of the contract that they had with the police at the time!

As usual in such instances with informants, although he had hinted at his own propensity to commit fraud, he glossed over the specifics of the other reasons why he had been dropped from the police contract. We discovered much later that he had 'assisted' a dodgy works manager, to whom the cleaning manager reported, in buying some IT kit out of the cleaning budget and laundering the bills through his company, out of which some of the kit had ended up delivered to the home of the 'dodgy' manager. The new works manager had made up his mind to make sure the cleaning company didn't keep their contract, but had gone about it in a wholly inappropriate way.

At the time I didn't have an investigative team and we made the mistake of hiring in a lawyer and an accountant to look into it for me. I was tied up on a far more serious case and couldn't spare anyone else to do the investigation. Between them, they failed to find any incriminating material or documents to support the informant's allegations and eventually I dropped the case.

Somewhat ironically, the cleaning company that had conspired against our East Ender crossed my path again, when I did have sufficient investigative resource to look into them. What we discovered was highly frustrating—and it is probably one of the reasons why I am so reluctant to let lawyers or accountants run my investigations. It turned out that when the East Ender lost his contract there were two rival bidders, one of which won and was the company he'd named as conspiring against him. What the lawyer and accountant had failed to find between them was that the other bidder had the same parent company and had only been set up to make it look like there was sufficient competition. A proper check of the records from Companies House would have exposed this at once.

 DISCLOSURE, DISCLOSURE, DISCLOSURE

Whether your case ends up in a criminal or a civil court and even for internal discipline and any subsequent employment tribunal, once you start to name your suspected fraudster or fraudsters, the rules of disclosure will apply to your investigation. At some point pre-trial or before a civil court hearing, your legal adviser will nod sagely at you, tap the side of their nose and sigh, 'Well, we'll have to give the opposition this under disclosure,[8] you know—such a pity those documents also came to light.' Do not let this concern distract you from the primary purpose of your fraud investigation, which is to establish the relevant facts, even if they make uncomfortable reading for others in the organisation. Only once the proper facts have been established can your top management finally decide what is in the best interests of your organisation, hopefully aided by your interpretation of what you (and your team) have found.

Disclosure is a two-way process and both parties in civil cases have to disclose relevant evidence for the case to the other party. Disclosure also applies in criminal cases but in UK law the suspect is not obliged to provide any evidence under disclosure that is self-incriminating. Relevant evidence from your point of view includes anything that you have found factually about the case that is relevant to the individual under investigation, *whether or not* it forms part of the case that you wish to put against the individual.

It can also include some details about how you have gone about the investigation, including any recorded key decision points. It does not include conceptual, strategic or tactical aspects of investigation planning but you will have to demonstrate that your investigation was proportionate and appropriate to the matter under investigation, hence why the decision-making process can be so significant.

Disclosure heightens the need to follow the principles that I outlined earlier. You have to begin with the end in mind and part of that is ensuring that you do not gather too much spurious evidence and that what you do gather is proportionate to the matter in hand. Also be cautious in your written communications internally about the case, particularly in emails and the like. It is all part of disclosure and an apparently biased remark, even if intended to be flippant at the time, can undermine a case later.

If you haven't recorded your key decision points then you may find yourself in difficulties when the court seeks an explanation of why you did what you did. It is an inevitable part of most fraud investigations that you start with incomplete information and as you gather more facts you may need to adjust the direction and effort of the investigation. If you took a decision early on and later found it was an error, judges are unlikely to criticise you where the basis of that decision is clearly recorded and it is obvious that you based it on the best available information at that point in time.

For disclosure or discovery, you do not have to provide all intelligence gathered but you do have to disclose all relevant evidence, even if it is unhelpful to your case. So, for example, if during observation of your suspect you recorded them committing a different fraud that you had decided not to pursue, that is still relevant evidence to disclose, as it is pertinent both to their behaviour and how you as an organisation have dealt with it. On the other hand, if you have an informant's report that the suspect has committed some other criminal or disciplinary offence, there is no need to disclose the existence of that intelligence as long as you haven't taken any action in this case because of it.

General principles and axioms**from Chapter 5**

▨ The initial allegation of a fraud is intelligence, not evidence.

▨ If a line manager or other employee obtains a confession from an employee without giving a caution, the evidence will still be admissible for any criminal proceedings.

▨ If an internal auditor or internal investigator obtains a confession without giving a caution, it will probably be admissible.

▨ If an external expert investigator is brought in, or the internal investigator is a retired police or customs officer then they will be expected by the courts to apply a PACE caution. If they don't caution a suspect their evidence will probably be inadmissible.

▨ If your end in mind is disciplinary, you don't need to worry about PACE.

▨ Gather your evidence in such a way that it would meet the necessary standards for a criminal case.

▨ The guiding principle is to maintain the integrity of any evidence that you gather.

▨ Original evidence is best, but properly certified copies obtained in a controlled way are also acceptable evidence.

▨ If it is not possible to remove evidence physically then it should be secured where it has been found.

▨ Once evidence has been secured, whether in situ or in your possession, you must be able to prove its integrity from then on.

▨ Email can be used as evidence—but beware—any relevant internal email will be seen for court cases, including any inappropriate management comment on an on-going investigation.

▨ Witness evidence is best gathered by formal means.

▨ Use the 'I will say ...' form of witness statement for disciplinary and civil proceedings.

▨ Disclosure is a two-way process and both parties in civil cases have to disclose relevant evidence for the case to the other party. It is also known as 'Discovery'. Since the Woolf reforms, these terms are interchangeable in the civil courts.

▨ Relevant evidence includes anything that you have found factually about the case that is relevant to the individual under investigation, whether or not it forms part of the case that you wish to put.

(Public bodies and authorities only)

■ If you have any interaction with an informant then under RIPA they are classified as a covert human intelligence source (CHIS).

■ If you decide to turn an informant about fraud or corruption into a CHIS, someone senior will have to understand the legal requirements to grant the required authorisation—or you could fall foul of criminal law.

Part III

PART THREE

Investigation
techniques

CHAPTER SIX

Using analysts to support the investigation

CHAPTER**SUMMARY**

T he role that analysts should play. Tasking analysts effectively. Using analysis to support proactive fraud detection. Making sure that you get the right product.

UNDERSTANDING THE ROLE OF A FRAUD INVESTIGATION ANALYST

Outside the world of the police and the intelligence services, only a few specialist investigative units use fraud analysts. When properly used, they are a vital tool in your investigations and can not only support an on-going investigation effectively but also proactively hunt out new areas and new frauds for investigation. Unfortunately, when not used properly or where they are inappropriately trained or skilled they can quickly become a liability and an unhelpful luxury. The trick is to get good, focused analysts who quickly understand the fraud investigator's needs.

Why do you need an analyst? Well, for a one-off investigation you may just be able to get by without one. However, if you work in an area where you find yourself conducting investigations on a fairly regular basis then you need analytical support. The best can not only analyse data from systems and sources but also spot potentially fraudulent trends or behaviour patterns in data and guide the investigators towards their targets.

When I had responsibility for the internal audit and investigations at the Metropolitan Police I had an investigations unit that consisted of a head of investigations, three investigation team leaders, each with two supporting investigators and separately from them a fraud awareness manager who also looked after two analysts. The analysts mainly supported the investigations teams but also provided support to my internal audit staff and we held joint tasking meetings for the analysts at regular intervals.

A good analyst has to have an eye for fraudulent behaviour in the data that they are examining. There are three main sources for properly trained fraud analysts: the military, the police and specialist government agencies (e.g., the investigations arm of HMRC, SOCA, etc.). In most organisations, despite the technical skills required, these sorts of analysts are not as highly rated as one might expect. Certainly in the policing environment qualified crime analysts, although essential support to detectives, were seen very much as the back-room staff. The best trained for general investigative work, in my experience, are funnily enough, those with a military background, especially if they have been trained at one of the better intelligence establishments. Ex-police analysts can vary considerably in quality and it is best to ensure that they have an aptitude for fraud work before they are taken on.

Research analysts are not necessarily the right type of analyst to use for fraud work. The profile of a typical research analyst is that they will be academically well trained and qualified and in many instances starting out on their careers either to become specialist analysts for particular industries or public bodies or even politicians and political parties. Many are extremely bright, mathematically and statistically literate and can no doubt turn their training and skills to fraud analysis if asked. The problem with this is that unless they discover a latent talent for the often pedantic and sometimes routine world of analysis for fraud investigation they may quickly become dissatisfied and move on or fail to perform effectively.

Research analysts tend to fall into two camps, either the painstaking researcher who can produce an in-depth analysis of the particular activity under review or the analyst who sees the broader picture and can analyse organisational data about trends and strategic issues. By and large, apart from analytical skills, which are broadly the same for all types of analyst, both these types of analyst are unlikely to be suited to the fraud analyst's role, which like the army intelligence analyst is much more geared towards examination of vast amounts of data looking for the unusual and the inexplicable rather than the norm and trends.

 ## TASKING ANALYSTS EFFECTIVELY

While an incompetent analyst will be unlikely to give you a good product, no matter how well you task them, a good analyst will be wasted if you don't ensure that you task them effectively. Analysts have a number of functions that they can perform. They can engage in proactive research to find as-yet undiscovered frauds, they can take suspicious material and examine it to see the patterns and they can present large volumes of data in charts and schedules so that investigators can grasp where to focus their efforts and on occasion see revealed contacts between individuals suspected of fraudulent activity that were not obvious from enquiries to date.

Proactive research

The best analysts will be constantly thinking about ways in which they can review data to detect fraud. There are a number of tools out there in the market place that can aid a proactive researcher. Techniques used here are often referred to collectively as 'data mining'. When used effectively they enable the analyst to pull out potential fraudsters from your business, financial and payroll systems for further investigation.

It is helpful if they can have live 'read-only' access to the main business systems of the organisation, that way they can run various data-mining and fraud comparison routines on the system data and pick out potential areas of the business for closer attention.

In its infancy data mining became an end in itself, much to the despair of people like me when the analyst or usually IT geek would turn up with a bewildering mass of data that they had just 'mined' from our systems in the mistaken belief that it was an easy route to a fraud. In fact it was an easy route to many wasted hours and days trying to find any meaningful evidence that related to the data that had been mined. Trends and data patterns that could lead to potentially fraudulent activities but generate a high volume of speculative hits are about as useful as a chocolate computer, since as soon as things heat up they start to melt away and everything gets horribly sticky when you try to do anything with it.

Day-to-day support, the National Fraud Initiative and background work

The analysts in my last job were the first port of call when the biannual information from the National Fraud Initiative hit our desks. They could quickly eliminate the many false positives and concentrate on detailed analysis of those hits that were most likely to need a fraud investigation. They acted as our on-going liaison with the Finance and Pay & Pension sections until we were sure that we had reduced the data to that which genuinely could represent potential frauds and could be turned over to the investigators for further enquiries.

If you have analysts, it is also important to have a background programme of work for those quiet moments when no urgent investigative matter needs their immediate and undivided attention. It is important for them too to know that if there isn't a headline case it is their function to make sure that through routine monitoring and checking they pick out developing risks and potential frauds in areas that have not yet been examined. Tasking meetings can be used to ensure that auditors, investigators and managers have identified potential areas where analytical review of the data could potentially assist further work on the ground.

Making sense of suspicious material

This is the high point of analytical work and where the best earn their corn. Investigators will by nature and inclination find themselves down in the weeds. If you have a long-running or difficult case you will find yourself drawn almost inevitably into that danger area as well. While precision of detail is necessary to bring home an investigation, it is also necessary to be able to step back and take a wider view of where gathered evidence is taking you and the analyst should be producing that type of material for you to examine and reflect upon while the investigators on the ground are delving into the detail.

It is particularly important that this type of analytical work is produced in 'real time' alongside the investigation, so that as new data is found it is added into the analyst's pot and either updated or new charts and analyses are produced for examination by those conducting the investigation on the ground. Analysts working on a particular case should be attending case meetings and producing required updates to help the tasking of further investigative work.

Producing patterns and links from data yet to be investigated

Again, this is another very productive area for an analyst. There are a number of computer applications that a well-trained analyst can use to present work processed in this way. A common one in police circles is called i2 and can present either timelines or visual wheels of data showing links between data such as names, addresses, phone extensions and phone calls. But there are other packages generally available that can be used by an intelligent analyst to produce the same results from the right data fed into their system.

This kind of analysis can be particularly useful if corruption is suspected between an employee and a particular contractor. Both email traffic and internal phone extension records (or work mobile/BlackBerry, etc.) can be analysed by such methods to pick out potentially suspicious communications.

 MAKING SURE THAT YOU GET THE RIGHT RESULT

If the analyst has the right skills and has been trained to use interrogation software on the most significant and useful systems within your organisation (e.g., the underlying financial system, payroll, HR record database, stock systems, creditor payment systems) and has the right 'nous' around fraud this part should be a doddle. You will be able to give them a clear steer at your regular tasking meetings and they will return brimming with useful results on the cases that had most significance to the investigative team.

Unfortunately it is very unlikely that you will find an analyst that has all these qualities and technical skills in abundance or indeed to the same levels. It is therefore important to ensure that any training and skills gaps are quickly identified and efforts made to plug them as quickly as possible.

The one area where an analyst's skills are always a bit of an unknown is their ability to pick up the signs of potential fraud. When we recruited anyone into the fraud side of the business we always tried to test out their abilities with real-time case studies before they were appointed. While this works well with investigators it isn't foolproof with analysts. But provided they are intelligent and know their technical stuff they can quickly pick this up from investigators or anyone with long experience of finding frauds.

I have seen two different models for structuring in analysts within an investigative set-up that work well and effectively. In the first, the model most familiar to me, fraud analysts reported through a manager to the head of investigations. They sat in on all unit meetings and had separate tasking meetings with the head of investigations and investigative and audit team leaders. In the other, fraud analysts were appointed at a more senior level, reporting directly to the head of investigations. In this model, there were no investigative team leaders but instead each analyst fulfilled that role with a small team of investigators reporting to them.

Whatever the preferred organisation structure—and a lot will depend on the amount of investigative resources available and the size of the team—without the right analysts properly managed you won't get the right result.

So, the key to getting the right result is

1. Have an analyst who is technically competent and capable of interrogating business systems.
2. Make sure the analyst is a trained user of one of the three main analytical tools (ACL, IDEA or i2).
3. Understand how to use the analyst.
4. Have regular tasking meetings where both analyst and investigators are present.
5. Keep the analyst's technical skills refreshed.
6. Use the analyst to help task the investigator rather than the investigator help task the analyst.
7. Don't let the analyst get self-indulgent. If no one knows what they are doing or why, make it your business to know and understand and, if necessary, challenge.

USING ANALYSTS DURING CIVIL AND CRIMINAL CASES

Analysts should be able to provide two main skills here. First, they should be able to prepare schedules, charts and visual representations from the data gathered by investigators and, second, they should be competent to make witness statements about how they have prepared the data, what manipulation has been necessary to produce it and, most importantly of all, what the data is telling them and why.

We used analysts extensively to support cases that we were taking through the civil courts, where often the investigators would have gathered enormous amounts of data that we needed to structure in a meaningful way so that it could be used in court if necessary. The analysts would help determine the structure of the data and then either prepare the schedules or check the schedules prepared by the investigators.

During our long-running saga at the Met with potentially fraudulent credit card usage, the analysts took the raw data from both AMEX and our own financial systems and produced schedules and charts of the most likely abusers. When we brought in a software solution to ease pressure on the volume of data being checked by the investigators, it was the analysts who quickly learned how to use the new tool and then started to produce potential suspects from its analysis of the data. That way I was able to avoid diverting hard-pressed investigators away from pursuing the guilty and at the same time then provide them with what in the end turned out to be an almost 100% hit rate of further potential frauds and abuses to examine.

General principles and axiomsfrom Chapter 6

- Analysts can be a vital tool in investigations and can support an on-going investigation effectively and proactively hunt out new areas and new frauds for investigation.

- When not used properly, or where inappropriately trained or skilled, analysts can quickly become a liability and an unhelpful luxury.

- A good analyst has to have an eye for fraudulent behaviour in the data that they are examining.

- Research analysts are not necessarily the right type of analyst to use for fraud work.

- While an incompetent analyst will be unlikely to give you a good product, no matter how well you task them, a good analyst will be wasted if you don't ensure that you task them effectively.

- If you have analysts, it is also important to have a background programme of work when no urgent investigative matter needs their attention. It is important for them to know that it is their function to make sure that through routine monitoring and checking they pick out developing risks and potential frauds.

- While precision of detail is necessary to bring home an investigation, it is also necessary to step back and take a wider view of where gathered evidence is taking you. The analyst should be producing that type of material to examine and reflect upon while the investigators on the ground are delving into the detail.

- Analysts working on a particular case should be attending the case meetings and producing updates to help the tasking of further investigative work.

- Use the analyst to help task the investigator rather than the investigator help task the analyst.

- Don't let the analyst get self-indulgent. If no one knows what they are doing or why, make it your business to know and understand and, if necessary, challenge.

- Analysts should be able to support civil cases by preparing schedules, charts and visual representations from the data gathered by investigators and be competent to make witness statements about how they have prepared the data, what manipulation has been necessary to produce it and what the data is telling them and why.

CHAPTER SEVEN

Technology that aids fraud detection

CHAPTER**SUMMARY**

C ommon tools that can assist. The internet. Spreadsheets versus databases. Using data interrogation software. Specialised data-mining tools.

COMMON TECHNOLOGICAL TOOLS AVAILABLE TO THE FRAUD INVESTIGATOR

The easiest tool available is free—the internet. Used wisely, it can provide unexpected assistance to a fraud investigator. Aside from that, other available tools include the now long-in-the-tooth spreadsheet—but beware, it has its weaknesses, simpler databases, specialist interrogation software (often proprietary to a particular organisation or commercial company) and data-mining tools that probe furthest into an organisation.

 ## TAKING THE INTERNET INTO THE FRAUD-FINDER'S TENT

When we think of the internet most people immediately think of the common search engines, such as Google and Yahoo, news and entertainment feeds, podcasts, some of the well-known applications such as social networking sites (e.g., Facebook) messaging through Twitter and the like and the ever-popular YouTube. In the hands of an expert the internet can be used to hunt down publicly available data that does not necessarily easily fling itself in front of you through a search engine, useful though they can be too. So what can be found?

Starting with the obvious, Google or similar search engines can be used to find out possible information about the fraudster or, in the case of a fraudulent company, any apparent information of their dealings or past misdemeanours. Reviews of regional and local news stories can pick up references to individuals of interest to an investigation.

Technically minded fraudsters will often want to use the internet to let on about their cleverness or just to share information with like-minded fraudsters. They may share illegal means of attacking organisations and they may join discussion groups or write blogs where they reveal their true feelings about your organisation. Although most will do this from an internet café or home email or internet access, an increasing number do it from the office computer.

Equally, IT-literate staff can often lead external fraudsters to your door, sometimes quite innocently. Using an internet specialist I have caught a systems administrator who was sharing details about our internal systems on an underground website hoping that IT-literate fellow users and hackers could help solve a software problem, which was kindly described in great detail, even down to the passwords needed to get into our system to look at the software! The specialist also identified a potential fraudster working for us who was sharing hacking information about illegal use of satellite television transmissions in a private internet forum.

The same specialist once tracked down an undercover business for me in less than half a day, proving that our controls were not as secure for that business as the operational manager thought. All that the specialist knew was the general business area in which the undercover company was hiding. He was able to track it down by looking at the spending habits of all UK companies in that line of business, picking out the ones with unusual habits and then narrowing them down by activity and looking for a company that didn't appear to have any relevant transactions in the business line that it claimed.

There are nowadays a plethora of tools available to your work IT department that are capable of identifying inappropriate websites and email traffic. Although most of these will be to prevent phishing or pornography coming in from the outside world, they can also be used to detect internal user activity either by keywords or known inappropriate websites, as well as monitor and recover email traffic, whether or not it has been deleted. In the past I've seen a systems administrator plotting to set up false accounts caught by their external traffic from the office, a disloyal employee who virtually spelled out how they were going to attack the organisation on a chat website and a manager who was writing pornography in work time for a dubious magazine but thought they had fooled us by deleting the material from their computer—they were wrong! All the above were caught when we checked their traffic from the office to the outside world.

If your IT department has tools to monitor traffic, make sure that the material that might relate to fraud isn't just enclosed in the usual note back to the line manager or HR for potential disciplinary action, along with the more usual internet abuses in the workplace, but also gets sent through to your team to examine as well.

 ## SPREADSHEET VERSUS DATABASE?

These are both obvious tools that almost any auditor or investigator worth their salt will be able to use to advantage during a fact-finding investigation or when analysing data from the main systems of the organisation. Each has its place, but for the investigator the spreadsheet must be used with particular caution.

During a number of our low-value, high-volume investigations in the Met around linguists, we had to revert to spreadsheet usage, much against my better judgement. In the end, although a database would have been far more secure and reliable, it was far easier for the investigators to compile the data into spreadsheet tables, particularly as we spent a fair bit of time on the earliest cases trying out different 'what if' scenarios, the one area where a spreadsheet always does well. But this also meant that we had to be particularly careful about controlling our 'audit trail' and we had to apply rigorous checks at the end to ensure that we had processed the right data and got the right result.

The advantages and disadvantages of using either for the fraud investigator are

Spreadsheet advantages
▨   Quick set-up time and easily understood.
▨   Can import data from most accounting systems directly.
▨   Can easily model different scenarios from the same data.
▨   Can do calculations without the need to set up a separate project.
▨   Easy to change and amend.

Spreadsheet disadvantages
▨   Even with an 'audit' feature it doesn't give you a complete audit trail, there are no date or time stamps to track who did what or when.
▨   Limited to the amount of data that can be imported.
▨   May automatically reformat key data; for example, a bank account number which starts with a '0' such as 01234567 is reformatted as 1234567, dates also get reformatted.
▨   Can't always see errors in formulae causing inaccurate calculations.
▨   Results can be amended or wiped by mistake too easily.
▨   Difficult to secure and will need backing evidence if used in court.

Database advantages
▨   Data is stored securely for each item captured.
▨   A complete audit trail can be maintained.
▨   Data can be manipulated and combined in reports without changing it.
▨   Can be used as reliable evidence for court.

Database disadvantages
▨   Someone needs to know it well enough to set it up accurately.
▨   Harder to use if investigator unfamiliar with it.
▨   Difficult to adjust if you don't capture the data in the right way first time.
▨   Needs data cleansing after a while.

In summary, if you have the capability to use a database, then that is generally the best option for storing and downloading basic data for the fraud investigation. However, there are times, particularly for a new investigation or an unusual fraud, where it can be better to use a spreadsheet initially.

DATA INTERROGATION TOOLS

There are two common data interrogation tools used in the audit and investigative world and one specific tool more commonly used by police and allied investigators. All three have similar characteristics although the last one is slightly different from the first two in the way in which it handles the data presented to it. In my experience, as these packages and their derivatives have developed over the years, they are now all so similar in what they can achieve that it doesn't really matter which one you use, as long as your team has staff appropriately trained and experienced to use it. Where you have analysts, these are part of the tools that I would expect to find in their armoury.

Commonly used data interrogation packages

The three most well-known and common data interrogation packages are, in no particular order, IDEA, ACL and i2. IDEA and ACL are, for all practical purposes, identical. Many years ago ACL was the market leader and IDEA lagged behind and was fundamentally a different product. That really isn't so today. ACL is probably still the more dominant across the audit world. Excel users often liked IDEA because of its similar appearance. Both ACL and IDEA have now adopted Windows and Excel standard tool bars. In addition there are other data interrogation software packages; for example, CPCP (see 'Using general sampling theory to advantage in a fraud investigation' in Chapter 10, p. 180) which runs in ARBUTUS, a spin-off development when one of the key ACL developers left to set up his own company. Both IDEA and ACL have over the years adapted their packages as the IT world has advanced and the end result is that it is hard to tell their features apart today. Many audit units will already have either IDEA or ACL although not all will necessarily have staff with the expertise and training to use them to best effect.

The third package, i2, is mainly a tool used by police investigators and analysts and differs from the other two in that it was designed to analyse crime data rather than financial data. Its great strength is the ability to identify logical relationships in a diagrammatic way, commonly known as link analysis. For example, you could analyse telephone traffic between internal extensions and certain suppliers; i2 can then represent this as a volume diagram with symbols for each of the telephone extensions and called numbers with their calls in and out radiating to other symbols in the diagram. Such a visual representation allows complex relationships to be easily understood, a great benefit when presenting evidence in court.

All three packages are in effect specialised databases that keep a complete audit and evidential trail, so that any expert can examine them and see exactly what manipulation—and when—has been applied to the data and output reports.

IDEA and ACL have all the advantages of a database while having some of the characteristics of a spreadsheet. They are designed to read in data from other systems and can interact both ways with databases or spreadsheets if need be. They both need training from specialists before letting anyone loose on them.

In the long-running saga that was my battle to deal with a dodgy vehicle repair and maintenance contractor (see Chapter 11) we used ACL extensively not only to analyse the financial data about the organisation but also to work through the maintenance records of over 5,000 vehicles, looking at the targets that triggered performance payments or penalties and measuring the accuracy of information supplied by the contractor in support of their many claims. It was one of our main weapons in proving that the contractor was not entitled to some of the million pound payments that they were seeking.

We used the same application in a not dissimilar way when trying to identify details of invoices for thousands of vehicles scattered across car pounds in London. In that case we had vehicles in and out of pounds, staying in pounds beyond the intended time and each vehicle registration and car type would just be one line on the invoice multiplied by the charge for the number of days it had been in the pound that month. At the peak of our problems one invoice had over 1,100 vehicles per month detailed on it for one of the three types of charges from the pounds. We simply would not have been able to work out what we were dealing with without using such an analytical tool to support our work.

Getting the most out of your data interrogation package

If you have analysts, make sure that they are fully trained and competent to use whichever package you have at your disposal. If not, then a member of the investigative team needs to be trained up and asked to act as the in-house 'specialist' for your interrogation package. If you are unable to do this, it is possible to buy in short term expertise, but be careful. In my experience this isn't usually that successful. The bought-in expert will generally be unfamiliar with your organisation, more costly than in-house staff and will need a significant amount of your or an investigator's time to manage them to deliver the tasks that you want rather than the ones that they'd much rather do—because they can do them easily.

IDEA and ACL (and i2 in a fraud context) are at their best when used to sort through data that may have been tainted by a suspected fraudster or fraudsters and produce reports showing what is in the data and what happens if parts of the data are compared in various scientific and comparative ways with each other. They are the buffer between the data in the main business systems and your reports and analysis of what you think you have found. By using them, you will have a complete evidential trail of how you have gone from the raw data in the system to a report identifying an anomaly or fraudulent transactions.

Their output can then be fed into more common user-friendly parts of Office or similar program suites so that the investigator or you can write up for management what has been found in a simpler and more impactful way, knowing that you can fall back on the detail in these applications to show how you have ended up drawing the conclusions that you have.

Common areas where these packages can be of particular benefit include

- Identifying payroll and pension fraud
- HR databases
- Invoice analysis
- Systems with a naturally high volume of regular transactions
- General accounting systems

USING SPECIALISED DATA-MINING TOOLS

These are some applications based around ACL or IDEA but which have been specifically developed to deal with a particular type of issue or fraud.

One that I used very successfully when I was Director of Internal Audit at the Met was originally developed in conjunction with the MoD and proved an invaluable tool in one of the last cases that I dealt with before my retirement from the Met in the autumn of 2009.

Corporate credit cards for cops—the system that should never have been

The Met developed a little corporate credit card problem, one that eventually received considerable press interest and made things a little awkward all round. In many ways it summed up a number of dilemmas and also the contradictory nature of policing in an urban environment. Eventually it became a major investigation for my team working in conjunction with the professional standards department of Scotland Yard (they conducted the criminal and/or disciplinary investigations into police officers while we reviewed all the financial evidence and in effect pointed the finger at those that needed further examination by the police).

The story that all was not well with the use of corporate credit cards by the police started circulating in the summer of 2007, when one national newspaper and then others ran stories about two counter-terrorism detectives who had been caught using their corporate cards for personal expenditure. One had spent some £80,000 gambling with the card and the other had gone on a spending spree for his family and himself until he was caught.

I had been aware of potential problems with the system for corporate credit cards for some time, following an earlier incident when an officer who did submit claims had made a number of false claims that my team had picked up and investigated. We passed the paperwork on to the internal police investigators and eventually the officer concerned had resigned and then later had been convicted of theft. Then in 2006 I had looked through the spending habits of officers who were making significant use of the corporate cards and had identified a number of potential abuses by a small number of police officers. We had been trying to get the police to sort the problems out for more than a year when the newspapers had picked up on these two cases, which the police themselves had detected. By that time I had been looking very closely at the expenses of one very senior police officer and had sought explanations as to his spending habits on the corporate card, which he had used as if it was for entertainment and hospitality when it was never intended for that purpose.

We monitored the amount being spent by all our cardholders on AMEX and realised that there was a huge and growing unreconciled balance. At its peak some £3.7m out of an £8.5m spend had not been accounted for at all. It was a massive amount of spent cash that had not been explained either by receipts or expenses claims. Of course, it was not necessarily fraud, it could all have been just tardiness, but we doubted that. Even so it was the best part of a year from the time we had sent over a list of potential fraudsters for further enquiries before the Met finally noted my concerns, coincidentally when the national newspapers picked up on the two fraudulent detectives and the then Commissioner sent a sharp reminder out through the management chain ordering all line managers and staff where there were outstanding balances to produce full explanations and submit the missing expenses forms.

The Commissioner's call led to a massive influx of belated expenses claims, and repayment cheques for 'personal use' came flooding in. In an ideal world we would have checked them all, but we simply did not have the available investigative resource or time. To try to focus our efforts on the more likely offenders, the Finance Department were initially processing the explanations and expenses forms provided, screening out those that they thought 'normal' and passing any that either had spend 'out of policy' (e.g., using the card for hospitality or local cash withdrawals) or where the explanations looked potentially fraudulent over to my team of investigators for a more in-depth review.

At the height of this investigation we were reviewing thousands of potentially fraudulent or wrongful use transactions for hundreds of detectives with corporate credit cards. Where it was patently obvious that something was amiss our only problem was the time that it took to put the evidence together. We had the expense claims of the individual officers and we had the original data from the credit card company to compare against. But we also had volumes of data where it was impossible to tell if anything amiss had happened.

The way the system had worked was that officers used their corporate credit cards and the bill was then paid by the Met directly to AMEX. Within three months the officers had to produce an expense claim to justify official spend on the card. This was an unusual system (as those who have reviewed corporate card expenditure before will realise) as normally employees pay their own bills on the corporate card and then seek reimbursement of the expenditure. Originally the system had been exactly that. The officers met their own corporate credit card bill and then produced their expenses sheets to have it reimbursed, but many detectives working away from the office or abroad or undercover complained that they could never get around to getting a reimbursement in time.

To ease pressure on hard-pressed detectives and other operational officers with corporate cards the Met's Finance Department had helpfully agreed to meet the AMEX bill directly provided the officers accounted for their expenses as soon as they could afterwards. What had been meant to be a helpful gesture to busy detectives, particularly after the horrendous events in July 2005, when almost every detective was switched to counter-terrorism work, had become a millstone round the neck of the Met. Very soon officers drifted into bad habits. As they knew the card was being paid off no one was in any rush to complete the paperwork. The longer this was left the harder it became for each of them to get around to reconstruct what the card had been used for and why. Aside from the small number of officers who started using the card for personal expenditure and as a state-provided personal loan others started making up paperwork to explain away expenditure, either because they had forgotten or lost the original receipts or because they had no reasonable explanation.

Because the Finance Department had only told the local finance managers in each operational command unit about this change, the police hierarchy (most of whom did not have a corporate card) didn't realise that line managers on the ground had an incomplete picture of who had a card. Many had little awareness that it was their responsibility to check their officers' spend each month, as they were too busy policing London to see it as a priority at that time. Most, if they did think about it, thought it was a responsibility of their local finance manager—but of course the local finance mangers had no responsibility for the management of the police officers concerned and were in no position to insist on completion of expenses forms.

The data from the credit card company contained insufficient detail to draw a conclusion for certain types of transaction (e.g., cash withdrawals), but we had our suspicions—for instance, if the corporate card had been used to withdraw cash but the reason given was illogical or no reason was given. It was also difficult to gainsay some of the explanations that we had been given where they closely matched the card information even though on the surface they seemed an odd thing for which someone would want to use a credit card. It was a case that started to consume a vast amount of our limited investigative resources and I needed to find a way to ensure that we targeted those that needed targeting and didn't waste our efforts on cases that were never going anywhere.

The answer came with a software application based on a variant of ACL, an alternative data interrogation tool to ACL or IDEA called ARBUTUS. This software application, called the Corporate Procurement Card Profiler,[1] (or CPCP™ for short) had originally been designed to work with Barclaycard and the Government Procurement Card. At the time, our corporate credit card contract was with AMEX (although, somewhat ironically, after the problems hit the headlines the Met switched to Barclaycard).

Once we had the software tweaked to work with raw data from AMEX we were able to review a number of possible pointers from behaviour both with individual cards and where several different card users appeared to overlap with each other by being at the same place at the same time. Some of the issues thrown up by the software were of limited use to us although they may have worked well for other organisations. By the nature of the job, operational officers worked unusual hours so data analysis suggesting it was odd for the card to be used at the weekend or bank holidays was little help as most of the time the officers in question were genuinely on duty at those times, an issue with potential 'false positive' results. At the time I left the Met, the software developers of the CPCP™ had taken onboard my observations and included departmental profiling which enabled the number of false positives to be reduced and more keenly focused on issues relevant to the way that the Met operated.

Despite the need to treat some of the results with caution because of the nature of the duties police officers perform we found some interesting data from this review that we hadn't picked up from the files and papers referred to us around card usage by police officers. It also picked out the two known worst abusers of their credit cards and put them at the top of the list of potential fraudsters and that gave me comfort too. Although we already knew about these individuals through other means it was comforting to know that the software would have detected them anyway on the basis of their spending habits alone.

One of the problems with checking corporate credit card expenditure, whether or not the organisation conducting the checks found itself in the extraordinary circumstances that we faced, is that it is at times impossible to see the wood for the trees, just by the sheer mind-numbing detail that needs to be checked for each cardholder. (At one time we were faced with the prospect that well over a thousand detectives, many of them either armed or working in specialist areas such as counter-terrorism or dealing with organised crime, appeared to have used their cards in ways that could have been construed as criminal and action might need to be taken.) The great advantage of the sort of software that we used on our cards is that it can pick out associations in the data that are virtually invisible to the investigator reviewing the documentation.

Because of the sheer volume of data (some 60,000 to 80,000 AMEX entries a month under scrutiny), we had put arbitrary limits around time periods and volumes in order to keep the investigation within manageable limits. We had agreed not to go back beyond April 2006 and had ignored anyone whose total spend since was below £1,000. What the software did for us was really twofold. It was able to look at all the available data and pick out anyone with a high hit rate of possible fraud, even if they sat outside the limits that we had set ourselves. Everyone picked out that way ended up being referred for investigation once we looked at their expenses claims—and these were officers misbehaving who we would otherwise have missed.

Second, it picked out patterns of inappropriate spend that we had not seen from the paperwork that we had already reviewed. One of the reasons for this was that each investigator was looking through a particular officer's claims and comparing them for the officer. Although we double-checked by putting each batch of claims through two different investigators we were still largely looking at one officer's claims in isolation. Unless we happened to know that they worked with another officer on a particular case we had no way of cross-matching the claims of officers working together except where they had identified this on the claim forms themselves.

In one particular instance the software picked out a number of officers who had been using cards in close proximity to each other for similar purposes. We were then able to cross-match claims that we would not otherwise realise were related and out of it identify a significant fraud being perpetrated by a small group among a number of innocent uses by other officers on the same operation. It still needed as much investigative effort to bring home the case, but had it not been for the software we would never have found the case in the first place.

Apart from the particular uses that I had for this software at the time, for other users it picked out among other things

▨   Cash withdrawals from the same location on four successive days.
▨   On-line betting with a procurement card.
▨   Claimed 'refunds' that weren't.

▪ A large quantity of alcohol in one purchase.

▪ A personal holiday paid for and hidden under several round amount payments.

▪ Double-billing where the card payment matches an expenses claim elsewhere.

Myths and legends

Some of you are probably thinking that these things couldn't possibly happen in your work systems. Let me dispel a common myth here. Many organisations will tell you quite fondly that their staff can either only use a procurement card with a limited number of suppliers or where they have issued a corporate credit card that they have a bar on it to prevent certain types of purchase.

If you know what you are doing, you can always get a transaction through outside the imaginary barrier that management think they have placed in the way. Dozy retailers and cash-based organisations will accept a procurement card that is supposedly off-limits to them. And if the staff have a credit card and are that way inclined, they will find it easy enough to get round any supposed bar (e.g., by drawing cash instead, at your organisation's expense with the added penalty of a credit card charge per cash transaction!). There are plenty of petrol outlets and small retailers where any card will be accepted.

Another myth is that a petrol card marked with the index number of an official vehicle can only be used to fill up that vehicle. There are always those with a convincing line that will be able to persuade a garage attendant to take it for the wrong vehicle and others don't even notice. The classic petrol fraud is to take a card for filling up a specific work vehicle and fill up petrol cans for later private use or their private car instead.

One of the other common myths here is that most managers actually check the expenses of their subordinates in a meaningful way. Had line management in the Met been more interested, many of the corporate credit card abuses would not have happened. Busy managers in most organisations can be tempted just to sign off expenses without really checking, and fraudulent managers will get colleagues inveigled either in approving dodgy transactions or participating in inappropriate activities so that they can't criticise the expenses habits of the manager.

General principles and axioms**from Chapter 7**

▪ In the hands of an expert the internet can be used to hunt down publicly available data that does not necessarily easily fling itself in front of you through a search engine.

▪ Technically minded fraudsters will often want to use the internet to let on about their cleverness or share information with like-minded fraudsters.

▪ If your IT department monitors traffic, make sure that the material that might relate to fraud isn't just enclosed in the usual note back to the line manager for potential disciplinary action but also gets sent through to your team to examine.

▪ A database is the best option for storing and downloading data for the fraud investigation. However, there are times, particularly for a new investigation or an unusual fraud, where it can be better to use a spreadsheet at the start.

▪ The three most well-known and common data interrogation packages are, in no particular order, IDEA, ACL and i2. IDEA and ACL are, for all practical purposes, identical.

▪ If you have analysts, make sure that they are fully trained and competent to use whichever interrogation package you have at your disposal. If not, then a member of the investigative team needs to be trained up and asked to act as the in-house 'specialist' for your interrogation package.

▪ One of the problems with checking corporate credit card expenditure is that it is at times impossible to see the wood for the trees, just by the sheer mind-numbing detail that needs to be checked for each cardholder.

▪ Credit card interrogation software can look at all the available data and pick out anyone with a high hit rate of possible fraud. It can pick out patterns of inappropriate spend that investigators cannot see in the volume of traffic.

▪ A fraudster can always get a transaction through outside the mythical barrier that management think they have placed in the way. Less scrupulous retailers will process a procurement card that is supposedly off-limits to them.

▪ It is a common myth that managers check the expenses of their subordinates in a meaningful way. Most only apply cursory checks or sign on trust.

▪ Fraudulent managers will get colleagues inveigled either in approving dodgy transactions or participating in inappropriate activities so that they can't criticise the expenses habits of the manager.

CHAPTER EIGHT

Considering covert surveillance

CHAPTER**SUMMARY**

W hat is covert surveillance? When—and when not—to consider covert surveillance. Using intelligence and evidence gathered through such means.

This chapter starts with a health warning. If you are contemplating using covert surveillance for the first time—*don't*! But if you have dabbled before or are being advised by someone who knows their business then read on!

◼ WHAT IS COVERT SURVEILLANCE?

First of all, covert surveillance is *not* sending round a team of private detectives to watch your suspect in their own home, even if you think they

are unloading half your store room there. That is a very good way to end up sued, arrested or both.

About the only time when there may be a legitimate reason for an internal fraud investigator to pursue such an option for an employee is if the employee works from home and it is part of their conditions of employment that the management reserves the right to check up on them at home. Even then, almost anything that might be done is either going to fall foul of the Surveillance Commissioner or breach the individual's (or anyone living with them) human rights.

> Covert surveillance in the context of an internal or contractor fraud investigation is about undercover methods to observe fraudulent activity in the workplace or involving contractors or staff at or travelling between work locations or business areas.

Some organisations already have staff with the power to conduct appropriate and proportionate covert surveillance on individuals in their own homes. The investigators with such powers include the police, intelligence services and Department of Work & Pensions Benefit Fraud inspectors. This section is not intended for them. It is for the fraud investigator concerned with protecting their organisation from fraudulent attack either by contractors, staff or organised criminals. Where members of the public are committing fraud against the organisation then it is unlikely that besides benefits fraud there will be any need—or indeed rights—for the organisation to conduct covert surveillance of an individual's home. If such surveillance is needed then it will have to come from a body with the legal power to conduct it.

One particularly tricky area has been insurance or early medical retirement fraud, especially where an individual claims to be incapacitated but is then seen physically doing that which they have claimed they cannot. Again, observing them in their own home may well turn out to be inadmissible or illegal or both. If, for instance, you check up on everyone who leaves work on medical incapacity grounds, you may be all right on equality legislation but the courts will not look kindly on speculative 'fishing expeditions' to catch individuals out without any grounds for the surveillance. In fact this is a very costly way of conducting business and I would never recommend such a 'blanket' approach to detect a potential fraud. It is far better to identify a potential fraudster target and then try and set a scenario whereby you can catch them out by covert surveillance on legitimate turf.

To keep on the right side of the law covert surveillance must be properly authorised by a senior officer and a proper record kept of the decision to conduct the surveillance. In the public sector that has to be someone who has the power to give a RIPA authority.[1] In the workplace, as a general rule of thumb, staff should have been put on notice that management reserves the right to check up on their activities at work. It is normal to have that sort of disclaimer on work IT systems, especially with the growth of email and the use of social-networking sites, but not all employers may have made it clear that they reserve the right to check up on their employees at work outside the use of IT.

WHAT MIGHT BE DONE AND WHEN COULD YOU CONSIDER IT?

Covert surveillance can be a very expensive way of trying to catch a fraudster and it is particularly important to recognise when it is the best and most suitable tool to use. History is littered with expensive tales of failed surveillance or evidence that backfired and burnt those conducting the investigation. That said, it is about the only known way where, done properly, you can give yourself a good chance of catching corruption and collusive behaviour between staff or between staff and contractors. If you catch any fraudster in the act you have two clear advantages. (1) You will have up-to-date evidence of their activities (which always goes down well with the police and the criminal side of things). (2) The trail is hot and you can pursue it vigorously, as the element of surprise is on your side.

So, let us consider the options and their context.

Camera surveillance inside the workplace

This is usually the most straightforward to set up and can produce the clearest results, if you keep it simple. Once over-elaborated, either something technical will go wrong or those under surveillance will cotton on and take evasive action. Some common examples where this can work include putting a camera up to observe a till operator or cashier that you suspect of fraud or cash theft, inside the issues or delivery area of a stock room where you suspect pilfering of stocks or inside an area where you store valuable business items. I am not talking here about security guards and security cameras, which will often already be in some of these areas. Indeed it is not uncommon for security guards either to be the culprits or to turn a blind eye or simply fail to observe the blindingly obvious. Covert surveillance will involve getting a specialist under some pretext into the work area either to install a secret camera and/or microphone or to have a hidden camera in operation about their person.

Cashier till frauds are often the easiest ones to detect with secret cameras, if they are suitably positioned. Straight overhead pointing directly down is often the best position if you can manage it. You can test what is happening by sending 'ringers' (i.e., your people) through at appropriate planned moments and then you can match their entries against the till records later to make sure that you are in sync with the customer transactions and the observed cashier behaviour. Even then you will probably have to gather many hours of evidence that will then have to be painstakingly reviewed to find evidence of fraud.

If you have staff 'clocking on' or off or employees on overtime where abuse is suspected then you may be able to position either a camera or a suitably placed investigator where the actual time the employee enters and leaves the work area can be captured and compared later against any claims that they make. For clock on and off for manual workers, it will pick up where individuals are operating a rota whereby one of them is clocking on and off for others.

Although a word of caution here, I once thought I had a 'clocking off' fraud in my NHS days, but ended up getting a surprise and a mouthful from my management for my troubles. The hospital group in question employed six staff as 'upholsterers'—a function I doubt that anyone would have nowadays. Anyway, I noticed from an examination of their clocking on and off records, that they almost always all clocked off within a minute of each other between 6:59 p.m. or 7 p.m. at night. This meant that they were getting regular overtime as well. I was convinced that this was the classic sending one along to do the 'clocking off' and the others had gone home hours ago.

A manager and I waited in a suitable area where we could watch the clocking off machine one night. At approximately two minutes to seven we heard this voice and footsteps coming nearer to us. All we could hear was "Left–right, left–right, do keep up lads!" We waited somewhat dumbstruck by this development. I began to suspect that I may have been a little hasty in my assumption of fraudulent behaviour. Sure enough, the senior upholsterer appeared with his team of five staff in a neat line as each one clocked off under his beady eye in turn before they left for the night. We discovered later that he had been a drill sergeant-major in the army and the habit hadn't quite left him. None of his staff would have ever dared to do anything wrong!

Electronic 'bugging' in the workplace

Modern electronic bugging devices are very sophisticated—the best are now so sophisticated that they can currently no longer be detected by electronic counter-measures, as they have outstripped the technology that looks for them. Although this is good news if you can afford to deploy the best devices—and you have someone capable of planting them without being spotted, it is also bad news if you suspect that someone is bugging you or your investigative team.

Internal electronic sweeps by organisations both commercial and governmental have for a long time been seen as part of ensuring the integrity of the arrangements in place to protect the organisation's data and internal information. However, to work successfully, they have had to rely on electronic devices that might confuse the sweep, such as computers, printers, digital phones and the like being powered down.

Nowadays there are tiny electronic bugging devices that can sit within the power circuits to other electronic equipment and when the equipment is powered off they will simply power down as well, making them virtually undetectable unless they are located by sight by whoever is conducting the sweep. Short of taking apart every plug, telephone and computer casing, simply not a viable option for almost everyone, there is little that can be done to ensure that such a bug hasn't been planted.

If you can get a bug planted in the work environment overnight or when the offices are closed, provided it is planted subtly enough, the chances are that it will not be detected. I have witnessed camera and sound bugs fitted in the simplest of office and warehouse arrangements without criminals who think they might be bugged finding them—despite conducting thorough searches, somewhat amusingly recorded by the very bugs and hidden cameras that they are searching for! However, as I noted earlier, not only is such equipment expensive, it also needs backup equipment, electronic storage and the cost and time of an investigator either monitoring in real time or running through hours or even days of digital recordings searching for the evidence.

These devices are most successful either where you are able to set up a 'sting' for your fraudsters by luring them into a trap where you can be reasonably confident that they will take the bait, or alternatively where you know where and when they are either discussing or carrying out their fraud and you can monitor them in real time in the act of committing fraud.

Undercover surveillance in the workplace

This can be very dangerous for the individual or individuals who act undercover. I have only ever used anyone in a significant role in this respect once—in a major corruption case and in that instance we worked in liaison with Fraud Squad officers who provided us with an undercover officer from another force, to avoid any local contamination. In the end, after four months' work, we had an excellent intelligence map of the extent of the corruption, even down to discovering that the ringleader pulling the strings was not our original target but another player who hid under their wing.

Unfortunately for us, careless talk by a senior officer who knew what we were doing blew out the cover of our undercover officer and the crooks slammed the door in our faces before we knew that they knew we were on to them. This taught me a valuable lesson about the need for constant vigilance around those informal networks that might betray your secrets.

It was a real case of Sod's Law, the odds were against such an informal link but they happened—and I had half a sniff of the potential problem but wasn't able to act on it quickly enough. I knew that the villain of the piece (as I thought originally) had a close past friendship with the secretary of the boss of this whole business area. The boss knew our secret, as we had needed his support to slip the undercover officer in there in the first place. He also knew about his secretary's former friendship with our target and as a result he was very careful not to let anything slip about our work in front of her. However, he brought in another senior officer to carry out a review of the area and, unbeknown to us, told the other senior officer about our undercover officer and where they were based, on the grounds that he didn't want him to do anything in the review that would cut across the work of our undercover officer.

This other senior officer spent a fair amount of time working in the outer part of the boss's office, alongside the secretary. They became very friendly and started going out at lunchtime together. This came to my ears through a work driver who spotted them canoodling in a smart restaurant that he had dropped them off at one lunchtime and he then mentioned it to me when we were having a little chat. (I've always found over the years that it is worth cultivating any support staff who provide services for senior managers; they will always know what is really going on and drivers, where they exist, are a first-class network of innuendo and gossip about their bosses!)

I realised the risk that this senior officer could leak information to a friend of one of our target villains, but it didn't occur to us until far too late that he might be privy to our secret—and in the classic Christine Keeler fashion, their pillow talk betrayed our undercover officer, who was very lucky to get out intact when the opposition made it very plain to her that she had been rumbled. Four months' hard work for our whole team down the drain because someone else couldn't keep a secret, not to mention the risk that a brave undercover officer could have been assaulted and physically scarred by an aggressive inner gang used to having their own way. One thing that had been reported back to us from the undercover officer was that if anyone objected to the working practices of our villains, they were taken to one side and given an old-fashioned 'seeing-to' until they saw the error of their ways.

We ended up with some excellent intelligence but absolutely nothing that we could use as evidence. To this day I can recall just how much detail I know about these particular scroats, but apart from the satisfaction of knowing that we were right to target them, it is completely useless information. That is one of the main risks and potential frustrations of covert surveillance. If you take it too far or your cover is blown you run the risk of ending up with even less than you had to start with.

So, if you do contemplate going down this route, do make absolutely sure that you have correctly evaluated the true risks and consequences of failure in it. If the surveillance is relatively short-term the chances are that you will have a better success rate. Don't use undercover individuals in the workplace if they are going to be in potential personal danger by it. Don't do it either if you can get a good chance of success without it. If there is absolutely no other way of getting to the bottom of fraudulent or corrupt behaviour then consider it. But even then if the risks are not worth the potential rewards it is best not done.

Undercover work beyond an hour or two is only for the well-trained and experienced few, not the many. It is one thing to act the 'mystery shopper', it is quite another to have to remember who you are and an entire fake history, as well as using the right jargon to fit in with the crowd that you are infiltrating.

Telephone and mobile phone bugging, 'tapping' and the like

The brouhaha that surrounded former Met Commissioner, Sir Ian Blair, when he secretly recorded the then Attorney General, Lord Goldsmith, during a series of telephone conversations in 2005 about the Stockwell shooting incident largely overlooked the fact that there was actually nothing illegal in what he did, as he was perfectly entitled to keep a record, albeit in this case a digital one, of the conversation that he was having with another senior official. Whether it was the right thing to do—or not—depends entirely on the motivation for making the recording and the use that was, or was intended to be, made of it afterwards.

It is not against the law to record a conversation to which you are a party and, depending on how it has been obtained, it can certainly be used as evidence in disciplinary and civil cases and in the right circumstances as evidence in criminal cases as well.

It is also quite easy to set up a telephone recording when either ringing from an office or receiving an expected call at an office. Any technical specialist can set the equipment up for you and you should be able to operate it yourself if necessary when the expected call is made or received.

Bugging someone else's phone outside of your organisation is, however, quite a different matter and the law can easily be broken and any evidence gathered become inadmissible if it isn't done properly. The requirements of RIPA and the various Wireless Telegraphy Acts have to be met. Such covert surveillance is best left to the experts dealing with organised crime and corruption and in truth should not be necessary for almost any fraud investigation that you are likely to have to do.

Dealing instead with something that can quite often crop up for an internal investigator—bugging a telephone conversation to which you are a party—can be a particularly effective way of dealing with dodgy contractors or overconfident internal fraudsters. If you can keep the conversation going long enough they may well drop their guard or drop a hint about something that you didn't previously realise should be of interest to the investigation. You must be careful of course, as if you are thinking of using the conversation for civil or criminal proceedings then the whole conversation will be the evidence, not the bit that proves your point. So if you've lied or misled in an inappropriate way in the build-up to get the information it could possibly backfire.

Generally speaking, the right result can usually be obtained provided the scenario has been prepared sensibly. Don't lie if you don't need to, people can often assume things if you don't spell them out. I tend to favour the half-truth, it is the same as conducting interviews; it is always easier to use the truth as a basis for weaving your web than a lie. You can ring someone up from the offices of the procurement department when you're there and say so—it doesn't mean that you work for procurement—just neglect to mention that bit. Equally you can say that you are an organisation interested in a particular matter without letting on that you are an investigator homing in on a fraudster.

One particular dodgy contractor, who provided the Met with services under the Dangerous Dogs Act, came to a sticky end when he was caught out by his own sub-contractor, who was furious when he told them that they were to overcharge deliberately and that he would then authorise their bills and split the profits. If they didn't go along with his little scheme he'd remove them as a sub-contractor.

The sub-contractor used an old-fashioned pocket dictating machine held to her telephone to record conversations in which the main contractor kept on urging her to carry out the fraud. She then very kindly sent us the tapes and suggested that we might like to play them! It was one of the most straightforward investigations that we ever conducted, we had transcripts made of the conversations and then our procurement department informed the contractor that (a) he no longer had a contract and (b) we were calculating the size of the overcharge and expected repayment. In the meantime we blocked that month's payment to the contractor as a down payment on what was owed. The hardest part of the investigation was working out the overpayment but we were sensible and went for obvious discrepancies. Armed with the knowledge of what he had suggested to this sub-contractor, it wasn't too hard to pick out what he'd done with the others.

 COUNTER-SURVEILLANCE, WHAT TO DO IF YOU ARE UNDER ATTACK

This happened to me in one difficult investigation into a particularly dangerous contractor. They found a way to keep themselves briefed on the progress with my investigation. To this day I don't know whether they were being fed by a high-up source in our organisation, perhaps one of the inner circle to whom I was reporting progress on the investigation, or whether they had simply managed to bug the office in which we held our regular progress meetings on the case.[2]

The technique I adopted to deal with this was not to appear to react as if I suspected anything. My then head of investigations and I went well away from the office, didn't tell anyone what we were up to and planned how we would deal with the risks. It was pointless sweeping the office—if we had found anything, to whom were we going to be able to link it back? And what would we gain? They might have a second device that we missed and we could lull ourselves into a false sense of security. Professional 'buggers' (if I can call them that) will often plant more than one layer of devices in the hope that if one or two are discovered the organisation or individual will relax and think that they have found them all.

On one investigation by a colleague he bugged a car where the villain used to sit and talk to his co-conspirators. Just in case, six bugs were planted, two a little obviously, two more discreetly and two as deep as he could get them. Sure enough, the villain spotted the obvious two and got concerned. He leapt out of his vehicle, had a good look around and then proceeded to work his way through the insides and underneath inch by inch. Eventually he spotted the two discreet bugs as well. Then by sheer bad luck for my colleague he dislodged one of the deep bugs and rendered it inoperable, even though he didn't notice it. Happily the one remaining bug did its job and the investigation had the intended result.

So, we didn't relax in our case. What we did was to plan everything on the basis that we were being 'bugged' by one means or another. From then on, we still held our briefing meetings on the investigation as usual, but I started introducing complete red herrings and some false information about both what we were finding and planning to do next. We then waited to see if anyone bit on any of the misinformation. They did. Now we were sure that we were being bugged or sold down the river by our bosses. We just carried on as if we were oblivious to this but held a separate series of briefing meetings off the premises in which we exchanged the real information and planned the actual investigation. And yes, I didn't quite tell the bosses everything that we were working on with the case from then on.

I didn't lie to my bosses in that case, but I may not have told them quite the whole truth![3] (That, by the way, is the best technique to adopt in a tight spot.) The successful fraudster will often stick as close as they can to the real facts, it is harder to break them that way (see Chapter 9, 'Fraud interviewing techniques') but the same rule also applies to the investigator. If you get challenged about what you are up to around a covert surveillance, tell as much of the truth as you can without compromising your real operation. It will always sound more convincing than a lie—and it has the advantage that you will remember it better if challenged about the same point by another member of the opposition.

An important point here, security is either 100% or compromised, both for your intended target and you. There is an old saying that you are as weak as your weakest link. So, it is better to be too cautious, even if you have to go through a few more hoops, rather than assume that no one would think of or be capable of turning the tables on the investigator. After all, there was that infamous incident a few years back when the Serious Fraud Office found that one of its highest profile investigations had been compromised by two junior accountants in the pay of its intended target.

 ## USING EVIDENCE AND INTELLIGENCE GATHERED THROUGH COVERT SURVEILLANCE

Legitimate covert surveillance material from the workplace can be used as evidence for discipline (including suspension or immediate dismissal), civil or criminal cases, provided that it has been obtained and held securely. If it was a one-off case then that is fine, as the covert equipment will have only been in place for a specific short-term purpose. Generally speaking it is more likely that covert equipment will need to be in place for a period of time, in which case a decision will need to be made about whether it is evidence or intelligence that is to be used to find evidence.

Key parts from a covert sound recording or modern digital video evidence can be used particularly effectively in interviews with those caught on camera or on voice recordings to demonstrate inappropriate or fraudulent behaviour.

General principles and axiomsfrom Chapter 8

▪ If you are contemplating using covert surveillance for the first time—*don't*!

▪ Covert surveillance in the context of internal or contractor fraud investigation is about undercover methods to observe fraudulent activity in the workplace or involving travelling between work locations or business areas.

▪ Covert surveillance can be a very expensive way of trying to catch a fraudster and it is particularly important to recognise when it is the best and most suitable tool to use.

▪ History is littered with expensive tales of failed surveillance or evidence that backfired and burnt those conducting the investigation.

▪ Cashier till frauds are often the easiest ones to detect with secret cameras, if they are suitably positioned. Straight overhead pointing directly down is often the best position if you can manage it.

▪ If you can get a bug planted in the work environment overnight or when the offices are closed, provided it is planted subtly enough, the chances are that it will not be detected.

▪ Camera and sound surveillance equipment is expensive, it also needs backup equipment, electronic storage and the cost and time of an investigator either monitoring in real time or running through digital recordings searching for the evidence.

▪ These devices are most successful either where you are able to set up a 'sting' for your fraudsters, or where you can monitor them in real time in the act of committing fraud.

▪ Undercover surveillance beyond the 'mystery shopper' time of an hour or two can be very dangerous for the individual(s) undercover, extremely expensive to run and a high-risk strategy with no guarantee of usable evidence at the end.

▪ It is not against the law to record a conversation to which you are a party and, depending on how it has been obtained, it can be used as evidence in disciplinary, civil and criminal cases.

▪ You must be careful if you are thinking of using your recorded conversation for civil or criminal proceedings, as the whole conversation will be the evidence, not just the bit that proves your point.

▪ If you get challenged about what you are up to around a covert surveillance, tell as much of the truth as you can without compromising your real operation. It will always sound more convincing than a lie.

- ■ Security during a covert surveillance is either 100% or compromised, both for your intended target and you.

- ■ Legitimate covert surveillance material from the workplace can be used as evidence for discipline (including suspension or immediate dismissal), civil or criminal cases, provided that it has been obtained and held securely.

CHAPTER NINE

Fraud interviewing techniques

If you know your enemies and know yourself, you will not be imperilled in a hundred battles; if you do not know your enemies but do know yourself, you will win one and lose one; if you do not know your enemies nor yourself, you will be imperilled in every single battle.

Sun Tzu[1]

CHAPTER**SUMMARY**

When you do and don't need to interview. Factual record interviews. Body language and behaviour. Understanding your style. Common pitfalls. Witness interviews. Hostile witnesses and interviewing potential suspects. What to do when you get a confession.

WHEN YOU MAY NEED TO INTERVIEW

During a fraud investigation it may become necessary to interview witnesses or indeed suspects, although (except for non-criminal or potential disciplinary cases) it is best not to interview suspects where the police may later wish to interview them.

" CONFESS NOW OR I'LL HAND YOU OVER TO PETER ! "

Determining whether, when and how to conduct formal witness interviews is an inevitable part of the fraud investigation process. Even where the matter is relatively straightforward and laid out clearly in the documents and records that you have gathered, someone with the appropriate authority is going to have to go on record to confirm that the evidence you gathered is genuine and is what it purports to be. Often, there will be a range of witnesses, from those who have handled part of the documentary or electronic processes through which the fraud passed through to those who were misled in person by a fraudster or who suspected or even got a confession out of a fraudster.

Apart from the most basic of fact-gathering interviews, there are techniques that the better interviewers use to ensure the best possible result from the interview. If conducting a specialised interview, such as a potential suspect or hostile witness, then the sage advice of the Chinese General, Sun Tzu, quoted at the top of this chapter particularly applies.

UNDERSTAND YOURSELF BEFORE YOU TRY TO UNDERSTAND OTHERS

One point I do want to emphasise in particular here, which applies as much to a general fact-finding interview as it does to interviewing a hostile witness or suspect, is that the key to success is to know your own natural style and how it is likely to be perceived by others. Various management and interviewing training courses will try and teach styles of approach but in truth if they do not come naturally to you then it will show and when it really matters you'll come unstuck in the interview. It is far better to use a natural style but make sure that you learn about the technical aspects of interviewing, so that you get the intended result from the interview.

Following my natural style I'm going to tell you a little tale here but bear with me, it is relevant. Way back in the late 1960s and early 1970s understanding the behavioural aspects of fact-finding interviewing became the 'fashionable' thing to research and speak about. Frederick E. Mints wrote a research piece for his doctorate in internal auditing on the behavioural aspects of audit interviews, published in the US in 1972. Mints was a great proponent of the 'participative' style of audit interviewing and it is no surprise that his research concluded that this was the best way forward after he had conducted a series of studies: first, with university students and, then, in the field with real internal auditors at a number of participating organisations.

However, for me, the aspect of Mints' research of most interest was not his thorough analysis of why all auditors should learn a participative, user-friendly approach to audit interviewing, but the anomalies that he also described that did not fit the general pattern of the rest of his research results.

During the field studies Mints asked his participating internal auditors to use a particular style of approach when interviewing. Style A was what he called traditional, an unfriendly and fairly brutal interview technique that treated the interviewee as potentially hostile—and not an uncommon technique for auditors in those days. Style B was less confrontational but businesslike and neutral in tone. Style C was the 'new' participative approach, attempting to engage with the interviewee, gain their trust and bond with them both over the audit and working together on the solution to any problems found. He allocated those styles on a proper random basis across all the participating internal auditors and then measured both how successful they had been in achieving their objectives and how well the interviewees had responded to the audit style.

Mints had two 'rogue' results from his studies, all the rest fitted into the expected pattern of behaviour. One 'rogue result' was from a pair of internal auditors who had been told to use Style C but whose results fitted the pattern elsewhere for Style A. It turned out that they had both been brought up in a culture in another country where the rules were the rules and everyone obeyed them. Try as they might, they could not convince the interviewees that they were truly going to participate with them, as they still came across as 'by the rule book' and hard-line. The other 'rogue result' was an experienced internal auditor who was asked to use Style A but came back with Style C results. It turned out that through his natural style over the years he had become well-liked and trusted by the employees in the organisation. When he adopted a Style A approach (whereas they might have reacted badly to someone else) they liked him so much that they went along with his more authoritarian unfriendly approach and still cooperated.

Mints didn't realise it at the time but he had the germ of another truth. You can amend your behaviour and you can learn the technical aspects of anything, given the right training, but your inherent style is you and in stressful situations or over a period of time that style will come through, regardless of how you try to alter or disguise it.

Learn to work with your natural style, not against it. And to do that you must genuinely and thoroughly understand yourself. Once you can be sure of that, then you can decide how you will use the principles and techniques set out in the rest of this chapter to best effect.

GENERAL PRINCIPLES FOR FRAUD INTERVIEWING

When you are interviewing a suspect you should try to ensure that you *never* ask a question to which you do not already know the answer. As a general principle this is a sound approach to follow and you should aim to gather evidence before such interviews with that key idea in mind. If you are not close to that position then you should, on almost any scenario that I can think of, refrain from interviewing your suspect.

An interviewer who goes into an interview without knowing what to expect from a suspect will have a significant chance of failure. Worse than that there is a real risk that a devious suspect will leave them none the wiser while at the same time learning that the interviewer doesn't have enough on them to cause any serious concerns.

If you know that you will be interviewing a potentially difficult witness and possible suspect then try to structure your interview around the methodology used by the police for such interviews. They use a structure known by the mnemonic PEACE. It stands for:

P	*Preparation and planning*
E	*Engage and explain*
A	*Account* (the part when the interviewee is answering your questions)
C	*Closure*
E	*Evaluate* (evaluation takes place after the interview has concluded)

In a police context there are specifics that they must do at each of these stages. For an internal investigation, it is best to bear this structure in mind but don't get too obsessed by the detail at each stage. It is just a simplified way of breaking down what needs to be covered at almost any formal interview.

With all fraud related interviews two basic principles apply

1. The interviewer must control the structure of the interview if they are to meet their objectives.
2. For the interviewer to have the best chance of establishing the truth or facts of the matter in question, they must relax the interviewee and gain their confidence.

This may sound counter-intuitive to some, but trust me on this. While it is conceivably possible that a weak or naturally very cooperative interviewee will give the interviewer what they want if they browbeat them, generally this is not so and if aggressive or threatening tactics are employed—or perceived by the interviewee to be employed—the chances are that the interview evidence will not survive any formal hearing or review.

There will be occasions when your need to achieve principle 1 above will conflict with your ability to achieve principle 2. It is always going to be a judgement call and wherever possible try to err in favour of principle 2. To control the structure of an interview you don't have to be aggressive or cut off the witness if they are wandering off the point, you just need to be assertive and take every opportunity to bring them back gently, politely but firmly to your agenda.

Before the interview begins, make sure that you have done all you can to dissipate any tension or concern of the interviewee. After the usual introductions it is always helpful to use a few ice-breaker questions, such as asking if they had a good journey or whether they would like any refreshments or water before the interview starts.

Once the formal interview starts you will need to deliver your questions in a neutral, almost deadpan tone. It isn't the particular style of delivery that is important, but the tone. By keeping a neutral tone you will help to relax the natural tensions that the interviewee will be feeling during a fraud investigation.

If the interviewee remains tense, don't be blown away by any outburst, aggressive reaction or indeed floods of tears, just keep calm and when the outburst has died down return to the question and make sure that you are putting it as dispassionately as you can. Don't be tempted to move on to the next question until you have exhausted any possibility of a sensible answer. If you keep calm and wait long enough (except in extreme circumstances) you will eventually get an answer.

There is generally no point in gaining control at the sacrifice of any relationship with the witness, although I have known occasions where it is clear from the off that the witness has no intention of allowing any relationship to develop and their entire line is to attack the interviewer. That is the one scenario where you must establish principle 1 and can decide to risk losing principle 2.

In the worst ever example of it—and I have seen a few—a witness about to be interviewed formally by me on a triple-decked tape machine[2] turned up wearing a bright red jacket (almost a banker that she'd come dressed for trouble) and with a prepared speech that she insisted on reading to the tape before the interview began. In the prepared speech she effectively rubbished our enquiries and challenged both my integrity and my right to conduct the interview. I'd like to say that I handled this very professionally but in fact at the start I allowed her to get under my skin and the first 40-minute interview tape was a study in how to record a growing frisson between interviewer and interviewee, complete with a thunderstorm in the background for added unnecessary effect.

Every time I turned up a page in the document bundle to ask questions I was asked a question instead. The classic being (me) 'I would now like you to turn to page 20 in the bundle.' (Witness): 'Why page 20? You haven't asked me about page 18 or 19 yet?' (Me): 'Because I am not going to ask you any questions about those pages.' (Witness): 'Well why are they in the bundle then?' I gave her a withering look and reiterated my request that she turn to page 20. This verbal onslaught was repeated by her in a belligerent tone every time I skipped over pages in the documents.

Then each time we finished with one of the bundles of documents the witness flung them down on the interview table in such a way that they flew at me and I had to sway nimbly to let them miss and crash to the floor as she waved her hand in a faint apology. At the first break (for exchange of tapes) as soon as the tape machine was off we squared up and had a spat at each other about the other's behaviour, until separated by my more experienced colleague who reminded her about her dignity and duty—and then took me on one side and reminded me that I had committed the cardinal interviewer's sin of letting her get to me.

After a 'coffee break' of a further five minutes I went back to the interview table now feeling suitably calm and pointed out to our aggressive interviewee that she could interview me at a future date if she wished, but as this was my official interview of her I would ask the questions from now on. I paused to make sure that she had taken that on board and then we started the tape machine again.

The interview lasted another six tapes, but I was now back under control and eventually on tape 7, many bundles of documents later, we had something approaching the truth of the matter, despite the hostile witness. Sheer persistence and determination got me there in the end but that was extreme and it is rare that an interviewer gets that degree of difficulty or opposition with the sustained aggression or intelligence to keep you at bay for such a long period of time.

It may surprise you but my normal interviewing style is quite deliberately gentle and friendly and not at all how the start of that interview had gone. My irritation had temporarily taken me out of my natural style and I nearly paid a price for it. I know that I get far more out of witnesses by a calm and friendly approach rather than a confrontational one, although it is always useful to prepare yourself for the witness that wants to be confrontational and then if they are you can deal with it calmly and stick to your planned script.

But it is important to remember that by the nature of a fraud investigation, even the most innocent of witnesses can be intimidated by your need to conduct a formal interview or take a statement. Intimidated, nervous or angry interviewees rarely tell the truth. They either give you what they think you want to hear or they only answer emotionally rather than factually. At worst they can set out deliberately to mislead you as their way of getting back at what they have wrongly perceived as threats to them.

General principles for interviewing a witness

Witness interviews for fraud investigations will often take some time, both to prepare and to conduct. With that in mind, the following general principles may help:

1. As with most aspects of human activity, remember the *six* Ps (proper planning prevents piss-poor performance).
2. Have everything that you expect to refer to with you at the interview.
3. Make sure that they understand approximately how long it will take and that apart from comfort breaks you expect their undivided attention until it is finished.
4. Don't forget the ice-breakers before the formal interview begins.
5. Make sure that you explain very clearly to the witness
   (1) who you are
   (2) who else will be present and why
   (3) the purpose of the interview.
6. With most witnesses, especially first-timers, it is helpful to give them a 'dry run' through the broad areas you are expecting them to cover and an indication of what you would like to glean from them.
7. Keep them on track as politely but firmly as you can.
8. Don't ask leading questions (e.g., 'You were at the desk, I take it?'—far better 'Where were you at that moment?' or, if you must, 'Were you at the desk?').
9. Don't ask multiple questions. People have a tendency to forget inconvenient ones and only answer the one that makes them feel comfortable.
10. Use closed questions to elicit facts and information where there is no room for debate (e.g. 'At what time did that happen?', 'Was it before or after you did X?').
11. Use open questions when you want to see what tale they are going to tell you or to let the witness put it in their own words (e.g., 'How did it happen?', 'What do you know about this document?').
12. Make sure that either you or your scribe is listening to every word from the witness. It is extremely easy to get so absorbed in the question that you are about to ask that you don't hear all—or any—of the answer being given to the previous question.
13. Only interrupt the witness if they are rambling completely off the point or have clearly misunderstood your question.
14. Try to keep use of language such that the witness understands you— and avoid professional jargon.
15. Don't forget to reflect back your understanding of what they have just said after each answer or group of related answers. (Particularly impor-

tant if you are writing down the witness statement before it is signed. This is a formal interview and you need to ensure that there are no misunderstandings when gathering your evidence.)

16. If you are not using recordings or timed tapes with built-in breaks, make sure that you take—and offer—a break if necessary in any interview that takes more than an hour.

Conducting straightforward, fact-confirming interviews

In theory this is the simplest to conduct and therefore it is just a matter of keeping your concentration going. You shouldn't need anyone with you to assist for these, but remember even in the most straightforward of interviews a chance remark from the interviewee may trigger off a line of enquiry or a thought about the investigation that had not occurred up to that point.

In these types of interviews you simply want the witness to confirm that something is the item, record or electronic document that it claims to be and that they have the authority to confirm that (i.e., they have reason by the nature of their work or location to know what it is). All you will then want is their signature and date alongside the simple 'I will say ...' statement that you have drawn up for them.

Conducting fact-finding interviews

This is the main type of investigation interview when you are not the police. Unless it is a simple straightforward matter you will either need someone to help you by recording it or you will need some kind of recording device operated by someone other than yourself. There are two reasons for this. First, accuracy is everything when gathering evidence and you can't afford to miss vital information—the presence of a colleague lessens the chances of that and gives you the opportunity to concentrate on questioning the witness. Second, you will need a formal record afterwards and in the rare event of a dispute about what was said or meant—or indeed how it was said—you are better protected by having a colleague in assistance.

By now you will be finding what I am about to say here a little repetitive, but I assure you one day you will thank me for it. As with the entire fraud investigation, you *must* begin a fact-finding interview with the end clearly in mind. If you don't you'll get sidetracked at some point in the interview and only realise later that you haven't gleaned some vital factual information or confirmation of other information that you needed.

Be organised and follow the general principles above. Avoid the temptation to rush the questions, make sure that the witness has said all that they want to say before you move on. Check regularly that whoever is taking notes is up to speed and if necessary wait for them to catch up. There is nothing more frustrating than to discover too late that the note-taker couldn't keep up. You can almost guarantee that they will have missed the most salient part or quote of the interview.

Conducting interviews of hostile witnesses and suspects

Generally speaking, the only time that you should plan to interview a suspect is when the facts that you gather will be used to determine whether they will face a disciplinary investigation for their involvement in an internal fraud. However, by the nature of fact-finding interviews, it is feasible that by accident or the usual Sod's Law you will find yourself interviewing a suspect.

When either you know or suspect that your witness may turn out to be hostile or is a suspect then make sure that you have closed off as many escape avenues to your questions that you can before you start. This includes clarifying that they know their organisation's ethical and anti-fraud policies and, if they deny knowledge, pursuing them about whether their managers allow or are against fraud and whether they themselves would commit fraud at the organisation before you get on to the meat of the interview. Then, if later on they are caught out on a question and try to claim that they didn't know it was wrong to commit the fraud in question, you can remind them of their answers earlier in the interview.

The general principles outlined at 1–16 above still broadly apply, but in these cases your initial preparation should also include any other witness evidence that you can gather before the suspect interview is conducted. It is important that, wherever possible, all other witnesses have been interviewed and any documentary or electronic evidence examined before this interview is conducted. It is far harder to get through or deflate a hostile witness if they sense that you don't have any facts at your disposal to challenge their evidence. The rule of thumb for a hostile witness or suspect is that you try to ensure that you know as many of the facts and the answers to questions as you can before you ask the suspect.

Once you have reviewed and prepared yourself with the evidence available from other sources (in this case sources that you will expect to be more reliable and less prone to mislead than your hostile witness or suspect), you are nearly ready to do battle. Now consider the wise words of Sun Tzu. Do you really know yourself? Unless you do you won't get past the first hurdle in a potentially stressful interview situation. Second, do you know the 'enemy'? Have you done your research into their background and views others have of them before sitting down to interview them?

For you, apart from the general benefit in life that comes from truly knowing yourself, there are aspects about how you behave in a stressful interview situation. What is your natural style when interviewing? How do you react when someone challenges a statement you've just made? Can you keep your emotions in check under provocation? Do you give away your feelings with tell-tale gestures or other body language signals? You must know the answers to these questions and also what strategies you can use to keep in control during an interview if you find yourself challenged in an area where you know your immediate emotional reactions might give you away, whether anger, surprise, embarrassment, fear or mental confusion.

If you have never been trained to deal with such interview situations, or have never faced them and don't know how you will react, then it is worth having some formal training so that you can get to understand how you behave in stressful interview situations, how others perceive your behaviour and what you can do to mitigate it, where necessary.

I used to work with a colleague years ago who was professionally competent but had an unfortunate 'bedside manner' with their own staff that they just could not see. Individuals were always complaining about their manner and asking to be moved onto one of the other teams. Eventually it got so bad that I had to take my colleague on one side during their annual appraisal and spell it out to them. They were horrified and utterly convinced that both their staff and I had got it wrong. For a while after that there was a frisson every time I tried to raise any staff matter with my colleague and an almost permanently hurt look in their eyes. Eventually the colleague moved on to another organisation and morale picked up considerably among my staff within a very short space of time. Then we heard tales of unhappy staff at my former colleague's new organisation, but every time we ever talked about staff, the former colleague remained oblivious and in complete denial, having convinced themselves that they were an excellent manager.

Anyway, I digress briefly but just to emphasise that you really do need to know how others see you before you get enmeshed in interviewing potentially hostile witnesses.

Hostile witnesses will usually bring along a colleague, union rep or 'friend' depending on your organisation's rules or arrangements. You must make it plain to them from the off that they are not there to interrupt or to answer questions on behalf of the witness/suspect. *Do not* allow any deviation from this. If they start to join in during the interview stop whatever you are doing and warn them that they will have to leave if they do that again.

Body language

For any general fact-finding interviews or interviews of hostile witnesses and suspects the body language on both sides is important. Numerous studies over the years have shown that a high proportion of the response that you have to another human being is caused by the interaction between their body language and the words that they use. The instinctive and natural human response is conditioned to react more to the body language that is seen rather than the spoken language that is heard. If the body language doesn't match the sentiments expressed by the words, it will jar in the mind of the observant interviewer as they are drawn consciously or subconsciously to the body language that they have observed.

Don't confuse body language with physical appearance. Studies of juries have shown that there is a natural propensity to see certain physical types and features as potentially guilty or potentially innocent, regardless of the quality of evidence against them in a particular case. Watch how the individual's body language varies when they are answering a range of different questions before you draw any conclusions about the veracity or otherwise of their answers.

You need to portray an exterior that is calm and in control—and not react to anything surprising that the witness says, keeping your body language as neutral as you can—unless you particularly want at a certain point to express visibly either your disagreement or incredulity. In the right circumstance you may want to convey that you think that they have just given you a load of codswallop but only do that as part of a planned strategy or tactic, not as an emotive reaction to what has just been said.

At the same time you need to watch the interviewee to see if you spot any tell-tale signs that not all is well with their answer to a particular question. When people are under stress they behave differently and if a particular question is causing stress only the very skilled liar will be able to prevent their own body language giving the lie away.

There is no 100% foolproof method of reading body language, as it varies between cultures and social backgrounds in the way it is displayed, but there are some generally common signs that can manifest themselves. Particularly for interviews in an organisation it is quite possible that you or a colleague may have come across the interviewee in a more normal work or work-related social situation. If you have, then that is particularly useful, as you should be able to identify when their body language is out of sync with the words that they are saying. If you can recall situations when they have exaggerated or been uncomfortable, you can keep an eye out for those signs creeping in during the interview.

Where you don't know the individual it is far harder to read the body language, but in a long interview you will start to get a feel for it. The good tester is a question where you are absolutely sure you have the right of it already and they try to give you a different explanation. What is their body doing, what sort of gestures are they using, has their eye contact subtly changed compared with other answers they've given? These are all hints that not all is well and once you have that 'test bench' you can treat with suspicion any answers where the same body language exhibits itself again.

But beware the eye contact business. Some people are very good at keeping it and others are not. You need to establish the norm for the individual before you can read evasiveness into an inability to keep eye contact or truthfulness in an ability to keep it. It is rare if someone is being evasive to signal it with just one small trait. If they are that good then they are going to be masking most if not all of their body language anyway and you will have to trip them up by exposing the illogicality of their lies under scrutiny.

Usually most people can't control their unconscious body language, particularly in the stress of an interview and there will be a set of associated gestures and physical signs, including reddening with embarrassment or shifting their position in discomfort that will signal they haven't quite told you the whole truth at that point.

We all have little ways of behaving that help us feel relaxed normally and pushed to extreme these can also betray the inner tension. I remember years ago, half-way through a job interview, where I thought I was about as relaxed as I could get, noticing that I appeared to be brushing imaginary crumbs off my left leg.[3] Watch out not only for these tell-tale signs in those you are interviewing but also in yourself—or you will give clever street-wise opponents unintended ammunition to use against you.

If you can, test yourself out with a trusted colleague and see if you have any traits under pressure that need to be controlled. In my younger days when I thought of myself as a regular tournament chess player, competing at weekend chess events, the stress of playing manifested itself in some very obvious traits, which became more extreme as the pressure mounted—and eventually persuaded me that even if my technique had now reached the standard to play tournaments at that level, I wasn't cut out to play regular chess under that kind of pressure. But I'd had no idea about the visibility of my give-away signs of stress until they were pointed out to me by a bystander watching at a tournament.

Somebody I once knew well got caught up in a business that led to their arrest. As the senior line manager I had to interview them formally over what had happened. This individual had worked for me for a number of years and we had often chatted about a range of work and non-work matters. Instinctively I knew how he behaved when he wasn't under pressure. When I started to interview him it became very apparent that every time he was thinking of either not giving me the whole truth or trying to put a favourable spin on something he made a particular gesture with his hands and he slightly adjusted his legs. I then watched out for this and each time it occurred I questioned him particularly carefully about the matter in hand before I moved on.

The use of silence

As well as reading body language another technique is getting the timing right. In that context silence can be a very powerful weapon in the armoury of the skilled interviewer and can be used to devastating effect. Before the merger of Revenue and Customs, many long-in-the-tooth Customs officials had built their career out of the ability to sit in silence after a particularly awkward question, to which of course they already knew the answer, waiting for their interviewee eventually to feel that they had to say something to them.

Inexperienced interviewers, as with interviewees, often feel uncomfortable if there is an unexpected silence and feel obliged to fill it with something. Learn to use silence to your advantage. If you lose your place in a momentary lapse of concentration just gather yourself in silence and peer at your papers until you remember where you were going. Don't feel any obligation to explain what you are doing. If you need to look up something before the next question take your time—if the interviewee starts to fill that silence then take even longer to find what you were seeking.

When you've asked a particularly awkward question and don't feel that you've got everything that you were expecting out of it just pause, deliberately take your time to look up the material for your next question and let the silence fall uncomfortably on your interviewee. You'd be surprised just how often they feel obliged to tell you a little more.

Wearing down a lie

Even if you don't pick a lie up from body language, all is not lost. The key difference between truth and lies is that although people may have different perceptions of the truth it comes from the same root of fact, but lies are not attached to the facts. Therefore under pressure it is harder to remember and recall consistently any detail that has been made up to support a lie.

If you interview 15 people about what was said at a briefing you will get 15 different answers (and this has happened to me!) but you will find a common core of what they can all recall. If you interview a liar they have to sustain their lie and they cannot fall back on memory to sustain it—and that is where you can start to find and exploit inconsistencies in their stories from the known facts of a matter or indeed any earlier interview that you may have had with them.

The secret therefore to exposing a lie is to return to the difficult subject matter as often as you can and from as many different directions as you can approach it. Once you get an inconsistent answer then work away at it comparing and seeking explanations. Eventually either they will admit the lie, weave a web around themselves or resort to bluster and indignity to try to deflect you.

If you have good evidence already in the bag that they are lying to you about a crucial aspect of the case then don't let them off the hook. Avoid unintentional threats as they risk jeopardising any confession later. (An intended comforting comment of 'you had better tell me all about it then' may look later in hard print shown to an employment tribunal or to a jury as a threat to the suspect.)

If they are persisting with a lie ask them if that really is the version of events that they want you to put on record. Make it plain that you don't believe them and that you have good reason not to believe them. Persist with the subject matter as long as you can, making them constantly break down the detail of the lie as far as they can take it. Eventually they may slip up and contradict something they've already said or refute a known fact, at which point you can point out the illogicality of the events they have described and ask them again for their explanation. You are entitled to play a variant of NIGYYSOB (see 'Game playing and transactional analysis') once you have them on the ropes, as the relationship is about to become a fruitful one of you (parent) and suspect (child).

Game playing and transactional analysis

Way back in the days when new management theories were popping out of the woodwork at an alarming rate, one technique—whose roots originated with the academic studies of a North American psychiatrist, Eric Berne,[4] who was interested in the interactions of his patients—became prevalent. It was taught to middle and junior managers in many larger organisations, me included. This was transactional analysis and it is still today a very useful and relatively straightforward technique to categorise in your own mind's eye the interaction between yourself and another (e.g., a hostile witness or suspect during an interview).

There are two aspects to transactional analysis that are useful to the investigative interviewer. First, Berne identified that an adult will move between three basic states of mind, which he called parent, adult and child. Each of those states has its own inherent characteristics and sets of behaviours associated with it. Second, Berne identified a number of dangerous verbal games that adults could play with each other, all of which had varying degrees of destructive influence on a relationship.

Berne's parent–adult–child model was that when two or more adults interact, they can only 'transact' (i.e., empathise or understand each other) when they are in complimentary states. Thus at its most basic, a child state can interact with another child, an adult with another adult and a parent with another parent. It is also possible to have a parent–child interaction that works effectively. However, if one party is in parent mode or child mode and the other one is in adult mode the transaction between them breaks down. In a workplace context the most effective state for meaningful communication is adult state to adult state. Where one party is not in adult mode the adult will need to find ways to move that party into the required state if they wish to have an effective interaction about work.

For the interviewer, this knowledge can be used not only to work out which state the hostile witness or suspect is in at any point in the interview,

Transactional Analysis – interpersonal relationships that work

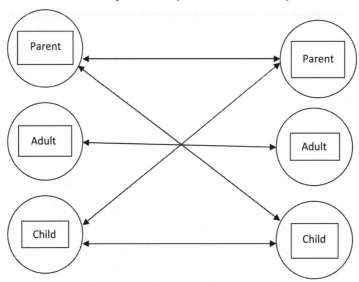

but also to change the interviewer's apparent ego state—either to break hostility and attempt to win the confidence of the interviewee or to put the interviewee under pressure by deliberately not allowing them to have an effective transaction with the interviewer. It can even be used to push an interviewee into child mode deliberately in the hope of an intemperate outburst by constantly asking questions coming from a parental ego state.

At the very least (if you don't feel confident enough to move away from the adult state in the interview) if you remain in adult state and observe from the language and body language which state the interviewee is in, then you can drag them back to adult state at appropriate points where you'll then stand a better chance of a meaningful transaction and getting nearer to the truth.

Berne's main research was, as the title of his book suggested, about the games that people play. Berne saw game playing in this context as potentially negative and destructive of self and others to varying degrees. Game-players were in child or parent mode, adults didn't play games and would move game-players away from their game by getting the transaction back to adult to adult.

Some example games

$NIGYYSOB$ = Now I've Got You, You Son of a Bitch

(I did warn you that Berne was from North America!)

This was a game played by a bullying or dominant individual—for example, a manager who would set a member of staff up to fail and then shout at them about the failure (i.e., an extreme form of parent mode).

$YDYB$ = Why Don't You, Yes But

(The original game from Berne's research.)

A child–child game in which one player announces that they can't do something and another suggests ways in which they can, but each time the first player finds a reason why they can't do it that the other party or parties has no means of gainsaying. The other party eventually exhausts all the alternatives that they can think of, leaving both feeling that they have got something from the game.

Blemish. Another parent-mode game, whereby the manager reads through a 50-page report but finds a small typing or factual error on an inside page and uses that as an excuse to downplay the quality of the work that has gone into the report.

$LHIT/Poor me$ = Look How Hard I Tried. A child-mode game played by managers or staff seeking sympathy for something that has happened but not wanting to accept any responsibility for it.

It is a natural human trait to want to look good to themselves and others in whatever company the individual is in at the time, even in a formal interview. Game playing is the means by which they can try to establish their superiority in an interview, to look good at the interviewer's expense, whether it be by presenting themselves as the victim, a variant of LHIT, or trying to out-psyche you and find out how much the interviewer knows by turning the tables during the interview and asking you the questions. Even out-and-out aggression or over-assertiveness is actually just a child-mode game to try to undermine the interviewer.

The important point here is that the interviewer must control the interview if they are to make any progress. Transactional analysis is a useful tool for recognising what is happening in an interview and to allow the interviewer to adjust their behaviour appropriately. For instance, skilled interviewers may well introduce game playing quite deliberately to manoeuvre a suspect in a particular direction in the hope that they'll paint themselves into a corner. Alternatively, if the interviewer's skill levels are not that advanced or the interviewer is not confident that they can bring a game off, then the best policy is to stick to an adult approach, if the suspect uses a parent or child mode in return, just stick to the adult mode, remain calm and eventually, although it may take some time, you will break them back into adult mode.

In the collaborative approach by a suspect they will try to draw you into their game, using body language and variants of LHIT/Poor Me to get you to react, either by nodding or other non-verbal signals of agreement. You must try and resist these. Although with most witnesses sympathy and empathy helps, even there you don't want to appear to agree with an opinion or justification for a particular action. With the hostile witness or suspect you need either to act neutrally or deliberately go on the counter-attack, preferably when they least expect it—and show the collaborative–manipulative suspect that their game plan isn't fooling you.

There is a similar tack to deal with belligerent witnesses, those that are outraged at your gall in daring to interview them. This can be a particular problem with relatively senior witnesses or suspects and it is simply just another variant of NIGYYSOB. You can throw them off balance either by the calm adult, carrying on as if they had said nothing, approach or, if you feel in the mood and can handle it, you can out-outrage the outraged. Most bullies in interview are either covering up embarrassment or feeling insecure, they are not usually prepared to trade verbal blows for any sustained period of time, as they are used to their minions running away in fear or not daring to answer them back. Whichever strategy you use to tackle them, the nub of it is to persist with the questions that you want them to answer until you do get a proper adult answer to each question, even if you have to keep on gently but firmly going back to the same questions.

Some extreme hostile interview scenarios

Sometimes a hostile witness will turn up with a representative and answer every question with a prepared 'no comment'. Remind them that this is an internal investigation and they have a duty to the organisation to assist your investigation. If you are unable to break them from this by conventional means remind them that they may face disciplinary action for their failure of duty and that you will have to report this to their management. Even if they are at the time suspended they still owe a duty to their employer and you are the employer's representative in that interview. Then after the abortive interview write to them seeking a written answer to all your questions within a fixed period of days. If that fails to elicit a response, then recommend them for dismissal.

If a hostile witness turns physically and violently aggressive it will give grounds for immediate dismissal anyway but stay calm and withdraw to a safe distance if you can. Revert to the written question method if they cannot be calmed down, unless, of course they have to be arrested for assault or are instantly dismissed.

 ## WHAT TO DO WHEN A WITNESS DECIDES TO CONFESS TO A FRAUD

This is a little trickier and it depends on the process that has led to this point and the intended outcomes of the investigation. While it is helpful to have a confession in the bank—and you should never, ever, stop a confession when you are an internal interviewer—you may need to take different next steps once they have finished confessing, depending on circumstances.

Confession when the police are going to be called in

If you have followed my earlier guidance, you will have started your interview process prior to any police investigation.

If you haven't and knowing the police were already investigating you've chosen to interview a suspect independently of the police investigation—and without giving a caution—you will almost certainly fall foul of current criminal case law and run the risk that the confession won't count in a criminal court. The only way in that circumstance you can get the confession to count for criminal action is if you stop the interview the moment that they start to confess and caution them in accordance with the Police and Criminal Evidence Act 1984 (PACE) and then ask them again. But the chances are that they will think twice about continuing with their confession once you have done that.

Alternatively, you can abandon any hope that the police will be able to use the confession for a criminal case and carry on taking it down, get the suspect to sign up for it and settle for the disciplinary action that can then be taken.

If you have interviewed them before the police have started their investigation, then let the suspect continue with their confession and don't concern yourself about PACE, as any confession obtained by you in your capacity as an internal investigator will still be usable for a criminal case. When the confession is complete get them to sign up to it and warn them that you will be passing it on to the police, who will probably wish to interview them as well about their confession.

Confession when the police are not going to be called in

This is simpler. Take their full confession first—and don't interrupt unless you think you have misheard something. Try to avoid any breaks until they have finished, although you may have to pause temporarily if they are very emotional during the confession. Once they have finished get them to sign up to it as soon as you decently can. Then take them back through it and try to tease out any points where you need to know more about how they did and anyone else involved in it. Not only will this confession do for any internal disciplinary proceedings, it is also usable if a later decision is taken to involve the police, since you did not intend it as part of a police investigation and were legitimately conducting the interview on behalf of your organisation at the point of confession.

General principles and axioms**from Chapter 9**

■ The key to successful interviewing is to know your own natural style and how it is likely to be perceived by others.

■ It is far better to use a natural style but make sure that you learn about the technical aspects of interviewing, so that you get the intended result.

■ Your inherent style is you and in stressful situations or over a period of time that style will come through, regardless of how you try to alter or disguise it.

■ Learn to work with your natural style, not against it. And to do that you must genuinely and thoroughly understand yourself.

■ When you are interviewing a suspect you should try to ensure that you never ask a question to which you do not already know the answer.

■ With all fraud related interviews two basic principles apply:
   1. The interviewer must control the structure of the interview if they are to meet their objectives.
   2. For the interviewer to have the best chance of establishing the truth or facts of the matter in question, they must relax the interviewee and gain their confidence.

■ By the nature of a fraud investigation, even the most innocent of witnesses can be intimidated by the need to conduct a formal interview or take a statement. Intimidated, nervous or angry interviewees rarely tell the truth.

■ Accuracy is everything when gathering evidence and you can't afford to miss vital information; the presence of a colleague lessens the chances of that and gives you the opportunity to concentrate on questioning the witness. In the rare event of a dispute about what was said or meant— or indeed how it was said—you are better protected by having a colleague in assistance.

■ Don't be blown away by any outburst, aggressive reaction or floods of tears; keep calm and when the outburst has died down return to the question and make sure that you put it dispassionately. Don't be tempted to move on to the next question until you have exhausted any possibility of a sensible answer.

■ Close off avenues of escape for suspects at the start of the interview both by gathering evidence from other witnesses first and by getting the suspect to agree what they know about the organisation's anti-fraud policies and whether they themselves would commit fraud or not.

■ Hostile witnesses will usually bring along a colleague, union rep or friend depending on your organisation's arrangements. You must make it plain to them from the off that they are not there to interrupt or to answer questions on behalf of the witness/suspect. *Do not* allow any deviation from this.

- You *must* begin a fact-finding interview with the end clearly in mind.

- Check regularly that whoever is taking the interview notes is up to speed and if necessary wait for them to catch up.

- The instinctive and natural human response is conditioned to react more to body language that is seen rather than spoken language that is heard. If the body language doesn't match the sentiments expressed by the words, it will jar in the mind of the observant interviewer.

- There is no 100% foolproof method of reading body language, as it varies between cultures and social backgrounds in the way it is displayed, but there are some generally common signs that can manifest themselves.

- Most people can't control their unconscious body language, particularly in the stress of an interview and there will be a set of associated gestures and physical signs, including reddening with embarrassment or shifting their position in discomfort that will signal they haven't quite told you the whole truth at that point.

- Inexperienced interviewers, as with interviewees, often feel uncomfortable if there is an unexpected silence and feel obliged to fill it with something. Learn to use silence to your advantage. If you lose your place in a momentary lapse of concentration just gather yourself in silence and peer at your papers until you remember. Don't feel any obligation to explain what you are doing. If you need to look up something take your time—if the interviewee starts to fill that silence then take even longer to find what you were seeking.

- The key difference between truth and lies is that although people may have different perceptions of the truth it comes from the same root of fact, but lies are not attached to the facts.

- The secret to exposing a lie is to return to the difficult subject matter as often as you can and from as many different directions as you can approach it.

- With the hostile witness or suspect you don't want to appear to agree with an opinion or justification for a particular action. Avoid nodding your head in apparent agreement. You need either to act neutrally or deliberately go on the counter-attack when they least expect it.

- The nub of it is to persist with the questions that you want them to answer until you do get a proper adult answer to each question, even if you have to keep on gently but firmly going back to the same questions.

- You should never, ever, stop a confession when you are an internal interviewer.

CHAPTER TEN

Advanced techniques in fraud investigation

There are lies, damned lies and statistics!

(attributed to Benjamin Disraeli but first frequently used by Mark Twain)

CHAPTER**SUMMARY**

Top-end anti-fraud activity. Using science to support fraud detection and investigation. Fuzzy logic and data interpretation. Hunting the hunter.

ADVANCED TECHNIQUES IN THE CONTEXT OF THIS BOOK

This chapter is not for the faint-hearted or indeed for those that do not need to employ complex methodologies or approaches in order to detect fraud. It is intended as an introduction to these aspects for those who would like to take their arsenal to this level and would like pointers to move in the right direction. I can promise that it won't be as much fun or as entertaining as some of the other chapters so please remember—you have been warned!

Elsewhere in this book I've touched on some aspects of advanced techniques, including considering covert surveillance and using the principles behind scientific sampling. Generally I like to keep fraud detection and investigation activity as simple and straightforward as possible; it avoids misunderstandings with the investigative team and it keeps me focused clearly on the end in mind during an investigation. Although most of the time this is the right approach, there are some matters needing investigation that can only best be cracked by using more advanced techniques.

But before considering using more advanced techniques, don't forget the principle behind Occam's Razor.[1] The simplest solution is often the best—however complex the fraud may appear.

THE APPLIANCE OF SCIENCE ...

Here I'm going to stray into the world of statistical theory for a while. Probability theory is generally understood, although its application beyond predicting the throw of a die or the chances of a spinning coin coming down as heads or tails often isn't, particularly when it appears to fly in the face of perceived wisdom or general understanding.

Statistical and probability theory can be built (and often is) into the software being used for databases and spreadsheets as well as more specialised audit and fraud tools. But in order to use such tools, you need to understand what this can or cannot do and what it means in terms that will aid your fraud investigation.

There are a number of statistical and probability areas that can assist the investigator. Perhaps the most useful areas are around sampling to find whether something probably is—or isn't—present in a given population, the likely variation in value of a population and the probability that a rare event may or may not have occurred. This last technique can be adapted to predict the likelihood of a fraud being discovered and then used to determine sampling sizes for finding frauds in large volumes of data. It isn't particularly helpful if there is a small population or only a few transactions involved in a potential fraud. However, in any area where there are many transactions or where there is a high volume of claims then statistical theory can help determine a result.

In essence there is one general theory that underlies this branch of statistics and that is that for any 'normal' population (see below for a definition of population) a random sample taken from that population will demonstrate the same characteristics as the population from which it was drawn. In fact statisticians would go further, for any large population with varying values (e.g., people and their height or weight) any samples taken will be normally distributed around the mean or average value of that population. This is a powerful piece of science which can be used to the investigator's advantage in the right circumstances. Like all tools in the toolbox it has its place but will not be appropriate in many circumstances. It is an area where an understanding of the concepts can be invaluable in deciding whether specialist help can assist the investigation.

Unfortunately not all statisticians use the same terminology to describe the same things but for the purposes of conveying the concepts (which is what you need to grasp if you are going to use or get someone else to use these techniques effectively for you) I am going to use my terminology as follows:

■ *Population.* Any group of homogenous items with a similar set of characteristics (e.g., invoices, claims, debtor accounts, stock items of a particular type).

■ *Random number.*[2] A number chosen randomly by computer or random number table (not a number chosen by a human being claiming it to be random!).

■ *Random interval.* An interval selected through the use of random numbers but then mechanically applied in equal gaps through a given population. Generally speaking, sampling theory requires randomly generated data to be selected. However, sometimes that is physically impossible or too time-consuming for the investigator to do. One way round this is to take the estimated size of the population and the size of the sample required then after a random start add on the same interval throughout the population and select those items for testing.[3] This is a technique that works best when the original documentation is still held or stored in manual records. In one extreme case I got my random interval with a stack of like-sized files by measuring several inches on a ruler and then repeating that gap throughout the entire stack of files. Where the original data is stored electronically it is generally best to take a true random sample and not use random intervals.

▧ *Attribute.* A characteristic of a population (e.g., an invoice coding or date).

▧ *Error rate.* The percentage or proportion of a measured attribute in a given population. As generally auditors and investigators are looking for a characteristic that shouldn't be there if all was well, it is often known as the 'error rate'.

▧ *Attributes sampling.* Taking a random sample from a population to measure the presence or absence of a particular attribute in that population to estimate its presence in the entire population. An attribute can never be present in more than 50% of a population— so, for instance, if you wanted to look for incorrectly coded invoices, the attribute would normally be the incorrect coding, which would be hopefully a small percentage of the population of invoices. If by chance you found that most of the invoices are incorrectly coded then that becomes the accepted 'norm' in statistical terms and the attribute is only now present in the few that are correctly coded— hence why in scientific-sampling parlance an attribute never exceeds 50% of the population.

▧ *Discovery sampling.* A variant of attributes sampling that is designed to ensure that you establish the probability that if there was a fraudulent item it has been detected.

▧ *Stop-or-go sampling.* Another variant of attributes sampling but this time using probability theory to estimate the chances that the population is fraud or error-free and therefore unlikely to be of interest to the investigator. It is generally a more appropriate technique for a systems-based auditor rather than an investigator.

▧ *Variable.* Unlike an attribute, which is either present or not, a variable is something that applies to every item in a given population (e.g., with people it could be height; for stock it could be number or value).

▧ *Variables sampling.* Taking a random sample from a population to measure the variability of that population and thereby estimate its range and true value.

▧ *Difference estimation.* A technique which uses a variant of variables sampling to get a more accurate and simpler result. However, it only works on populations where there is a high degree of differences between book and actual (e.g., between a stock ledger and what is found in a stock count).

▨ *Monetary unit sampling.* A variables sampling variant based on Poisson distribution theory, which is around the likelihood of small or large values appearing. Very popular at one time with the National Audit Office. From an investigator's point of view it is of limited interest. Where this technique is used the external auditor will have ended up selecting all the largest value items in a population of invoices to check. Any fraudster worth their salt will have ensured that they haven't submitted an invoice that would be picked up for testing in that way. (Or, if they have, that it was a massive one-off hit and they are now living beyond extradition range!)

▨ *Confidence* (not to be confused with *Precision* below). Confidence is a measure of how likely that a given error rate (attributes plans) or average value (variables plans) at a certain precision is representative of the population from where the sample has been drawn. It is best illustrated by a simple rule. The only way to be 100% confident of a result with 100% accuracy (i.e., plus or minus 0% on precision) is to test and measure every item in a population. Sampling theory is about how to get a result that is almost certainly nearly as accurate but by sampling (i.e., testing and investigating) far fewer items than the total available for examination. Although scientists will use a whole range of values for confidence, for the average investigator or auditor it is only the very highest values that are of interest.

What statistical theory teaches us is that you can have a very high degree of confidence that your sample does represent the population from which it has been selected without needing to select a very high proportion of the population. It sounds counter-intuitive but there is proof out there that it works. It is, for instance, quite feasible for a population of, say, 100,000 invoices to get a 99% confidence that your sample is representative with a sample of perhaps no more than 600 invoices whereas you would need 100,000 invoices to get 100% confidence.

▨ *Precision* (or confidence limits). This is a little trickier as it is different for attributes-based plans and variables-based plans, even though the theory comes from the same root. In an attributes-based sampling plan precision is usually expressed as a plus or minus percentage around the error rate that has been found in the sample. For a variables plan it is a plus or minus percentage of the average value of the sample. Precision and confidence have an inverse relationship to each other. For a population of N items and a sample size of n (where n remains a constant number) any increase in confidence weakens precision and any increase in precision weakens confidence. To increase both the accuracy (precision) and the confidence a larger sample value for n is needed.

WHERE ATTRIBUTES COME TO THE FORE

With both attributes-sampling plans and variables-sampling plans you are trying to estimate what is going on in a large population of items (say, invoices) without the need to examine a large number of them to answer that question. In both cases the theory is well established and scientific formulae can measure the result of any given sample taken from any large population. Indeed they are often built into spreadsheets and some audit and investigative software.

There are two main uses of a general attributes-sampling plan that can be of interest. When such a plan is used the analyst or investigator estimates the likely level of error (or fraud), determines how confident and precise they want the result to be and from that will have a random sample size that needs to be selected and examined by the investigator. If the result from the sample selected comes to an approximation of what was expected then you both know the level of fraud and that your assumptions were a good guess from the base data at your disposal. If the result turns out to be much higher or lower than expected then you can recalculate and work out either if you need to sample more items or the chances are that the level of fraud is so low that it does not warrant the level of investigation originally intended.

A general attributes plan will therefore either enable you to confirm that what you thought was going on is going on or it will tell you that something fundamentally different is happening. It won't measure the value of a fraud but it will measure the likelihood and frequency of a fraudulent transaction or item turning up.

A general attributes plan can also help measure multiple events that might signify fraud but where they themselves are not a monetary value. A good example of this would be in the context of either ghosts on the payroll or fraudulent invoices. In both instances you may know that throughout the population certain events should occur for each item, but if they don't, or are in error, then there is a chance that fraudulent activity has taken place. If your analyst can pull out all items that fall into that category, it may be the answer, but if the number of items that are hitting the categories pull out too much data you may simply not have the resource to find out if this is error or fraud that you are seeing.

If you take pay entries as an example, missing NI number, unidentified budget codes, salaries that don't match others or duplicate bank accounts can all potentially be signs of fraud. And for invoices, incorrect coding, mis-calculated invoice values, incorrect VAT code are all potential signs of fraud. In both instances their likely level in a population can be measured by the use of a general attributes-sampling plan.

Using stop-or-go sampling to eliminate areas where there is no fraud

One way round a high level of hits from the analyst's work is something that Lockheed Aircraft Corporation called 'stop-or-go' sampling in their original scientific research in the 1940s. This arose out of the need to work out the probability that a supply aircraft was going to make it to a particular war zone and back without being shot down or being forced to abandon its mission by engine failure and the like. The end result was a sampling plan that is particularly useful to disprove things. So, if you think it is unlikely that what the analyst has found indicates fraud then you would use stop-or-go sampling in the hope that it could be quickly shown that there was a very high probability that the population was 'clean' and contained no fraud.

How this would work is as follows:

You take a small sample of randomly chosen items—say 30 items—from the population. You then check each item to see if it is fraudulent. If you find no fraud then you can cross-match your sample size on a stop-or-go table and it will tell you the probability that there is no fraud or that the fraud is below a certain level in the entire population. If that result isn't accurate enough you take a further 20 items and see if they are fraudulent. If none of them are then the chances that the population is clean will improve statistically quite rapidly as will the chances that the true level of fraud is below a lower percentage than before. For instance, if your organisation is a retailer prepared to accept a pilferage rate of 3%, then provided your sample suggests that the pilferage rate is no more than 3% you can stop and move on to some other investigation.

The only problem would be if you found a fraudulent item in either your first or second sample above. It immediately worsens the probability of a low level of fraud in the population and you will need to test more items—if a further fraud is found then chances are there is significant fraud, if it isn't you may conclude that any fraud is below an acceptable level for your organisation.

When I was working as a lecturer at the Civil Service College in the 1980s (now known as the National School of Government) I worked alongside two statisticians and, at my request, between them in their spare time they worked out the probability theory behind the Lockheed stop-or-go tables. As a result I was able to create my own stop-or-go table and also find one or two errors in the originally published tables. This meant that for any sample size I could calculate the probability of the population being clean and the likelihood that the true error rate was below a certain percentage.

Discovery sampling as a means to detect fraud

One variant—discovery sampling—will give an accurate assessment that if there was any fraudulent item in a population you have probably found it in your sample. To achieve that result though its sample sizes are far larger than normal samples and in some circumstances may be prohibitively large.

My general view is that the investigator is unlikely to need to use discovery sampling. If a fraud is frequent or common enough it will show up in general testing. If it is very infrequent, then you are only likely to be interested on the rare occasions; when it is infrequent but each fraudulent transaction is of a significant value, in that scenario discovery sampling may be the answer you need.

■ THE VALUE OF VARIABLE SAMPLING

If you are trying to estimate the likely value of losses through a fraud but cannot check everything in a population then variables-sampling plans can help answer that question.

Using difference estimation to calculate the value of a fraud

Probably the most effective plan in that context is difference estimation. Although it is frequently considered in the context of stock losses and frauds for stocktaking exercises it can in fact be applied successfully to any financial population where your fraudster has been at work. As long, of course, as the population is sufficiently large and the number of fraudulently submitted items so great that pulling them all out and proving them isn't a viable investigative option at this stage of your enquiries.

If you know what items should be valued at, or the normal value of items that haven't been fraudulently inflated, you can measure the difference between the two for at least 50 occurrences and provided that you have selected the sample randomly from which these 50 occurrences have been measured, you can extrapolate for the population to estimate the likely total value of the fraud. In case that makes no sense, I've set out a shortened example below. In reality you'd need at least 50 differences to do this or there is no guarantee of the accuracy (precision) of your result.

Item	Normal invoice value	Fraudulent value	Difference
1	£300	£500	£200
2	£250	£400	£150
3	£400	£600	£200
4	£600	£700	£100
5	£425	£600	£175
6	£875	£990	£115
7	£350	£500	£150
8	£225	£350	£125
9	£175	£350	£175
10	£500	£650	£150
Total	£4,100	£5,640	£1,540
Average	**£410**	**£564**	**£154**

Total number of invoices by fraudster 1,000

Average value of tested fraud × total invoices = **£154,000**

(estimated size of fraud)

This example is an over-simplification for the sake of clarity but statistical theory can easily work out the amount of variability in the differences and from that either a statistician or the appropriate statistical tables can calculate the likely accuracy of the estimate for the invoices that haven't been tested in this way. For instance, that might be expressed as follows:

> We have calculated via difference estimation that the true value of the fraud is £154,000 ± £15,000.

With the difference estimation calculation for a suitable sample size it will also be possible to estimate how confident you can be that the sample you have taken is representative of all the invoices that you could have tested.
So the final expression could be:

> The true value of the fraud is estimated to be £154,000 ± £15,000 at a 99.7% confidence that the sample data is representative of the whole population.

How could anyone argue with that sort of precision!!

If that is really too much fine-tuning then as long as the method above is applied to a minimum of 30 and preferably 50 items then why not just use that as your best estimate of the fraud, particularly if you are at the stage when you are thinking about a freezing order and your affidavit. It has the advantage of being simple and methodical and is as defensible as anything until you have had the chance to delve further into the fraudster's invoices.

▦ USING GENERAL SAMPLING THEORY TO ADVANTAGE IN A FRAUD INVESTIGATION

I'm not a statistician by training or inclination—I was for 38 years a 'frauditor' and the frauds that I either found or came to light on my watch are the events that inspired much of my thinking and work activity. However, I recognised how some of the basics of scientific sampling theory could be used to advantage in my world. For instance, most of the sampling plans I've just outlined are based on the premise that a number of samples taken from any large population, even if that population itself is in some way skewed, will form a normal distribution around the mean value of the population. This is potentially helpful when looking at a low-value, high-volume fraud or any area where there is a vast number of transactions in which you need to find the fraudulent ones.

An example of how this might help runs as follows:

Let's say you have hundreds of contractors or sub-contractors supplying minor works and maintenance, including Dodgy Dan, who on the surface just looks like another typical sub-contractor sending in invoices. Every month thousands of small invoices from Dan and many others are being processed. He's below the radar and doesn't obviously stand out among the others. It is just possible that you might pick him up by the application of Benford's Law (see 'Financial/Accounting patterns' in Chapter 2, p. 26), which would certainly be the cleanest and easiest way if he stands out by having an average first digit higher than others.

If Dan isn't outstanding on first digits then another way that could be tried using the principles from sampling theory is to take the average value of his invoices and compare them to the average value of invoices of similar sub-contractors. Don't forget to pick out at least 30 and preferably 50 invoices of each sub-contractor. Then by calculating the average value of their invoices and comparing that to the average value of all invoices in the same time period you can map how close or far away they are from the average value. If Dodgy Dan is behaving the same as the majority then his number and value of invoices will be close to the average value of the population. If he's doing something quite different then he'll be off by a significant amount—either far too low or far too high.

To determine whether Dan's difference from the norm is significant or not you could simply rely on your frauditor's instinct but if you want to be more scientific or the boss is tough to convince the easiest way would be to draw up the normal distribution curve for the results (which should form a nice bell-shaped curve) and measure how far Dan's results are away from the norm in terms of variance, which is usually measured in standard deviations (to a statistician standard deviation is the square root of variance, to me it is more simply a measure of variance on any particular bell-shaped curve). One standard deviation = approximately 68% of the possible values of any bell-shaped curve, 34% either side of the mean value. Bell-shaped curves can have a sharp peak towards the middle or be relatively flat. If yours is relatively flat then it is telling you that there is a wide variation around the mean value naturally. In such circumstances it is harder to show that those away from the mean value are specifically that different. But, generally speaking, if you were looking at a large number of small suppliers of the same type of service or product then you would expect to see a fairly close grouping around the mean average (i.e., a sharp rather than a flat peak) so anyone who wasn't that close would stand out.

While it isn't particularly significant if Dan is within one standard deviation, you will certainly be interested if he is more than one standard deviation away from the average value: 90% of the values within any bell-shaped curve are contained within 1.96 (approximately two) standard deviations, and 99.7% of the values in a bell-shaped curve are contained within three standard deviations. Turning that around, if Dan had, say, an average value for his invoices that fell between two and three standard deviations away from the mean average, that is telling you that the chances are that Dan is in a tiny minority as 90% or more of the average invoice values of other contractors are closer to the average than his are. And if Dan is in some way unique, it suggests that there is something potentially fraudulent about Dan's invoices.

I do hope you've been able to make sense of the last few paragraphs. I did warn that this chapter may be a little more challenging!

▦ FUZZY LOGIC AND DATA INTERPRETATION

This is a highly specialised area but there are software companies out there that make tools that can review almost any file written in any computer language and make sense of them. One particularly powerful tool can reconstruct text from another software application, even if you are unable to decode the application in question.

Fuzzy logic is the art of getting a computer program to think more like a human being. We spend our lives making estimates and judgements based on incomplete information while our brains fill in the blanks for us. At its most basic, it is the reason why we can walk without falling over, even when we are not looking at the ground beneath our feet. For a long time that kind of judgement, with a wide number of variables, was simply beyond computers. Now it isn't.

I have seen a software tool that can pick out and accurately translate what is being said inside virtually any work system, coded or otherwise. It works by going right back to the binary code in the other application and then uses fuzzy logic to determine the most likely meaning of the code it has found.

These tools are generally not suitable for the one-off or occasional investigation, unless it is a technically complex fraud of significant size. Such software tools have to be used by forensic computing experts but the investigative frauditor needs to know when they might be used and how to find them. I cannot name specific brands here as the companies concerned are often sensitive about which companies are being promoted in a market place that is for once dominated by the smaller specialised players.

If you want to find such a product then any forensic computing specialist worth their salt ought to know how companies can be tracked down and who can provide it to you. Any business that is competent to take an image of a hard drive and crack passwords in a secure manner suitable for an evidential trail in court is likely to know where to find these specialists, if they don't have access to such software themselves.

A word of warning here, by their nature such tools are not going to be cheap to use so be sure that they are the only way to resolve your investigation or you could find that you are committing considerable resource to this for little obvious benefit. But if you particularly need to crack what has gone on inside a system or where someone has tried to hide or scramble their files then there are a range of software applications that specialise in making sense out of it when it really matters, including a number that already provide specialist services to government organisations, the military and the police.

 ## HUNTING THE HUNTER

One of the fundamental problems facing most fraud investigators is that their work starts after the horse has already bolted. Fraud is one of those areas where the first the investigator is likely to know is when they are off on the trail of something odd that has been discovered or has happened. It is hard to get ahead of the game but in some areas it is possible.

In his seminal book *Corporate Fraud* Mike Comer describes how in the commercial world his team once entrapped a corrupt senior manager by appealing to the senior manager's natural dishonesty and greed. The fraudster was conned by an approach from a bogus head-hunter. He was then put through an interview process as if he might get the job and told he was the only significant candidate but then left to stew. When eventually patience and curiosity got the better of him and he rang up to ask if he'd got the job he was told that he hadn't, as he had come across to the interviewers as very honest but they were really looking for someone who could duck and dive more than that. He then proceeded to tell them that he wasn't that honest, even describing the main fiddle that they had been trying to nail him for in the first place!

If you are in the commercial world then you can get away with this sort of approach and then fire the individual concerned. Unfortunately in the public services it is a little harder and could backfire very messily at an employment tribunal. Tempting though it is at times, I cannot therefore in all conscience recommend such an enterprising step for local and central government investigators.

That doesn't mean that in the public services there aren't some proactive things that can be done. For example, as an experiment some

years ago one of my previous employers, Her Majesty's Treasury, were looking at ways to open up their computer systems to the outside world
without compromising internal security. (This was in the days when the
budget was still an un-leaked secret and no Treasury system had any direct
link to the outside world.) To establish the risks that they faced, a standalone link was set up to the outside world, running a webpage about HM
Treasury with some links to genuine but non-sensitive data. They were
inundated with hackers and attempts to corrupt the files. But now they
knew the risks, they were able to build links that could resist known attacks.

The same principles can be applied to fraud investigation. If you know
where your main risks of fraud lie, why not put out some bait in the water
and see what sort of fish can be reeled in? With a bit of luck you'll be able to
make sure that they never get a contract or work for your organisation
and if you are particularly subtle, they may leave themselves exposed to
criminal charges or civil action.

General principles and axioms from Chapter 10

▪ The simplest solution is often the best, however complex the fraud may
appear.

▪ In any area where there are many transactions or where there is a high
volume of claims, statistical theory around large numbers can help determine a result.

▪ Statistical theory teaches that you can have a high degree of confidence
that your sample does represent the population from which it has been
selected without needing to select a very high proportion of the population.

▪ There is one general theory that underlies this branch of statistics and that
is that for any normal population a random sample taken from that population will demonstrate the same characteristics as the population from
which it was drawn.

▪ A number of samples taken from any large population will form a normal
distribution around the mean value of the population. This is potentially
helpful when looking at a low-value, high-volume fraud or any area where
there is a vast number of transactions in which you need to find the
fraudulent ones.

▪ One of the fundamental problems facing most fraud investigators is that
their work starts after the horse has already bolted. It is hard to get ahead of
the game but in some areas it is possible.

Part IV

Fraud types

CHAPTER 11

Catching your crooked contractor

CHAPTER**SUMMARY**

C ategorising crooked contractors. Methods and approaches for tackling contractor fraud. Real-life case study: the one that should never have got away with it. Using Companies House to best advantage. Due diligence.

▓ TO CATCH A CROOKED CONTRACTOR ...

With effective systems it is possible to weed out the obviously fraudulent, bogus and corrupt contractors before they get through to your organisation—some of the procurement process checks that can be done are briefly outlined in Chapter 2. However, fraud and corruption with contractors comes in several different layers. I've set out briefly below those that are most likely to cross your path and that can be tackled, provided that you have the right resources and the right backing from specialists within your organisation.

The main case study in this chapter is from my own real-life experience and still one which feels very personal, although at the time of writing it is 10 years since my first investigation into this company and its contract with Scotland Yard. It was an example where, for what was considered a valid political reason at the time, police management did not fully support my investigations and in the end decided to live with the contractor as the lesser of two evils. Over the lifetime of the contract they paid a high price for that, as did eventually the owners, management and staff of the contractor.

▪ COMMON CATEGORIES OF CORRUPT CONTRACTORS (IN ASCENDING ORDER OF SIZE)

1. The sole trader/self-employed contractor.
2. The mendacious middle manager/supplier representative.
3. The small works and maintenance or service supply company.
4. The dodgy supplier of goods.
5. The 'too big for its boots' company.
6. The big firm that has fallen on hard times.
7. The corrupt multinational that can't help bribing.

I have not included on this list either the out-and-out fraudsters who have no intention of supplying any goods or services, since the characteristics here are more akin to financial fraud and theft, or the undercover company, where they win a contract with you in order either to spy on your organisation or steal its resources from the inside. They are an entirely different kind of problem, since their prime purpose is not to steal from the contract that you have with them, but to use that contract to enable an advantage to be obtained elsewhere. These are the most dangerous fraudsters of all and I will deal with them separately—as they are the Trojan fraudster (see Chapter 12).

The sole trader (or self-employed contractor)

By and large there are three points where they are likely to try to rip you off. (1) If they are employed for specialist work there will be a proportion of them who will have lied about either their qualifications or their skills and you will end up paying for work that they were never competent to do and where no real value is obtained for what has been done. (2) If they are paid on piece rates or hours actually worked then they will inflate the number of pieces of work completed or the hours that they have performed the work. (3) If they provide a specialist technical service they will try to find ways in which you need to give them more work to do the job and they will try to stretch out the time that it takes them to complete their work, to encourage you to offer additional payments.

The mendacious middle manager

In this case the company that employs the middle manager may in itself be perfectly respectable and may have passed all your usual tests during the procurement process. However, they are a fraudster and they make their money by doing dodgy deals with corrupt approaches either or both to their own sub-contractors and those in your organisation who can provide them with more money. The commonest version of this is the 'let's then split the invoice' trick. A real example from manager to organisation illustrates this quite neatly.

Real case: Cleaning up on the cleaning contract

The regional manager of a medium-sized cleaning contractor invited the contract supervisor from their main client out to lunch and they had a few drinks to help the lunch go down. Time went by, the alcohol flowed and he made his approach when he thought the right moment had arrived. 'Look George, it's very simple—and foolproof. You just put an order in for extra work at a few outlying units that don't need it, make sure you put a special reference for me on the order. The order comes to me, I sit on it for a few weeks then I send you the invoice. All you've got to do is certify it for payment and then later we'll split it 50–50.' George thought about this for a few moments, trying to clear his head. 'But won't someone complain if no one turns up to do the work?' 'Not if you sit on the unit's copy of the order the same way as I'm sitting on my copy before I send you the invoice. My guys won't be expecting to do the work and your guys won't be expecting to see them. That way no one need ever know and we can both make a profit!'

After some further liquid encouragement, George thought he'd give it a go. Life was hard enough and a contract supervisor was just an office worker who wasn't that well paid and had little or no chance to earn any overtime. All went well on their little scam for a while, but the boss of the cleaning contract supervisor was a wily old fox and he realised something was up. So, the twosome became a threesome and more fake invoices were needed to service what had now become a three-way split of ill-gotten gains.

One day George was feeling a little rueful about how he'd got sucked into this and had a separate lunchtime meet with the regional manager from the contractor who'd originally made him an offer that he had found so tempting. Neither was too happy about the way their 'silent partner' had muscled in and was taking a third of their profit for no risk to himself, leaving them both vulnerable to further demands out of their profits. George felt particularly 'at risk' as it was his immediate boss. They had one or two too many glasses while drowning their sorrows and their conversation and mutual commiseration got louder until it was easy to hear from where someone else was lunching, two tables away from them. As luck would have it, the 'someone else' worked in the engineering part of the same client organisation. He overheard enough to understand what was happening and went back to the office and reported it up the line. A quick management check showed that they had paid far too many invoices in this area and they called in the police as well as launching a disciplinary process. The two internal employees were suspended and the regional contract manager was fired by his company.

When George, his boss and the contract manager were each accused of the invoice fraud in interview under caution, each one blamed the other two but denied their own active involvement. The CPS looked at the case and concluded that the chances of a successful prosecution were low as the only witnesses were clearly all unreliable and it was not therefore in the public interest to take the case to court. It took two years to get to that point and throughout this time the two employees were suspended on full pay and the disciplinary process held in abeyance pending the result of the criminal case.

George eventually resigned at the recommencement of the disciplinary case after he had already had two years suspended on full pay. His boss 'got off' on this one but was demoted for an entirely unrelated scam on another contract that had by now come to light.

No money was ever recovered from the contractor for the overpayments as they blamed their now-fired employee and the member of the client staff equally and with the collapse of the criminal case no one was pursued by anyone in the civil courts either. It could hardly be described as a satisfactory outcome for the client organisation.

This case is also a good example of the problem of trying to deal with corruption through the criminal route. It is hard enough through the civil courts and ten times harder in the criminal courts. The main difficulty about criminal prosecution is that the standard of proof is 'beyond reasonable doubt' and the accused are presumed to be innocent until either proven guilty or they confess. For internal discipline or civil courts all that is required is a 'balance of probability' and there is no presumption of guilt or innocence.

Had I been there at the time (it was an organisation I joined after this incident) I would have advised as strongly as I could against the way they went about the internal investigation and their reliance on the police to bring home a criminal case against the three individuals concerned. With the approach that I would have advocated, dealing with the disciplinary case immediately and considering civil action, they could have long been dismissed—after a proper disciplinary hearing—and I would not have worried about the outcome of a criminal case, any more than the contractor did in dealing promptly with their corrupt manager.

The small works or service supply company

They will often have 'got in' by offering cheap rates or charges just below that of their rivals. They rely on the fact that they are hidden among a number of other small suppliers providing similar services to a larger organisation and that they won't easily stand out from the crowd. Often they will try and form cosy relationships with those that they know are going to be either responsible for commissioning work from them or certifying that the work has been done so that they can get payment. They commit fraud because they want more money than they can get from the contract by legitimate means and, sadly, all too often it is very easy for them both to commit fraud and to sustain it without detection, with or without any collusion with those responsible for overseeing their work from your organisation.

Common tricks are: (1) sending in invoices for work that was never ordered—and then badgering support staff until they get a retrospective order; (2) turning up to do work that wasn't ordered and persuading local staff that the work is needed; (3) claiming excessive piece rates or day rates for work that was never done or only a fraction of the work was done; (4) overcharging on agreed rates (they will get away with this one in organisations where those on the ground either haven't seen the contract or don't have a current price list); (5) sending in 'duplicate' invoices and regular statements to see if your people are foolish enough to pay on them as well.

Real case: Slashing the sash window bill

The minor engineering maintenance bill was climbing and management couldn't work out why. Expenditure on the more significant—but still minor—

maintenance companies was rising slightly (those with individual job orders up to £10k a time) but nowhere near as much as the expenditure for jobs that individually cost less than £1k and were 'lumped together' in monthly management reports because they were relatively insignificant. At its peak. expenditure on minor 'insignificant' works had reached £200k a month (it was meant to be £20k per month!) and we were called in to help get to the bottom of what was going wrong on an area that on the surface had to be low-risk.

At the time we didn't use the Benford's Law analysis, but we sussed the same problem. There were an incredible number of invoices coming through from several minor maintenance suppliers at £900–£999, just under the limit when they would get more analysis in the management information that went further up the line. It was obvious that either on their own or with inside information certain contractors had worked out that if they kept each individual works and maintenance invoice under £1k the organisation would just pay their bills without checking.

Looking at the worst offending minor maintenance contractors, we identified two in particular who seemed to have had a considerable amount of business in comparison with the size of their company and the work that they were allegedly providing. One had earned over £500k in small jobs and was run by a husband and wife team operating out of a small flat. Another, when we tested out some of their jobs, had been claiming for re-painting warning signs in boiler rooms at two-monthly intervals (instead of two-yearly) and had claimed for replacing window sashes at £950 a time at locations that had no sash windows!

Both contractors were immediately dropped and we all waited to see if anyone on the ground complained that they weren't getting the service that they needed. All went very quiet—and stayed that way. Our problem had been solved!

The dodgy supplier of goods

These fall into a different category to dodgy service providers and in many ways because of this it is much easier to get on top of any potential fraud and deal with any problems. They can be just as hard to take through the courts, though, as often dodgy suppliers will naturally look for someone on the inside to corrupt, usually with a cash bribe of some kind, although these can come in many forms. On one occasion it just took a nice lunch out to persuade a procurement clerk to turn a blind eye to over-ordering and over-supplying from a particular contractor. By its nature such corruption is hard to prove and often the corrupted employee eventually pays a far higher price than the dodgy supplier.

The classic dodgy supplier approach is either to provide substandard or even illegal goods (a common issue with software purchases) or to persuade a junior procurement official to order products that were never needed in the first place. I've set out an example of each practice below from my own knowledge and experience.

Real case: Stolen software sold to specialist detectives

Unless you have dealings with or know someone who works for the police, not many people appreciate that policing in the United Kingdom is divided up among a number of entirely different-size police forces, the smallest of which are no bigger than one of the 32 borough command units of the Met (and the Met has over 60 command units in total). By and large, except where they have pooled resources with a nearby force, the smaller forces have very small teams—often just one or two people—to deal with a major business function, such as procurement.

One such small force found that, in a moment of unexpected enthusiasm, its assistant chief constable had volunteered them to take the lead in purchasing software and related Microsoft products to run a sensitive police system that linked to every specialist police unit of a particular type in the UK. Their procurement officer didn't know where to begin but this didn't faze the assistant chief constable. He had a pal down the golf club who was always telling him that although he ran a car dealership, he could—and did—buy and sell computer equipment as well. His pal was happy to oblige such a prestigious policeman and got his team to round up the computer equipment and software that was needed, after signing a contract to supply it to the force concerned. However, these were hard times and it was going to cost a fortune upfront to buy all the software licences before they supplied the kit in working order to the police. So, they in turn told their suppliers that they needed to get the kit a bit cheaper or not pay for the licences until they had sold their products on. Their suppliers hit on an ingenious solution. They used one copy of Windows and related products and cloned it to every computer they supplied, thereby keeping the car dealer's—and their own costs down.

When the first systems were linked up for trials and testing the police immediately discovered that they had been sold cloned software and operating systems by another force, but worse was to follow. When they checked the operating system references with Microsoft it turned out that even the original copy had been pirated and neither the supplier nor the assistant chief constable's pal had ever had a legitimate copy of any of the operating systems.

It seems patently obvious that this was never the proper way to go about such a specialised procurement but no one checked up on either the bona fides of the golfing 'pal' or the legitimacy of the supply arrangements. Had proper tendering processes been applied there would have been far less risk of such an embarrassing faux pas by the police force concerned.

Real case: Disposable gloves that refused to be disposed

The NHS uses a lot of consumables and one item that is always needed is pairs of disposable surgical gloves. The average operating theatre and surrounding clinics will get through a fair few in the course of the year, although not quite as many as one North London hospital group once found it was consuming.

The fraud literally popped up out of their drains at the main hospital where the operating theatres were located. Various parts of the sewerage system had been getting blocked a bit too regularly and then one day a whole section of drains across a wide part of the hospital grounds started overflowing and spitting up thousands of surgeons' gloves, many still in their sterile packs before use. Management were now alerted and on the case. The trail led very quickly back to the surgical stores. Inside, every spare space had been taken up with extra boxes of disposable gloves. The storekeeper complained to them that he had constantly told the surgical procurement officer not to order any more but they kept on turning up. In the end, desperate for space, he had been going out last thing at night with the procurement officer and throwing them either directly down drains or those sinks where they could find a big enough waste disposal unit to put them in.

The procurement officer admitted his part in the fraud almost immediately—and with clear relief that it was now a weight off his mind. It had all started innocently enough, when he had accidentally duplicated a monthly order for the disposable gloves and both deliveries had turned up on the same day. When the stores told him what had happened, he immediately rang up and left a message for the contract manager at the firm to ask them to take the extra gloves back. They came round to see him and explained that it wouldn't be possible to take returns on this item, however they realised how awkward this must be for the procurement officer—so, if he would just let it go and take any grief for over-ordering they would give him a one-off backhander to keep quiet. He was tempted by this easy money and took the proffered cheque.

To his horror, the following month another payment arrived by cheque in an envelope marked for his personal attention only, with a note attached thanking him for his cooperation. He got in touch with them and asked what they meant. They explained it very simply and starkly to him. He was to carry on with the duplicate orders every month—and, in return, he would receive a suitable little reward by cheque each time they received a duplicate order. 'B-But', he stammered, 'I haven't placed a duplicate order this month.' 'That's all right. You will—now you know what the cheque is for!' 'And if I don't?' 'Well, I wouldn't want to be in your shoes. We didn't ask for last month's order but you cashed our cheque even so, didn't you? Not sure how your bosses would view it if they were sent a copy of that cashed cheque in the post.' He knew then that he was hooked and had little choice if he was to avoid instant disciplinary action—and almost certain dismissal. At first he had found ways to fill up spare spaces but eventually he and the storekeeper had simply run out of places to put the gloves.

This fraud lasted about a year and a half before its somewhat spectacular denouement and in that time the procurement officer had ordered 5 million more gloves than the hospital actually needed, at an estimated overspend of more than £400,000. Money the organisation could ill-afford to waste. No one had noticed the upward spend on disposable gloves in that time.

I am expecting a resurgence of this type of fraud until we are well clear of the aftermath of the recession. The original classic was the great carbon copier paper fraud of the 1970s, which particularly hit the wider public sector hard, especially the NHS and local authorities, but they weren't the only victims and many medium-size commercial organisations also fell for it. Although the use of carbon paper by typing pools and secretaries is long since consigned to the bin of history (as, generally, are typing pools and secretaries too) the principles behind the fraud are as alive today as they ever were. And mediums such as Facebook make them much more likely than back then.

The whole carbon copier paper fraud worked on a very simple con. The fraudster would identify the individual responsible within the target organisation for placing orders for their product. They would find out as much easy background information as they could glean about the individual, at the very least their full name, any known hobbies and whether they were married, etc. (nowadays a piece of cake with Facebook). They would then ring them at work, sounding like the original long-lost friend. A typical conversation might go as follows: 'Hi, Paul, it's Mike. How's it going? Haven't seen you since the Reading Half-Marathon—I was well impressed. Anyway, I'm calling 'cos my boss is a bit worried. We had an order from your guys for 50 reams and we seem to have misplaced the order. Could you give us an order ref so we can deliver?' Nine times out of ten the confused recipient would give them a new order number and tell them to use that for now and they'd catch up with the paperwork later. Once armed with an order number, the invoice was sure to follow. If they were ever challenged about a missing delivery for the order that had never been placed, someone would turn up and deliver the unwanted carbon paper. In some instances they were able to repeat the trick for months, developing a genuine relationship with the bewildered procurement officer along the way.

The 'too big for its boots' company

Such companies bid for work that is way beyond their reach, either through greed or incompetence—or both—and then try to hang on to their ill-gotten contract through thick and thin. They are a nightmare to deal with and if your organisation isn't strong enough to beat them off they will bleed you dry for years.

The worst case I ever saw of this haunted me like a badly recurring dream for the best part of seven years. Its example is the case study to which I am referring at the beginning of this chapter and I've set out a potted version of it below—even today it pains me to think that this was the one big case where I failed to persuade my own management to do the right thing at the right time. We had plenty of evidence but things fell into that 'too difficult' box for senior management and once they'd made their minds up they found it easier to live with the consequences that to face up to what we were finding during our investigations.

Never underestimate the psychology of the moment. It is very hard psychologically for someone to undo something that they have done. Instinctively they want to defend their previous decision and then they start to look for ways to build on it. It takes a very strong mind—and nerve—to admit failure and change tack completely.

For most senior managers in the public service it is the 'kiss of death' for their career if they admit or are seen to have caused a major organisational failure. Hence even when all the evidence is screaming that this is going to be a disaster, whoever has already taken the decision to press ahead finds it almost unpalatable even to consider any other option. They are committed to their choice and things start to move in that direction. As each week goes by it becomes not only psychologically but also physically more difficult to reverse direction or take a fundamentally different decision. Eventually the organisation's resources have been realigned with the original decision and at that point it also becomes impractical to change that original decision, however flawed it may now be seen to be.

This also highlights one of the very real practical problems of investigations into potential contract fraud and abuse when the scenario is moving on and not waiting for you to complete your work and report back to top management. Field investigators generally want a very thorough and bullet-proof investigation, but that all takes time. In such scenarios you will find yourself torn between the need to produce some substantial evidence for senior management—as nothing less than that is going to change their minds—and the need to get a quick result, which, by and large, is going to come at the risk of not having found all the evidence or finding a piece of apparent evidence that later gets disproved, thereby throwing doubt on the validity of the whole investigation. This was very much the position that we found ourselves in for the real example set out below.

Real case: Outsourcing to an off-shore opportunist

This story starts in the late 1990s when a well-known building company decided to outsource its vehicle repair and maintenance business, which was not exactly core to its main operations. They encouraged a management buy-out who duly took over the business but to succeed the new team needed some capital. They took out a loan with 3i—a well-known and perfectly respectable investment company at the time. But, as with most capital providers, 3i expected a good rate of return on their investment. The new company felt under pressure and were concerned that they couldn't ever make any serious money while so much of their profits were needed to pay off their debt to 3i.

And then they fell into the wrong hands. They were tempted by an offer of new capital and the chance to repay their loan to 3i from another investor, in return for handing over the control of the company to new management, which they then did. But their 'White Knight' had no substantial funds of their own and had no intention of putting their hands that deep into their own pockets. To pay off 3i in turn they borrowed from another major capital investor who was tempted into their business. The capital investor was only tied into the business for a year but this was represented to the outside world as an on-going deal. On the back of this the company, which had by now teetered along for four years without ever making a profit, decided to bid for a major public-sector contract with the police. They had just lost out in a bid for a RAF 'White Fleet'[1] repair and maintenance contract and were looking around at the same time as Scotland Yard decided to seek bids to repair and maintain its vehicles, including the emergency response teams.

Originally there were six short-listed bidders and an in-house team. However, when the final bids were opened, only this teetering company and the in-house team had put a bid on the table. This was a bitter blow to the bid organisers, who were committed to a programme of outsourcing during the late 1990s and were completely inflexible about it. They had committed to outsource the repair and maintenance of the operational fleet by a certain date and they were determined to meet the target.

The in-house team were so convinced that they would win against such a small and unprofitable company that they greedily inflated their bid. They were convinced that any business analysis would have told the Met's management that the small company left in the running was unable to run the business. To their horror they had badly miscalculated. Their bid was so high that it was impossible to accept it, leaving the only question as to whether the teetering contractor's bid was sound or not. Despite the fact that the only remaining bidder apart from the in-house team had an annual turnover of only £3.5m and had never made a profit—and had bid for a £57m contract—they were successful and were awarded the contract in November 1998, with a planned start date of 31 March 1999.

When the initial euphoria wore off the contractor realised just how big a mouthful they had bitten into. They had 29 staff and the MPS transferred a further 70 staff to them, along with several workshops and garages. Their computer system had never been geared up for such a large amount of data and the need to keep so many thousand vehicles operational and on the road at any one time. They recruited nearly eighty sub-contractors to help them with the work, even though they had just signed a contract limiting them to a maximum of 25 contractors. Many of the sub-contractors were unused to a police environment and had no previous experience of maintaining or repairing police vehicles. Within weeks of the contract actually starting in May 1999 the first signs that all was not well started to emerge. Fast-response police vehicles had specially strengthened suspension, harder brake discs than a normal car and specially formulated brake fluid that boiled at a higher temperature, to recognise the enormous strain that emergency response vehicles were under when hurtling around the capital. Many of the sub-contractors were simply not geared up to this and a lot of mistakes were made in the first few weeks.

Worse was to follow. Within a couple of months the contractor had consumed most of their working capital in setting up the business and with a negative cashflow had nothing left with which to pay their sub-contractors, so where they thought they could get away with it, they simply didn't. The larger sub-contractors muttered a bit but took a longer term view, as after all this was a contract with the police who had always paid their bills before. However, many of the smaller sub-contractors were now facing a financial crisis as a result and became extremely unhappy. One sub-contractor threatened to impound police vehicles until they were paid by the main contractor and others complained vociferously to anyone who would listen, including members of my audit and investigation team out in the field. We started to take an interest and in the autumn of 1999 dispatched a couple of our investigators out to a few local police units to find out what was going on.

They came back with a tale of operational disaster. Police officers were so disillusioned with the repair and maintenance contract that they were hiring in vehicles for everything except the emergency response fleet. A number of police units complained that when repaired vehicles were returned to the unit they had arrested the drivers supplied by the various sub-contractors, who were wanted on outstanding police warrants. One police vehicle had lost engine mountings during a high-speed car chase, leaving the police driver shaking when they realised the possible consequences, others had been given the wrong brake fluid and had put officers and members of the public's lives at risk in consequence.

I immediately reported our concerns to the Commissioner's Office and an urgent 'Gold Group'[2], chaired by the Assistant Commissioner with overall responsibility for emergency response policing, was set up to sort matters out.

In the meantime the contractor had twice changed the bank accounts into which they wanted us to pay their bills and was exhibiting all the classic signs of a company that had simply run out of money and couldn't handle the contract. However, they continued to persuade the powers that be in the MPS that despite the teething troubles they could manage the contract. They were telling the senior management that they had plenty of funds and were in the process of building a new HQ (they never did—and only rented their existing one)—it was just a temporary cashflow difficulty.

What we suspected but couldn't prove then—and only found out years too late—was that the company was technically insolvent for the last three months of 1999, hence why they hadn't paid their subcontractors during that period. Although we were paying them their dues under the contract they had leaked too much cash in gearing themselves up from such a small company to run such a large business.

The company's accounting year finished then on 31 December and just days before, on 22 December, they finally persuaded another investor to put a cash injection of £10m into the business. They had already lost their previous backer in October and had lost £1m of their capital as a result. Part of the £10m was used to repay the previous investor and the rest went largely into damage limitation on the debts that they had already run up. This was not the position represented to the new investor in the management accounts that the company produced at the time and, seven years later, the new investor won a court judgement against the company's then-responsible officers for fraudulent misrepresentation of the management accounts. The judgement awarded £10m damages and costs against the then-chief executive, finance director and management accountant of the company.

I had been trying to persuade my management to let me into the company to force them to show us their records but this was resisted both by the company and the Met's top management, over concerns about getting off on the wrong foot with the contractor. As a result I was unable to discover any of the internal management and financial data that became visible to a court years later, despite my deep suspicions at the time.

With my then-boss's agreement I had already arranged for the business insolvency partner of a well-known accountancy firm to go through this company's known accounts and financial information, to give us an up-to-date assessment of the financial strengths and weaknesses of the company. In essence this was a belated 'due diligence' review. The accountancy partner was appalled by what he saw. His detailed report listed a string of poor practices and accounting transactions of dubious legality. Even the internal transactions between the various sub-companies of the businesses were adrift by more than twice the annual turnover of the company. He was astonished that they had persuaded any external auditor to sign off their previous year's accounts.

On the back of this I was asked to hold a meeting with the contractor and seek their explanations on the key points of concern. During this period in early 2000 the Met also suspended briefly all work by the contractor and sub-contractors on the emergency response fleet while vehicles were checked and they ensured that the right parts, especially brakes and brake fluid, were being put into the emergency response vehicles. This action hit the headlines at the time, but the work we were trying to get done about the financial position of the company remained hidden from the public gaze.

With my expert business insolvency partner alongside me and a member of my investigative team in support I met with the chief executive and the finance director of the company to try to get an adequate explanation on our main areas of concern about their financial affairs and the way they were conducting their business. They ducked and dived and we ended the meeting feeling that we hadn't really got a straight answer to anything that we'd asked.

To my amazement I then got a call later in the day from my boss to say that he understood I had been provided with adequate explanations and that I was now satisfied. I pointed out that nothing could be farther from the truth. Neither my expert nor I were satisfied with any of the explanations that we had been given. Indeed on several points the contractor's chief executive had stated that they would need to get back to us and had not provided any explanation at the meeting, even though, at their request, we had supplied them with a list of our questions well in advance of the meeting.

However, what of course I didn't know was that the MPS top management had already decided to carry on with the contractor and neither my concerns, nor the specialist accountant's report, nor complaints from staff in the field cut any ice any more with the management. (Later my boss took me on one side and told me that I was never satisfied by anything and I wasn't seeing the bigger picture for emergency response vehicles and the need to get the contract back up and running.)

The Gold Group set up to deal with the crisis changed management and I was no longer asked to provide reports to it. A police commander with the then-MPS Director of Procurement was sent to meet with the contractor and sort matters out. In the end, despite my objections and misgivings, in the spring of 2000 management upped their payments, speeded up the payment cycle and softened their performance targets.

A joint project between the MPS and the contractor was set up to kick-start things again and the £1m it cost to take over the contract while emergency vehicles were checked was offset against a large claim from the contractor for additional costs.

After some battles both with the director of procurement and the commander made responsible for the vehicle repair and maintenance contract I managed to knock some holes in the more spurious aspects of the initial £5m claim but in the end, some months later when the Met had by now taken over responsibility, the contractor got a one-off payment of an additional £2.5m to keep the contract going.

Outcomes from the outsourced vehicle repair and maintenance contract

I have set out in 'Using due diligence to deal with dodgy contractors' (see

p. 205) an example of the kinds of due diligence tests that an expert can apply to the business and financial information of a contractor.

Although by now our investigative attempts had been halted by my own management, I continued to look around aspects of the contract and we identified a number of valuable systems issues for the future that helped in the next generation of large outsourced contracts for the police. However, we continued skirmishes through the years with the contractor and had to keep a constant eye; they seemed to be up to every trick in the book to try and squeeze more cash out of the contract and I needed to be at my most vigilant to stop their more blatant attempts.

In 2003 the commander who had overseen the contract retired from the MPS and was allowed to join the board of directors of the contractor that he had been responsible for overseeing. I was outraged but there was nothing to be done, as no police rule prevented such an occurrence (and at the time of writing there is still no rule or regulation to prevent such a thing happening again). Finally in 2006 the contractor lost out in their bid to retain the MPS contract and we could move on. Oh, and in case you were wondering, during the rest of my time at the MPA, up to my retirement in 2009, we never had any trouble with the contractor that replaced the over-ambitious and greedy company.

So, what was the final reckoning of it all? If the Met management at the time hadn't have been so rigid about meeting their original timetable and objectives, they might never have appointed this over-ambitious and greedy small company. If any proper due diligence had been done, rather than looking purely at cost and operational promises, they would have realised that the company was not financially sound and not geared up to run such a large business. Nor did they have any particular expertise in vehicle repair and maintenance. By not doing proper due diligence we had a difficult contract that in direct costs leaked some £5m more than it should have done, the cost of hire vehicles went through the roof to the tune of another £3m to £4m a year and a fortune was spent on management time sorting out the various crises along the way.

Had management not have been so weak at the time I would have been able to get access to records that the contractor kept hidden from me and we would have discovered their deception and had grounds for an early termination of the contract. The people I feel most sorry for are the former MPS staff that were transferred to the new contractor and took their pensions with them. Eventually the contractor failed to meet their obligations and many staff left in some disillusionment. Others found themselves left out in the cold when the contractor finally lost our contract.

The big firm that has fallen on hard times

They will still look like the business and will be anxious to impress your organisation that they are still the big, successful company that they once were. This is where a proper due diligence approach can save the day. Without it organisations can catch a severe cold. It is a particular problem if the company has existing contracts or has been used by the organisation for a few years. People get comfortable with what they know and forget the ongoing 'business maintenance' part of the contract, particularly with service rather than supply contracts.

No matter how good the working relationship with a contractor, that should not blind the organisation to the need to keep an eye on the available financial information about the company. Indeed, if there is a good relationship there should be no difficulty in getting the company to share relevant internal management financial information with you that will offer comfort that they have their cashflow under control and are neither spiralling into debt nor running out of cash. If they have set up a separate company or special purpose vehicle for your contract then you should be able to see a good set of on-going and relevant interim financial information before they produce their draft annual accounts each year.

The corrupt multinational that can't help bribing

I'm not going to give an example here as it is simply a scaled-up version of the scenarios presented between 'The small works or service supply company' and 'The big firm that has fallen on hard times' (pp. 191 to 202). If the final BAE report is ever published, it should make interesting reading. However, what I will say is this. As a rule in this country we seem to somehow think that we are the 'fair play' nation and there is a tendency to associate corruption and lack of 'fair play' with Third World countries and some of the more ruthless Eastern European countries. If thought of nearer to home, people tend to look at Greece and Italy as countries with a significant problem on bribery and corruption and not the UK.

While the UK may not have the highest levels of corruption and bribery shown and found in certain countries, it is also nowhere near the top of the tree for squeaky clean nations. Just look at the corruption index regularly prepared by Transparency International if you are finding this hard to believe. The least corrupt nations in Europe are all Scandinavian, with Norway resting in first place at the time of writing.

Another issue that everyone tends to forget about is just how much of the bribery and corruption in Third World countries is triggered by the attitude and wealth of multinationals based in the UK and the Western world bidding for work in these countries.

Anyway, enough of the homily for now and I'll get back to my bedtime reading about greedy MPs, their expenses and the effect it all had on the nation and the perception of the UK Parliament around the world!

▪ USING COMPANIES HOUSE AND FINANCIAL ASSESSMENTS TO BEST ADVANTAGE

The best option with a fraudulent or corrupt contractor is to try not to take them on in the first place. However, for some of the reasons already outlined in this book, that is easier said than done. If your procurement department is up to scratch they will be using two obvious sources about companies before allowing them to get on shortlists for potential contract awards. First, they will have online access to Companies House and will be able to call off their own set of the basic data about the putative bidder before them. This can then be compared with or added to anything provided by the company. Second, they will have the online services of one of the main credit-rating agencies for companies (as opposed to people) such as Dun & Bradstreet.

There is one fundamental problem with both Companies House and Dun & Bradstreet type information. While it may very well be accurate, it is also by its nature historical, it will only tell you about the past activities and performance of the company in question and it is no help at all with a brand new company or a 'special purpose vehicle' (i.e., a company set up by one or more other companies to run that specific contract or service).

The important point about Companies House information is that it has to be supplied by law and there are severe penalties for lying or providing false information to Companies House. There are in theory also penalties for sins of omission, failing to provide required information in the appropriate timescale, but I have always found that Companies House rarely ever pushes this and takes a lenient line, unless the company in question significantly delays its reporting of required statutory information.

From a fraud investigation perspective, Companies House data is useful as you can analyse what you have now against what was last reported. And you can cross-check certain information on the Companies House database. The subscription isn't expensive and we used to call off data and reports online on a regular basis in our investigative department. I authorised the monthly bills for whatever we had downloaded the previous month and it was never that expensive.

Useful checks to apply to Companies House data

First, you need the name and registration number of the company or the name and date of birth of a key director. It is always best if you can work from a known company registration number but if you have incomplete information then the best place to start is with the known company name. From the Companies House database you should then be able to identify the right company, although be careful here. There are a lot of similar-sounding and in some cases same-named companies, often entirely unrelated to each other.

Once you have the right company then you can check to see if it is a principal or parent company or the subsidiary or wholly-owned company of another. Ultimately you need to trace the parent company as this is where the buck will stop for any later financial or fraud problems. Are the ultimate owners under UK or EU tax law—or are they off-shore in well-known tax havens?

Check the main directors of the company and just go to the directors' database on Companies House to see what other companies they may—or may have had—an interest in. See if any of the directors crop up in other businesses or were directors of similar businesses that have gone into receivership or ceased trading.

From the Companies House database you can call off annual returns and the like, all of which can reveal information about the company that can be compared against what they are telling you.

You can also see the history of your company, has it filed its returns and its accounts on time? Does it have a history or is it so recent that there are no accounts or returns held for it?

The Companies House copy of the accounts should also be pulled off and if possible checked against any supplied when applying for your contract. The annual commentary from the chair or other main officer of the company is also a useful source of information, since they will often include information about the current year while reflecting on the previous year's accounts. If you have a history, look at what the company has said about its plans and growth in the past. How accurate were the predictions?

USING DUE DILIGENCE TO DEAL WITH DODGY CONTRACTORS

Due diligence covers both organisational competence and its financial affairs. Here I am concentrating exclusively on the financial aspects of due diligence enquiries. They are best done by a specialist in either business insolvency, business recovery or a related discipline, such as financial investigation of company fraud. Not all accountants have the necessary skills for this work.

When I was trying to deal with the dodgy contractor in the real case above (see p. 197) I used such a specialist and he earned his corn with me, even if ultimately our organisation's management didn't want to listen to what we had to say. That was politics, rather than anything about the quality of his work. What I did learn from working with him, is just how many pointers to a potentially fraudulent company can be picked up even from their legitimate and published accounts. I have set out below a number of the items he picked out from the accounts that I gave him, along with a brief explanation of the issue each time. It is not a comprehensive list but does cover many of the main pointers to look for with a dodgy company.

My investigators and I had gone through four published annual accounts of this company, which called itself a plc, and apart from noting that its turnover was rather small for our contract and it didn't seem ever to have made a profit, we hadn't gleaned that much more.

Our hired-in specialist noted the following, among other points:

▪ **Although the company was a public limited company (plc) it was in fact a private plc as it didn't trade its shares, which were all owned by either an investor with a seat on the board or held by off-shore trusts that had as their beneficiaries the three senior directors of the company.**

This gave two clear signals about their attitude and behaviour

(1) By making it a private plc no one was ever likely to be able to bring a prosecution or a civil case for any breach of company law by a director

that caused a loss to the company, even where for a public plc a director would have been given a prison sentence for such a breach.

(2) If the company did make a profit, or was eventually sold, the directors were intent on avoiding UK tax laws as far as they could.

> ▨ **The Chief Executive and the Finance Director were both the co-directors and owners (with their wives) of companies that had been paid for their services from the parent plc. A look at the accounts for both these companies showed accumulating corporation tax liabilities over the years.**

This was particularly serious and showed potential criminal offences under the Companies Acts by both of them (but see note (1) above).

(1) They were effectively paying themselves a salary as directors of the plc, through the artifice of these companies that they owned jointly with their wives and which had no other significant work other than the payment from their plc. These salaries had eaten up any left-over profit in the company each year.

(2) Some of the payments from the main company were shown in the accounts as prepayments and could also be illegal.

(3) The accumulating debt on corporation tax year on year meant that they were in fact paying no tax on their earnings from these companies, another potential criminal offence under tax legislation as that is evasion (illegal), not avoidance (a right).

> ▨ **The main 'holding' company in the group of companies that had been set up had assets of only £200k.**

This company had been used to provide the 'parent company guarantee' for the special purpose company that had been set up to run the £57m contract—an annual contract value of approximately £8.3m. This was a meaningless parent company guarantee. Where the parent company hasn't got enough assets you should always seek a bank guarantee instead.

> ▨ **Inter-group transactions could not be reconciled to the balance sheet.**

Our specialist identified inter-group transactions that appeared to show £13m of business but when he unpicked them there was only £7m of real business; thereby they had made the company look more active and larger than it really was. He also identified from this that it was impossible to reconcile how much cash was held, a worrying pointer to potential problems.

▩ **The company had capitalised massive amounts for IT systems and payroll development in comparison with the money spent in these areas.**

It is perfectly legitimate to capitalise development costs and a proportion of payroll and the like, but there are limits. This was a small company with few employees, they had capitalised almost all the money that would have gone into running costs in this area, stretching well beyond what would normally be considered reasonable.

▩ **The group had cumulative unpaid dividends to its preference shareholder that meant four years into the contract the shareholder would be entitled to payments of £17.5m, money the company simply did not have.**

This showed that the company was living on borrowed time and entirely reliant on the good offices of its main shareholder, who had injected capital into the company at the last moment. He had waived his dividends until such time as the company made a profit but was entitled to 'pull the plug' if the money wasn't forthcoming, two years before our contract was due to end.

▩ **Bank security had been eroded by continuing losses in the two years after the company had won our contract.**

Two of the main companies in the group were showing an apparent and misleading healthy cash balance, but on unpicking this the company had net current liabilities. A company in that position might not be able to pay its debts as they fell due. The company's operating profits were insufficient to pay the interest on its loans.

Our specialist also noted with concern that the company's book value was £13.8m but its potential break-up value was only £6.9m. He felt that it was very highly geared and at significant risk of financial failure in consequence.

General principles and axioms**from Chapter 11**

■ With effective systems it is possible to weed out the obviously fraudulent, bogus and corrupt contractors before they get through.

■ It is hard enough to deal with corruption through the civil courts and ten times harder in the criminal courts.

■ For internal discipline or civil courts all that is required is a 'balance of probability' and there is no presumption of guilt or innocence.

■ Deal with disciplinary cases immediately and consider civil action, don't wait for police enquiries to start.

■ The classic dodgy supplier approach is either to provide substandard or illegal goods or to persuade a junior procurement official to order products that were never needed in the first place.

■ Never underestimate the psychology of the moment. It is very hard psychologically for a manager to undo something that they have done. Instinctively they want to defend their previous decision and then they start to look for ways to build on it.

■ It takes a very strong mind—and nerve—to admit failure and change tack completely.

■ Effective due diligence, particularly of the business and finances of any major or critical potential contractor is worth its weight in gold.

■ Due diligence is best done by a specialist (e.g., a business insolvency accountant).

■ The best option with a fraudulent or corrupt contractor is to try not to take them on in the first place.

■ No matter how good the working relationship with a contractor, that should not blind you to the need to keep an eye on the available financial information about the company.

■ There is one fundamental problem with both Companies House and Dun & Bradstreet type information. While it may very well be accurate, it is also by its nature historical.

■ The important point about Companies House information is that it has to be supplied by law and there are severe penalties for lying or providing false information to Companies House.

■ From a fraud investigation perspective, Companies House data is useful as you can analyse what you have now against what was last reported. And you can cross-check certain information on the Companies House database.

CHAPTER TWELVE

The danger that is a Trojan fraudster

Yes, I know that address, that's Big Frank's house. He's a successful armed robber, very successful. It's a large detached house with electric gates, swimming pool and guard dogs. I wouldn't go anywhere near him if I were you.

A police intelligence collator's advice to my team in January 1996, while we were trying to track down a provider of minor maintenance work who turned out to be a Trojan with a three-year maintenance contract at Scotland Yard

CHAPTER**SUMMARY**

W hat is a Trojan fraudster? How effective vetting can minimise the risks. Rooting out employee Trojans. Dealing with organised and contractor Trojans.

▪ SO WHAT EXACTLY IS A TROJAN FRAUDSTER?

Trojan fraudsters come in broadly two types, each equally potentially lethal to your organisation. There is the employee Trojan—and often these will infiltrate at a surprisingly low level in the hierarchy. Then there is the contractor or organised Trojan where either a company or a number of

" DO YOU THINK HE'S A TROJAN ? "

deliberately placed employees will conspire to use your organisation to commit serious fraud or set out to destroy the organisation by fraudulent and corrupt means.

THE NEED FOR EFFECTIVE VETTING OF NEW STAFF AND CONTRACTORS

The key to trying to prevent a Trojan fraudster from infiltrating your organisation is to have an effective means of vetting applicants as staff or contractors. Unfortunately many organisations simply do not have an effective system at the point of recruitment. Most central government and government agencies and bodies rely heavily on a vetting system designed to protect national security and avoid terrorists working for the state. Local authorities do not generally have any standard checks when recruiting new employees or contractors, although most will apply similar checks to the information supplied in the application form or submitted CV. Larger commercial organisations may have more sophisticated means of checking applications and those working on certain types of government contract will use the government's national vetting system as well.

The only common checks that most organisations apply at the recruitment stage are to check references from a previous employer. A proportion will also ask for personal referees and a number will follow these up when appointing a candidate. Many ask for an employment history but I cannot think of any HR departments in my experience where once they have a potentially successful candidate anyone then checks out the validity of the employment history since the individual left the education system.

Any apparent gap in the employment record should be a cause for concern, starting with working out when the candidate left school or university and comparing that information with stated institutions and their claimed age at that time. It is a modern trend only to ask for the employment history over the last 10 years but I would always want to know about the entire history since leaving the education system.

Trojan employee: Example 1

I can give an example of how ineffective this type of checking can be from one of my earliest cases at Scotland Yard, in the late 1990s. In Chapter 2 in the 'Behaviour at work' section (p. 21) I outlined the case of a fraudster found entirely by chance when two police officers arrested another individual while under the influence of drink or drugs. Documents in the back of the arrested individual's vehicle showed contact with an MPS employee working in the HR Department on what was known as the 'Back Record Conversion Team'. When the police subsequently arrested the MPS employee, they found a briefcase in his possession containing information stolen at work for use in fraudulent activity.

The Back Record Conversion Team was at the time taking manual HR records about individual employees, weeding out any information no longer needed and then preparing the files for input into a new electronic HR system. This was a very dangerous part of the organisation in which to find a fraudster. So, how had he evaded our recruitment checks in the first place?

The Trojan in question was skilled at getting work in government organisations, when the police investigated (with our help) we realised that we were at least the third government body to have employed him. He was also not working alone and it became apparent that there was a bond between several corrupt individuals working at a cross-section of organisations in the public sector that had been deliberately targeted.

One of the golden rules of this type of fraudster is that they are not overly ambitious. They don't set out to get an important position in the organisation, they'd much rather have an administrative or supporting role. First, the standards needed to get the job are usually lower and the quality of other candidates less strong, thereby increasing the chances that they will be successful in getting the appointment; second, they attract less attention in support and back-room jobs, giving them more time to carry out their nefarious activities; and, third, they usually are successfully gambling that less rigorous checks will be applied to the filling of less important posts.

We caught another 'administrative' Trojan when by chance a member of my staff bumped into him in a canteen and remembered him and his fraudulent activities from a local authority where they had both previously been employed. It was another example where the authority in question (and the local police) had failed to get home the criminal case and had backed off from sacking him outright, even supplying a reference for his current employment with no mention of the action they'd tried to take and why.

Our Back Record Conversion Trojan had been very careful about how he had engineered his own 'back records' when making his original application for the first administrative job that he had got in the MPS, as a clerk involved in payroll preparation. His first government post had been with the Charities Commission, who indeed seemed to have lived up to their name by employing him. He provided references of a previous commercial employer, one 'Johnson & Company', whose 'personnel office' subsequently provided a written reference in glowing terms.

The Nigerian passport he provided as proof of identity contained an interesting clue. It gave his height in metres and centimetres. On his application and in person his height in feet and inches was nearly a foot taller than the metric measurement on the passport that he produced, supposedly with his picture as an adult only a year before. However, although their HR office copied the passport for proof of his identity, no one noticed the considerable height discrepancy.

While our Trojan fraudster worked at the Charities Commission they kindly paid for him to have some accounting technician studies and even sent him on a course to learn about auditing! He was well regarded in the office and whatever he did there that he shouldn't have never came to light.

Two years later he resigned from the Charities Commission after he applied for and got an administrative post in a sensitive area of the Ministry of Defence. For this job he managed to produce a UK resident's passport with him at his right height. They of course applied some stringent vetting checks around his home address and who he was and then passed him through their national vetting process for the post that he then took up. He gave two references, the Charities Commission and 'Johnson & Company'. This time 'Johnson & Company' appear to have changed address but the reference is returned with the same company stamp seen by the Charities Commission.

Whatever he was up to at the MoD never came to light either but he had more trouble than at the Charities Commission and after a period of unexplained absence—when they discovered that the telephone contact number he had given them didn't work and they couldn't find anyone at the address that he had given them either—they sacked him in absentia and never heard from him again.

One can only speculate, but in view of his other known activities it is quite possible that under another name and identity details he had been sent to prison, hence why he appeared to have no gainful employment from the time the MoD noticed that he had gone missing to the time nearly a year later when he applied for an administrative job with the HR department of the MPS.

Of course, he now had another problem, as plainly he could not put down on his application form that his last employer had been the MoD, or any check would have revealed that they had sacked him after he had gone AWOL on them. So, creatively, he solved the problem by putting down his home address at the time as his last employer's address, and put the contact details for the office as his then home telephone number. I am sure that you will have anticipated the name of the company by now, it was of course our old friend 'Johnson & Company'—at what as well as being his home address was also the same address given to the MoD as his previous employer's address. He now no longer showed them as his employer before the Charities Commission but instead showed that he was previously unemployed or a student. When the local MPS HR manager checked out the employment with 'Johnson & Company' by ringing this 'office', his wife obligingly answered the phone and gave a glowing reference for him. Later on a duly completed written reference in similarly glowing terms turned up from 'Johnson & Company' with the obligatory company stamp used on the two earlier references.

There was a further twist of irony, not lost on us when all this came to light later. His wife was at the time employed as a temporary local clerical assistant at the local police station! As she was only employed as a temporary clerical cover, no one had bothered to apply any checks other than putting her name and address into the basic criminal records check, where nothing untoward had shown up.

Had any of the HR staff at any of the three organisations got someone to check out this company with Companies House records, they would have discovered that although there was indeed a 'Johnson & Company', it had no connection with any of the addresses that had been used by the fraudster, nor were any of its directors those named on the letterheads for the references sent in to his future employers. He had simply picked the most generic company name that he could think of—but even so a careful check would have revealed the fraud before anyone had employed him.

This type of Trojan fraudster is always catholic in their tastes and will turn their hand to anything of potential advantage. In the time our Trojan was with us (before events beyond his control blew his cover) he cross-fired a dud cheque, stole a valuable ring, fraudulently altered police warrant badges passed out to his fellow gang members, ran a fake charity using police systems and stole a number of differing blank documents on police letterheads. He also copied bank account and personal details for a number of staff with the intention of committing identity thefts later on. (He also tried to fiddle his season ticket loan while a payroll clerk, got caught and was recommended for dismissal—but unfortunately given a second chance by a lenient senior HR manager! At times one can only despair . . .)

The Trojan was able to commit such a wide range of frauds and thefts because during his time as an administrative officer with the MPS he was employed as a payroll clerk, then as a clerk in a police station and finally back to HR again on the back-record conversion of files. In each area of the business he found new frauds and fiddles to turn to his advantage.

Trojan employee infiltration: Example 2

This type of Trojan was particularly prevalent 10 years ago and is making a comeback in government organisations since the 'credit crunch' triggered recession.

A national government agency based in the Midlands employed a number of lawyers to conduct business for it. All the senior lawyers had an assistant/PA but there was still the usual volume of business/financial paperwork generated by lawyers that cluttered up too much of the time of the PAs when they were needed for notes at meetings and sending out correspondence. They decided to recruit an administrative assistant to process the basic paperwork. They advertised locally and had a number of written applications, one of which was far better written than the rest and caught their eye. They invited the individual concerned along with one or two of the other better written submissions, although the Trojan's application was by some distance the best. When they interviewed him, he was charming. However, just to be totally sure, as the job involved some basic financial work, they invited him and two other short-listed candidates to attend a short written test, where they would do some basic numbers and written work. What no one then noticed, although subsequent research identified, was that the person who turned up to give such a charming interview was not the man who turned up for the written tests, nor, one suspects, were either of them the one who completed the original application form. However, between the three of them the organisation thought that it had found the perfect candidate for the job and the charming man was hired.

At first all seemed to go well and the charmer soon won the trust of the senior lawyer, who, in addition to the work intended for the new administrator, started getting him to process some of the cheques received by the organisation. What the lawyer didn't notice, but his PA did, was that this charmer went missing for about two to three hours every Wednesday either side of lunchtime. As is often the case when internal staff realise something isn't right but lack the immediate courage to speak up, in case they are wrong, the PA said nothing to her boss, although muttering to friends and family outside of the office about how the charmer seemed to be able to get away with taking extra long lunch hours once a week.

Eventually, on a Wednesday when he was taking his long break a problem cropped up with one of the cheques that he was supposed to have processed, when the finance department queried why it hadn't come through to be banked, even though it had been received by the lawyer's office several weeks previously. A quick search of the desk area in his absence found that there were other cheques shown as received which had also not made their way to get banked. At this point alarm bells started to ring and they checked everything that he had handled. The charmer had diverted any cheques that were not properly completed or where they were easy to alter into an account run by him as if he was the lawyer. The money had then been quickly withdrawn in cash once the cheque cleared. When the charmer returned from lunch he was confronted and looked suitably stunned. He seemed in considerable distress and was allowed to go home after the welfare officer had a word, but told he was suspended and would have to come back in to explain in due course. They never saw him again. His address turned out to be lodgings where several people shared the accommodation and no one admitted that they had ever seen him there. Someone had collected post for him but no one had noticed who or when; the front door was often left open and mail dumped in the hallway for all the apartment flats.

It was clearly a fraud that would eventually come to light in any half-competent organisation but it became obvious as they investigated further that this was an organised gang who would use 'hit and run' tactics, keeping up the fraud until discovered and then melting away. They operated in a team of four to six, deciding each time who would be the best to put up for a particular job and then the rest of the team would make sure that they used their skills to get the chosen individual the job.

The reason why the charmer disappeared every Wednesday also came to light when a check at the local job centre showed that someone of his description under another false identity at the same apartment block was signing on every week and collecting his dole!

Tightening the noose on employee vetting

Checks applied at the recruitment stage in central and local government, as well as commercial organisations, are generally ineffective in detecting known and likely fraudsters, except where Criminal Records Bureau checks are required to prevent the wrong type of employees being recruited by organisations dealing with vulnerable adults and children where the information may crop up as a by-product of criminal records checks.

The police have long been aware of their own vulnerability to infiltration by criminal Trojan employees, not intent on financial fraud but often on stealing or altering police information about themselves and their partners in crime. In part the access that the police have to prior criminal records and intelligence databases about suspected or known criminal contacts helps in the fight against this kind of infiltration, as does the use of undercover police officers, their own Trojans, to infiltrate the criminal gangs that try to infiltrate the police. However, generally speaking, such databases and methods are not available to most organisations in the wider public sector or the commercial world.

So, what can be done? Well, it is possible to tighten checks but if your organisation is either unwilling or unable then you need to take other preventative measures as well as detective checks to try to root out the fraudsters who will assuredly be there in any organisation of any size.

In my last job we would always press HR to conduct more rigorous checks at the recruitment stage, as it is far better to root out fraudulent putative employees at the application stage, rather than discover after they have been recruited that they are fraudsters. Most will have had to lie somewhere on their application form and that should be capable of discovery during final checks. I quite accept that it would be too labour-intensive, almost impossible and quite pointless to subject every application form from potential employees to a rigorous check, particularly as it is a sad fact of modern life that an increasing number of applicants seem to think that embellishing or lying on a CV is not the criminal offence that it is. If they get a job as a result of such a lie then it is worth remembering that they have committed an offence of fraud by false representation and you are well within your rights to have them sacked for it, as long as you go about the process in a proper way (see the real-life example below about how *not* to go about it!).

However, once a long-list or short-list has been drawn up of candidates for potential selection it is worth considering checks of factual information supplied about previous employment history, including testing whether business referees appear to be genuine organisations and that is their right phone and address details. Personal referees, unless someone at the organisation making the appointment happens to know them already, are an almost pointless check. They are hardly going to say anything unhelpful about someone that they know well enough to act for as a personal referee. All it shows at best about the candidate is that they know someone prepared to act as their referee.

It is also important that when candidates turn up for selection interviews or tests they are asked to bring original documentation about themselves to be checked. If possible passports and ID cards should be checked visually against the candidate who turns up and if there is a staged selection process of any kind then the original candidate should be photographed for comparison with the candidate who turns up for the next stage.

If a fraudulent employee manages to get through these checks then there are tests that can be applied by the audit or investigative department—or indeed by a sophisticated HR department itself. Although some checks are not in themselves conclusive, it is back to the 'Peter's pointers to peculation' principle. More than one check suggesting a problem then it looks serious; if it is just one, then it depends on the nature of which one it is.

However, I must give you a word of caution here. If you do not want to fall foul of employment legislation and wish to avoid the potential for being on the losing side of any future employment tribunal brought by a recruited employee who is subsequently sacked following your further enquiries into their background, then make absolutely sure that your actions are both fair and proportionate. Again this is best illustrated by an example. This one happened to a colleague—and I gained no satisfaction at all from telling him 'I told you so' when it all went pear-shaped.

Real-life example: The over-embellished reference and CV

The Finance Department was recruiting to get in an accounts technician to support the accountant dealing with financial forecasts. They interviewed six short-listed candidates and appointed one of them, coincidentally the only black candidate. The others were either Asian or white.

Once the individual was appointed it quickly became apparent that he knew nothing about accounts or anything that one would expect an accounting technician to know. Line management became concerned and went back to re-examine the CV and references that he had submitted. The main business reference was from a previous employer. At the time of appointment no one in HR or from line management had bothered to contact any of the referees to check out the references provided.

At this stage I was asked by my colleague if I had any advice to offer as to how they should proceed. I advised that they should check the references of all the short-listed applicants and not just this individual. It would have been better if they had done it at the time, but better late than never. My colleague took a different view and argued that as this individual had already been appointed the other applications no longer mattered. I pointed out that no one had been checked at the time and this was a retrospective check that would be seen by any subsequent tribunal to be a deliberate attempt to find a reason to sack the individual rather than following our lengthy and drawn-out 'limited efficiency' or staff appraisal processes.

My colleague thought I was being too cautious and pressed ahead with the check just for the successful candidate. Sure enough, it turned out that not only had he considerably enhanced his CV, but also the previous employer was a one-man business that had used him for some part-time help in the office—and not in relevant work for the job that he now held. A discipline board was held and the employee was sacked for lying in his application and embellishing the reference. He duly launched an employment tribunal case on the grounds of race and inequality of treatment. The tribunal held that retrospective checking of the application was a deliberate act that had not been applied to other candidates and was based on perceptions of the candidate and therefore direct discrimination.

Had my colleague done as I had suggested, it would have cost more time and money to start with, but it would not only have confirmed whether other candidates should have been on the short-list but also would have given him Asian and white comparators who had been treated the same, thereby reducing considerably the chances of a successful claim against the organisation on the grounds of racial discrimination.

Checking for fraudulent recruits

Things that can be checked include the much maligned—and abused—National Insurance number. If they were born in the UK it is possible to check if the NI number is genuine by comparing the code to their stated date of birth. The final code changes according to the time of year and the start codes can be identified to a particular year. For those born overseas with UK employment rights, their NI number should coincide with the time when they were first granted employment status.

It is not uncommon to find duplicate NI numbers and they are not always a fraud. Sometimes the payroll section has wrongly entered the employee's code; sometimes the pay section is using a holding code, awaiting confirmation of the right code. There are also a large number of bogus codes that the system will accept. At one point at its worst, there were some 13 million more NI numbers issued than people of working age registered in the UK! However, if you find an unrecognised code or one that doesn't look right it is a good pointer to a potential fraudster.

Do they frequently change home address or bank account details? If there are frequent examples of this I would take a keen interest in finding out why.

If it hasn't already been checked, check out the employment history for any gaps or unusual employers.

 ## THE TROJAN COMPANY

Although this differs from the Trojan employee it can be detected by some of the same methods, although it is often even more dangerous than the employee. They will want to be your contractor to get something tangible out of you to which they are not entitled. Sometimes they will be 'sleepers', looking to build a cosy history with your organisation before they strike; in other instances they will be trying to take advantage from day one. In my experience dealing with the police this has been a particular problem for the business side of policing. Often the Trojans have combined fraud with more nefarious motives and attempts to glean intelligence about police activities that might threaten their criminal organisation.

Even without the criminal records incentive in non-police organisations, most will have a range of potentially dodgy contractors and sub-contractors in certain obvious areas of business, including anything from security guarding to minor works and maintenance and catering. These are all areas of business where the basic pay and wages of the contractor's employees or your in-house staff will be relatively low. They are also the very areas where Trojans are most likely to strike. They will ruthlessly undercut competitors in areas where the margins are low anyway to ensure that they get the contract. Once they are in they will set about getting their payback out of your organisation.

The simplest type is the Trojan security company, who either provide security guarding or security devices, but in fact use them to spy on your organisation or to steal assets when most of the workforce has gone home for the night. In similar vein Trojan cleaners will sweep business offices, quite literally, looking for useful documents and papers about your business that they can turn to fraudulent usage. When I ran the Audit Department for Scotland Yard I always insisted that our offices were only ever cleaned when we were present to supervise and could ensure that they didn't see any sensitive papers. No cleaners were ever allowed access after the staff had gone home and the offices shut.

Trojans who target intellectual property rights can be particularly hard to detect, although proper analysis of their company information provided to make their initial bid should show up obvious discrepancies (e.g., companies with no obvious previous history in that line of business, the company with a parent company based well beyond UK and EU borders, the company that shares directors or major shareholders with a known rival).

The low, low, lowball bidder

I recall one case where the successful contractor's bid was almost a quarter of the value of the next highest bidder. Even though any procurement department that was on the ball would have been highly suspicious of such a discrepancy in bid prices, because they were a tightly squeezed public-sector organisation they awarded the contract to the cheapest bidder anyway. The contractor duly repaid them six months into the contract by persuading the procurement department that the contract needed a 'minor' amendment to reflect the actual business that they were doing for the organisation. This 'minor adjustment' with an associated pricing schedule was agreed without any consultation with the main business areas using the contract.

On the surface, the 'minor adjustment' shouldn't have cost the organisation much more, although it did mean that if the contractor was unable to collect monies owed by members of the public, the organisation had agreed to make good the difference and pursue the non-payment itself. Within a further six months the contractor's monthly bill for this item of the contract had risen from £nil to £400K, with the amount claimed effectively doubling each month. Within a year the contract was £5m over budget, not bad for a relatively minor back-room contract originally awarded for less than £1m a year. At that point a team of management and audit stepped in and put a stop to the nonsense, but never did recover any of the extra £5m.

Sleepers, wolves in sheep's clothing

Because of the nature of the job at Scotland Yard, with its responsibilities across all of London except the City[1]—and in some cases representing the UK's interests across the world[2]—we had a particular problem with these, especially in the areas of minor works and maintenance and back-room support activities. They were invariably after our internal information and also wanting to know specifically how much information the detectives who dealt with organised crime knew about them as well. The police were fully aware of this, but despite best efforts some still managed to get under our radar.

Real case: Armed robbers who dropped in to fix the Flying Squad's offices for them

I know it sounds so unlikely that it is hard to believe, but it actually happened in the 1990s to the world's most famous police force. This was my first fraud and corruption investigation after I became Director of Internal Audit for the Metropolitan Police in 1995 and it opened my eyes as to how such Trojans could get under the radar of Scotland Yard itself.

I've always been Napoleon's 'lucky general' when it comes to fraud and this case was no exception. I stumbled across the company run by an armed robber by accident when a quantity surveyor mistakenly misspelt the name of a contractor during a search for companies connected to another case that never really got off the ground. (We knew the main contractor in the other case was capable of corruption and bribery but we were too late on the scene to catch anything untoward by the time we had the allegation about them. Corruption is always hardest to prove and particularly so if the trail is even slightly cold.)

When I pulled out the contract file for the mistaken company I realised immediately that something was indeed wrong. They gave an address of a business park and a mobile phone for contact. But by chance I knew that part of the suburbs of London well and I knew that there was no business park in that area—it was in fact quite a smart residential district. I'd only been the Met's Director of Internal Audit for a few months so I asked a long-serving Met employee who was now one of my senior internal auditors where I could check out the address. He told me about police intelligence collators in each command unit, who would know if there was anything known about that address. We rang the local one up and got the astonishing reply:

> Yes, I know that address, that's Big Frank's house. He's a successful armed robber, very successful. It's a large detached house with electric gates, swimming pool and guard dogs. I wouldn't go anywhere near him if I were you.

We were completely taken aback. I don't know what we expected to find out, but it wasn't that. He gave us some interesting details, not only about Frank, but also his 'wife', who under a different surname was shown on our records as the boss of the company employed by the police, supposedly operating from the 'business park' that we now knew was a private address. I went back and had a further look at the contract files. How on earth had an armed robber ended up with a contract from the police to provide minor works and maintenance to police stations and specialist police units in southeast London?

Looking through the paperwork Frank only appeared as the Contracts Manager with his wife as the Managing Director of the company. However, the original submission to be included as a police contractor was signed by Frank as the MD; it had only changed when they responded to the invitation-to-tender notice that had been sent out. Two other curiosities also stood out from the contract files. The Finance Department provided basic financial checks on new companies and at the time had a junior member of staff in the Works Department to do that for each new contractor. He had called for the latest set of accounts lodged with Companies House and on checking had found discrepancies between them and the accounts submitted by the contractor with the bid. He drew these to the attention of a senior works manager, but was overruled and a note put on the file that 'as both sets showed the company in profit' it was no bar to their award of contract. Quite extraordinary—whatever happened to the offence of false accounting? And I never did find out whether the overrule was incompetence or corruption.

The second curiosity was about how this firm had got on to the list of invited bidders in the first place. Originally the Met had wanted to invite a bare minimum of 24 firms to bid for minor works and maintenance, dividing the Met into four inner and four outer regions, each of which would have three bidders vying for the work. However, initially they had only found 23 firms prepared to make a bid. They had asked a specialist surveying company to suggest some more names. They in turn had gone to a small company being used on another contract and asked them, as they were already on the Met's list, if they knew anyone else. This company, A, had recommended a small company B to fill the spot. (B was, for some reason, quite a common name for a company, hence why my tame quantity surveyor had originally picked out B for closer scrutiny and not the company that he had intended to draw to my attention.)

Both A and B now had my full attention, and that of any spare member of audit staff that I could lay my hand on (I didn't have a specialist investigative team at the time, that came later). While my staff started hunting through invoices to check out the work that had supposedly been done by A and B, I pulled the contract files for A as well and gave them close scrutiny. It paid off. A had been on the Met's list of minor works contractors for a few years but when I looked back at their original references something struck me immediately. A was effectively a two-man company with two directors who ran and owned everything, supported by a varying army of permanent and temporary workers, depending on the job in hand. One director of A had an unusual surname, so it was a bit of a give-away when the firm that had provided their reference to get on the books in the first place turned out to include the same man as one of their three directors!

There was also something odd about the business address of A; although it clearly was a business address this time, it still rang a bell with me. I went back and looked at B's contract file. The answer lay in their annual return[3] submitted to Companies House. These clearly showed that—as Frank and his wife had already used their home as their business park address—it would have been a bit awkward to show that they were also living there, so they had used A's works address as if it was their home address! So, there we had it, if they didn't know each other why would they have done this. And since we knew one was a convicted armed robber, who was the other one? Later we discovered that he had shotgun offences and was known to the police as a money-launderer for criminal gangs. A good companion for the first one!

At the time, on the grounds of the sheer volume of minor works and maintenance staff with contractors—and the constant turnover of them— although they were vetted the Works Department did not issue photo-passes, so we had no idea who had really turned up on some of the jobs that they had done. What we did discover—and it led to urgent remedial action by the police—was that Frank, our armed robber, had been responsible for carrying out routine maintenance work inside part of the Flying Squad's HQ in southeast London. One can only speculate what may have been gained by our Trojan from those visits.

Whatever type of organisation it is, if there is something that a Trojan can gain by infiltrating it they will. On the surface it seems incredible that a convicted armed robber's company could have so easily ended up with a contract to work for the police. But they had help from others to 'get in' and once inside the tent were accepted as part of the 'background noise' supporting the police to do their work. That is why the ones that target low-level work and contracts can be so dangerous, as frequently no one notices them there until it is far too late.

If the organisation that you work for doesn't think it could be targeted by a Trojan, just get them to read this chapter and think again!

General principles and axioms**from Chapter 12**

▪ The key to trying to prevent a Trojan fraudster from infiltrating your organisation is to have an effective means of vetting applicants.

▪ Any apparent gap in the employment record should be a cause for concern. It is a modern trend only to ask for the employment history over the last 10 years but I would always want to know the entire history since leaving the education system.

▪ One of the golden rules of the Trojan employee fraudster is that they are not overly ambitious. They don't set out to get an important position in the organisation, they'd much rather have an administrative or supporting role.

▪ This type of Trojan fraudster is always catholic in their tastes and will turn their hand to anything of potential advantage.

▪ Checks applied at the recruitment stage in central and local government, as well as commercial organisations, are generally ineffective in detecting known and likely fraudsters, except where the information may crop up as a by-product of Criminal Records Bureau checks.

▪ It is far better to root out fraudulent putative employees at the application stage, rather than discover after they have been recruited that they are fraudsters. Most will have had to lie somewhere on their application form and that should be capable of discovery during final checks.

▪ Areas of business where the basic pay and wages of the contractor's employees or in-house staff will be relatively low are also the very areas where Trojans are most likely to strike. They will ruthlessly undercut competitors in areas where the margins are low to ensure that they get the contract. Once they are in they will set about getting their payback out of your organisation.

▪ Trojans who target intellectual property rights can be particularly hard to detect, although proper analysis of their company information provided to make their initial bid should show up obvious discrepancies.

▪ Trojan cleaners will sweep business offices, quite literally, looking for useful documents and papers about your business that they can turn to fraudulent usage. Don't let contract cleaners 'do' the office unsupervised!

▪ Whatever type of organisation it is, if there is something that a Trojan can gain by infiltrating it they will.

CHAPTER THIRTEEN

Low-value, high-volume fraud: the investigator's nightmare

CHAPTER**SUMMARY**

T ackling high-volume fraud where each individual transaction is relatively low-value. Successful strategies, including multi-tracking. Using specialist expert witnesses to assist the investigation. Real-case studies, including NHS practitioners and police linguists.

DEFINING LOW-VALUE, HIGH-VOLUME FRAUD

By low-value, high-volume fraud I mean frauds where each individual transaction or false invoice or claim is in itself minor (say, less than £500), sometimes less than £100, but by the nature of the activity there is a very high number of claims or invoices to investigate per potential fraudster and the total value of the fraud is significant to your organisation.

Almost any area where professionals or technical specialists are paid piece rates can fall into this category. Common areas where this type of case crops up include NHS practitioners (doctors, dentists, opticians and chemists in particular), linguists, minor works and maintenance contractors and procurement or credit card abuses by internal staff.

WHY TACKLING LOW-VALUE, HIGH-VOLUME FRAUD POSES PARTICULAR PROBLEMS

Such frauds cause a number of potential difficulties for the would-be investigator.

First, by their nature the amount of documentation or electronic records to review to be able to find evidence of fraud in the first place is often far more voluminous than for other types of fraud. It can be practically difficult to locate and often the electronic records will prove initially hard to link to any supporting information, making analysis of the issues and focus of the investigation at the planning stage (to begin with the end in mind) more tricky and easier to get wrong.

Second, in almost every instance the fraudster has made a vast number of potentially fraudulent claims with an army of supporting records and documents that will need to be checked. This can tie up valuable investigative time, and effort can often be dissipated for increasingly smaller returns trying to establish the true extent and volume of the fraud. Even the best of investigators can get bored or careless, and if a tight grip isn't kept time and money will be wasted pursuing trivia for no additional gain.

Finally, other than for internal disciplinary cases it can be harder to prove—either to get a conviction in a criminal court or to persuade a judge about the true size of the fraud in a civil court. In both scenarios, estimation has yet to be accepted by the courts prior to a successful outcome and therefore you will find yourself limited to a case based around that which you can actually prove, whether beyond doubt for the criminal or on balance of probabilities for the civil case.

ISSUES TO TACKLE DURING THE INITIAL INVESTIGATION PHASE

Once you have a suspicion that someone is committing this type of fraud, there are some specific steps to take that can help you bring home a successful case. During the planning and scoping phase it is important to get as good a grasp as you can on the extent of the fraud being committed.

The principle to adopt here is not dissimilar to the approach used in scientific sampling techniques. Now, don't switch off before I go any further—but if you are of a nervous disposition or twitch if anyone starts talking statistics, please sit down, get a nice cup of tea (or glass of wine if you prefer—I usually find claret works best for me), make yourself comfortable and read on. The pain will pass and this is genuinely a very effective approach that I have used successfully in the past.

Where a statistician doesn't know the likely error (for 'error' read 'fraud' in our terms) for calculating the sample size in attributes testing they take a random sample of between 30 and 50 items and check the level of error in those. That is then used to estimate the size of the full sample and in turn measure the true error in the whole population under review. The point is that the results of samples can be estimated from a small sample and then the true results of the whole sample replace the original estimate thus giving a more accurate sample estimate, but, importantly, *without the need to check everything to find out the true level of error.*

Just to recap here *error* = fraud, *population* = all the claims or invoices that you are trying to check and *attributes* = whatever characteristics the population has to be classed as the same population.

These techniques are well established but, unless you are a trained statistician or find these things fun, it is best first to follow the simple approach that I will outline below. If you do that and find you need professional help later, a statistician or similar specialist will be able to build on the work that you have already done.

Example background

Let us assume that you have suspicions about a linguist who is employed as a part-time contractor. There is a standard UK approach by the major users of linguists. Linguists are often paid as a piece-rate contractor, either per 1,000 words or part thereof translated into English or per hour of attendance at an interview or where a translation is needed in person (e.g., a diplomatic meeting).[1]

Like all piece-rate workers your linguist will have to submit claims to be paid for their work. They are a busy linguist translating a main language and put through about 500 claims a year with an average value this year of £200 each. In the last four years they have submitted 2,000 claims and received about £360,000. (In case this sounds unreal, the worst linguist case we investigated in my last job had earned over £600k in part-time work in just three years!). You need to establish whether there is any substance in your suspicions but you can't afford the time to go ploughing through the invoice payment records to find the original details of 2,000 claims that then need checking against the organisation's local records. In this instance the linguist is submitting claims for both translation work and attendance at formal interviews.

Example method

Step 1   Take the most recent period where all records will have been processed and claims paid. I would recommend a period of months for this, possibly up to six months. Trace and recover some vouchers that have been paid that fall in each month. You can go as low as five or six a month, as long as they are spread out across the time period in question.

Step 2   Examine the selected vouchers to see if they look potentially suspicious. If they do, send someone off to find the supporting organisational records to compare against the claim that has been paid. (If you are an auditor reading this, it is a bit like an expanded 'walk-through' test).

Step 3   Now look at your results and put them in a simple table so that you can see the value of claim, what was claimed and the value of and details of items that from the underlying records you would now challenge.

Step 4   If more than five records in the whole sample that you have taken are causing you significant concern then it is worth gearing up the investigation and pulling more records. To do this, go back to the earliest period that you can find documentation for where significant claims were being made by this linguist.

Step 5   Repeat Steps 2 and 3 with the new data. Compare the results with the original data. Does the level of fraud look worse, about the same or less or non-existent?

Step 6   Based on your comparison of the two periods make a rough estimate on the value of the potentially fraudulent over-claims that you have found of the total fraud by multiplying the average value of error that you have found by the total number of claims. Now you will know whether it is worth any kind of full-scale investigation.

Once a decision is taken that the case is worth a larger scale investigation, you need to go back to basics and remember to keep the end in mind here. With low-value, high-volume frauds the main aim is to stop the fraudster and get your money back.

Stopping the fraudster will be relatively straightforward for a part-time contractor, but as they will have been paid over a period of time and will have probably spent most of their ill-gotten gains you will often have to resort to tortuous legal methods if you are going to stand a chance of recovery. Most of the serial fraudsters that I have come across in this category can be divided into two clear groups. They have either spent it all and there will be little to recover or they will have horded it and turned it into assets that you can recover, such as property.

For those that have horded their assets, if they meet the criteria set out in Chapter 16, go down the freezing order route as soon as you can, before they realise that they are under investigation and start trying to put assets beyond your reach.

Right, so the investigation is under way in earnest and you will have to take a decision about the outcomes that you are hoping to achieve now you have a fair idea of the extent of the fraud.

If the criminal prosecution route is a chosen option, you can still continue with a civil recovery case as well, but you need to think carefully about what will go where. Unless you get an obliging fraudster who feels a strong urge to confess to everything, thereby saving the need for an extensive investigation, you will have to bear in mind that the criminal case will inevitably be for a fraction of the amount that you are trying to recover from the fraud. (In one case, we got £250k back through the civil route but the criminal prosecution was only for £5k.)

Options, options—twin track or not?

Investigators in the NHS and similar often talk about 'twin-tracking' or even 'triple-tracking' a case, where there is a high volume of small-value claims by the same fraudster.

Twin-tracking simply means running the civil case or disciplinary case in parallel with the criminal case, a route I've often used for this type of fraud. In theory you can run an even wider range of options—and they are worthy of consideration at this stage. For instance, if you have a professional, as in the case of a doctor or accountant, why not consider civil (court action), criminal (police investigation/charges), regulatory (apply to get them struck off by their professional body or regulator) and disciplinary (trying to get them dismissed from the position that they hold with you)—effectively quadruple-tracking the case. The only limitation to be conscious of in trying to multi-track a case is your available investigative resources to support the work involved. There are a number of pros and cons to such an approach to consider.

Multi-tracking—the pros

- ▧ Gets the attention of the fraudster.
- ▧ Spreads and increases the options to get a result.
- ▧ More likely to gain a financial settlement or recover assets from the fraudster.
- ▧ Stops the fraudster more effectively.
- ▧ Inflicts damage and sends a clear message of a strong anti-fraud approach.
- ▧ Prevents the fraudster finding it easy to fool other similar organisations.

Multi-tracking—the cons

- ▧ Can be more labour-intensive for the investigative team.
- ▧ Need to watch deadlines and timelines carefully for each track.
- ▧ Can be a more expensive approach.
- ▧ Can drag the publicity for the case out to the organisation's detriment.

All in all, I am in favour of multi-tracking where it is practicable and where a clear roadmap can be seen. It will hurt the fraudster more than it will hurt you and it does enhance the chances of getting a civil settlement out of them where you are owed money.

Setting the investigation off on the right foot

Once it is clear that there is a significant fraud of this type from the sample exercises, your first twin-track decision must be to decide whether this is the right moment to involve the police. If you do decide to call them in— after reading what I've had to say in Chapter 15 'Dealing with the law' (we used to have no choice but to call them in at this point in my last job)—then try to find about 10 to 12 classic and unambiguous examples of individual fraudulent claims/invoices. Preferably go for a recent period if you can, but it isn't the end of the world if you can't. The most important thing is that you give the police at least 10 good examples to pursue for the criminal case. They may run with all 10 or whittle them down further, but once you have handed over your '10 best' it will be entirely up to the police.

If the twin-track decision is to bring in the police and you have a good working relationship it should run smoothly. Occasionally we used to hit hiccups, not because we didn't have a good general relationship but because individual detectives would come and go, sometimes not realising we already had a working relationship with their department. By and large police officers instinctively trust another police officer above an investigator or auditor in the organisation that has reported the fraud to them, so even if you do have a good relationship, be prepared for a change of investigating officer meaning that you have to build the relationship all over again. It is one of the frustrations of dealing with detectives that they will frequently move on and be replaced without any obvious handover or passing on of accumulated knowledge to the next one.

Once 10 good examples have been extracted from your case for the criminal investigation, by all means still keep the details in the overall fraud calculations but concentrate your efforts on building up the civil case as quickly and accurately as you can with other examples of fraudulent claims or invoices. Remember that for both civil and criminal proceedings each fraudulent claim or invoice will be seen as a standalone item and will need to be proved to the appropriate standard for the intended proceedings.

With every significant linguist case that we pursued, we went down the twin-track route and all were resolved in our favour before we reached the day of the civil proceedings. Those that led to criminal charges against linguists all resulted in convictions, although not necessarily on every count. This twin-track success was partly because we prepared our cases very thoroughly and partly because we kept up constant pressure on the fraudsters with every means at our disposal through our lawyers.

I cannot overestimate the need to take extreme care in these types of cases if you go down the civil claim route. By their nature the detail will be both repetitive and tedious—and with the best will in the world even the most diligent of investigators or reviewers will make mistakes or lose concentration for a moment when compiling the records. We used to double-check absolutely everything—and then get it reviewed again by someone who had not been involved in preparing our schedules, spreadsheets and databases.

The key problem is that while, say, at the affidavit stage of a freezing order you can get away with a fairly broad estimate, on the reasonable grounds that you are acting in deliberate haste, that will not do for the civil courts. You might have correctly scheduled 1,000 fraudulent claims, but if the opposition can find just a handful where your team has miscalculated or made even a rounding-up error they will pounce on it to challenge the validity and accuracy of your whole claim against them.

We were absolutely ruthless with our own civil claim and if necessary would sacrifice any individual item in the claim where we were not 100% sure. If there was any room for doubt, we always gave the benefit of it to the fraudster. That had the double benefit of taking the wind out of the opposition's sails when, inevitably, they would challenge our disclosed evidence and also encouraging their solicitors about the strength of our case at the same time. We may have sacrificed a few thousand pounds potential claim that way, but we successfully brought home every high-volume case that we took on civil recovery.

I have set out below the key stages of a real twin-tracking case with a linguist who defrauded some £250k from the Met in a four-year period. She worked as a part-time linguist for the Met for nearly 20 years, but had only started to defraud to a significant level in recent years at the time of our investigation. Our official records were difficult to track back in time and eventually we limited ourselves to a four-year period where we knew we could produce any supporting evidence that would be needed by a court.

Real case: Lost in translation as a linguist finds a licence to print money

Miss X, a self-employed linguist engaged by the MPS, was sentenced at Southwark Crown Court for nine counts of false accounting arising from claims made for services that she had not provided. She received a three months suspended sentence to run concurrently and ordered to pay £2,000 costs and £2,000 towards legal aid. The amount involved in the nine counts was in the region of £5,000. Prior to Miss X being charged the Metropolitan Police Authority (MPA) commenced civil proceedings to reclaim £226,000 from her that they alleged was obtained by the submission of false claims. Those proceedings were adjourned pending the criminal trial.

This was the bald statement from the MPA after her conviction on 9 out of 10 counts. The investigation and pursuit of civil and criminal claims took my team the best part of two years to bring home.

How had we come to pursue Miss X? Initially, we were investigating another linguist whose self-employed claims proved to be fraudulent to some 50–60% of the value of the claims actually made. In checking claims made by the other linguist, it became apparent that in a three-year period from 1999 to 2002 Miss X had earned more than any other linguist, including the known fraudster, in every single year. In all she had been paid over £600k in these three years and had also received police commendations for her hard work. The sheer volume and cost made us suspicious and, using the method described above, we took a sample of her claims over a six-month recent period for closer examination. We then extracted the supporting case files at police stations for her work and compared the evidence from them and from records kept in police custody suites with the claims that had actually been made. We found some extraordinary differences that needed explanation.

Once we had convinced ourselves that there were no innocent explanations for the claims that had been tested, we took our 10 best examples and showed them to the police responsible for checking the behaviour of other police officers. Although Miss X was not a police officer, police officers had signed her false claims before they had been paid and that needed investigation.

We agreed to twin-track, in fact it was triple-track as we also got the Met to suspend her contract while police pursued their criminal enquiries and we continued to gather evidence for our civil case. Once the police had started to make enquiries but before any arrest or interview we realised that we might need to take out a freezing order.

When the police eventually arrested her at home[2] it became apparent that she owned more than one property and had a large amount of cash in her possession. Once we knew that we acted swiftly to make sure that we could secure our Police Authority's (and the tax-payer's) interest by taking out a freezing order in the High Court on her bank accounts and property. We had already got a fair estimate of the size of the fraud but had only looked at a small sample of the total number of claims that she had made. We fleshed this out as best we could between the freezing order being granted and the hearing where, as we expected, objections were raised by her lawyers to our order.

We kept our freezing order despite the objections but our lawyers were approached by hers immediately after the 'objections' hearing. After discussion, the lawyers agreed between them that Miss X would pay £240k into the High Court in return for agreement that we would release the rest of her assets. What this in effect meant was that provided we could prove our civil case in due course on 'balance of probabilities' the court would hand this sum of money over to us. However, if we could not, it would have to be returned plus interest to Miss X.

Miss X was released on police bail after her arrest. Police bail is not quite the same thing as bail directly from the court. Police bail is a device that is normally used for a fixed period of time while the police complete their enquiries but before charges are laid. It is granted by the custody officer after an individual has been arrested. It is usually limited to 60 days from the date of arrest and as a pre-condition requires the arrested person to return to the police station at a specific date or face further arrest.

Eventually Miss X was charged and appeared at the magistrates court where the case was deferred. By now, a number of months had already passed since her original arrest, which in itself was a couple of months after we had started our investigation. Our lawyers then agreed with her solicitors to stay the civil proceedings until the charges that had now been placed were resolved in the criminal courts. We had expected and planned on the basis that this would happen as criminal always takes precedent over civil.

During the intervening period we continued to flesh out our evidence for the civil proceedings. In particular we looked at ways to estimate the likely total value of the fraud without having to find the supporting evidence for every single claim. We sampled as many claims as we could scattered across the four-year period under examination but while we could detail all the claims from the information available to us, we could only at that time check custody records for prisoner interviews by physically locating them in police stations across London (nowadays, on the new police electronic systems, custody records can be examined online without the need for lengthy travelling around different police units). If the records involved translations for a particular case, we needed to locate the case files and then wade through everything to find all the translation work contained within them. It was difficult and tedious work, and several months after we had started it we only had a very limited number of actual supporting records to disprove her claims, even though we suspected that all of them had either been inflated or were entirely bogus.

We were then helped by discovering that Miss X had worked on one particularly significant case where she had translated many documents from French into English. Somewhat ironically, it was a fraud case and Miss X had set about defrauding it with a will. She had persuaded the detective sergeant running the case to let her use his computer in the office to translate some of the documentation and in the end this proved to be her undoing. Where she was working in the office she claimed the number of hours, as it was more advantageous to her than the translation rate per 1,000 words. Unfortunately for her we were able to get a complete record of when she had been given access to the computer and also when she was physically on the premises. It bore no resemblance to her actual claims.

In one instance used for the criminal case the police found that she had marked in her diary that she was making a false claim from us, as she knew that she was going to be translating at an international diplomatic conference the same weekend that she claimed double-time hours from the Met. She tried to claim in court that she was working for us on the plane flying to and from the conference, but as on the original claim she had said she was in the police station, the jury didn't accept that attempt to wriggle off our hook!

In the end, we were able to identify over £140k of false claims relating to this fraud case, more than half the total fraud by this linguist that we could confidently identify. While this was helpful and we took appropriate witness statements to back up the work ready for the civil case, we still had a difficulty about the many hundreds of claims for custody visits and smaller cases that we hadn't yet matched to the original documentation. We knew that as the law stood (and still stands at the time of writing this) we would need to prove that each individual claim was false if we were to justify our freezing order amount when we finally stepped into the civil court.

Another concern pointed out to us by our legal team was that once the criminal case was resolved we would only have a limited time at our disposal before we would be required to disclose the details of our case against Miss X to her lawyers. Indeed, if we could not respond to requests from her lawyers within a month without any extenuating circumstances we ran the risk of losing large chunks of our case before the scheduled hearing date. After careful consideration, we provided a list of all the claims that we believed were inflated or false, but we did not at this stage show all the detail that we had gathered. We knew we would have to disclose it eventually but at this stage we could sail close to the wind without exposing ourselves to any legal rebuke. We were telling the opposition the truth and providing answers to their questions, just not all of the truth about how far our enquiries had—or hadn't—got to date.

Our lawyers advised us that this would be a good time to prepare expert witnesses to testify at the civil court hearing. After discussion we decided that we needed two of them. (1) A forensic accountant to advise whether we had got the financial case right and the calculation of the value of the fraud could be justified and (2) a statistician to look at the records that we had recovered, the gaps and where we only had partial information and give some theoretical backing to the assumptions that we would need to make.

Both the forensic accountant and the statistician proved hard work for differing reasons. The forensic accountant kindly spotted a flaw in the way we were presenting information and calculating our numbers. As a result we had to re-work a fair chunk of our summary data until he was prepared to certify that it was accurate and clear enough for court. With this sort of expert witness, although they are only advising you, it is madness not to present the information the way that they expect, as you run the risk that a clever cross-examining question or an interruption from the judge will expose that you were at odds with your own expert.

The statistician, who turned out to be a really nice man, as well as considerably cheaper than our forensic accountant (I never did like parting with the public purse when we employed other professionals to assist!), caused us difficulties at first as, try as we might, we could not see where his logic and use of statistical terminology was taking us. Eventually the penny dropped and we adjusted our data and tests to reflect his advice. We were still left in the position that we could not prove every item in our case, but we now had a raft of professional evidence to suggest that we had been as thorough as we could be.

After discussion with counsel we felt that we could take our chances and maybe set a precedent on the use of statistical evidence, particularly as, if the worst came to the worst, we could fall back on the non-statistical evidence, which was around the £140k defrauded from that single case. (It is a source of concern to me even today that statistical evidence can only be used to determine the size of a fraud once the fraudster is convicted—and not as part of the case against them before conviction.) Counsel noted, wisely, that often when money has been paid into the court as a result of a freezing order, the party deprived of the money gets, over time, used to the idea that it may be lost to them. Thanks to the criminal case it was nearly two years from the date of the freezing order to the point when the actual hearing for the civil case was due to start, a long time indeed to have £240k beyond the fraudster's reach.

Our lawyers kept up the pressure on the opposition's lawyers with a string of exchanges and in due course when the opposition finally pressed us on the totality of our position we provided a complete listing of every claim made by Miss X as well as some of the accounting and statistical analyses that we were going to rely on to justify the size of our freezing order and civil action.

The date of the hearing got ever closer but we held our nerve despite the risks. Eventually, just a day before the hearing was due to commence, Miss X and her lawyers caved in and rather than fight us in court offered up the full sum that had been paid in to discharge the freezing order.

So, in conclusion the case was a long, hard struggle that took two years to bring home. Our legal costs (including expert witnesses) came in total to some £90,000, nearly double the original estimate of our solicitors. However, we achieved four key successes, which collectively more than justified our expenditure on the civil case.

1. The fraudulent linguist was no longer able to defraud the public purse.
2. They now had a criminal conviction.
3. We had recovered £240,000 of fraudulently obtained assets.
4. We knew that we had sent a clear warning message out to all those linguists that may be tempted to defraud our organisation.

The proof of the pudding for point 4 came when we examined the average spend per linguist in the two years after our investigation became known to other linguists with the same period before. We found that the average value of their claims on a then £9m budget had dropped by a staggering £2m a year.

While we were of course elated at the success of our strategy, part of me was a little saddened that we did not get to be the test case in the civil courts for the use of statistical evidence to back up the size of a civil claim. But then there is no pleasing some people!

The dodgy doctor who didn't go down

We will all have had prescriptions for something at some point in our lives, but what those outside of the NHS probably don't realise, is that the form itself is a 'script' and each item on it, of which there may be several or just one, is the 'prescription'. Fraudulent prescriptions therefore create the same difficulty as other high-volume, low-value frauds. You have to prove the degree of fraud on each script to bring home a successful criminal or civil case.

I once ended up monitoring a case for NHS Audit at the Old Bailey. It was the classic NHS practitioner's fraud, involving a chemist and several doctors. It taught me some valuable lessons about how not to pursue a case and how difficult it is, even today, to persuade a jury that doctors are capable of committing fraud too. So, are you sitting comfortably? Then I'll begin this tale of woe!

'Simon' was a chemist who had expensive tastes. He liked to entertain and enjoyed visiting the local casino a bit too regularly. One day, providence lent him a hand in the form of an overworked local GP who was getting a little bored with a number of his elderly patients who had regular prescriptions but because of the nature of some of their conditions (and the state of technology a few years ago) couldn't just get a block of automated prescriptions.

The GP suggested to Simon that if he left a script or two with him, he could fill them in when these patients arrived at the chemist and then all the GP would have to do would be to sign the bottom of each script at a convenient later time to him. This worked fine for a while and then Simon offered an improvement. Why didn't the GP just sign up a few script pads in advance during his quieter moment and then pass the pads to Simon? Simon would then process them on and the GP wouldn't have to worry any more. The GP liked this idea and readily agreed.

Months went by when one day, out of the blue, the GP happened to be in the chemist's premises. He saw Simon and said that as he was there, he'd better just have a look at a few of the scripts to remind himself what had been given to his patients. Simon started to look a little uncomfortable and suggested that there was no need. His suspicions aroused, the GP now insisted that he saw the scripts that were waiting to go to the Prescription Pricing Authority. Simon explained that he might not like what he saw. He admitted that he had been adding on bogus prescriptions to each script after he had dispensed whatever the patient was really meant to have.

Now at this point the GP could have turned him in to the local Family Practitioner Committee and that would have been the end of Simon and his fraud. But he didn't. He agreed to keep quiet provided Simon split his fraudulent income with the GP, by 'cashing' cheques every now and again but at the same time handing over some of his takings from the till. This went on for a while but soon another GP at the same group practice indicated that he knew what Simon had done and that if he didn't split with him as well, Simon would be reported to the authorities.

Eventually Simon was splitting his fraud with three GPs, all at the same group practice, which had in total eight doctors, although we knew afterwards that the other five had no idea what was happening. How you might ask can I be so sure about that? Well, at the time every doctor had to sign each script, but as most doctors' signatures are indecipherable then the script was also stamped with their name and surgery address. At this group practice there were script pads knocking about with eight different doctors' stamps on them. But when NHS auditors analysed all the fraudulent scripts, one fact screamed out of the pages at them. Although a proportion of other GPs' script pads naturally ended up used by the wrong GP, either in error or because their own were not to hand, in all cases where Simon had made a fraudulent entry, whichever of the three GPs had signed it, they had always made sure it was on one of the non-participating five GPs' scripts! (That way, any costing of expensive scripts would not have detected that these three GPs were the culprits.)

The fraud did not come to light through diligent audit work or someone at the group practice finally doing the right thing and reporting Simon. Remarkably, eventually Simon turned himself in and confessed to the fraud, naming the three GPs as his accomplices in his crimes. He did this partly out of guilt but mainly because it was getting very hard to make enough fraudulent claims to pay off the three GPs and still have enough left for his own expensive needs. He'd got to the point when like a runaway personal loan he was doing all the work feeding ever-increasing and demanding creditors but with no benefit for himself out of his own fraud!

The case was handed over at an early stage of the investigation to the local CID. They decided that there wasn't really enough prima facie evidence on one of the GPs, the last one to get involved in the fraud, so papers were passed to the Crown Prosecution Service who recommended that they charged the two remaining GPs and Simon. As luck would have it, one of the two GPs had a heart attack at the magistrates committal hearing and collapsed and died on the steps of the courtroom. My somewhat unsympathetic view was that they had been called to account by a higher authority. The important point here is that in such circumstances any evidence gleaned from or witness statement made by that individual is lost from the case. Unfortunately for our case, the GP that died, along with Simon, had pleaded guilty. The surviving GP hadn't.

When the case got to the Old Bailey, Simon admitted his guilt, gave his evidence naming the remaining GP as one of his accomplices and beneficiaries from the fraud and was duly remanded for sentencing at the end of the case. The GP entered his 'not guilty' plea. It was at this point I realised that he had hired one of the then most famous (and expensive) defence counsels in the land, George Carman QC. Carman was a master of his craft at the height of his powers and found himself up against a typically wet-behind-the-ears, new barrister provided by the CPS. It was a no-contest from the off. The case set out by the prosecution was clear enough to me, but then I had the benefit of having seen the evidence and being an auditor/investigator by trade. (Although judging from the eventual summing up, it was clear enough to the judge, too, even though they cannot drop hints or take sides!)

But the prosecuting counsel alienated the jury. He kept on reverting to Latin phrases and you could see them looking puzzled every time he did it. He forgot that it was the jury, not the judge, who needed to be impressed by the evidence. He also did not explain the evidence of the wrongly signed scripts at all well and it was obvious to me that the jury were struggling to follow his points on them. In contrast Carman had clearly realised that his client couldn't win an argument about the evidence, so he made no attempt to challenge it, just leaving our hapless prosecutor to dig his own Latin grammar grave unaided. Instead Carman produced character witness after character witness to say how the GP had gone out of his way to do them some personal favour in various delicate medical matters. Carman spoke to each of them—and the jury—in a most ordinary but deliberately calm and clear voice, being careful not to use any language or legal phraseology that might confuse them about his client.

We could all see the end result coming and it was no surprise when the jury acquitted the GP. Simon was then brought back in for sentencing and the senior police investigator stood up and told the judge that Simon had cooperated fully with the police investigation and that they believed the evidence given by him and against the GP, despite what had happened in court.

After the case concluded I found myself next to the jury foreman on the way out of the court, as they had all traipsed round to the public gallery to see what sentence Simon got (two years and a £20k fine, in case you were wondering). The foreman asked me about my interest in the case, as they had noticed me there every day and wondered if I was a relative or a journalist. I explained that I had been representing the interests of NHS Audit. That led to some raised eyebrows and pointed looks and I began to realise that officialdom might not be that popular with the average jury. Even though I knew it was against the rules, I couldn't then resist asking why they had found the GP innocent. 'Well,' said the foreman, looking directly at me and without any hint of irony. ''E was a doctor, wasn't 'e. 'Ad to be innocent.' That got me going and before I could stop myself I had pointed out that the other doctor in the case had pleaded guilty but died on the steps of the Magistrates Court. The foreman looked taken aback for a second and then without a word they all walked off, not once looking back in my direction.

This is one of the cases that have reinforced my belief that in almost every instance, obtaining a criminal conviction should be seen as the icing on the cake, not the intended end in mind of an investigation. If it happens, all well and good, but the chances are in a fraud case that without damning evidence or a confession, you just can't expect to get a conviction and you are better off planning your campaign without a successful criminal case as an intended outcome.

General principles and axioms**from Chapter 13**

■ Low-value, high-volume frauds cause a number of potential difficulties for the investigator. Evidence is often voluminous and they can consume disproportionate amounts of investigative time for the results obtained.

■ This type of fraud is harder to prove in court as each individual claim is treated as an individual fraud, meaning that they all have to be proved if you are to make a civil recovery or gain a criminal conviction.

■ To improve the chances of success in dealing with such cases, first get a good grasp of the extent of the fraud by randomly sampling items across the most recent six months and then if they reveal a pattern of fraud go further back in time—but do not go beyond a time where the records and supporting proof can no longer be found.

■ It is easy to lose track on a complex or lengthy investigation so it is particularly important to remain focused on the end in mind, which should be to stop the fraud and recover your organisation's assets.

■ Either this type of fraudster will have dissipated the stolen assets (e.g., on drugs or gambling) or, commonly, they will have salted them away in property or accounts where you can attack them with freezing orders.

■ Civil cases or disciplinary cases can be multi-tracked in parallel with a criminal case. If you go down this route it is best to start the civil or disciplinary proceedings first.

■ Once a criminal case starts, it will take precedence over a civil case and almost inevitably the civil proceedings will have to be parked at some point until the trial is over. *But* this is not the same for disciplinary cases, which should continue and be resolved as soon as it is practicable.

■ Multi-tracking gets the attention of the fraudster and spreads and increases the options to get a successful result, but it can be more labour-intensive for the investigative team. On balance, I favour multi-tracking, particularly on civil, disciplinary and professional body complaints.

■ The most common type of multi-tracking is twin-tracking between the criminal and civil cases or criminal and disciplinary cases. Your prime focus must remain on bringing home the civil or disciplinary case in these instances, while supporting the police where needed.

■ When dealing with the police, make sure that your preparation is thorough before the first contact.

■ To deal with the criminal aspects of low-value, high-volume frauds pick out your 10 best examples of fraudulent claims and pass them over to the police. If they can run with a high proportion of these for the criminal case it will not only enhance the chances of a successful prosecution but will also free you up to continue with your investigation.

- It is easy to get careless and make errors with a detailed and repetitive investigation. Make sure everything is double or triple-checked if you are going to use it in a criminal or civil court. All the opposition needs to do is find some errors in a few calculations and they will throw doubt on your whole case.

- Be ruthless—if you are in any doubt about the fraudulent nature of an individual claim then resolve it in favour of the fraudster and move on. Only put forward your best and most reliable evidence for a civil claim.

- Use expert witnesses to help refine the case and support your evidence before the court hearing.

- Remember that once a criminal case is resolved and a civil case restarted, there will only be a few weeks before you will be obliged to disclose your evidence to the opposition. Use that time wisely!

- Once you are sure of your case, hold your nerve. Very few fraudsters, once they know the quality of the evidence, will want to end up defending themselves in a civil court. As long as your lawyers keep the dialogue open, there is every chance that a settlement offer will be made late in the day.

- Don't plan your campaign around an expected criminal conviction. Your case must be strong enough to survive even if the criminal prosecution fails.

CHAPTER FOURTEEN

Pay and pension frauds

CHAPTER**SUMMARY**

The main types of pay and pension frauds. Gross and net-pay reconciliation. Classic cases and how to detect them. 'Ghosts' and 'echoes'. Modern difficulties. Using your analyst effectively to detect payroll frauds.

RECOGNISING THE TYPES OF PAYROLL FRAUD THAT MAY BE COMMITTED

Pay and pension fraud come in three basic types: those committed by pay and pension staff (and sometimes HR staff, depending on their access to pay information), those committed by individual employees or their relatives and those committed by line managers. Each tends to have its own particular characteristics.

Typical pay/HR staff frauds include creating extra staff on the payroll (known in the trade as 'ghosts') and diverting the payments to a bank account under their control or keeping on staff after they have been notified to take them off the payroll but changing their bank account details so that the payments are diverted (these are known as 'echoes'). Ghosts and/or echoes in one form or another are among the most common type of significant payroll fraud.

One of the more extraordinary examples of ghosts in a public-services organisation occurred in the army payroll part of the Adjutant General's Office just a few years ago, coming to light in 2005, with an estimated £2.5m of potentially fraudulent payments. It all started with one army private working as a payroll clerk in the Adjutant's Office, then responsible for the army payroll, who took advantage of slack management controls and the sheer size of the payroll to add in a few ghosts of his own, all carefully opened with bank accounts from where he could collect the pay. Another member of the pay section spotted what he was doing and challenged him. Now this could have gone one of two ways. No prizes for guessing which way it went. They probably justified it in their own minds on the grounds that they were lowly paid army privates and clerks, deserving of better rewards. So, now they had two payroll fraudsters adding ghosts to the payroll. This caught the eye of a supervisor and so it started to spread. Eventually management noticed that quite a few lowly paid privates and junior ranks were walking about in expensive clothes, had lots of gold jewellery and owned luxury cars. But by the time this came to light a number of payroll staff were involved in committing or supporting the frauds and had effectively created a bogus battalion of some 600 imaginary soldiers!

 PAY RECONCILIATION

It is one of the disappointments of the way we are today that it is almost impossible to find a wholly effective pay reconciliation system in most large organisations—and yet that is one of the classic means of detecting errors and frauds affecting pay and pensions. To maintain effective control there must be reconciliation somewhere between the cash drawn for staff pay and the financial records of what the payroll says should be disbursed to staff. Gross-pay reconciliation takes the whole payroll, including the employer's contributions and tax deducted for HMRC, and compares it with the financial records of the organisation. Net-pay reconciliation takes the cash calculation due to staff from the payroll and reconciles it to the cash paid to employees for that payroll period.

It is vitally important that pay reconciliations are run by staff independent of those that can generate payroll entries or arrange for cash to be paid for staff. They should get payroll information from independent direct read-only access to the real payroll and cash information in similar fashion from the organisation's financial system. Where the two systems share a common database, as is frequently the case nowadays, it is even more important that those with the right to input and alter records are identified and that no staff processing pay can get at both sides of the information.

▪ CLASSIC PAYROLL FRAUDS COMMITTED BY PAY AND PENSIONS STAFF

Charity doesn't always begin at home ...

The first major payroll fraud that crossed my path was committed by the Chief Salaries and Wages Officer at a hospital group in the southeast of England. He was responsible for a large number of payroll clerks in the days when much of the processing was still done manually before entering into the mainframe computer that ran the payroll itself. I was with the external audit team at the time. We had an old-fashioned boss who insisted on doing gross and net-pay reconciliations himself and leaving the rest of the payroll to us, as he saw this as a fitting split of responsibilities between senior and junior staff. As we discovered later, he had also given himself the cushiest part of the job—and unfortunately through over-familiarity with what he was so used to auditing entirely failed to spot the payroll fraud being committed under his very eyes!

Ultimately the fraud came to light in almost comical circumstances. We had done our usual annual audit of the accounts and our boss had done his work on pay reconciliations without spotting anything unusual, even though this was the only place where there were any obvious clues to the fraud that was being committed.

Shortly after our external audit visit had finished the hospital group had appointed a new member of internal audit. As part of learning the basics he was sent off to do a payroll audit and—as part of the audit—to look at net-pay reconciliation. He took advice from a more experienced colleague and set about trying to understand the balance on the net-pay reconciliation account.[1] One thing that puzzled him and he just couldn't understand was that when he looked back over each month's reconciliation for the last 12 months the balance on the account had gone up every month. As his colleague had taught him, that simply doesn't happen. By their very nature net-pay account balances vary up or down from one month to the next and over time you'd expect to see a pattern within a range of values, not either constantly increasing or constantly decreasing. He looked further back in time and realised that the balance had started to creep up two years ago but the rate had really accelerated in the last few months. It looked like something had gone wrong.

It was quite common in the NHS in those days for the Chief Salaries and Wages Officer to be personally responsible for net-pay reconciliation, as they were considered to be independent both of the staff actually processing the payroll and the staff making payments to their employees. A lot of lower paid support and ancillary staff at hospitals were still paid in cash and it looked like it was the reconciliation of this payroll that was causing the problem.

The new internal auditor went round to the office of the Chief Salaries and Wages Officer and asked if he could have a word with him. The Chief Salaries and Wages Officer appeared at the door to his office but didn't invite the internal auditor in. The internal auditor showed him his notes where he was trying—and failing—to audit the net-pay reconciliation and asked if he could help him. The Chief Salaries and Wages Clerk looked at his attempts to reconcile the net-pay control account. He scribbled away furiously for a minute or two then looked up at the internal auditor. 'Look, I'm too busy right now—I'll sort this out in a minute or two.' With that he grabbed the internal auditor's working papers off him, ushered him out of the doorway and slammed the office door shut, locking it behind him, leaving the auditor out in the corridor. He was a bit taken aback but politely found a chair outside the office and sat down and waited. Time went by, half an hour, then an hour, but there was no sign of the Chief Salaries and Wages Officer emerging from his office, where the door remained firmly shut and locked on the inside.

After a while, regular payroll staff walking up and down the corridor noticed that the polite young auditor was still sitting outside the Chief Salaries and Wages Officer's door, and had been there by now for the best part of two hours. One of them went up to him and asked him if he was all right and why he was sitting there. 'I'm waiting for your boss,' he explained, 'He's checking my working papers for me.' 'I don't think he is, young man', the payroll clerk commented, 'We all saw him drive off in some haste about two hours ago!' 'But, the door is locked still and he hasn't come past me.' 'You must have nodded off, dear—he definitely isn't in his office.'

Now in some alarm, the young internal auditor went back to the office and told his boss what had happened. The two of them found the Head of Finance and explained their concern. He went back round with them to the office and peered through the keyhole, with the key still in the lock. He couldn't see anyone in there. They went then round outside the building where they found the office window open next to the fire escape. They then checked the Chief Salaries and Wages Officer's car parking space and sure enough no car was there. The Head of Finance called in the hospital carpenters and they broke into the office, to find papers scattered everywhere, amid signs that the Chief Salaries and Wages Officer had left in great haste. There were also several empty spirit bottles randomly scattered about the office and a strong smell of stale alcohol.

In hindsight they all realised that he had often turned up in the morning looking quite dishevelled and had been spotted taking a nip out of a bottle during the day in recent months but no one had thought to tackle him about it as he was seen as a nice but rather eccentric and erratic individual. Nor had it occurred to anyone to wonder what it was that had driven him to need to take a nip or why he'd become increasingly dishevelled over recent years.

While turning to drink or drugs can be one of the pointers to a potential fraudster it is unusual, except in the case of habitual gamblers or Class A drug users, to find a fraudster who shows no outward signs of the money gained from the fraud. This fraudster drove a battered old estate car, dressed shabbily and was not known for expensive holidays or interests. He had a wife who worked full time at another hospital and they didn't have any children. He was heavily involved in national hospital charities, sitting on the board of one of them, but that was it. His only apparent problem was alcohol and he hadn't been seen drunk at work. The bottles in the office had caught most of them by surprise. On the surface, not the classic profile of a middle-aged male fraudster.

Three days later everyone was still trying to piece it all together (he didn't return to work) when they had a visit from the police from a town some 40 miles away, to tell them that their missing Chief Salaries and

Wages Officer was currently in police custody and being assessed for his mental welfare prior to facing a possible criminal charge for theft. He had driven to a bed and breakfast hotel and had booked himself in there but after a couple of days the landlady had become very concerned. He wouldn't leave his room and she could hear him constantly sobbing and crying out. Worried that he would self-harm she had called the police. They found him surrounded by payroll records from the hospital and clearly in a highly agitated state. When he saw the police he broke down and admitted without any prompting that he had been committing payroll fraud. They searched his car and found the boot absolutely stuffed with empty pay packets for hospital employees who were normally paid in cash. Some of the empty pay packets were up to 10 years old. (It is another common trait with this type of fraudster, for some reason they feel obliged to keep an evidential trail, probably in this case as the only way that he could remember what he had done.)

After the police had finished with him he was charged and eventually convicted and sentenced to three years' imprisonment. In the meantime the true extent of his fraud became apparent. He had started it when the main computer payroll system had been changed, some 10 years earlier. While the system was going through its teething troubles, there had been a number of problems with permanent records of total pay and deductions for individual staff accidentally getting changed or deleted. It had been a particular problem for new staff and anyone who had left in the financial year. To counteract this, all the chief salaries and wages officers in the region were given some emergency input forms, so that if one of their records was wrongly altered or deleted, they could send in the form and the computer pay staff at the regional computer centre would alter the records to what they had been told was the correct figures for the staff at that hospital group.

Our fraudster realised that if he altered records of employees who had left, using the emergency input form, he could adjust the balance on the net-pay control account reconciliation, to cover for any cash theft and make the accounts appear in balance again.

But how did he get his hands on the cash payments to support staff to be able to steal them in the first place? This was boldness and simplicity itself. Because cash payments were high-risk the cash for the payroll was counted and put into packets by his staff and then collected by a well-known security company before transmission to each hospital where the wage packets would be handed out to the ancillary workers. Unknown to his staff—and not in any pay manual procedures or even the contract with the security company—security staff were under orders to bring the trays of pay packets to the Chief Salaries and Wages Officer for a final check before they went out to the hospital pay points. He would simply help himself to some nice juicy-looking fat pay packets and put a note in to the local hospital to say that the payroll had generated the wrong amount and they were to reimburse the worker directly out of petty cash this week. When in due course they put this through on their cash disbursements he would use the emergency input form to adjust the records of former employees by the amount that he had stolen. That would then counterbalance the effect of having apparently 'paid' some employees twice, once through the payroll and once through petty cash.

All the money stolen through this fraud had been donated to national hospital charities, hence his seat on the board of one of the most prestigious bodies, as a reward for his 'generosity' to their cause over the years. As time went on, he had become more agitated by what he was doing, had started to turn to drink and had lost control of which packets he had stolen when. As a consequence he had got behind in putting through the emergency input forms. The fraud had started to catch up with him as the balance on net-pay reconciliation grew in proportion to the alterations that he had either forgotten about or not yet got around to making.

Had my boss at the time paid more attention, instead of ticking through each month's net-pay reconciliation balance into the records for the next month, he might have noticed a steadily growing balance where it simply shouldn't have ever been.

There's a ghost in the machine

In 2006 NHS Payroll Manager Joy Henry was jailed for four years for a ghost employee scam that ran between 1999 and 2003 before it was discovered. In all Joy and her co-conspirators defrauded a NHS Trust of nearly £600,000. The case highlights some classic points about this type of fraud and about the time it takes to bring cases home in both criminal and civil courts.

Joy Henry ran a 'nurse bank'. This is basically an internal agency payroll that allows the NHS to tap into nurses and other hospital staff who are no longer working full-time but may be available for short periods of part-time work as agency or interim staff to cover for shortages or periods of leave. Unlike most regular payrolls, which run on a negative pay system (i.e., the basic assumption is that the employee worked that month and is entitled to their pay), agency payrolls, internal or external, usually run on positive pay systems where some kind of timesheet or overtime claim form or electronic docket is needed to generate payment.

Joy became involved with a man who didn't work at the NHS Trust but who persuaded her to put him on the payroll and generate payments to him. He used his contacts to get others to take part in the fraud by appearing to be genuine workers and getting Joy to set them up on the system as staff on the agency bank. They then had false payments generated to them while appearing to be genuine agency staff. In all some 10 ghost employees were set up and paid during this four-year period. The bogus employees took their cut from the fraud and then passed the rest of their ill-gotten gains back to Joy and her partner.

Joy's partner fled the country when the fraud was discovered, leaving her and the other conspirators at the mercy of the criminal investigation that followed. At the same time the NHS Counter-Fraud Service were able to assist in the recovery of £250k of the fraud and institute legal proceedings for the rest. Although Henry had tried to delete the fraudulent records from the computer system, they were still able to trace them through the use of computer forensic techniques. Virtually the day before the criminal trial Joy Henry finally pleaded guilty to one count of conspiracy to defraud.

The civil proceedings were of course put on hold until Joy Henry's criminal trial concluded. And because of this, although the charges were a mixture of money laundering for those receiving the cash and conspiracy to defraud for the rest, the judge in Joy Henry's trial deliberately made no confiscation order under the Proceeds of Crime Act and left that as a matter to be pursued through the civil courts, since civil proceedings had already commenced. In my opinion this is the best option, since criminal proceedings will often be limited by the charges that have been put and the degree of admission of guilt by the fraudster. Since criminal has precedence over civil, had they both been trying to recover stolen assets at the same time it would have been a recipe for disaster and confusion in court.

How a government agency managed to get two fraudsters for the price of one

The Government Paymaster General's Office, among other functions, used to pay the pensions of civil servants. An enterprising junior executive in the section that dealt with pensioners worked out that with a few suitable changes, he could divert monies intended for pensioners or their estates to a bank account that he had set up under a false name. He picked on two targets and in both cases he was creating a classic echo.

His prime target was unmarried pensioners on death. If he received notification that one of them had died and that the pension should cease, he would simply delay processing the stopping of the pension but change their bank account details to his own account and pay it to himself for a few months. He relied on the fact that there would be no reconciliation likely to affect their estate or any relative's tax position on probate.

His second target was also unmarried pensioners, but this was for the refund of pension contributions to widows or widowers. The original civil service pension scheme was—and remains—non-contributory, although new civil servants can no longer enter this scheme. However, there was a 1.5% contribution towards the widows' or widowers' pension if the employee died before retirement. But if they reached retirement age without ever having had anyone entitled to a pension on their death, they could get their contributions refunded. This was not automatic and a request had to be made. Sometimes, by the time the request was received, the unfortunate retiree had already died. In these instances instead of refunding the contributions to their estate, the fraudster simply refunded them to himself.

Sooner or later a sharp-eyed relative would have realised something was amiss but there were no internal procedures at the time that would have picked up either of his frauds. So, how did they come to light, if it wasn't internal controls or aggrieved relatives? Breathtakingly, he turned himself in and confessed to the frauds!

He had set everything up and had diverted about eight people's payments in a relatively short space of time when for some unknown reason he just got cold feet and admitted the fraud to his management, even telling them the details of the bank account to which he had diverted the money.

It was at this point that management took the decision that ended up getting them two fraudsters for the price of one. In a moment of madness that I can only describe as naive beyond belief, they not only publicised that they had caught a fraudster (not in itself a bad idea) but also explained how the fraudster had been able to commit his fraud! This publicity was then sent out in the monthly magazine to all staff.

Unsurprisingly, another enterprising member of staff immediately copied the same fraud! Luckily for the Paymaster General's Office the new fraudster was as naive as the management and left a trail to their fraud that was picked up when a relative did challenge why the estate hadn't had some expected funds.

Just to be clear here, I am fully supportive of giving the right publicity when internal fraud is discovered—and I would certainly advocate making sure that all staff knew that an internal fraudster had been caught. Not only might it deter others thinking of committing frauds, someone may as a result realise that they have seen another fraud being committed, and finally it can be good for the morale of the rest of the staff, the majority of whom will have behaved honestly and will want to see strong management action against those who don't. But the golden rule here is that you *never give out the intimate details of how an internal fraud was committed*. It will automatically attract the attention of copycats, especially if there has been no significant system change as a result of the already discovered fraud. The smarter fraudsters will already know how to do it, but why make it easier for those with fraudulent intent who were not already capable of committing the fraud? It simply puts the organisation at more risk than it faced before.

 ## CLASSIC PAYROLL AND PENSION FRAUDS BY EMPLOYEES OR RELATIVES

The commonest pay fraud is one of duplicate payment or overpayment. This either happens because of a fraudulent act on behalf of or by the employee or because there is a human error and they gain financial benefits to which they were never entitled. Once an employee knows that they are receiving something to which they are not entitled from their employer, whether or not they have caused it to happen, it is a crime for them to try to keep or spend the money.

For some reason, many employees who are accidentally overpaid seem to think that they have no duty to inform anyone and can happily keep the money or spend it without committing any offence or indeed facing any likely retribution. In fact you can pursue them in civil as well as criminal law and this has been the case now for the best part of a decade! If you are a caring organisation you will probably give them the opportunity to repay the 'overpayment' once it comes to light—and may agree to a staged repayment. However, it is still a potential fraud and should be treated as such. At the very least they have committed two disciplinary offences. They have failed to check their payslip information—a requirement of almost any employment anywhere—and they have had something that was not theirs by right of employment. If they knew what was happening or had been warned or spotted it on the payslip, then that is gross misconduct and the organisation should consider dismissal.

One of the simplest errors that I saw taken advantage of by the employee was the case of a police constable who happened to have first initials of P.S., also the payroll code for police sergeant. Needless to say, this confused staff at the contracted payroll provider and they moved his pay on to the police sergeant pay range. Even though this was patently not his pay he continued to receive it for a whole year before he was picked up by a data-matching exercise.

A variation that also happened to my last organisation was when a detective was permanently transferred to a similar organisation in another part of the country. There was an oversight at the payroll centre and they continued to pay him even though he was now working for and being paid by another police force. He happily continued to receive two salaries for a year before it was finally picked up through a data-checking exercise. And yes, the local professional standards unit for police discipline did arrest him and he was eventually charged with theft. A career ruined because he didn't tell anyone that he had been overpaid—he thought he could get away with spending the money, as it wasn't his fault that the initial overpayment occurred.

Another common problem that can be difficult to put right after the event is failure to recover allowances and loans through the payroll when staff are leaving or retiring.

CLASSIC PAYROLL FRAUDS COMMITTED BY LINE MANAGERS

Almost always these tend to be the wholly bogus employee—a ghost. Just occasionally one will indulge in a few echoes as well, but it tends to be predominantly ghosts. The problem about echoes is that unless you work in pay and pensions it is usually hard to suppress the central information that shows you are still paying someone who has left. Eventually HMRC, the NFI (National Fraud Initiative) or another employer are going to pick it up. Line manager frauds (and manager frauds with smaller sub-contractors) have been particularly rife in the building and construction industries and with support companies (e.g., cleaning, security guarding and facilities management). Any area with a high staff turnover and use of temporary staff can be particularly vulnerable to line manager fraud.

If the line manager has the power to hire and fire locally then their easiest target will be bogus temporary staff, created in a not dissimilar fashion to Joy Henry (see p. 249) except that they will submit the information to the HR and pay people rather than manufacture it at the centre. Short-term employees can often pass through without hitting many of the points in an organisation where you'd easily be able to prove or disprove their existence—and the smarter fraudsters won't keep each one on the books too long.

Where local powers to hire and fire exist the line manager is king—or queen—of their empire. Payroll frauds committed in these circumstances are always among the hardest to detect. If the fraudsters are not greedy and stay within their budgets and allocations they will not stand out on any review of normal financial data. If there is a local personnel/HR employee they may cotton on, but if it is a centralised organisation then those at the centre are unlikely to spot anything amiss.

If your organisation has parts of its far-flung empire where local managers have these powers then my best advice is truly random surprise visits and check of all staff physically present on a particular day or time. Unless it is a very small and self-contained work area you will need to go mob-handed to do it effectively. Even in a well-contained area I would recommend a bare minimum team of two just to protect the integrity of your team—preferably more if they can be spared. A surprise spotcheck won't necessarily catch a fraudster immediately, but it will eliminate genuine employees from your enquiries and reduce those for whom you might consider further checks.

By and large line managers don't get the chance to commit pension fraud, by the nature of what would be needed to generate a pension payment.

 ## USING ANALYSTS EFFECTIVELY TO DETECT PAYROLL AND PENSION FRAUD

I have covered the use of analysts in depth in Chapter 6. Where you have an analyst who knows their business they will have a range of tools at their disposal that enable them to interrogate pay and pension data.

Matching internal organisational data

There is a surprising amount of data held within most organisations that can be usefully analysed and pointers picked out to potential frauds and abuse.

Ghost and echo detection

In most organisations there isn't an effective nominal roll any more. There was a time when every HR department had a comprehensive record of all employees that could be independently matched against all employees being paid by the organisation. By its nature an effective check between the two would throw out any ghosts created either by line managers or payroll staff. In larger organisations and where pay and HR data share databases, this check is no longer of much validity, even if it can be done. There are a couple of alternatives, not foolproof, but better than not looking because of either a shared database or non-existent nominal roll.

First, if every budget head is doing their job, you should be able to match employees cost-coded to their department to the number of staff that they believe they have on their books. There are bound to be some discrepancies here with larger organisations as staff move about between sections, but if you run this exercise across the whole organisation at a given point in time then it should be possible to pick out genuine anomalies from errors caused by time-lags in processing staff information.

Second, go to the IT Department and get the current list of active email addresses for employees and, wherever it is held, the list of current telephone extensions for individual staff. Neither of these is a perfect solution (e.g., it won't deal with employees who don't use a computer and who are not on a phone extension). But for the majority of administrative and managerial staff comparing this list with paid employees will work. It should be particularly effective in identifying potential ghosts.

Employees in receipt of the wrong allowances

I remember a particularly useful check for staff receiving shift allowances that identified several hundred employees who were no longer on shift work but still in receipt of shift allowance. Equally it is possible if your organisation pays regional allowances, such as London weighting, to find out if any employees whose regional code tells you they are not working there are still in receipt of an allowance for that region. My last organisation used to pay an inner and an outer London allowance. Using our analysts we managed to find over a hundred employees still receiving an inner allowance when based in the outer region.

Employees committing other frauds

Another useful check is to compare your creditor bank account details with employee bank account details. Where there is a match, is it due to employee expenses not paid through the payroll or is it because the employee is also a contractor—and potentially a fraudster?

The National Fraud Initiative and its part in detecting pay and pension fraud

All bodies to which the Audit Commission appoints auditors are required by law to participate in the NFI. The NFI has statutory authority to conduct data-matching exercises across a wide range of public-sector and, more recently, private-sector bodies who can participate on a voluntary basis for the purposes of preventing and detecting fraud.

Data matching for the NFI involves comparing computer records held by one body against computer records held by the same or another body to see how far they match. Computerised data matching allows potentially fraudulent claims and payments to be identified. Where a match is found it indicates that there is an inconsistency which requires further investigation. No assumption can be made as to whether there is fraud, error or other explanation until an investigation is carried out.

Once the data-matching process is completed, the output is returned to the relevant participating body for consideration and investigation via secure NFI software. Responsibility for investigating any matches rests with the participating bodies.

In my last organisation we would receive the output from the NFI exercise every two years. My analysts would then work in liaison with finance and pay and pension staff to eliminate false positives and get down to a hard core of potential frauds. The NFI is constantly changing and, generally, expanding but the most relevant aspects from a pay and pension perspective have been

Pensions

▪ Matching Department for Work & Pensions (DWP) deceased

records to pensioners to identify any that are deceased. This can replace the time and expense of sending out paper life certification forms.

▪ Matching pensioners' data to payroll data to identify individuals who may have gone back into employment but have not notified their pension scheme and as a result an overpayment of their pension has occurred (i.e., the pension should have been abated).

▪ Matching deferred pensioner data to DWP deceased records to help locate pensioners that the scheme may have lost track of so that payments can be made to family members or dependants.

Pay

▪ Matching employees with the same core details (such as forename, surname, date of birth, address or national insurance number) to employees on other organisations payrolls to identify individuals who may be committing employment fraud—either by failing to work their contracted hours because they are employed elsewhere or are taking long-term sickness absence from one employer and working for another employer at the same time. (Once the part-time data is sifted out it can identify those who have either been overpaid because their last organisation hasn't stopped their salary or who have managed to find a way of having two or more full-time jobs at the same time.)

▪ Matching employee details to UK Border Agency records to identify (1) employees who appear no longer to be entitled to reside in the UK having been refused asylum or are not entitled to work; and (2) employees who appear to have no right to remain in the UK because their visa has expired; or no right to work because of their visa conditions or their right to work is limited (i.e., they are in the UK to study).

The benefits of having an analyst to examine the output, once it has been refined to remove false positives, is that they should have the expertise to compare the NFI data with the live systems for your organisation and draw up a hit list of targets for the investigator(s), as well as pulling off the most up-to-date information on any individuals of concern. It also makes sure that investigator activity is focused on those cases with the highest chance of a successful outcome.

Our main pay-and-pension hits out of the NFI at the Met were always around deceased pensioners. They fell into two categories and our analysts could quickly identify which. Most would be time-lags in the system where someone had recently died but the machinery hadn't yet caught up. A few would be more sinister and an investigator would be despatched to follow up and get back any overpayment.

Other sources of external data

If you have doubts about the existence of an employee or suspect that someone has used a genuine individual as cover for their fraud then there are some external sources that can help cross-matching that you can do yourself, in addition to NFI checks or as a substitute if your organisation cannot be involved in the NFI. I have set out below some of the possible and most readily available options. None are foolproof or absolute, but taken in conjunction with other tests may help identify ghosts or echoes on the payroll.

- *Companies House.* If they've ever been a director then address details, etc. should be here.

- *Electoral Roll.* Not everyone registers, but if they are on it they should match the payroll and HR information. You can buy disks of it from reputable sources and check the ones of interest in house.

- *Telephone Directory.* As above, not all register or have a landline phone nowadays but it can still be a useful source of information.

- *Land Registry.* Property purchases have to be recorded. Appropriate investigative organisations can ask, others may need to pay a fee.

- If you have an address but are not sure if it is genuine or matches the occupant you can also consider a more direct if potentially risky approach. Find a cover story that doesn't involve an out-and-out untruth and ask the neighbours—but if it all goes horribly wrong it wasn't my idea!!

- *Credit reference agencies.* Certain organisations are registered as legitimate reference agencies and can check on your behalf with the more well-known agencies—useful if you don't want to show up at this stage of your enquiries as having instigated a check. I used to use one such internet-based intelligence research company to find out legitimate but hidden public domain information about individuals without the search linking back to my investigation.

▦ *Internet search engines.* An often overlooked source. They won't help with people who have very common names or the same name as someone famous but if people have appeared in a local newspaper, been to court, run a business or been involved in a social or business event then their name or contact details might crop up on a search engine. I remember once identifying an ill-health pension fraudster through a search engine because they ran a guest house, helpfully complete with their personal details, which advertised on the internet.

General principles and axioms**from Chapter 14**

- Ghosts and echoes are the commonest form of payroll or pension fraud.

- Pay or pension frauds can be committed either by HR or payroll staff, employees and/or their relatives or associates or line managers where they have autonomy for staff appointments.

- Effective independent gross-pay and net-pay reconciliation should highlight any potential area of concern—but in many large organisations this is a weakness.

- Pay records can be cross-referenced to email and telephone directory records to help prove the existence of staff.

- Random and surprise checks are the most effective way to find line manager payroll fraud—make sure you never carry out any surprise raids on your own.

- Use analysts to examine unusual or unexpected patterns and to compare staff payment details against other sources such as creditor payments.

- Publicise fraudsters that have been caught—but don't publicise how they have been able to commit their fraud.

- For those in the public sector the National Fraud Initiative will help identify payroll anomalies such as employees with two full-time jobs and deceased pensioners still in receipt of pension, as well as potential illegal workers.

- There are a number of external sources that can be used to check with internal data when looking for payroll fraud, including the electoral roll, telephone directories and credit reference agencies.

- Don't forget the internet as a potential source of information to prove or disprove the existence of employees.

Part V

Getting the right result

CHAPTER FIFTEEN

Dealing with
the law

CHAPTER**SUMMARY**

R eporting fraud to the authorities. Dealing with the police. Relevant
criminal law. Relevant civil law. Employment law. Staying within FOI
and DPA requirements.

REPORTING A FRAUD TO
THE RELEVANT AUTHORITIES?

There comes a point with every fraud allegation and its subsequent
investigation when you have to decide for the first time whether what you
have found constitutes a crime and whether you should report it to the
police. For much of my working life over the last 20 years I have dealt with
organisations where there was little choice. If we had the evidence, then

our procedures and internal rules have required that we report the discovery of fraud to the police. However, in many public-sector and private-sector organisations the internal rules and procedures do not make it a requirement and there is a choice to be made.

Fraud is a crime and if there is prima facie evidence of it then there is a civic obligation on the organisation to make the matter known to the police. There is no legal requirement as such, although every citizen should do their duty. Nor is there any legal duty to report the matter immediately—or as soon as practically possible—after discovery of the prima facie evidence. As I noted in Chapter 3, the last thing the local CID will want is a tangled web of fraud with a pile of paperwork to wade through before they have any opportunity to work out for themselves whose collar they need to feel and why they should be feeling it. If you are going to take a fraud case to the local CID, then 9 times out of 10 it will need wrapping up in a neat bow with a large illuminated arrow pointing to an obvious suspect. Bear in mind that although you will probably end up dealing with a detective, only a very small proportion of detectives have any significant experience in fraud investigation and there is no guarantee of being given anyone at the local CID with the appropriate experience or training in such matters.

If you have clear evidence of fraud once the initial intelligence or allegation is checked out, then the team set up to review decisions must take a view about reporting it—or not—to the police. It is not a decision to be taken lightly and needs to be balanced practically between moral duty and organisational need. Once a fraud has been discovered and is under investigation you will pass through a number of subsequent points when you will need to decide what, if anything at all, should be reported to the relevant authorities, whether the police, trading standards, professional regulatory body or the Serious Organised Crime Agency (SOCA), who deal, among other matters, with suspected money-laundering reports.

Reporting a fraud to the police at an early stage of the investigation is clearly appropriate in some cases (e.g., when the fraudster has already absconded and you have no means of tracing them at your disposal or, the opposite scenario, when they voluntarily confess and hand back whatever they have gained). In the continuum of possible scenarios between those two options the decision to report a fraud to the police at a very early stage of discovery may—or may not—be appropriate.

In that case, how do you decide whether or not to report a fraud? A lot depends on the nature of the fraud and the end in mind that you intend to achieve by your investigation. If the case will be entirely disciplinary then there is no need yet—or possibly at all—to report it to the police. If your organisation's intended outcome of the case is not yet clear to you but the fraud is, then further clarification with your top management of where the case may end up will help decide if it needs yet to be reported to the police or other authorities outside your organisation.

▪ DEALING WITH THE POLICE DURING A FRAUD INVESTIGATION

If you have a good working relationship with the local CID or Economic Crime Unit (the modern posh name for what the rest of us still fondly think of as the Fraud Squad) then by all means sound them out informally at an early stage, possibly before you are sure that there is any substance in the allegation or information. But do not formally report a fraud to them until you are absolutely sure that it is the best way to achieve your organisation's objectives and to stop the fraudster.

Even when you have a good working relationship you can hit a snag dealing with the police, as individual detectives may come and go from their team, often without any warning—and sometimes when you are in the middle of a case. If you do have a good relationship, be prepared to have to build the relationship up all over again. It is one of the frustrations of dealing with detectives at every level that they will move on and be replaced without any apparent handover or passing on of accumulated knowledge to each other. Despite the many good contacts that we had with the police when I was the Director of Internal Audit for the Met, we could still find ourselves caught out by a sudden posting of a detective and the need to build a rapport on the case again with a new detective.

Dealing with the police for the first time

To develop an effective working relationship with the police it is important to understand both (a) how they are organised and (b) how they interact with organisations and people.

Police organisation

Contrary to popular myth, apart from SOCA there is no single United Kingdom police organisation. England and Wales have 43 separate police forces, Scotland has a further 8 and Northern Ireland has just 1. They vary in size and territory from relatively tiny forces such as Dumfries and Warwickshire, both with barely 1,000 police and support staff, through to the Met in London, with 55,000 police and support staff, an organisation larger than the Navy or the RAF. Each force has its own arrangements for dealing with fraud cases, although the national lead on fraud policy rests with the City of London Police, a small force sitting inside the boundary of the Metropolitan Police but with responsibility for major fraud investigations in the City's financial district.

All police forces are divided up for operational purposes into units, known as BOCUs or OCUs (BOCU = Basic Operational Command Unit— except in Greater London where it stands for Borough Operational Command Unit). A BOCU will usually have a number of separate police stations and units within a geographical area under its control. Unless either you have a massive fraud to report or happen to have found a contact in the force's Economic Crime Unit, your first contact will be assigned to the local BOCU Criminal Investigation Department (CID). The first thing the police will want to know, apart from who are you and why you are there, is where you believe the crime was committed. That is because, with a few exceptions, it is always the physical location of the crime that determines which force and which of their BOCUs has responsibility for resolving the crime.

Nowadays every CID office has some financially trained detectives, often involved in pursuing criminal assets under the Proceeds of Crime Act. The chances are, however, that the first detective you find yourself talking to at the BOCU will not be in any way either a fraud specialist or aware of the niceties of how financial matters work in your world.

Police interaction with organisations and people

If you do not have an established working relationship or have not had to deal with the police before on a fraud investigation then there are certain steps that you will need to take, or you will find the experience taxing and frustrating and the police may appear to you at first sight to be surprisingly unhelpful and unsympathetic.

It is part of a detective's training to be naturally suspicious and if they don't know you they will be cautious until they are satisfied that they have established your bona fides and that you have come to them about a matter in which they should be interested. Part of that initial caution with some detectives can include an air of diffidence or disinterest when they first talk to you. Others will sound really interested and keen on what you have to tell them, but after that initial contact you hear nothing and then find it almost impossible to find that detective to speak to again.

If you find yourself on the receiving end of such an experience, remember it isn't in any way personal and the average detective will be working on a wide range of cases simultaneously, so until you have had the opportunity to build a relationship they will tend to file you away in the background while they deal with what they will see as more pressing matters.

Hopefully the potential problems that I've outlined above won't be your first experience and you will find a detective who does take the time and trouble to listen to your case and understand your business. Generally the police are a 'can do' organisation by nature and detectives would much rather be getting on with a case than sitting about in an office.

Steps to take on initial contact with the police

First, try to find an appropriate detective to deal with for the initial contact and advice. If you have any trusted friends or colleagues who know of one willing to talk to you then that will almost certainly be the best route. If you don't have that kind of contact, you will probably have to turn up in person at a local police station near to your business. While it is possible to ring up, the chances are that a non-emergency call will get referred to a general desk and it is unlikely the police officer or support person answering the phone will be able to deal with the case. Tests have shown that in the busier forces, it is hard to get a first-time outside call through to the relevant CID in such circumstances and unless there is an urgent need to detain a potentially fleeing fraudster, it is not justifiable to call the 999 emergency numbers to report a fraud.

It will help if you cultivate the view that you are interested in getting advice from them, rather than seeming over-anxious to report a fraud at first. Even then, some police officers will immediately want to take the case over and run it as a purely criminal investigation. They are less likely to do this and more likely to listen to your organisation's point of view if you know your stuff or have an investigator who knows their business well enough or has a background that might earn their respect.

Second, if you are thinking of reporting a fraud formally, get your preparation right before you speak to the police. It is no good turning up with a bunch of paperwork, telling them it contains a fraud and then waiting for them to look through it and agree. They will expect you to have already done that part of the work and to point out to them why you think that you have a fraud to report. It doesn't mean that they then won't go and do exactly the same as you've already just done, taking twice the time and asking apparently unimportant or irrelevant questions as they go along, but have patience here, they'll want you to convince them that you know what you are talking about and that there is the real possibility that a crime has been committed.

Third—and perhaps most importantly—police officers are trained to see a crime in terms of the legal process associated with it. Before they accept that a fraud has been committed, they will want to see the elements that make up a potential criminal charge of fraud laid out clearly before them. This is one key area where a police officer differs from the non-police auditor or manager.

To most of us a fraud is clear and apparent from what has been discovered. To a police officer, nothing is clear until they know how the evidence has been discovered, whether it is factually accurate, whether there is corroborative evidence and/or reliable witnesses and whether the elements that would make up a criminal charge are all present.

For example, if a bidder for a contract submitted a set of false accounts to you would that be a deception? Well, that may seem self-apparent, but in law under the Theft Acts 1968 and 1978 there were three key ingredients to a deception—and they all had to be met to create the offence.

- First, it had to be practised (i.e., achieved in this instance by the would-be contractor submitting the false accounts).
- Second, it had to be believed—did you believe they were genuine when in fact they were false?
- Third and finally, it has to be acted upon (i.e., you had to take some action because you believed that the false accounts were genuine, such as awarding a contract to the bidder submitting the false accounts that otherwise you would have awarded to someone else).

▪ FRAUD AND THE RELEVANT CRIMINAL LAW

If you are considering the need to go down the criminal route, you will stand much more chance of persuading the police to take on the case if you can demonstrate all the key elements of an offence under the Fraud or Theft Acts from what has been discovered in your investigation to date.

A retired detective superintendent and good friend of mine used to liken this to the ingredients of a cake. Without all the key ingredients brought together you could not make a cake, even though each ingredient could be recognised and used on its own. To make a criminal offence, all the key ingredients must be present in the same matter and in the same time frame.

The Fraud Act 2006

The Fraud Act 2006 repealed sections of the earlier Theft Acts and other legislation that dealt on the fringes of fraud. It is now the most significant Act for dealing with criminal fraud. [1]

The Fraud Act 2006, s. 11, has replaced criminal deception under s. 1 of the Theft Act 1968 with the offence of 'Obtaining services dishonestly'. In effect it has brought the offence into the modern world and in doing so has changed the necessary ingredients of the cake. For a service to be obtained dishonestly the ingredients are now that:

1. The service has been provided to a person or over the internet on the basis that payment has or will be made for it.
2. The recipient of the service intended to avoid payment for it.

It is a far simpler recipe than the old Theft Act offence of deception and broader based (except that deception to avoid a fee due would not be an offence here, although it would potentially be an offence under s. 1 of the Fraud Act).

If you examine the key three sections of the 2006 Fraud Act, it is possible to understand how this works in the mind of the law and help yourself to be able to manage police officers' expectations.

Sub-section 2(2) Fraud by false representation

(2) A representation is false if—
    (a) it is untrue or misleading, and
    (b) the person making it knows that it is, or might be, untrue or misleading.

(3) 'Representation' means any representation as to fact or law, including a representation as to the state of mind of—
    (a) the person making the representation, or
    (b) any other person.

(4) A representation may be express or implied.

(5) For the purposes of this section a representation may be regarded as made if it (or anything implying it) is submitted in any form to any system or device designed to receive, convey or respond to communications (with or without human intervention).

Sub-sections (2) to (5) of Sub-section 2(2) clearly set out the ingredients that need to be present for the crime of fraud by false representation. It is worth comparing this with the definition of deception earlier. Unlike deception, which needs to be acted upon, it is sufficient for a crime of fraud by false representation that it is untrue or misleading and the person making it knows that it is or might be untrue or misleading.

Sub-Section 2(3) Fraud by failing to disclose information

A person is in breach of this section if he—
    (a) dishonestly fails to disclose to another person information which he is under a legal duty to disclose, and
    (b) intends, by failing to disclose the information—
        (i) to make a gain for himself or another, or
        (ii) to cause loss to another or to expose another to a risk of loss.

The important ingredient here is that it must be a *dishonest* failure to disclose. Accidental or good-faith failures to disclose are not fraudulent in the eyes of the law, whatever their consequences may have been. The police will have to prove beyond all reasonable doubt that the fraudster deliberately chose not to disclose information *and* that they intended by so doing either to make a gain or cause a loss.

Note here that whether the fraudster personally gains is immaterial. The gain may be for another or the effect of the fraud could be to cause a loss to the victim(s). It is the effect of the fraud on those that it is perpetrated that is important rather than whether the fraudster personally benefitted by their fraud.

Sub-section 2(4)   Fraud by abuse of position

(1)   A person is in breach of this section if he—
    (a)   occupies a position in which he is expected to safeguard, or not to act against, the financial interests of another person,
    (b)   dishonestly abuses that position, and
    (c)   intends, by means of the abuse of that position
        (i)   to make a gain for himself or another, or
        (ii)   to cause loss to another or to expose another to a risk of loss.

(2)   A person may be regarded as having abused his position even though his conduct consisted of an omission rather than an act.

All these three parts of Sub-Section 2 of the Fraud Act are written in the context of an individual defrauding another. However, the Act itself clarifies the full extent of its meaning in relation to sole traders and companies committing fraud in two further parts.

9   Participating in fraudulent business carried on by sole trader, etc.

(1)   A person is guilty of an offence if he is knowingly a party to the carrying on of a business to which this section applies.

(2)   This section applies to a business which is carried on—
    (a)   by a person who is outside the reach of section 458 of the Companies Act 1985 (c. 6) or Article 451 of the Companies (Northern Ireland) Order 1986 (S.I. 1986/1032) (N.I. 6)) (offence of fraudulent trading), and
    (b)   with intent to defraud creditors of any person or for any other fraudulent purpose.

In other words, where a fraud is committed that is either already defined under the Companies Acts and the body is a company to which those Acts apply, then it is dealt with under those acts. Otherwise it is picked up by the Fraud Act.

12   Liability of company officers for offences by company

(1)   Sub-section (2) applies if an offence under this Act is committed by a body corporate.

(2)   If the offence is proved to have been committed with the consent or conni- vance of—
   (a)   a director, manager, secretary or other similar officer of the body corporate, or
   (b)   a person who was purporting to act in any such capacity, he (as well as the body corporate) is guilty of the offence and liable to be proceeded against and punished accordingly.

(3)   If the affairs of a body corporate are managed by its members, subsection (2) applies in relation to the acts and defaults of a member in connection with his functions of management as if he were a director of the body corporate.

This is particularly useful, as it makes it clear that for the purposes of the offences under Sub-Section 2 of the Fraud Act, they apply as equally to a corporation and its responsible officers as they do to a private individual. But don't forget the point about ingredients. To prove a fraud under S12(2) above you need to be able to show that there was connivance, not an easy offence to prove.

So, in summary, the Fraud Act is a pretty comprehensive piece of legislation. Only time and case law will tell whether it is a good piece of legislation or not. The early signs are encouraging, but at the time of writ- ing this book it hasn't faced any significant challenges of interpretation and they will be the real test of its applicability and suitability.

It is a relatively straightforward and all-embracing Act that covers fraud committed by individuals and organisations, as well as any means by which those frauds may have been committed, whether electronic, physical or personal. In that way it has dealt with many of the inherent difficulties and weaknesses in the old Theft Act sections that it has replaced where they crossed with modern technology and internet-based fraud and it has also removed the need for some areas of the even older Prevention of Corruption Acts to be so urgently updated (although I dream of the day when they too are modernised and fit for purpose).

But the key point of this section is to emphasise that once you take a matter to the police, they will be thinking about it in the context of the law and, for fraud, that will generally mean in the context of how they interpret the Fraud Act and whether you have or can make available to the police the means to establish sufficient evidence against an individual for them to be charged with an offence under the Act. If you don't have anything that appears to be sufficient evidence or the means to obtain it they may offer you advice but they are unlikely to commit any resources to mount a criminal investigation.

As cases in criminal courts have demonstrated in the last decade, it is generally far better for an organisation and far more fruitful if you can establish all the relevant and obtainable facts before you go to the police. It is also helpful if you have already started the ball rolling on any internal disciplinary procedures, including line manager interviews, as well as any planned civil recovery action or freezing-order applications.

The Criminal Attempts Act 1981

This is an all-encompassing piece of legislation that is still relevant since the Fraud Act came into force. Although it covers a range of attempted crimes across the whole spectrum of the criminal justice system it can equally be applied to fraud or theft. Where an individual attempts to and intends to commit an offence of fraud or theft, *whether or not*[2] they can physically commit that offence, then they can be guilty of a criminal attempt under this Act.

Misconduct in a Public Office

Misconduct in public office is a common law offence that can be traced back more than 200 years to the case of *R v Bembridge* in 1783. More recently it has been used to charge police officers who have deliberately failed in their duties, although in Victorian times it was often applied to town hall officials. In 2007 the Crown Prosecution Service defined its key ingredients as

(a) A public officer acting as such
(b) Wilfully neglects to perform his duty and/or wilfully misconducts himself
(c) To such a degree as to amount to an abuse of the public's trust in the office holder
(d) Without reasonable excuse or justification.

All the ingredients have to be proved for the offence to stand. The courts have declined to rule on the position of private companies providing services previously provided by public officials who could be charged with misconduct, but the general expectation is that if pressed they will take a narrow view of the definition of a public servant.

Misconduct in a Public Office has been used more in the last decade than in the 50 years preceding it (last reported year of usage to Parliament, 2007, for 21 cases). However, as can be seen from above, proving each and all of the ingredients is in itself a stern test. It is still rarely used and is reserved for the most serious cases of misconduct where no other offence might be charged. It carries a maximum sentence of life imprisonment.

It is not to be confused with, although similar to, the common law criminal offence and civil tort of misfeasance. In common law in addition to misconduct in public office there are also criminal offences of misfeasance (deliberately providing the wrong service) and malfeasance (deliberately providing a harmful service). These are often more appropriate and easier to prove for fraud-related cases than misconduct. For example, personal use of an officially issued corporate credit card by an officer of an organisation could lead to them being charged with misfeasance.[3]

Prevention of Corruption Acts 1889–1916

These are effectively dead ducks waiting for the final coup de grâce. In recent times public officials are far more likely to face charges under the Fraud Act or to be charged with misconduct in public office.

The problem here is that this outdated legislation requires a public official to prove that they have not acted corruptly when challenged, although the alleged corruptor does not face the same burden of proof. Aside from the 1976 Race Relations Act and the subsequent Race Relations (Amendment) Act it is the only piece of legislation on the UK statute books that requires the accused to prove their innocence and is in direct contradiction to the general principle that the accused is innocent until proven guilty.

As a result, the CPS has been reluctant to use the Prevention of Corruption Acts except in extreme cases and judges have been even less keen to see it come before them. All attempts to reform and replace these Acts have so far failed to make it through the legislature, although interestingly Ireland did update its version of these in 2002.

They have, however, been partially revived in the UK for the purposes of dealing with overseas bribery and corruption under Part 12 of the Antiterrorism, Crime and Security Act of 2001. I have reproduced all of Part 12 here, including the revealing comment that 'presumption of corruption' is only to apply under the two sections (108 and 109) repeated below.

Part 12   Bribery and corruption

Section 108   Bribery and corruption: foreign officers, etc.

(1) For the purposes of any common law offence of bribery it is immaterial if the functions of the person who receives or is offered a reward have no connection with the United Kingdom and are carried out in a country or territory outside the United Kingdom.

(2) In section 1 of the Prevention of Corruption Act 1906 (c. 34) (corrupt transactions with agents) insert this subsection after subsection (3)

''(4) For the purposes of this Act it is immaterial if
   (a) the principal's affairs or business have no connection with the United Kingdom and are conducted in a country or territory outside the United Kingdom;
   (b) the agent's functions have no connection with the United Kingdom and are carried out in a country or territory outside the United Kingdom.''

(3) In section 7 of the Public Bodies Corrupt Practices Act 1889 (c. 69) (interpretation relating to corruption in office) in the definition of ''public body'' for ''but does not include any public body as above defined existing elsewhere than in the United Kingdom'' substitute ''and includes any body which exists in a country or territory outside the United Kingdom and is equivalent to any body described above''.

(4) In section 4(2) of the Prevention of Corruption Act 1916 (c. 64) (in the 1889 and 1916 Acts public body includes local and public authorities of all descriptions) after ''descriptions'' insert ''(including authorities existing in a country or territory outside the United Kingdom)''.

Section 109   Bribery and corruption committed outside the UK

(1) This section applies if—
   (a) a national of the United Kingdom or a body incorporated under the law of any part of the United Kingdom does anything in a country or territory outside the United Kingdom, and
   (b) the act would, if done in the United Kingdom, constitute a corruption offence (as defined below).

(2) In such a case—
  (a) the act constitutes the offence concerned, and
  (b) proceedings for the offence may be taken in the United Kingdom.

(3) These are corruption offences—
  (a) any common law offence of bribery;
  (b) the offences under section 1 of the Public Bodies Corrupt Practices Act 1889 (c. 69) (corruption in office);
  (c) the first two offences under section 1 of the Prevention of Corruption Act 1906 (c. 34) (bribes obtained by or given to agents).

(4) A national of the United Kingdom is an individual who is—
  (a) a British citizen, a British Dependent Territories citizen, a British National (Overseas) or a British Overseas citizen,
  (b) a person who under the British Nationality Act 1981 (c. 61) is a British subject, or
  (c) a British protected person within the meaning of that Act.

Section 110   Presumption of corruption not to apply

Section 2 of the Prevention of Corruption Act 1916 (c. 64) (presumption of corruption in certain cases) is not to apply in relation to anything which would not be an offence apart from section 108 or section 109.

■ INVESTIGATING WITHIN THE LAW

The Regulation of Investigatory Powers Act 2000 (RIPA) is covered in more detail in Chapter 5 'Gathering and using intelligence and evidence' and Chapter 8 'Considering covert surveillance'. The Police and Criminal Evidence Act 1984 (PACE) is covered in Chapter 9 'Fraud interviewing techniques'.

Aside from PACE, RIPA and associated Acts around lawful interception of telecommunications, etc. the two most common areas of modern day difficulty are the Freedom of Information Act 2000 and the Data Protection Acts 1984 and 1998. Failure to deal with the requirements of either act can lead you into hot water or cause the loss of either a civil or criminal case.

They are not, however, the demons that they are often represented to be. Following a few simple precautions can ensure that you do not fall foul of them and that your investigation remains suitably confidential until it needs to become more public. Both FOIA and DPA are mutually exclusive, by that I mean that if you are required by law to do something under one Act then you cannot be compelled by law to do something contradictory under the other Act. The Data Protection Act covers all organisations and indeed individuals, whereas the FOIA only applies to you if you are either a public authority or your organisation is providing services to a public authority, such as payroll or data management.

The Data Protection Act 1998

To avoid falling foul of the Data Protection Act during a fraud investigation it is important to make sure that any—and only—personal data relevant to your enquiries is acquired securely and safely, held securely and, once the purpose for which it has been gathered has passed, destroyed or otherwise disposed of in a secure manner. There is nothing in the Data Protection Act to prevent the proper acquisition of personal data to which you have legitimate access where it is relevant to an official investigation.

It all sounds simple enough but as some high-profile cases from government departments in recent years have shown, even the most apparently secure of public-service organisations can manage to lose personal data in inappropriate ways. Perhaps the most staggering—and also relevant to an investigator—was in 2007 when the National Audit Office asked HM Revenue and Customs for some limited personal data on 25 million individuals in the UK. Although the NAO made it quite clear that they only needed certain data fields, the staff holding the data concluded that it would be too difficult to split out that data from that required by the NAO for their audit. Instead, the complete database was downloaded and sent on disk via a well-known courier company, but never arrived. It cost the head of HMRC his job.

Unlike the NAO I don't like to trust third parties to deliver the information that I want, especially where there might be room for interpretation. If you can't collect the data electronically by your own means, then the first thing is to see if it can be physically placed on a storage device that you can either collect in person or send a trusted individual to collect. If you require physical files or records that contain personal data, then go to where it is held and acquire it there, wherever possible. Once the relevant data is in your possession then make sure that it is secured in such a way that only you or a nominated investigator has access to it; the same principle applies to any personal information that needs to be copied as part of the investigation.

And now for the Freedom of Information Act 2000

In the month before the Freedom of Information Act was about to become law many officials in the public services found themselves ensconced by a shredder removing reams of documents and files from office cupboards and shredding their contents. So, why were they doing this? It certainly wasn't an attempt to undermine the spirit of the Act which many genuinely welcomed. Well, originally DPA requests had only been applied either to indexed or electronically available records and files, but in 2000 the FOIA extended this to include any record or document that could be recovered that was relevant to the request, even if held in unstructured or partial files. There were still some limitations (e.g., if the cost of responding to the request was prohibitive or the request was deemed vexatious—and I'll return to that one) but if documents subsequently turned up, either under disclosure or during other enquiries, then officials would have been in deep trouble under the Act.

This is particularly relevant also to employment law, where there are defined periods for the appropriate holding of information either about those who have applied for jobs or employees and in certain circumstances any disciplinary information held about them. By and large HR departments tend to be over-cautious here and destroy information that would have been quite helpful for the investigator if only it had been kept a little longer—but this is an area where you'll have to live by the legal advice obtained by your organisation.

Investigations do have some protections but they are not a 'blanket' right, as public-sector auditors investigating a fraudulent manager in one case in Scotland found when he was able to get a court ruling that under the FOI he should have been allowed access to their audit report into his affairs. Although the legal system is different in Scotland compared with the rest of the United Kingdom, on matters that come out of European and Human Rights legislation, the law is largely the same, it is just a matter of local judicial (or in this case Information Commissioner) interpretation. Despite this ruling, any factual investigation in support of a potential criminal investigation is exempt from FOIA requests at the time of the investigation—although not in perpetuity thereafter. It may well also be that some of the data and reported information is exempt but the rest is not. This is frequently the aspect of the FOIA that catches most investigators out.

You can exempt certain matters either where they would interfere in future criminal or indeed civil proceedings or where the information requested is of no legitimate relevance to the individual making the request. The same does not necessarily apply in disciplinary cases—and remember from earlier that under disclosure rules once either civil or criminal court proceedings start you will be required to share the relevant factual data gathered for the investigation with the representatives of the fraudster.

Sometimes those connected with a case or with a particular bee in their bonnet will submit request after request under FOIA, either seeking variants of the same information over and over again or taking each previous answer to create a further set of questions that they now want answered. If your nominated officer is doing their job they should spot this kind of behaviour and write back to the individuals concerned to warn them that they will be considered 'vexatious' under the Act if they persist with the same line of questioning. The questioner has the right of appeal but it is a weapon that can legitimately be used to stop fishing expeditions by fraudsters and their friends.

So, to sum up. There is no such thing as a 'blanket' right for the investigator to ignore either a DPA request or a FOIA request. However, it is legitimate to protect an on-going investigation until such time as any aspect of criminality in the case has been resolved. Even then, the advice may be that some information will be released in response to a request, even if part of that information is redacted until other matters are resolved.

CIVIL LAW AND FRAUD

In Chapter 16 'Dos and don'ts of civil litigation' I have set out the process by which you can launch freezing orders and other weapons at your fraudster. A freezing order is a particularly useful weapon in the war to get stolen assets back. This section, however, is an outline of the key areas of civil law that are likely to crop up during a fraud investigation and is intended to make sure that you haven't overlooked any obligations and requirements that make come back to bite you later.

Of particular importance here is employment legislation. If relations break down between an employer and an employee, it will either fall to an employment tribunal or the civil courts to resolve the matter, although ACAS will often offer both parties the opportunity to resolve their dispute outside the court system. An employment tribunal is, in law, a civil court for hearing statutory matters of employment where individuals may bring cases against their employers in person.

It can be quite easy for the unwary investigator to cross the line between a legitimate fact-finding investigation and breach of an employee's rights under their contract of employment and thereby trigger an employment tribunal case. It is back to my basic point that the investigator sticks to their fact-finding role as far as possible. If subsequently a decision is taken to pursue disciplinary action against an individual on the basis of the facts established by the investigator then, if necessary, the investigator can assist whoever is appointed (either the line manager of the employee facing disciplinary action or an appointed panel of managers) to establish the relevant facts for the disciplinary process.

If despite your best efforts you find yourself named as a respondent in an employment tribunal case it is important to make sure that you have all the relevant documentation to show what you did, why you did it and when you did it. Tribunals are generally concerned about the attitude of mind but are entitled to draw third-party inferences to establish that (i.e., they can accept hearsay evidence if they think that it is relevant) and will take their decision on a balance of probabilities. Once an employee can demonstrate to a tribunal that they have grounds to believe they have been acted against unfairly the burden of proof will then fall to the organisation to show otherwise. While this can be quite daunting, it is also worth bearing in mind that only a very small percentage of employees and ex-employees are successful at an employment tribunal.

If, as a result of an investigation, an organisation decides to terminate its contract with another organisation, the other party can and may take civil court action against the organisation, potentially naming the investigator. It is unusual and normally the investigator will be covered by their organisation. Any professional owes a duty of care, but that duty of care is first and foremost to the owners of the organisation that employs the professional, not to any outside parties or external reviewers or other parties with whom the organisation has had a relationship.

It is here that the legal maxims that 'fraud is odious' and that a fraudster shall not profit from their fraud need to be remembered. In a civil court, if you are attacked, it becomes legitimate to defend yourself with any relevant evidence to the attack that has been launched. For a fraudster to take you to court is a high-risk strategy that only the most foolhardy and brave would even attempt. It gives you carte blanche to introduce all relevant material from your investigation and if the court concludes that the individuals have been acting fraudulently it could cost them dearly.

General principles and axiomsfrom **Chapter 15**

■ Fraud is a crime and if there is prima facie evidence of it then there is a civic obligation on the organisation to make the matter known to the police.

■ There is no legal requirement to report fraud as such, although every citizen should do their duty.

■ If you have clear evidence of fraud then the team set up to review decisions must take a view about reporting it—or not—to the police. It is not a decision to be taken lightly and needs to be balanced practically between moral duty and organisational need.

■ Do not formally report a fraud to the police until you are sure that it is the best way to achieve your organisation's objectives and stop the fraudster.

■ To report a fraud formally, get your preparation right before you speak to the police. They'll want you to convince them that you know what you are talking about and that a crime has been committed.

■ To a police officer, nothing is clear until they know how the evidence has been discovered, whether it is factually accurate, whether there is corroborative evidence and/or reliable witnesses and whether the elements that would make up a criminal charge are all present.

■ To make a criminal offence, all the key ingredients must be present in the same matter and in the same time frame.

■ Under the Fraud Act 2006 the key ingredients of a service obtained dishonestly are:

1 The service has been provided to a person or over the internet on the basis that payment has or will be made for it
2 The recipient of the service intended to avoid payment for it.

■ It is far more fruitful if you can establish all the relevant and obtainable facts before you go to the police. It is also better for your organisation if you have already started the ball rolling on any internal disciplinary procedures, as well as any planned civil recovery action or freezing orders.

■ To avoid falling foul of the Data Protection Act during a fraud investigation it is important to make sure that any—and only—personal data relevant to your enquiries is acquired and held securely and, once the purpose for which it has been gathered has passed, destroyed or otherwise disposed of in a secure manner.

■ There is nothing in the Data Protection Act to prevent the proper acquisition of personal data to which you have legitimate access where it is relevant to an official investigation.

▪ Any factual investigation in support of a potential criminal investigation is exempt from FOIA requests at the time of the investigation—although not in perpetuity thereafter. It may well also be that some of the data and reported information is exempt but the rest is not. This is frequently the aspect of the FOIA that catches most investigators out.

▪ There is no such thing as a 'blanket' right for the investigator to ignore either a DPA request or a FOIA request. However, it is legitimate to protect an on-going investigation until such time as any aspect of criminality in the case has been resolved.

The dos and don'ts of preparing for civil litigation

The Metropolitan Police do seem to pay their interpreters rather well.
Order granted!

His Honour Judge Richards, when faced with a freezing-order application on a linguist
who had fraudulently claimed a quarter of a million pounds from the police in
four years for part-time work

CHAPTER**SUMMARY**

W hen and when not to consider civil litigation. Freezing orders and
their place in your armoury. Keeping the civil case going in parallel
with a criminal case. Expert witnesses and how they should be used.

WHEN—AND WHEN NOT—TO CONSIDER LITIGATION

Mike Comer summed this up succinctly in his 1998 book *Corporate Fraud*
when he noted that if you were considering civil litigation then you should
dig two graves. What he meant by this is that you should only consider civil
litigation on those rare occasions when it is the most appropriate route to

attempt to recover the fraudster's ill-gotten gains. It is an expensive business and the cost will often outweigh any gain. Having said that, I have used the civil litigation process successfully on a number of occasions to recover fraudulently obtained assets and also successfully defended a position when others have instituted civil litigation against my then-employers.

So, when should you consider civil litigation? First and foremost, it has to be for the right reasons, none of which should include the desire to 'get even' with the fraudster. It is all about practicality and ensuring recovery of fraudulently obtained assets that you cannot get back by easier means. If considering whether to institute civil proceedings my starting point is, first, to consider whether the fraud is sufficiently large enough and, second, whether the fraudster is likely to have the wherewithal to repay it if a case is brought home successfully against them. It is no good winning a civil judgement against a heavily indebted gambler who stole and wasted your money on feeding their gambling habit. You still won't recover anything worth getting back and you'll have all those mounting legal bills to pay.

In deciding whether the fraud is large enough to pursue through the civil courts I have a general rule of thumb that seems to work. First, don't bother to consider civil action if the potential sum recoverable is less than £100k. Second, if the potential sum recoverable is £100k or more ask your solicitor or legal adviser for their best estimate of the likely legal costs in bringing home the case. They will estimate in a range, being cautious individuals. Say the low point is £60k. Double it to £120k and look at the value of what you might recover. If it is £120k or more then go for the civil action to recover it, if it is less, walk away and forget it. This doesn't mean that where the sums don't add up you can't try something that looks like you are starting proceedings, as sometimes a solicitor's letter, suitably worded, can encourage the fraudster to repay monies anyway that you couldn't have afforded to pursue through the courts.

You may be thinking that when you win the civil case you will be awarded costs by the court anyway, so why should you worry about the legal costs? The primary reason is that the chances of the litigation actually reaching court are very slim, as most cases are settled before the big day, sometimes on the steps of the courtroom on the day itself! As all settlements will include a degree of compromise between the two parties' legal representatives, the chances are that you will only recover a small part of your legal costs to that point. And, strange as it may seem, most of the legal costs occur before you get to that big day in court.

▥ TO FREEZE OR NOT TO FREEZE—IS THAT THE QUESTION?

If you are going down the civil litigation route for recovery and you have the opportunity to take out a freezing order,[1] my instinctive reaction is to go for it. There are risks and you need to understand them fully first, but in terms of impact it gets the fraudster's immediate and undivided attention.

When considering whether to go for a freezing order you must show sufficient grounds to have it granted. A key ground is if you believe there is a risk that the fraudster will attempt to put their assets beyond your reach. This is a strong argument but also one that holds less water if you have spent several months investigating before you decide to go for it, as the judge may then conclude that as the fraudster doesn't appear to have done a runner or dissipated their assets up to this point then it unlikely that they will do so now.

The only occasion that I went for a freezing order a long time after we started an investigation—and got it—was in the middle of a fraudster's criminal trial, when they had known that we were on to them for more than a year by then. They were found guilty but given a month on bail before sentencing. In court they asked the judge if they could visit Iran to see their sick mother during that month. Amazingly the judge agreed to this, provided that they bought a return air ticket. My people heard this in utter—and stunned—astonishment and rang me immediately. I signed a hastily prepared affidavit and we then rushed round to the High Court with our lawyers and were granted a freezing order on the spot. Curiously our fraudster then decided that he didn't need to go to Iran after all, but would rather talk to us instead about how he could release his assets from our freezing order!

Phase 1 of deciding to go for a freezing order is to sit down with your solicitor to ask them to choose the appropriate junior counsel to represent you on this matter, as only counsel can go to the High Court and ask a judge for a freezing order. Junior counsel simply means counsel who hasn't become a QC. They are considerably cheaper than a QC (and in my experience far cheaper than the average solicitor!) but will usually have many years' experience of fraud-related work or be a bright and up-and-coming spark in that field on their way to later glory.

Phase 2 is the bit that can cause sleepless nights. You (or a nominated investigator involved in the case) will need to sign a suitably prepared and witnessed affidavit setting out the broad facts, why you are seeking the freezing order and a justification for the amount that you are seeking to have frozen. If any of this later turns out to be untrue and you should have known it, you can find yourself on the wrong end of a legal judgement and personally liable for the consequences. Even though the freezing order will be for a specific amount, its immediate practical effect is to freeze temporarily all the assets of the fraudster, hence why it is an excellent way to get their undivided attention.

Once the affidavit has been agreed your counsel will see a High Court judge sitting 'unrobed' (i.e., dressed normally and in a smaller side court) and put your case. You can be present but you are not allowed to speak and there are no witnesses called. It is advisable therefore not to turn up mob-handed, or you may get some very curious looks and a possible challenge from the judge. The judge will ask counsel questions and counsel will explain as best they can. The decision is almost immediate and will happen once the judge has finished reading the affidavit. The important thing to understand at this point in the process is that you are under no obligation to tell the fraudster—or their legal representative—that you are taking out the freezing order. At this stage it is a one-sided procedure, the opposition is neither present nor represented.

Once an order is granted—if it is granted—then the judge will set time aside to reconvene in around seven days' time with the opposition present when they will have the opportunity to object to all or part of the freezing order. This is a period of frenetic activity as you will need to flesh out the supporting documentation to the amount frozen as much as you can before the court reconvenes. The affidavit will have been accepted as an estimate but if you can't back it up with some evidence when you get back to court there is a real risk of the freezing order being withdrawn by the judge.

Provided you have done your homework, any objection to the freezing order should fail. There are then three likely possibilities at this point:

(1) You may revise your estimate of the value of the fraud and the judge may adjust the frozen amount up or down as a consequence. A dangerous course unless there are very good reasons for the wrong value on the original affidavit. Your counsel may be asked some probing questions about the reasons for the revision and it will throw future doubt on your professional credibility.
(2) The judge may accept an argument from the fraudster's lawyers and reduce the size of the freezing order. Disappointing if it happens, but c'est la vie!

(3) The fraudster's lawyers may offer to put a sum equivalent to the freezing order into court care in return for the release of the freezing order. If they do this the judge will release your freezing order, as the money will now be kept by the court until you have resolved your litigation with the fraudster. If they then agree to pay or are ordered to pay it to you, you will get the money equivalent of what was originally frozen. (If you fail to win the civil litigation the money will then be returned to the fraudster, plus an agreed rate of interest, to rub salt in your wound. And almost certainly, if that happens you will end up meeting all their costs as well. But you will have been very poorly advised if you are pursuing a case where the odds are not heavily in favour of winning.)

It is of course possible that once their lawyers see your affidavit they may seek to pay you immediately in which case you will withdraw the freezing order as soon as you have the money. I have never had that experience myself, but I am sure somebody out there will have.

CIVIL AND CRIMINAL CASES—GETTING THE RIGHT RESULT

If you do find that you are pursuing a case through the civil courts and the police are also pursing the same individual(s) for a criminal case there are certain rules of the game that you will need to bear in mind to make sure that you can still get your civil case home. The last thing that anyone will want is to end up with neither case coming home. However, there is a tendency for most senior managers to get over-awed once the police get involved and to lose sight of the original end in mind that you had for the fraud case that you've put in front of them.

Having spent most of the last 14 working years of my life closely involved with as well as probing and prodding the internal processes of the police, I am perhaps less in awe than most, simply through a closer familiarity with their workings and their ways than most people get the chance to have, unless they were a police officer or worked inside police organisations in a former career.

So, let's be very clear about the considerable risk that criminal prosecutions will either fail or the outcome will be unsatisfactory for your organisation. Criminal cases for fraud or corruption are rarely successful. For every high-profile prosecution and conviction there is a whole mountain that never got past the Crown Prosecution Service when the police submitted the paperwork. And then for those that do get through, many juries simply feel out of their depth with fraud cases and unless the expert witnesses are particularly clear and the crimes obvious, they will be reluctant to convict. Since 'burden of proof' is a higher standard than disciplinary and civil action, that also has to be borne in mind and can lead to a 'no result' where even the police officers in the case are convinced—and have convinced you – they will get a conviction.

Your organisation and you will not want to have to rely on a criminal case; you should treat them as the icing on the cake—and if they are successful well that's great, but whatever else you rely on, *never ever rely on a criminal investigation to bring home a successful outcome for a fraud case*. Even where the criminal is convicted, the case will usually have been brought on a small sample of provable offences. Ultimately any financial award back to your organisation will be limited by how many of the charges were brought home. For example, if they are charged on eight counts but only four are successful, they are still convicted but you are not going to get the sums involved in the whole fraud or anything like them awarded to you. And if the judge decides the organisation was negligent, you might not get anything at all.

Since criminal cases often take a long time to get to court there may well be nothing of value to have awarded. I had a case in recent years where we had 9 out of 10 counts in our favour but the criminal damages were a fraction of the monies we got back through our civil action. Without the civil litigation we would only have scratched the surface of the fraudster's ill-gotten gains.

So—the golden rule—if you can't recover your money without civil litigation, start the civil case as soon as you can. Do this either by launching a freezing order or through your solicitors formally notifying the opposition that you intend to take legal action to recover the stolen money.[2] Do this whether or not a criminal case has already started, although preferably try to get the ball rolling before the criminal case, as it will be more beneficial in the long run. It also gives you greater scope as once the criminal investigation does start then you cannot take any action that might be seen as prejudicial to the criminal case, but of course, within reason, you have carte blanche until the criminal investigation officially starts.

Civil and criminal cases in parallel

The first rule of the game is that the criminal case, once launched by a police investigation, takes priority over the civil case. This is why I can't emphasise enough the need to get your civil case started, if there is to be one, before the police have really got under way. By getting in first you not only gain the advantages of gathering evidence and conducting internal interviews without having to worry too much about Code C of PACE; you also get the opportunity to seize control of the fraudster's assets before they have time to consider their options during the inevitably lengthy police investigation.

If you've taken out a freezing order or they have agreed to pay a sum into the civil courts then until the matter is resolved you will have protected your position and can happily let the police investigation and any subsequent appearances for the usual police bail and criminal delaying tactics carry on while you refine your evidence.

I can almost guarantee that the fraudster's lawyers will be in touch as soon as they are arrested or find they are likely to be facing criminal charges asking that the civil case is stayed until the criminal matter is concluded. And you will almost certainly get some pressure from the police investigator not to tread on their toes with the civil case. So, as long as you've taken the appropriate legal precautions, you can park the civil court part and use the time to firm up your evidence ready for the day when it can be used, either to assist the police case or for your civil litigation.

Ah, do I hear a cry of 'wait a minute, Peter' there? Surely you can't use the same evidence for civil and criminal cases that are simultaneously running? Well, regardless of what some police officers may tell you, you can. The problem is that you can't have the evidence in two places at once, so particularly for high volume fraud cases it is easier and cleaner to give the police a few of the best evidential examples for the criminal case and to work on the rest to evaluate the civil case. However, in many such cases that I worked on in my last job, we were able to give our best examples, but still used them in the civil case scenario. This was partly because we had gathered our initial evidence to criminal standards, partly because we did the initial fact-finding investigation and not the police and partly because if they subsequently formed part of a criminal award back to us we then deducted the value from the sum we were claiming in the civil courts, while still using the evidence to influence the outcome of our case.

One of the long-term advantages of having started the civil action and then putting it on hold during the criminal case is that freezing orders and monies paid to the court—or a neutral third party—get the fraudster used to the idea that they no longer have that sum of money available to them. Psychologically this can make a big difference and make it much easier after the criminal case to get your hands on the sum that you wanted back in the first place.

The 'phoney war' scenario

Once you have started civil proceedings, whether or not there is a twin-tracked criminal case, you will enter what is best described as the 'phoney war' period, when little appears to be going on apart from increasingly irascible letters from your solicitors to theirs and similar veined replies from their solicitors to yours. My cynical view of this period is that it justifies the solicitor's monthly bill, as I don't think they can bring themselves to produce one without new charges on it!

Be prepared for the strident and robust tones of the legal correspondence, which can often come as a bit of a shock when your organisation would normally correspond in polite, balanced and measured exchanges. It is largely 'puff' and frankly I have sometimes pointed out to my solicitors that I don't believe a suggested letter needs to be that emotive to get the desired result. Once the initial bow shots have been fired and both sets of solicitors have tried to send their most robust letters suggesting that the other party should fold and throw in their hand, it will settle down to a series of attempts by the opposition to throw your investigation off-track, either by raising irrelevant issues or by demanding detail that you can't yet or don't yet want to provide.

The civil court judge will allocate a time when both parties' legal representatives will meet with the court for a case management hearing. Everything that you are going to rely upon will not only need to be ready for that hearing it will also have to be disclosed to the opposition's solicitors in sufficient time for them to have considered it before the hearing. It will include any witness statements, summaries and documents. If, for any reason, either your opposition or you think that the other party is not disclosing something relevant that they hold, then either party can make reasonable enquiries to get 'discovery' before the case management hearing. It is only once the case management hearing has taken place that either a date will be set or the judge will ask for some actions within a given timescale before a court date will be set. Almost certainly at this stage, particularly if neither party is showing any willingness to negotiate a settlement, the judge will order a mediation day before the court is prepared to see the case.

Mediation by mutual consent of the parties

In an ideal world both sets of solicitors see reason with the case and you sit down and mediate by mutual arrangement. If you can reach that position it is a better option than court-ordered mediation as you won't have to pay for a mediator provided by the court, which can be surprisingly expensive, as it will probably be a part-time judge or someone of similar legal standing.

In my experience, you are more likely to get mediation by mutual agreement when the criminal case has come home. That focuses the mind of the now-convicted fraudster and the gap between conviction and sentencing, where there is one, will often encourage the fraudster to be seen to do a deal, in the hope of a lighter sentence.

I have some fond memories of mediation by mutual agreement although in one instance, where we didn't have a realistic chance of a criminal prosecution, it did backfire a little and we only recovered just about enough to cover our legal costs to that point—and that proved to be a hard fight. With that one exception, our other cases proved more fruitful and much easier to get a result.

With this type of mediation, you can either leave it to the solicitor or you can do it yourself with the solicitor acting as your adviser on the day. I have done both, depending on circumstances—and neither approach is better or worse than the other, it just depends on the particular circumstances of the case and the nature of the opposition. Either way, or any combination between the two, it will involve detailed case meetings with your solicitor to agree how you will approach the opposition and also to determine and agree your strategy for mediation.

The overall strategy should not be dissimilar to any other type of negotiation. You need to determine your ideal, realistic and fallback positions and prepare the evidence that you'll need on the day accordingly. It is often quite useful to make a starting position offer, to put the opposition on the back foot if you can. The approach that we favoured was to offer just in advance of the mediation day that we would settle for an all-in sum and no further legal action would be taken against them. The reason for this was to encourage them that they would save a day's legal costs and also to show the courts later, if all went wrong, that we had been trying to make a reasonable attempt to resolve our dispute.

Real case: Example of mutual mediation—The linguist who was lost for words

We had a bit of luck with one of our linguist cases, not only did we get a criminal conviction for all of the '10 best' examples that we gave to the police, but also the judge in the criminal case was known to have a harsh view of fraudsters. In the gap between conviction and sentencing the counsel and solicitors for the fraudster approached us with a view to a settlement—it was obvious to us that they were desperate to go back to court with the civil case resolved before the judge passed sentence.

In this instance my Head of Investigations and I decided that we would participate directly in the negotiations ourselves, with our solicitor present to step in if necessary, but mainly there to cover the legal aspects that had to be done on the day. The fraudster turned up with his criminal case barrister, a sharp and well-spoken individual who, as it turned out, was clearly only focused on criminal law and hadn't grasped the subtleties of a civil action. They didn't have a separate solicitor with them and in the end my experienced Head of Investigations and I made mincemeat of them both, all our solicitor had to do was hold the coats.

They started off by challenging the validity of our evidence beyond the '10 best' cases that we'd given to the police for the criminal case. For every type of fraud that had been committed my Head of Investigations gently placed different cast iron examples from our schedule of false claims in front of the opposing QC. On each occasion a dialogue passed between the two of them, the QC then tried to raise some implausible objections, we saw them off between us and eventually the QC conceded the point and we went on to the next one. This went on for a little while, until it became more and more apparent that they were running out of arguments and ideas to challenge our evidence.

Once it was clear to all that the validity of our evidence had been conceded, the QC tried a different tack. He looked airily at me. 'You took out a rather belated freezing order on my client.' That was true, but as it had been granted and upheld, I said nothing and just gently grinned. It seemed to infuriate him and his next outburst unintentionally finished his own client off, all I had to do afterwards was give the smoking embers a gentle but firm prod. 'Have you taken out a freezing order in any other similar cases,' he asked rather peremptorily. 'Yes,' I replied. 'And how much was the last one for?' 'A quarter of a million pounds.' At that point his client reached out for a full glass of water and started to raise it to his lips with a rather unsteady hand; it didn't escape my attention. Before the QC could stop himself he fell into his own trap. He gave me his best haughty look. 'And how much did you recover at the end of that case?' I leant forward and looked straight at him, with just the slightest hint of a smile. 'The whole amount.' Whatever the QC was about to say next was interrupted by a choking sound from his client, who proceeded to swallow the rest of the contents of his glass of water as quickly as he could, while scattering a fair bit of it over the table in front of him as he was shaking so much. We got our full settlement within 10 minutes.

Mediation ordered by the court

Mediation ordered by the court will start off as a formal affair. A mediator will be selected and both parties have to agree to meet the mediator's costs. A day will be set aside but in effect the mediation will be expected to last until either a deal is done or a point of irreconcilable difference is reached. Neither party can really afford to be seen as the one that walked away to scupper a deal, as it can strongly influence the views of the judge about final settlement when the case comes to court. And since these cases are only heard in front of a judge, it isn't helpful to be seen to be the party dragging your feet unless you have good reason.

Although you won't want to be seen as the villain of the piece if mediation fails, with a good case you will be in a stronger position than the opposition and can afford to play the game of poker longer than they can. But be prepared, it will be labour-intensive on the day and eventually it will be you, not the solicitor, who will have to take the final decision about the amount of settlement and whether or not to settle.

Proceedings will start with preliminary discussions between the mediator and the opposition and the mediator and your team. You will usually be billeted in separate rooms from the opposition for the mediation. At this stage the mediator is just taking each side through the rules of engagement for the day and sounding them out about their expectations of any settlement.

The mediator will then often act almost as an agent provocateur, suggesting to your side that you are being over-ambitious or asking if you could settle for a lower figure than originally suggested and suggesting to the opposition that they need to be prepared to offer more than they have stated in private to the mediator. Strength of case determines the position here but there is a long way to go at this stage, so don't feel obliged to go soft because the mediator suggests it. The mediator won't start talking possible settlement sums anyway until they feel that they have got both parties into the same ball park.

If you do reach a point when the mediator is pressing for changes that are within the game plan for settlement, then it is at this stage that decisions need to be taken about how much of your costs and lost interest since the case started you are prepared to sacrifice in return for a clean deal on the day. Both parties will be expected to sacrifice on costs, as they are saving the cost of the rest of the legal process if they do settle through the mediation.

A final word on tactics. If you have, as you should for this route, a strong case and for whatever reason the opposition won't get into the ball park, not even within range of your fallback position, it is unfortunate but it isn't the end of the world if you don't settle on the day. It doesn't preclude a further round of mediation—although probably an unlikely outcome—and it doesn't preclude further direct negotiations between the two parties in the run-up to the hearing.

Real case: Example of court-ordered mediation— A settlement that exceeded expectations

In one particularly difficult case we had a fraudster who fought us tooth and nail every inch of the way through the civil proceedings. His lawyer and accountant specialised in ridiculous challenges and requests for spurious information. We stayed proceedings for the criminal case, which eventually convicted on 8 out of 10 of our best examples. The case dragged on and we had been unable to find any justification that would warrant us taking out a freezing order, so we had only the criminal conviction as leverage at the mediation.

Before the mediation day we offered to settle the whole case, with each party bearing their own legal costs, in return for £210k from the fraudster. The fraudster's lawyers made a counter-offer of £38k and that was the position that we took with us into the mediation. On the surface it was an insurmountable gap between the sides.

The fraudster had hired a particularly expensive but good law firm to put their side to the mediator and we had our usual competent solicitors supporting our side. Because the case was complex—a classic small value, high volume fraud (see Chapter 13)—we had to send in a complete investigative team of three and stacks of documentation to support the evidence for our claim. In addition they had a solicitor and assistant and my Head of Investigations coordinated the team there on that day. Negotiations started early but the initial indication from our solicitors was that they thought a deal would be reached by early afternoon. On the back of that we agreed that the team would contact me when the deal was near and I would come over to take the final decision on whether we would settle or not.

The hours went by and I began to get concerned as no contact was forthcoming. Eventually, concerned, I wandered across to the negotiation rooms in the late afternoon to see what was happening. I arrived to find that they were just about to contact me as the first offer had finally been made (we later discovered that there had been earlier offers but the mediator had considered them so paltry that he hadn't bothered to waste our time by putting them to our team). The first offer we were aware of was therefore to settle for £177k, a considerable improvement on the fraudster's first offer of £38k and only £33k short of our starting position. We discussed it at length. I thought about it and informed the mediator that we were turning the offer down. I got some curious looks from one or two of our negotiating team, who thought we had done well to get that far. I was adamant that if they were prepared to get that close they'd get closer.

An uncomfortable couple of hours passed, by which time it was getting quite late in the day (we were already into an extra payment to the mediator as it was beyond the normally allocated time for a settlement), when a further offer came in at around £200k and we then seriously started to pass counter-offers back and forth about how much interest and costs each side would forgo.

Eventually when it was all drawn up both parties signed up to a payment in full settlement to us of £238k. It was only after we had packed up and had time to relax that the truth dawned on us. We had walked into the mediation prepared to settle all-in for £210k but after a hard day's negotiation had walked away with £238k! The fraudster's legal team had ended up costing him £28k more than we would have settled for without the mediation. It was an unexpected bonus for the day's efforts.

▦ TRACING ORDERS AND OTHER WEAPONS

Tracing orders come into play if either you haven't been able to get a freezing order or your fraudster has done a runner or has no apparent cash asset that can be recovered. They enable you to get a legal claim over the money owed, provided you have either a successful civil claim, a court judgement in your favour or grounds for seeking one (such as bankruptcy of a company through fraud), at which point your lawyers can trace the route that the missing asset took once it passed into the possession of the fraudster and legally acquire the asset in whatever form it now takes.

For example, if Freddie Fraudulent has taken his stolen cash and bought a painting or a car with it, then you can claim the painting or the car instead of the cash, provided that only your money was used to buy it. It gets more complicated if it has only bought part of the asset. If the asset has increased in value, in some circumstances you can also get back the profit made from it as well. The same principles apply to property although it can be a nightmare where the fraudster doesn't cooperate.

There are a whole variety of related orders, including search orders, which can also be used to try to discover assets owed by a fraudster. It is far better if at all possible to get in at the start and freeze assets or get signed agreements for the handover of assets. For instance, in cases where monies have been fraudulently obtained and turned into property investments, it is perfectly feasible to exchange a freezing order for a charge over property owned by the villain, provided that there is sufficient asset value in it. However, once you are going down the tracing-order route, the chances are that it is going to be a very long time before you see any of your assets, if at all.

I am not going to say any more about tracing orders and the like, as the concept is simple but the art complex and a matter that legal and accounting experts specialise in and charge accordingly. It is a very quick way to have the meter running hot on your legal and accounting costs, especially if the asset has moved through several hands or resides outside the UK.

▮ USING EXPERT WITNESSES TO BEST ADVANTAGE

With any civil case you will, unfortunately, have to find your way through the minefield—and cost—of using expert witnesses. In my experience, with one very notable exception, they never came cheap. When solicitors are estimating the costs of a civil action they are usually mainly thinking about their costs, the cost of counsel, court fees and so on. However, for any financial information you are now going to need, as a minimum, an independent forensic accountant who will examine your work looking for faults and then write a report for the solicitor, to whom they will report for pay and rations purposes (but don't worry the solicitor will pass the full cost on to you later!), although the working relationship will almost certainly be an iterative one between the forensic accountant and the internal investigative team.

So, what will the expert witness forensic accountant be doing for their money?

First, they will have been independently selected—you may make a few suggestions and hopefully the solicitor will get the hint but for civil actions you won't be able to choose your favoured forensic accountant. Strangely, the courts might not think that you have been entirely objective in your choice if you do it yourself! (It is a different matter if you find you need a forensic accountant during your investigation, then you can select your own, by whatever criteria are appropriate for the work that you want them to do—but if you do this and end up going to court, you will generally need a second forensic accountant to confirm that what they did for you has been done appropriately.)

There are certain forensic accountants who specialise in court work and who are used to being an expert witness. They are usually the best choice. However, don't just roll over with whoever your solicitor comes up with or colleagues suggest, ask to see their track record in court. And by this I don't mean the track record of their firm if they're part of a larger organisation. I want to know about the track record of the individual or individuals that I'm being offered and for whom I'll have to pay. Some basic questions you need to ask are

- Are they more used to defence than prosecuting?
- What is their percentage of being on the winning side?
- How often have they actually stood up in court and given evidence?

If they are more used to defence than prosecuting but have a high success rate then it wouldn't worry me—but I would expect at least a 90% on the winning side from their history. If their track record shows that they haven't been in court that often then any loss above one case would make me concerned that they simply didn't yet know enough about winning the case for their client. I wouldn't want them to cut their teeth on my case— I'd rather have a more experienced forensic accountant with a personal track record of successful evidence-giving in court.

I once had the forensic accounting specialists of a major accounting firm bid for a piece of work, and when I cross-questioned them I teased out that their leading 'expert' had only been a witness in court four times and had lost one of those four cases. That simply wasn't good enough and I went to a specialist with a longer and better track record.

Unfortunately quality costs, hence my point earlier about litigation being potentially an expensive route to take. However, if you are going to end up in court, it is better to go in with the best expert witness that you can afford, as they are far more likely to provide a clear professional evaluation to the judge.

In a number of our cases we used a forensic accountant who was a defence specialist but understood—and had written books about—how the court system works with expert evidence. He had hardly ever lost a case but sadly died suddenly a few years ago. For most of our cases we used his expertise to re-examine the way we were presenting our evidence.

None of our cases ever got to the actual civil court proceedings as in every instance our opposition folded before we got there, albeit on one occasion just the night before—it pays to keep your nerve in this game of poker! This was partly down to our good case preparation and quality of evidence and partly to the additional explanatory and presentational points that we had to do to satisfy our forensic accountant expert before he was prepared to sign off our work as accurate for court purposes. Once the opposition's experts looked at our prepared material, they were advising their clients that they needed to settle with us.

General principles and axioms **from Chapter 16**

- Only consider civil litigation on those rare occasions when it is the most appropriate route to recover the fraudster's ill-gotten gains. It is an expensive business and the cost can outweigh any gain.

- In considering whether to institute civil proceedings, first, decide whether the fraud is sufficiently large enough to be cost-effective and, second, whether the fraudster is likely to have the wherewithal to repay you.

- If you are going down the civil litigation route for recovery and you have the opportunity to take out a freezing order, go for it!

- When considering whether to go for a freezing order you must show sufficient grounds to have it granted. A key ground is if you believe there is a risk that the fraudster's ill-gotten gains will be dissipated before you can recover them.

- If any of your freezing affidavits later turn out to be untrue and you should have known it, you can find yourself personally answerable to the court.

- Although the freezing order will be for a specific amount, its immediate practical effect is to freeze all the assets and accounts of the fraudster

- You are under no obligation to tell the fraudster—or their legal representative—that you are taking out the freezing order; it is a one-sided procedure.

- Once an order is granted the opposition will have the opportunity to object to all or part of the freezing order.

- Criminal cases for fraud or corruption are rarely successful. For every high-profile prosecution and conviction there is a whole mountain that never got past the Crown Prosecution Service when the police submitted the paperwork.

- Never, ever, rely on a criminal investigation to bring home a successful outcome for a fraud case.

- The golden rule: if you can't recover your money without civil litigation, start the civil case as soon as you can.

- The criminal case, once launched by a police investigation, takes priority over the civil case. This is why I can't emphasise enough the need to get your civil case started, if there is to be one, before the police have really got under way.

- Regardless of what some police officers may tell you, you can use the same evidence of fraud for the criminal and the civil case. (But you can't have the evidence in two places at once, so it is easier and cleaner to give the police a few of the best evidential examples for the criminal case and to work on the rest to evaluate the civil case.)

■   One of the long-term advantages of starting the civil action and then putting it on hold during the criminal case is that freezing orders and monies paid to the court get the fraudster used to the idea that they no longer have that sum of money available to them.

■   You are more likely to get mediation by mutual agreement and a settlement of the civil case when the criminal case has resulted in a conviction.

■   Be prepared, court-ordered mediation will be labour- intensive on the day and eventually it will be you, not the solicitor, who will have to take the final decision about the amount of settlement and whether or not to settle.

■   With any civil case you will have to find your way through the minefield— and cost—of using expert witnesses. They rarely come cheap.

■   There are forensic accountants who specialise in court work and who are used to being an expert witness. They are usually the best choice. However, ask to see their track record in court before agreeing to them.

■   Quality will cost, hence my point about litigation being potentially an expensive route to take. However, if you are going to end up in court, it is better to go in with the best expert witness that you can afford.

Part VI

PART SIX

Fraud in context

CHAPTER SEVENTEEN

Fraud risks, fraud awareness and whistle-blowing

CHAPTER**SUMMARY**

A ssessing the risk of fraud in an organisation. The benefits of fraud awareness training in preventing and detecting fraud. Fraud hotlines and whistle-blowing. Strategic aspects of fraud awareness.

ASSESSING THE RISK OF FRAUD IN THE ORGANISATION

One of the main difficulties in assessing the likely risk of fraud in your organisation is that the actual level of fraud at any point in time will always be an unknown factor. The only way to estimate with any degree of potential accuracy is to know where all the weaknesses lie within the business controls of the organisation and where things have gone wrong before and frauds have come to light. Even then, the cleverest fraudsters may well be committing frauds that are unlikely to see the light of day.

Measuring the level of fraud more generally within the UK has been a matter that has exercised both the government and all the major accounting bodies that provide forensic and investigative services. Known frauds are often expressed as a small proportion of actual frauds, perhaps no more than 10%, but there is no sure way of knowing this. It is a concern within organisations where I have worked that has troubled me as well. There has to be reliable ways within an organisation to allocate resources but how do you determine how much effort needs to go into anti-fraud work when you don't know how much fraud is happening to the organisation in the first place?

One answer to this conundrum is to conduct a full fraud risk assessment and use the results of that to determine how much resource should go into anti-fraud work. Those of you with an audit or risk management background will be familiar with the concept of risk analysis of an organisation. As the Chief Internal Auditor of two different government organisations over 20 years I had a risk analysis model of the organisation that fed into my rolling audit needs assessment, determining priorities and level of need for audit resources but for much of that time I had no objective means of linking this to the need for investigative staff and resources.

In recent years the inability to determine the need for investigative resources by something more scientific than the reply I usually got from my Head of Investigations when I asked the question had troubled me. (After a discussion about next year's budget bid and how I would allocate my available resources between auditors and investigators he would look at me, smile gently and comment 'Well, Peter, we're always busy!') Towards the end of my tenure at Scotland Yard we did finally develop a separate fraud risk analysis that built on the model that I had developed for determining internal audit need. While I cannot guarantee that it is by any means perfect, I offer this general model as a logical means by which you can assess the risk of fraud within your organisation.

■ A MODEL FOR ASSESSING THE RISK OF FRAUD IN AN ORGANISATION

Step 1 is to identify all the business activity of the organisation and, where it is known, the level and adequacy of internal control in each business activity. I had this as the basic core of the risk analysis model that I used for determining my audit need. I measured certain factors and by that I could develop a simple arithmetic model that enabled me to determine the inherent level of risk in each business system. The factors I found most useful to measure were

- expenditure;
- income;
- other funds affected (e.g., investments, where expenditure might be small but a huge chunk of the organisation's assets could be at risk);
- adequacy of control;
- sensitivity (e.g., whether a system failure would be a PR disaster or cause senior management to resign);
- time since the last audit;
- impact on the organisation of a catastrophic failure in the system; and
- likelihood of a catastrophic failure in the system.

It is a golden rule that in any risk assessment methodology the scoring system has to be simple and consistent, if it is to be able to make any meaningful comparisons.

My risk factors were all scored on a five-point scale, where 5 was the worst or most significant and 1 was the best or least significant. For the three items expressed in monetary value, I took the range of values that could be there and divided them across the five-point scale. This had the desired effect as well of giving due weight to income, as the organisation spent five times more than it earned (I always consider each £1 of income is worth £5 of expenditure, since you only know what you can see of income—you don't know what has been suppressed. But you can always see all your expenditure, even if it hasn't gone quite where you expected it to go. So by having a five-point scale for income and the same scale for expenditure, although expenditure was five times as much, each point on the income scale became worth five times the monetary value for expenditure). They were then added together and taken as a percentage of the maximum score, so that they could be ranked for each system in the organisation.

The model was designed for both current and inherent risk (current risk being the assessment at the moment when we 'turned the handle' and

inherent risk being the innate risk of the system compared with other systems, regardless of any current or immediate information). Once this was
completed at the beginning of the planning cycle I always checked its reality, both by going through it with my senior management team but also by
seeing all the top management of the organisation and taking their views
on where they saw the risks in their area of the business. Armed with this,
phase 1 of the model was now complete and it could be used to determine
high, medium and low-risk systems for audit work. Its output now needed
to be re-configured and enhanced to use for a fraud risk analysis.

Step 2 was to look at all the business systems and group them according
to the type of fraud risk that they might face. For example, what was the risk
of cash theft for the payroll system? What was the risk of corruption in the
procurement system? And so on. Eventually this gave a grouping of systems
with similar fraud risks to each other. Each group was then weighted in
two ways: first, in accordance with the risk score from the risk analysis
model and, second, according to known frauds and attempted frauds that
affected each system within the group. A combination of this then gave an
overall ranking of the particular fraud risk for the organisation.

While we kept the scoring on this as 'behind the scenes' supporting data
for the model for use of resources that I put to our Audit Committee and my
management, to develop awareness in the organisation and to visualise
our model more effectively the output was used to produce a giant sliced
pie chart with the key fraud risks identified and colour-coded in ranked
groups. It proved a very useful tool for fraud awareness training where it
was quickly dubbed 'the Wheel of Misfortune' by police officers and middle
managers!

Such a model will obviously vary from organisation to organisation,
but I suspect that the generic risks and the general batting order that came
out of the model are probably true of every public body and authority and
many of the medium and larger sized organisations in the private sector.

What the fraud risk model showed for us was a generic batting order as
follows: [1]

■ Lowest risk (of frauds or significant value to any frauds committed)
   —false loan applications by staff
   —false property theft claims by staff

■ Low risk
   —working while on sick leave

—deceased pensioners still paid
—theft of cash

▪ Medium risk
—ghosts or echoes on the payroll
—employment under false pretences
—dishonest use of corporate credit cards

▪ High risk
—roster manipulation for allowances
—false overtime claims
—inflated or duplicate invoices for goods supplied

▪ Highest risk
—local theft of cash received
—false creation of suppliers
—unauthorised purchasing
—inappropriate supplier relationships
—invoices for goods or services not supplied.

In all we were able to identify 43 main areas of likely fraud and about 60 risks of different types of fraud in total. One of the many interesting points that came out of this work was the realisation that most of our biggest fraud risks lay in the area of procurement where, by and large, when things went wrong the amount of money at risk was considerable.

One of the low risks of fraud identified was the theft of monies within the organisation, by this I mean funds put into bank accounts to run various activities. It was a comfort in a way that the methodology threw this out as relatively low-risk, as the reason why I had gone to the Met in the first place had been to sort out the mess after a major scandal broke when it was discovered that the then number 2 in Finance had helped himself to just over £5m from the funds for a covert operation over a period of almost eight years.

Equally though, this shows the difficulty in getting an accurate assessment of fraud risks. The £5m fraud is still at the time of writing the most significant fraud that has come to light ever perpetrated by a police official on their own organisation in the UK and is only exceeded for any official across the public services by Gordon Foxley's audacious and corrupt behaviour in dealing with the procurement of ordnance at the MoD in the 1980s. As such, although clearly a rare event, it only takes one such fraud to have a major and catastrophic effect on an organisation. The question we had to ask ourselves was: Should more credence be given to likelihood or impact? Our view here was that it was now 14 years since the scandal, there hadn't been one of such size before it and at the time of writing there hasn't been one of similar size since. So, on balance, we had to rate the chances as about as likely as a major catastrophe bringing the whole of London to a complete standstill.

THE BENEFITS OF FRAUD AWARENESS TRAINING IN PREVENTING AND DETECTING FRAUD

It has become increasingly popular as part of good governance to raise levels of fraud awareness among staff in an organisation. Apart from the obvious benefit of ensuring that employees are more likely to recognise and report fraud to the right authorities as a result, it also in my experience has two other benefits. It helps get the moral tone of the organisation right, in turn reducing the risks of certain frauds being perpetrated and, second, it also generates information about current and potential frauds that can then be pursued at an earlier stage than might otherwise have happened.

If you work in local government or public authorities, there is a very useful toolkit called Changing Organisational Cultures developed by the Audit Commission that can be used as the starting point for fraud awareness training. It has been recommended in the 10th Report by the Parliamentary Committee on Standards in Public Life for use by all public-sector organisations. Although it starts with some basic (but important) statements about culture and controls, it gives a sound basis for fraud awareness training and enables the organisation to be able to benchmark itself with other public authorities, before and after a programme of fraud awareness training.

For those that are not in a position to use the Audit Commission's toolkit it is based around a number of concepts and steps that can be applied to any organisation. The key ingredients are

1. A survey across the organisation of the current level of fraud awareness and what is—or isn't seen—as appropriate behaviour around fraud.
2. Workshops to discuss ethical scenarios, anonymous voting to see where people really stand on specific scenarios, coupled with comparison of the group with the organisation and wider bodies.

3. Tests of the degree of knowledge of how fraud should be reported and the routes available to managers and staff to report fraud.
4. Genuine case studies based around frauds that have happened at the organisation with lessons to be learned.
5. Reinforcement of the message from the very top.
6. Follow-up programme to keep awareness levels up and to test whether attitudes and knowledge have improved since the original survey.

The benefit of the toolkit for those bodies that are entitled to use it is that the Audit Commission will trap results anonymously on its own website and then feed back those results for your organisation alongside benchmarking information from the wider public sector. Although this is based on pre-set questions each organisation can tailor additional questions. We certainly needed to do that so that we could capture demographic information about the employees who were responding to the questionnaire. In my last job we also needed to amend some of the individual wording to avoid misinterpretation of specific questions in the context of our organisation.

When we ran the workshops they were a joint effort with the Audit Commission. We wrote to all staff beforehand and told them that the workshops were going to happen. Because of the sheer size of our organisation (over 50,000 employees) it wasn't viable to run half-day workshops for all staff. Instead we deliberately targeted top management, middle management and those with significant financial responsibilities. They were all asked to complete the initial questionnaire and then participate in a workshop.

At the same time we prepared a shortened version for top management. That in itself was, to my mind, one of the successes of using this approach. Top management enjoyed a shorter workshop, stayed, paid attention and bought in to the messages from the workshops. It meant that we could send out the summary material prepared for us by the Audit Commission with a ringing endorsement from the very top about the value of the fraud awareness programme, particularly the ethical scenario training and the lessons that could be learned from it.

▨ WHISTLE-BLOWING ARRANGEMENTS AND THEIR PLACE IN FRAUD AWARENESS AND DETECTION

I've already set out the issues around the use of informants/covert human intelligence sources during an investigation in Chapter 5 'Gathering and using intelligence and evidence'; this section is instead about what can be done as an organisation to ensure that the mechanisms are there to enable effective whistle-blowing arrangements. By and large these are aimed at existing and former employees, although occasionally they may involve members of the public.

The Public Interest Disclosure Act and Public Concern at Work

Fraud whistle-blowing can either be to an external body, senior management, the Audit Committee or to part of the organisation that is there to investigate fraud. It is covered by the Public Interest Disclosure Act (PIDA) of 1998, which applies equally to the public and private sectors as well as charities. PIDA is intended to cover all forms of malpractice that an employee might wish to report without fear of reprisal or punishment, provided that the employee has acted in good faith and is neither malicious nor mendacious. It includes health and safety issues and illegal actions by companies (e.g., shipping arms to a banned country). It encourages all organisations to have appropriate internal arrangements for whistle-blowing and the law expects that these routes are exhausted before any whistle-blower goes public with their accusation.

PIDA also provides protection in law for whistle-blowers where an employee has a contract or former employee a compromise agreement forbidding whistle-blowing, provided that the whistle-blower has acted in accordance with the wider public interest and not for any personal reasons.

In general, most large organisations now have both internal and external arrangements for dealing appropriately with whistle-blowers and employees have a choice of route depending on their circumstances. A charitable organisation called Public Concern at Work, founded five years before PIDA was passed, exists to act as the external whistle-blowing route of organisations' employees where the employer has paid for the independent external whistle-blowing resource to be provided by it. It also provides training to employers and employees on how to go about whistle-blowing and responding appropriately to concerns raised by a whistle-blower. Its website provides guidance and advice on how PIDA may—or may not—apply to a particular circumstance.

Despite the view on Public Concern at Work's website that the vast majority of whistle-blowers are dealt with fairly and their concerns addressed by their organisations without the need to take the matter further, my own experience has been that whistle-blowers in organisations generally have a hard time of it if they are reporting fraud or corruption. In some spectacular cases the organisation itself has gone under and the whistle-blower has along with their colleagues lost their job. In others the organisation's management has rounded on the whistle-blower and they have found it difficult to get a fair outcome for their concerns.

Whistle-blowing and the investigator

There are two different aspects of whistle-blowing to bear in mind for the internal investigator or auditor. First, it is a potential route to the start of an investigation as the whistle-blower may provide the initial allegation that kicks off an investigation. Wherever possible, you should therefore aim to ensure that your organisation's internal whistle-blowing arrangements give the opportunity for employees to contact your investigators or you directly with their concerns.

In my last organisation we set up an automated internal fraud hotline which staff and contractors could contact 24 hours a day to leave messages that we would then follow up within a guaranteed working day of when the message had been left. At intervals and when we conducted fraud awareness training, staff would be reminded of the hotline and its purpose. We always guaranteed confidentiality but not necessarily anonymity, as by the nature of some of the matters that might be reported, that simply wasn't possible.

Generally the response to our fraud hotline wasn't that great, despite efforts to market it. We got a few good cases out of it, including a major investigation into corporate credit card abuse, but also a lot of wrong referrals, where employees had discrimination or bullying concerns about which we could do little other than try and put them in touch with the appropriate individual in HR. Another problem was that we also had a number of cases over the years of malicious fraud reporting by employees seeking revenge on colleagues, when these became apparent we then investigated the individual who had made the false report of fraud.

The second aspect of whistle-blowing relevant to the internal investigator or auditor is that by the very nature of the fact-finding enquiries that an investigator will conduct in a case, they may discover matters management would rather suppress, creating a potential for the investigator themselves to become a whistle-blower.

If you find yourself in a scenario where you could be a whistle-blower on your own senior management, my advice is to be very clear about what you need to do and weigh up the potential consequences of any actions that you may take. If at all possible, you have to raise the matter first with your own line management and try to persuade them to push for the organisation to do the right thing. If you are unable to persuade them, or they are complicit in the matter that you have discovered, then you have to try going directly to the top person in the organisation.

I have been a whistle-blower only once in my career and I well remember the considerable stress and strain that my family and I were put under as a consequence. It had all started innocently enough when one of my audit staff came in one morning looking a little smug. She then informed me that she knew who had won an outsourcing contract for the organisation, as her partner was a close friend of the managing director of the winning bidder and the two had discussed it at the local conservative club the previous night. I was somewhat underwhelmed and pointed out that she had to be mistaken, the short-listing had still to take place, let alone award of contract. She checked with her partner that night and reported back the next day that it was indeed just as she'd told me. We thought about this and waited to see the eventual outcome. Sure enough, two months later the contract was awarded to that self-same company and our suspicions were fully aroused.

On the day the award of contract was officially announced I seized all the papers and commenced an immediate investigation. After working through the seized documents, I discovered that my own line manager had personally taken the final decision and signed the suspect award of contract. We carried on with our investigation despite that but when I wrote the matter up I went above my boss's head directly to the top man in the organisation.

Even before the opprobrium that was heaped on me for daring to by-pass my boss, I had already been put under considerable strain by senior managers. During the period between starting the investigation, when I received various discouraging and threatening remarks from the two senior colleagues who knew what I would find, through to the point when I fell out of favour with my own boss once I had discovered his involvement, I was put under increasing pressure to abandon the investigation and not take it to its logical conclusion. Every time I attended any management meetings I would be berated about my single-mindedness in pursuing the matter. I was made to feel petty and stupid for pursuing it and repeatedly told I was vindictive rather than motivated by the desire to get to the truth. Eventually I withdrew from all meetings involving these senior colleagues or my boss.

Once I issued my investigation report directly to the head of the organisation, by-passing my normal reporting line, two things happened. First, I was effectively ostracised by my boss and his colleagues and, second, I was given a new temporary boss who himself was ordered to investigate me and my investigation. (I found out later that on receipt of my report the top man had rung up my boss and berated him for his lack of control in letting a member of his own staff bypass him! Then, of course, the top man had actually read my report and realised that he had to do something.)

The member of my staff who had originally thought that she was just giving me a bit of inside info was horrified by what had happened and the pressure that was heaped on me personally. It may seem a strange thing to say, but ultimately I was grateful for what happened. I wouldn't want anyone to go through what I went through in those months at work, but it taught me far more about my own character and resilience under pressure than I could ever have learnt without it. In a crisis of conscience at work most of us hope that we would do the right thing, even if it was unpopular with our peers and management, but until it actually happens you don't know if you really have the strength of mind and ethical clarity in your own head to come through it in one piece.

Eventually, three months later and six months after the start of my investigation my new boss concluded that I had been right all along. My reward for this was to be called to a secret meeting with the head of the organisation who told me that I must have the hide of an elephant to do what I had done. He agreed with my findings, noted that what I had uncovered was gross incompetence by officials trying to engineer a particular result—rather than corruption—and then proceeded to tell me that he was burying my investigation, as what I had found was too politically embarrassing to see the light of day.

I knew at that point that my career was finished there and I looked round immediately for another job, which by chance I was able to get without the need to resign or fight my previous employer in the courts. I had a young family to think of at the time and although I was determined to stick to my principles with the investigation I was equally determined not to put their circumstances at risk by making any futile grand gesture that wouldn't change anything.

My advice to anyone who finds themselves in similar circumstances over a fraud investigation is to do whatever you can internally within the organisation to put matters right but if they won't do the right thing then you must find a way to leave, it is no longer the organisation for you. Whether or not you then choose to go down the external whistle-blower route will depend on the circumstances—and how much harm it may do to your own family if you do. If you can afford to speak up and deal with the stress that follows then by all means do so, but don't put your health and well-being at risk unnecessarily; it isn't you that has done wrong it is those that you are pursuing. It is a sad fact worth bearing in mind that life isn't fair and very few get their just desserts, either good citizens or villains.

STRATEGIC ASPECTS OF FRAUD AWARENESS

If the organisation is to stand any chance in the fight against fraud then it is important to make sure that it has the structural elements in place to encourage employees and contractors to behave ethically at work. At the highest level the organisation needs an anti-fraud and corruption strategy approved by the board or top management and published in overview documents or websites about the organisation.

The most important aspect of a good anti-fraud and corruption strategy is that it mustn't get bogged down in the detail of process. Far too often organisations produce laudable but dry tomes that then deteriorate into a list of low-level processes, with the end result that only auditors and fraudsters ever bother to read them. Keep it simple and strategic and then you'll be able to link everything else on anti-fraud and corruption, from ethical standards, appropriate use of email and internet access policy through to reporting processes, whistle-blowing arrangements and who will conduct investigations underneath its all-embracing umbrella.

Next, employees and contractors must be individually informed both of their responsibilities not to commit fraud and their duty to report fraud or attempted fraud on the organisation if they find it. For both staff and contractors the contracts should include standard clauses about the dire consequences of a fraudulent act by them. They need to know that you are a zero-tolerance-to-fraud organisation and that transgressors will be punished. Finally there can be a set of procedures provided to employees so that they know how to deal with fraud should it arise in your organisation.

General principles and axioms**from Chapter 17**

■ The actual level of fraud at any point in time will always be an unknown factor. One answer to this conundrum is to conduct a full fraud risk assessment and use the results of that to determine how much resource should go into anti-fraud work.

■ It is a golden rule that in any risk assessment methodology the scoring system has to be simple and consistent, if it is to be able to make any meaningful comparisons.

■ Most of the biggest fraud risks for a public authority lie in the area of procurement where, by and large, when things go wrong the amount of money at risk is considerable.

■ Raising levels of fraud awareness among staff in an organisation ensures that employees are more likely to recognise and report fraud to the right authorities, gets the moral tone of the organisation right and generates information about frauds that can then be pursued.

■ If you work in local government or public authorities, the toolkit called Changing Organisational Cultures developed by the Audit Commission can be used as the starting point for effective fraud awareness training.

■ Fraud awareness training will only work effectively if the very top of the organisation is seen to endorse it both in word and deed.

■ Fraud whistle-blowing can be to an external body, senior management, the Audit Committee or part of the organisation that is there to investigate fraud.

■ My own experience has been that whistle-blowers in organisations generally have a hard time of it if they are reporting fraud or corruption.

■ Whistle-blowing is a potential route to the start of a fraud investigation. Wherever possible, you should ensure that your organisation's internal whistle-blowing arrangements give the opportunity for employees to contact your investigators or you directly with their concerns.

■ By the nature of the fact-finding enquiries that an investigator will conduct in a case, they may discover matters management would rather suppress, creating a potential for the investigator themselves to become a whistle-blower.

■ If you find yourself in a scenario where you could be a whistle-blower on your own senior management, be clear about what you need to do and weigh up the potential consequences of any actions that you may take. Raise the matter first with your own line management. If you are unable to persuade them to act, or they are complicit in the matter, go directly to the top person.

■ Do whatever you can internally within the organisation to put matters right but if they won't do the right thing then you must find a way to leave, it is no longer the organisation for you.

■ It is a sad fact worth bearing in mind that life isn't fair and very few get their just desserts, either good citizens or villains.

■ At the highest level the organisation needs an anti-fraud and corruption strategy approved by the board or top management and published.

■ The most important aspect of a good anti-fraud and corruption strategy is that it mustn't get bogged down in the detail of process.

■ Employees and contractors must be individually informed both of their responsibilities not to commit fraud and their duty to report fraud or attempted fraud on the organisation if they find it.

■ For both staff and contractors, contracts should include standard clauses about the dire consequences of a fraudulent act by them.

■ There should be a set of procedures provided to all employees so that they know how to deal with fraud should it arise in your organisation.

CHAPTER EIGHTEEN

So, you're a fraud-finder too?

CHAPTER**SUMMARY**

This chapter is a series of tests based on the preceding chapters. The tests are self-contained but intended to give you a view of where your own strengths and weaknesses lie with regard to the role of a fraud-finder

 FRAUD BASICS

(you should be able to do this in your sleep; 100% right—what else could I expect?)

Multiple choice scenarios

F1. I rate each £1 of income as equivalent to £5 of expenditure in terms of fraud risk. Is that because

(a) Income frauds are five times more likely to occur
(b) Expenditure is usually higher than income in most organisations
(c) With expenditure you know what you've spent, with income you don't know what you haven't received
(d) Income frauds are usually smaller frauds and the value of what can be recovered is also smaller.

F2. When conducting a surprise cash-up it is important that you

(a) Make sure you know how many cash points or tills there are before you start
(b) Do not go on your own but take a colleague to assist/witness
(c) Keep the cashier with you until the cash-up is completed and they have agreed and witnessed or signed for the cash sums found
(d) All of the above.

F3. Teeming and lading is a precursor to more extensive fraud. But how can you spot a teeming and lading fraud?

(a) By checking the total banked against the amount recorded in the ledger
(b) By comparing cash received with the total banked in each period
(c) By regular reconciliation of paid cheques with bank records
(d) By conducting a surprise cash-up.

F4. When might you want to apply Benford's Law?

(a) To help reconcile cash to bank during a surprise cash check
(b) To find potentially fraudulent patterns in amounts of payments or receipts
(c) To detect missing income
(d) To check whether a company has a valid VAT number.

F5. Benford's Law only works for

(a) The first digit in any numerical value
(b) Numbers of items that are out of sequence
(c) Values of items that are greater than 1
(d) Things that can't be found.

F6. Which one of the following statements is true?

(a) Corruption is easier to prove than fraud   True/False
(b) Stock ledgers and bin cards are the same thing   True/False
(c) Fraud is easier to prove than corruption   True/False
(d) Ponzi frauds are named after the Sicilian town where the first one was discovered.   True/False

F7. Which one of the following statements is false?

(a) There is a legal maxim that fraudsters must not profit from their fraud   True/False
(b) The Fraud Act 2006 defined fraud as a criminal offence for the first time in England, Wales and Northern Ireland   True/False
(c) Bin cards are the most accurate and up-to-date record of stock in a store   True/False
(d) Corruption by its very nature involves two or more corrupt-minded individuals.   True/False

F8. Which of the following should arouse suspicion?

(a) A nervous cashier
(b) Discrepancies in the make-up of the amount banked, but the total banked agrees with the amount received
(c) Someone who is never available to see or who goes sick after you have started your enquiries
(d) A company that only has a mobile phone and an email address as the means of contact
(e) None of (a) to (d)
(f) All of (a) to (d).

F9. Why should you look closely at their expenses when trying to stop a fraudulent manager?

(a) Because they may have left clues in their claims about where the money went
(b) Because it will help identify any accomplices to the fraud
(c) Because they might have defrauded their expenses
(d) Because they are likely to have defrauded their expenses and it is often the easier fraud to prove.

F10. Which of the following is—or isn't—a crime?

(a) Teeming and lading
(b) Borrowing from the petty cash overnight and paying it back
(c) Fiddling the mileage on expenses
(d) Moving jobs without paying back all of a season ticket loan
(e) Keeping an accidental overpayment of salary
(f) Accepting lunch in return for turning a blind eye to a dodgy invoice submitted to your organisation by a contractor.

(1 mark awarded for each correct answer—maximum for 'Basics section' is 15 marks)

Right, that was the easy bit. Now you're suitably warmed up, they get a little tougher to answer!

PLANNING AND MANAGING INVESTIGATIONS

P1. Which of the following individuals should run your investigation for you?

(a) A forensic accountant
(b) A police officer
(c) A lawyer
(d) Any of the above
(e) None of the above.

P2. List three key players who should be present at the initial planning meeting prior to the start of the investigation. *(1 mark for each correct player)*

P3. You should always begin an investigation with

(a) legal advice about the risks
(b) a forensic auditor in support
(c) the end in mind
(d) a formal interview of the potential suspects
(e) an unannounced raid to seize evidence.

P4. On which two of the following should the early effort of a fraud investigation concentrate its priorities?

(a) Stopping the fraud
(b) Finding the fraudster
(c) Getting back the money lost to the fraud
(d) Interviewing the witnesses
(e) Interviewing likely suspects.

P5. Which one of the following is not a recommended 'end in mind'?

(a) Preventing further losses to the fraud
(b) Ridding yourself of a fraudulent contractor or employee
(c) Stopping a fraud where you can't identify the fraudster
(d) Calling the police and waiting for the criminal investigation to start
(e) Stopping collusion between staff and contractors.

P6. What should you try to avoid at all costs late on a Friday afternoon?

(a) Going to the pub or a wine bar
(b) Interviewing a potential suspect
(c) Planning a new investigation
(d) Interviewing the person making the initial allegation
(e) Seizing available evidence.

P7. Expenses can be a short-cut route to

(a) A successful outcome in a fraud investigation
(b) Ensuring that you stay within budget
(c) Finding the missing money in a fraud
(d) Finding out if your own staff are honest.

P8. There are 10 basics of effective fraud investigation management.

The first one is to select the right team for the investigation. Give yourself *1 point* for each of the remaining 9 that you can recall without looking them up. Give yourself a bonus *5 points* if you can recall them all.

P8. If you are the senior investigator on the case you must ensure that

(a) The team is working flat out until the case is cracked
(b) All new evidence passes across your desk and you read it

(c) No one interviews a witness until you say so
(d) All the evidence has been fully documented before you interview
(e) All the evidence is secured before you interview.

P9. The difference between intelligence and evidence is that

(a) There is no difference, it depends how you use the information
(b) Intelligence is innate, evidence has to be discovered
(c) Intelligence may be evidence but evidence can't be intelligence
(d) Intelligence isn't part of your evidence but evidence can form part of your intelligence
(e) Intelligence is communications, verbal or oral, evidence is physical.

P10. When should you administer a PACE caution?

(a) When interviewing a suspect prior to a police investigation
(b) When interviewing a suspect facing internal disciplinary action
(c) When interviewing a suspect after a police investigation has started
(d) When interviewing a witness to the fraud
(e) When a witness unexpectedly confesses to a fraud during an interview.

P11. When gathering evidence you should gather it to the same standard as for a criminal case because

(a) It is a requirement of the police and the courts
(b) It is a simpler way of gathering evidence
(c) It will be admissible if needed for a later criminal case
(d) That is what your lawyer and forensic accountant will expect
(e) You can use the same documentation for civil and criminal cases.

P12. Which of the following statements are true and which are false?

(a) To secure evidence properly it has to be in your own cabinet or cupboard
                                                                        True/False
(b) Original evidence is always best   True/False
(c) Documents must be protected by placing in clear plastic wallets
                                                                      True/False
(d) Electronic images of hard drives are not acceptable as evidence
                                                               True/False
(e) It is better to gather too much evidence rather than too little
                                                            True/False

(f) An ESDA test checks for missing pages in documents   True/False
(g) An ESDA test checks for indentations on the paper   True/False
(h) An ESDA test identifies credit card abuses   True/False
(i) Email traffic can only be used as evidence with the sender's permission.
                                                                 True/False

P13. Witness evidence is best gathered formally. Which of the following methods is acceptable (A) and which isn't? (N)

(a) Using a multi-deck tape machine and microphones   A/N
(b) Using a digital recorder   A/N
(c) Writing it out longhand with the witness   A/N
(d) Taking it down over the telephone   A/N
(e) Interviewing the witness on your own and secretly recording them
                                                                         A/N
(f) With a colleague taking notes   A/N
(g) By writing to the witness and seeking a written signed reply.   A/N

P14. Who or what is a CHIS normally known as? What do the initials stand for?

P15. What do the initials RIPA stand for? What bearing does RIPA have on use of a CHIS?

(total possible marks for 'Planning and managing' section = 50 marks)

Well that was certainly a little harder. For P9 and P10, I will allow *1 mark* for one of the 'wrong' answers as well as *2 marks* for the 'right' answer, since they aren't 100% clearcut. This next section is both harder and easier— you'll see what I mean!

▌ INVESTIGATION TECHNIQUES

It1. What is the primary function of an analyst?

It2. Which of the following skills should an analyst be able to demonstrate?

(a) An ability to understand numbers and be at ease working with them
(b) An ability to use interrogative software (such as ACL, IDEA or i2)

(c) Technical proficiency in extracting data from the main business systems of the organisation
(d) An instinct for fraud
(e) Ability to learn how an investigator hunts out fraud
(f) All of the above
(g) Some of the above (please specify)
(h) None of the above.

It3. Give three advantages and three disadvantages for a spreadsheet as opposed to a database. Which is generally better to use for gathering and presenting financial evidence?

It4. There are three commonly used data interrogation software tools. What are they and how do they differ, if at all?

It5. Covert surveillance in the workplace can be risky and expensive, but can produce good visual and sound evidence of fraud and corruption. Which of the following statements about covert surveillance are true or false?

(a) Covert surveillance at work is illegal if innocent staff are recorded

True/False
(b) It is safer to use a hidden camera than use an undercover agent

True/False
(c) It is legal to record someone travelling from their workplace up to the door of their home address without their knowledge   True/False
(d) Bugging a telephone conversation between yourself and another party is a breach of the Human Rights Act and therefore illegal   True/False
(e) Telephone bugging can only be done by the police and security services

True/False
(f) Electronic sweeps will detect all planted bugs—provided that equipment is turned off before it is swept   True/False
(g) Covert surveillance material can only be used for intelligence and not as evidence unless staff are warned in advance.   True/False

It6. When interviewing a potential suspect what should you try never to do?

(a) Ask a direct question
(b) Ask a question that they can't answer

(c) Ask a question that you don't know the answer to already

(d) Ask a question that you do know the answer to already.

It7. What does the mnemonic PEACE. stand for and who normally uses it?

It8. There are two basic principles to all fraud-related interviews. What are they?

It9. When is the one occasion when it is OK to abandon the second principle in order to achieve the first principle?

(a) When you are just gathering a short statement about basic facts

(b) When you are confronted by a hostile witness

(c) When you are trying to build a rapport with a witness

(d) When the witness has just confessed to a fraud.

It10. What is transactional analysis a theory about?

(a) How to find out if someone is telling the truth

(b) How to ensure a participative interviewing style

(c) The games that people play and how to control or negate them.

(d) None of the above.

It11. Which of the following should you know before interviewing a potential suspect?

(a) Any other witness statements and evidence relevant to the suspect

(b) Your own style and potential weaknesses in interviewing techniques

(c) How you will react under pressure

(d) Answers to as many questions as possible that you are going to ask

(e) The intended outcome of the interview

(f) All of the above

(g) Only (a) and (e) above

(h) Only (b) and (c) above.

It12. For general interviews I've listed 16 pointers that you should try to remember. The first one is the six Ps. Write down as many as you can remember of the rest. Score *1 point* for less than 5, *2 points* for 5 to 10 and *3 points* if you get 10 to 14. Give yourself *10 points* if you get all 15 remaining pointers (I did warn you that life isn't fair).

It13. What must you begin a fact-finding interview with—and also any investigation.

It14. What should you do if there is silence after a question in interview?

(a) Repeat the question in case the witness failed to hear you
(b) Move on to the next question
(c) Apologise for any confusion and start again
(d) Wait in silence for a while and see what happens.

It15. If a hostile witness or suspect has a colleague or representative with them

(a) What must you make clear at the start of the interview and
(b) What must you ensure during the interview?

It16. Which three of the following should you do if you suspect that a witness has just lied to you?

(a) Move on to the next question after noting their answer carefully
(b) Explore their answer in more detail
(c) Return to the question by as many different routes as you can
(d) Challenge the veracity of their answer by body language as well as verbally
(e) Immediately terminate the interview
(f) Ignore their answer and don't note it down.

It17. What should you do if a witness suddenly decides to confess to a fraud?

(a) Stop the witness and immediately give a PACE caution
(b) Suspend them and the interview at once
(c) Carry on, record the confession and get their signature to it
(d) Suspend the interview and re-convene when they have a formal representative with them

Warning: skip the next three questions if you have decided not to use advanced techniques just yet.

It18. (a) What is the difference between attributes and variable sampling?
(b) What is a random interval sample and what risk does it run that a random sample doesn't?

It19. If you took a number of random samples from a large population of invoices which two of the following statements would be true?

(a) They would have similar characteristics to the population that they've come from
(b) They would be normally distributed around the mean value of the population
(c) They would form a Poisson distribution
(d) They would have exactly the same average value per invoice.

It20. Difference estimation is a variant of variables sampling that is particularly useful to

(a) Detect very rare errors in a large population
(b) Work out when the population is largely clean
(c) Work out the likely value of a fraud when there are at least 50 fraudulent transactions in the population.

(I did warn you! Maximum marks available in 'Investigation Techniques' = 50)

FRAUD TYPES

Ft1. Name three things that can be checked at Companies House about a contractor.

Ft2. What is due diligence? When is the best time to conduct it?

Ft3. What is a Trojan fraudster?

Ft4. Why are low-value, high-volume frauds difficult to investigate?

Ft5. There are three broad groups of likely fraudsters for pay and pensions. One is the employees themselves. Who are the other two?

Ft6. How does a ghost differ from an echo?

Ft7. Name three tests that can be done on pay and pensions using the National Fraud Initiative. (*1 mark for each*)

Ft8. Why is proper, independent net-pay reconciliation important?

(a) To ensure that the pay to staff has been made up correctly
(b) To identify anomalies in allowances being paid to staff
(c) To identify leavers still on the payroll
(d) To identify and resolve discrepancies between cash and payroll totals.

Ft9. When reporting a discovered fraud to the staff in an organisation, what should you never under any circumstances explain?

(a) How the investigation was triggered
(b) How the investigation team was selected
(c) The detail of how the fraud was committed
(d) How much was stolen and how much has been recovered.

Ft10. Why shouldn't you explain the answer at Ft9?

(the 'Fraud types' section is worth a maximum 15 marks)

▓ GETTING THE RIGHT RESULT

Gr1. What is twin-tracking?

Gr2. When should you consider civil litigation?

(a) When there is not going to be any criminal investigation
(b) When the fraudster has confessed and offered restitution
(c) When the employee is believed to have dissipated their fraudulent earnings
(d) When the cost of the litigation is likely to be exceeded by the gain and the fraudster is known to have sufficient assets to pay
(e) You should never consider it.

Gr3. What is a freezing order?

Gr4. When are you most likely to be granted a freezing order?

(a) When there is a significant risk that the fraudster will hide their ill-gotten gains
(b) When the criminal investigation has been launched
(c) After the criminal investigation has been launched
(d) When you have gathered all the evidence and know precisely how much has been stolen
(e) When under disclosure you find out that the fraudster has sufficient assets to claim.

Gr5. Which of the following statements are true or false?

(a) Fraud is a crime in Scotland but not the rest of the UK   True/False
(b) Fraud has only been identified as a crime in England and Wales since the 2006 Fraud Act became law   True/False
(c) If you discover a fraud at work you have a legal duty to report it to the authorities   True/False
(d) If you discover a fraud at work you must immediately report it to the police   True/False
(e) If you discover a fraud at work you have a civic duty to report it to the authorities   True/False
(f) If you discover a fraud at work you may choose later to disclose it to the relevant authorities.   True/False

Gr6. The three key parts of the Fraud Act are the offences of fraud by false representation, fraud by failing to disclose information and fraud by abuse of position. In all three cases the act by the fraudster must be dishonest. What 'either or' must the fraudster also have intended in order to commit the offence under each of these sections? *(2 marks if you get them both)*

Gr7. Which is potentially the more serious offence? Why?

(a) Misconduct in public office
(b) Misfeasance.

Gr8. What is the difference between misfeasance and malfeasance?

Gr9. What is the connection between the Data Protection Act and the Freedom of Information Act?

Gr10. Which of the following statements are true or false?

(a) The FOIA only applies to public bodies and their contractors

True/False

(b) Investigations are exempt from the Data Protection Act   True/False

(c) There is nothing in the DPA to prevent acquisition of personal data relevant to an investigation of fraud   True/False

(d) Investigation reports are exempt under FOIA   True/False

(e) Investigations into a crime are exempt from the requirements of FOIA

True/False

(f) Exemptions under FOIA cannot be blanket   True/False

(g) Individuals cannot make requests about themselves under either Act

True/False

(h) Repeated FOIA requests can be refused as vexatious   True/False

Gr11. When running a parallel civil and criminal case, what should you never, ever rely on?

(a) Getting the affidavit agreed by the High Court first
(b) Getting the criminal case home successfully
(c) Getting a sensible result from the CPS
(d) Keeping the civil case going if the criminal fails.

Gr12. Is it allowable to use the same evidence in both criminal and civil courts for the same fraud case?

Gr13. If planning a twin or triple-track action you should

(a) Report the crime first to the police and then consider the other options
(b) Wait until your suspect has been arrested and charged before commencing disciplinary action
(c) Start the fact-finding and kick off any disciplinary or civil action before the criminal case starts
(d) Do none of the above.

Gr14. What is the difference between disclosure and discovery?

(total marks available for 'Getting the right result' = 27)

Section	Actual marks	Possible marks
Fraud basics		15
Planning and managing		50
Investigating techniques		50
Fraud types		15
Get the right result		27

Maximum possible score = 157 markso

- If you scored between 140 and 157 award yourself the full diploma as a frauditor.
- If you scored between 120 and 139 award yourself a certificate as a fully fledged frauditor.
- If you scored between 100 and 119 hold the celebrations—you are a part-qualified frauditor.
- If you scored between 80 and 99 then have fun, but you need to re-read some of this first.
- If you scored between 50 and 79 I'm not convinced that you were really paying attention!
- If you scored below 50—are you sure that this is the right career for you?

See Appendix A for the answers and scores for the questions!

CHAPTER NINETEEN

Current trends with fraud and corruption

Laws are like spiders' webs: if some light or powerless thing falls into them,
it is caught, but a bigger one can break through and get away

Solon (ca. 600 b.c.)[1]

CHAPTER**SUMMARY**

R ising levels of fraud in a post-recession climate. Office of Fair Trading
reports, Northern Ireland Audit Office and works contractors. Other
corruption and fraud in public and private businesses. Fraud risks and
issues to address in your organisation.

RISING LEVELS OF FRAUD IN A POST-RECESSION CLIMATE

The aftermath of the 2008 collapse of the financial system in the UK on the
back of World recession will be with us for many years to come. One immediate consequence is that as the levels of bankruptcy and company failure
have spread out like a shockwave from the financial sector, so has the need

for fraudsters and shysters to turn their attention to areas where they are more likely to get ill-gotten gains. Whenever the economy is in a poor state it has two inevitable consequences for fraud. First, existing fraudsters will find some of their ready sources drying up and will have to turn their attention to newer and softer targets and, second, an increasing number of hard-pressed individuals will turn to fraud as their means of survival in lean times. The National Fraud Authority[2] estimated fraud in the UK at a staggering £30.5bn for 2008, more than twice the estimated figure for 2006. £17.6bn was fraud against the public sector.

For those that work in the wider public services, whether in central government, agencies or local authorities, these are dangerous times. The government is generally accepted as a good payer of bills owed. Therefore when other potential targets are falling by the wayside as smaller and medium-sized firms either go to the wall or tighten their belts—one side effect of which is to discover and stop more fraud in which they are the victim—the fraudsters will turn their attention more and more to what they perceive as the soft under-belly of public services.

For those that deliberately waste funds, whether greedy politicians, corrupt officials or dodgy contractors, the French have a word that feels just right—*gaspillage*—sounding like a mixture of grasping and pillage in English. Individual wasters thus become *un gaspilleur* or *une gaspilleuse*. It was reports of unnecessary wastage of public funds that got the Office of Fair Trading interested in the goings on of, first of all, roofing contractors and then from that major works and construction companies with public-sector contracts.

 ## THE OFFICE OF FAIR TRADING AND WORKS CONTRACTORS

The Office of Fair Trading (OFT) caused havoc among major building and construction contractors when in April 2008 it produced a damning *Statement of Objections* for 112 companies it claimed were involved in bid-rigging, particularly against the interests of public-services clients.

Bid-rigging is straightforward collusion between bidders, a clearly corrupt act intended to cause a gain for the eventual contractor and a loss to the party inviting the tenders for the work. What the OFT found was that if, say, contractors A, B and C were invited to bid for a works contract, contractor A would do a deal with B and C to make sure that they bid higher than A's bid. In return either contractor A would return the favour in a future bid by B or C, or they would 'arrange' to use B or C's services as sub-contractors or consultants, effectively splitting the profits from contractor A's successful bid between them.

An example of how this would have worked in practice:

Contractor	Competitive bid	Actual bid	Excess profits	Split of excess profits
A Plc	£195,000	£245,000	£50,000	£30,000
B Ltd	£195,000	£254,000	—	£10,000
C & Co.	£195,000	£257,000	—	£10,000

The OFT followed their 2008 *Statement of Objections* up in September 2009 with fines totalling £129.5m for 103 firms, many of whom had admitted bid-rigging in order to abate the size of the fine that they ultimately received. The OFT had conducted a similar exercise into roofing contractors in 2004 but that was nothing on the scale of this investigation. In all the OFT found some evidence of bid-rigging by 1,000 firms in 4,000 contracts that it examined, but by the nature of these types of investigation it concentrated its efforts on those with the most clear-cut and serious examples of bid-rigging.

The OFT has two clear advantages over the rest of the field when it comes to investigating potentially fraudulent practices in the building trade. Unlike you or me it has the power to seek explanations from any contractor and by law they are required to comply. There is, curiously under our legal system, no right of silence here. Second, it can offer amnesties and fine abatements in return for companies spilling the beans on their involvement in corrupt acts and the naming of their co-conspirators. In the murky world of dodgy contractors, this has proved to be a very powerful weapon at the OFT's disposal.

Bid-rigging is particularly hard to find when looking at how an individual organisation has awarded contracts for particular construction or works and maintenance contracts. About the most likely time when it may stand out is if the organisation has put a number of tranches or separate contracts out for similar-size and designed projects, when a comparison of successful with unsuccessful bidders will show if they have been rotating themselves at your expense. Generally it is neither that clear-cut nor easy to spot. However, there are ways in which the odds can be narrowed into finding out if you are likely to have been the victim of such corrupt sharp practice.

First of all, in the area of works and construction, check out the listed named-and-shamed companies in the OFT papers which you can look at easily enough as an on-line PDF file. In my old outfit we found that we had used a number of them, but there were very few occasions in which they had been bidding against each other. Where they had bid against each other we became more interested.

Next, look for companies that often appear to be bidding against each other for your work. Look at dates of bids, sizes of jobs and the winners on each occasion. Are there any patterns that seem unlikely? Do the winning bids seem to alternate between a few favoured firms? Are the winning bidders small companies who seem to have beaten off larger concerns?

One of the problems with any kind of bidding to supply support services, from works and construction through to facilities management and catering services, is that companies know each other in the same field of activity and can be tempted to develop cosy relationships, even considering merging and joint ventures after you have invited them to bid as separate entities. If that happens, I'd take a close interest in where they had previously claimed to be bidding independently for earlier work.

We had one example of this where the bidders fell out with each other before they had submitted their joint bid. None of us had any inkling that there had been a problem at the time of contract award, which had seemed on the surface a routine matter of seeking bidders to run a pan-London service for the organisation. The size of the original contract award was well under £500k and it had not registered on our radar as worthy of any particular attention. But a year after the contract had started, when the winner's greed became their downfall over an entirely unrelated matter, the consequences put them straight into the arms of the very firm who had been their spurned partners when they won the contract with us. The spurned partner then took their revenge and for several years we had to fight a strong rearguard action to make sure that we did not become the public service fall guys for a commercial dispute, as both parties tried to blame us for the failure of the contract.

Because we ended up fighting a rearguard action I went back to the original contract award files and read the correspondence in detail. I then compared it with information that we had acquired during the dispute and what we had been unaware of at the time suddenly became very clear to me. It was a sad and sorry tale, but it should have been picked up by our procurement people at the very beginning, the clues were all there.

Contractor A had won the contract with a bid that was a quarter of the value of contractors B and C, the only other bidders out of seven companies invited to bid. This was ridiculously cheap, compared both with the other bids and the current cost of providing the service—and on those grounds alone they should have ruled out contractor A as they clearly had not understood the contract.

What was buried deep in the papers was that A had approached several of the other bidders and offered to give them work if they backed off. B and C had decided to bid but had met A. Contractor C had then combined with one of the other invited bidders D and they had presented a joint bid. A had then approached E (a major player) and suggested that they too did a joint bid. E had agreed to this and had notified our procurement that it was their intention so to do. A kept E going on this until the night before the bid submission closing date. At almost the last second A switched allegiance to F instead and they presented a joint bid. E was forced to withdraw, as they had no time to put together another bid. F had originally indicated that they would bid with G, who also now found themselves without a bidding partner and withdrew.

A won the contract, but soon had a serious cashflow problem, so serious that F started to run out of cash too and felt obliged to look for help. They found a French backer to keep them going. A then renegotiated a better contract with our organisation and for a while all seemed well. The contract renegotiation had a significant impact, costing us an extra £5m in six months, at which point we became seriously concerned and the senior management responsible for the business area asked me to step in as a matter of urgency to try to get to the bottom of what had gone wrong.

In the meantime the original owners of A sold out their interest to F's new French backers. The ink was hardly dry on this when the French company found themselves taken over by their biggest rival in France. Their rival already had another UK subsidiary through which they ran their UK businesses—company E from our previous bidding war! E did not look kindly on A but as they couldn't turn them into a cash cow they proceeded to strip their assets and lay the blame at the door of our now tighter contract. A was put into administration by E and a six-year-long legal battle then ensued between E and our organisation as to who was really responsible for A's failure.

Realistically, I don't think that we could have picked up any of the attempted bid-rigging without a whistle-blower, but if our procurement people at the time had been on the ball, the original villains of the piece would never had been awarded a contract in the first place. Even after they were awarded the contract, the subsequent renegotiation wasn't properly evaluated and ended up draining public funds at increasingly rapid rates until we were able to put a stop to it. For certain types of contracts, if you do suspect bid-rigging has taken place, it can be worth hiring in a specialist (e.g., a quantity surveyor who specialises in construction or works), who can give you an estimate as to whether the prices that you are paying reflect the market or are over the top.

If straightforward bid-rigging is happening, contractors will seem on the surface to each have a reasonable share of the available work. However, there are other variants that may be easier to detect. Where only a few firms are directly involved in the bid-rigging they will be trying to persuade others that they don't want the work, in which case only a common core of contractors will cling to you through thick and thin.

Almost the opposite end of the spectrum occurs when a member of the organisation's own staff is either accepting bribes or has a personal connection with one of the bidders. In these instances there will be no bid-rigging from firm to firm but the favoured contractor will win a disproportionate amount of the available work. That leads me on to discuss the findings that have certainly fascinated me in the Northern Ireland Audit Office's report early in 2009.

SUSPECTED CONTRACT FRAUD IN PUBLIC BODIES IN NORTHERN IRELAND

On April 29th 2009, the Northern Ireland Audit Office (NIAO) issued report NIA 103/08-09, entitled *The Investigation of Suspected Contract Fraud*. I would recommend this document as an invaluable read for anyone contemplating an investigation into works and contractor fraud. It is also free as it can be downloaded over the internet by anyone.

It starts off rather sonorously, in the way of responsible public auditors, but the case studies given and its summary of what happened fascinate me for two reasons. First, in describing the efforts by the internal auditors and others within the Belfast Education and Library Board to deal with whistle-blower allegations and potential works frauds it highlights why they were initially unable to get to grips with the allegations. It also highlights very clearly that those who are not sufficiently trained in dealing with fraud investigation will approach it in a less effective way and will be too reliant on police advice that ultimately is unlikely to progress the matter for the organisation. The NIAO has set out some good practice to tackle the frauds and abuses set out in the cases within the document but they also show on every occasion that mistakes were made in the investigations and opportunities missed by internal management to bring matters to a successful conclusion at a much earlier stage.

However, I must offer a word of warning about some of the messages in this very worthy document from the NIAO. While I absolutely agree that some of the systems and control weaknesses that were found directly contributed to the frauds and abuses that took place, the converse is never true. In other words, if the controls aren't there, it is always easy for the fraudulently intended to have their wicked way with the organisation, but if the controls are there it doesn't mean that the frauds will somehow miraculously stop. It just means that it will be harder for fraudsters to commit fraud, but it is almost impossible to stop a determined fraudster, especially if they manage to persuade others in the control framework to allow them to circumvent the controls or weaken checking mechanisms.

It is a very good test of how much of the fraud investigative advice in this book has stuck (or was already known to you) if you read each of the NIAO case studies carefully and pick out what went well, went wrong and where management or auditors did things that I would have most strongly advised against.

 ## OTHER RECENT INTERNAL AND CONTRACTOR FRAUD TRENDS

CIFAS,[3] a not-for-profit UK company limited by guarantee, provides anti-fraud training and advice to the public and private sectors as well as monitoring fraud trends. Since the recession hit, CIFAS has noticed a significant rise in certain types of fraud in the UK, particularly identity theft and misuse of bank accounts for fraudulent purposes, both of which had increased by more than 30% from 2008 to 2009. For both 2008 and 2009 it reported rising levels of fraud, noting an 11% overall increase in frauds in the UK in 2009. Of particular significance in the context of the themes in this book, CIFAS has noticed in the last two years an increasing number of employee frauds—and a proportionate increase in female staff committing fraud, reflecting the general trend of evening out the numbers of fraud perpetrators between men and women as we have moved away from the male-dominated middle-management workforce of most of the last century.

Similar studies by organisations in the US show that the trend towards increasing volumes of internet-based frauds against individuals is increasing. In particular, apart from the more well-known scams, such as the hoax email where the sender claims to have access to vast funds but needs someone in another country to receive them in return for a cut of the profits, with the usual request for the bank account details of the greedy and gullible that follows any response, the US has found increasing levels of what might best be described as modern day teeming and lading.

In these latest scams it is financial institutions that are often the victims, although any organisation that provides funds or grants to commercial organisations could find itself a potential victim. So, how does this work? Generally, a bogus organisation is set up that apparently provides a vague 'service' to other organisations. It then proceeds to create and send out a quantity of invoices to these other organisations, thereby generating apparent evidence in its accounts that it is owed a considerable sum of money. On the back of this it then borrows funds from a financial institution. In the meantime the more alert recipients of the invoice have noticed that they haven't had any services from this company and have started rejecting the invoices or threatening action against the company if it continues to invoice them. The company then cancels these invoices and sends out a further batch to new targets, making sure that the total value exceeds those that they are cancelling. On the back of this the financial institution is lulled into a false sense of security and may even allow increased overdraft or borrowing facilities. As soon as the cash has been moved safely out of the company it melts into the night, never to be seen again.

 ## CURRENT FRAUD RISKS AND ISSUES TO ADDRESS IN ORGANISATIONS

I have set out in Chapter 17 a model for analysing the risks of fraud in your organisation. Appendix C to this book is the so-called 'wheel of misfortune' setting out the main risks of fraud in my last organisation and which is also briefly described in Chapter 17. If you start at midday on the chart and go clockwise the risk of significant fraud increases until the highest risks, just before returning to the midday clock position. What we found was that our most significant risks of fraud were mainly around procurement and contracts. As a general rule this was also a reflection of the amount of money at risk, since procurement activity was running at about £850m per annum and one dodgy contract could represent many millions of waste whereas the worst individual cash or income fraud in the last 10 years had been less than £100k.

Whatever the results of such an analysis for your organisation, all the current evidence suggests that fraudsters are increasingly targeting public-sector organisations. Modern fraudsters can attack from outside through either hacking directly into your systems or by being internet-based fraudulent traders, helped by the automated nature of much electronic procurement today. Others will be Trojans, looking for the internal opportunities once you've taken them into your company and then finally cash-strapped or pressed employees or existing contractor's employees are more likely to turn to fraud to supplement their earnings in a recession and its aftermath.

Therefore a key part of the defence mechanism for the organisation has to be around the strength and speed of response of electronically based internal controls, including firewalls and real-time-updated anti-virus software.

Organisations also need to ensure that for existing contractors and would-be new contractors there are adequate business-monitoring processes in place. All too often, even if the organisation has conducted an effective due diligence process before contract award, there is a tendency to see the contract management as monitoring the interaction and performance between the contractor and the organisation, without any monitoring of the wider business performance of the contractor or any press coverage that might suggest the contractor has any financial difficulties.

At the Met we had a regular forum that exchanged information on a closed loop to update and evaluate the risk of fraud and failure with our main contractors for both goods and services. It had representatives from contract managers, senior procurement officials, Finance and my Head of Investigations. It meant that we had an effective early-warning system when any major suppliers looked to be in trouble and we could dust off the appropriate contingency plans.

A combination of analytical checks for duplicate payments and unusual or recent changes of contractors coupled with a Benford's Law analysis (see Chapter 2) of current payments should enable any unusual invoicing activity by contractors to be highlighted and potential fraudsters detected before they have become too much of the background scenery to be picked out by normal checks and safeguards.

With employees, whether the organisation's own workforce or working for contractors, there are two key measures that I would recommend. First, I would urge that organisations ensure they have rigorous vetting of recruits, including adequate checks of previous employment history, to lessen the opportunity of Trojans targeting the organisation. Second, I would encourage organisations to have a continuous fraud awareness programme and ethical scenario training for staff. Primarily this is to enable the organisation's own employees to become an effective weapon in the fight against internal and contractor fraud, although it will often bring the added bonuses of identifying risk areas that the top of the organisation had overlooked and throwing up information about potential frauds that would not otherwise have been reported.

In the fight against fraud, you need both the broad strategic overview of risks to be able to offer a degree of assurance to the organisation and careful analysis of potentially fraudulent activities. Once an area of potential fraud is selected for examination, there is no point in adopting half-measures, as a cursory review is generally worse than no review at all. At least if you know you haven't reviewed an area in depth you know the risk is still there, but if there has been a review that didn't dig deep enough you'll end up drawing false comfort about the level of fraud in that area—and in the current climate that confidence could come back to haunt you later.

CHAPTER TWENTY

Conclusions and
the way forward

CHAPTER**SUMMARY**

W hat this book has and hasn't tried to cover. Where to gain further
knowledge and experience. Useful sources for further study and
experience. Concluding thoughts.

THE JOURNEY'S END OR JUST THE BEGINNING
OF THE STORY?

To a certain extent that is entirely up to you. I've written this book as a
starter for 10. It gives you all the basic knowledge necessary to conduct or
manage a fraud investigation in the workplace, whether dealing with
fraudulent staff or contractors.

It isn't a comprehensive guide to the fraud investigator's art but it does cover all the steps necessary to get an investigation off the ground with every chance of getting a successful outcome. As with all specialist activities, there is more that can be learnt and developed in every aspect that I've covered.

Much of my experience has been practical rather than theoretical and for that reason this book has been aimed at those who would wish to be or who have found that they have become practitioners of the art of fraud investigation. This book is packed with as many examples from my own knowledge that I can recall both good and bad. That way I have tried to set out the practicalities of how investigators are likely to make mistakes as well as how to correct them and get it right first time during investigations.

▪ MEETING TRAINING NEEDS

If you feel that you need more training to back up some of the material in this book there are a number of possible options from one-off seminars on particular aspects to particular courses and modules where you can learn more about the technical aspects of fraud investigation. The major body for internal auditors in the UK, the Institute of Internal Auditors (UK and Ireland) provides some specialised seminars and one-day events, as do the Association of Certified Fraud Examiners (ACFE), the Chartered Institute of Public Finance and Accountancy (CIPFA) and the Fraud Advisory Panel, an independent charity that specialises in advice and seminars around fraud-related matters. One-day events can be useful to get up to speed on a particular aspect but are no substitute for more concentrated training or practical experience.

At the time of writing there are only a limited number of training routes for the practical fraud investigator that I would personally recommend, although there may be more specialised training available in certain employments of which I don't have sufficient information to comment one way or the other. For instance, if you work in the NHS and are not already part of the training programme run for the NHS Counter-fraud Service then that would probably be your best initial route, although for those not in the NHS I would not recommend it as the best available option.

One of the problems with choosing fraud training is that there is no officially recognised standard core of training or qualifications that can be applied to all fraud investigators. It is something that even the police haven't managed to set as a national programme, although it has been discussed and considered on a number of occasions. Various academic institutes vie with each other to promote particular diplomas and university standard post-graduate courses, but at the professional level there is not yet any dominant qualification that is recognised by most organisations and across the public and private sectors as entitling the holder to consider they can practice as a fraud investigator.

The strongest contender at the time of writing trains fraud investigators in the public sector. It is the most relevant training for those involved in practical investigations in the public sector, rather than academic study and is the CIPFA Certificate in Investigative Practice. The reason why I particularly like this one is that it is modular and you can either choose to do all the training or if particular modules are more relevant than others then you only need to do those modules. It is also generic for the public sector rather than concentrating on one type of public organisation.[1]

In the private sector it is harder to make any specific recommendation. All the major accountancy firms with forensic arms provide internal training for their staff and a degree of external training, although it is not a particularly cheap option. PwC started their fraud academy in the summer of 2009 but it is early days yet and I wouldn't want to pass judgement until they've started churning trained fraud experts out the other end of the academy.

FRAUD INVESTIGATION—ART OR SCIENCE?

Whenever a group of long-in-the-tooth or retired fraud investigators get together the conversation inevitably turns towards the apparent dearth of expert investigators in the modern world. We all tend to see our past through rose-tinted spectacles and investigators are no different in that respect. However, I have to say that my own experience in trying to recruit skilled investigators on setting up an investigative team in 1997 through to my retirement in 2009 showed me just how difficult it was. Fraud investigators only come from a limited number of pools and some of those pools are themselves limited in scope. For instance, it is rare to find a benefit fraud investigator who has covered many, if any of the aspects of fraud investigation that I have concentrated on in this book, as their entire process is such a specialised area within the world of fraud investigation.

Organisations often recruit ex-police officers without recognising that having been a police officer does not mean that the individual has any particular expertise in fraud investigation. They should all know the law and how to deal with the criminal courts, but very few have genuine fraud investigation experience.

The problem of finding police officers with good fraud skills was exacerbated by two significant events. First, the Detective Training School at Scotland Yard was effectively closed during a period of rationalisation of police training, only re-emerging in anything approaching its former glories in 2005. Then, partly because of a series of major corruption scandals, originally in the 1970s and then again at the start of the 1990s, a decision was taken to move police officers about far more between locations and also for the first time between detective branches and uniformed officers. This decision to break 'tenure'[2] was done largely to get round the increasing problem that the younger and inexperienced officers were often the ones in the front line of the more dangerous parts of inner cities where experience really counted and the older, more experienced officers often gravitated to the relatively quiet leafy suburbs—and then a number of them were understandably reluctant to take any job opportunities back to the rough and tumble of inner-city areas.

As with all things, the law of unintended consequences struck. Detectives had long considered themselves the elite, once a police officer made it into the ranks of the detectives they stayed there until they retired or resigned. Moving some of them at every level back into the uniformed side felt like a demotion to many, while uniformed officers felt that they were suddenly working with or being managed by people whose last experience of working on the streets as part of a visible team was far too many years ago for comfort. Equally, uniformed officers who became 'instant' detectives suddenly found they were being flung into a world for which they had little training and were quickly dubbed the 'plastic' detectives by those who had been to Detective Training School and had learnt their trade as detective constables or working their way up the detective hierarchy.

The result of this to the outside world looking for trained investigators was twofold. When 'tenure' was first changed, a number of the more experience investigators quickly left and many ended up with forensic accounting firms, or senior security officer jobs with commercial organisations. Then, as the years went by, more and more of the officers moving into specialist investigative units such as fraud squads had not had the detective training or experience that their predecessors had, with the result that it became harder and harder to find well-trained and experienced ex-police officers who had a sufficient knowledge of fraud investigation techniques.

Other organisations, such as HM Customs and Excise, a source over the years of high-quality investigators also had cut back on training and the merger with Inland Revenue did no favours in retaining specialist investigators with good experience. Probably the only area where there has been a growth in investigative expertise is in the world of computer and IT fraud, where both the weapons and the investigators have become more sophisticated at a rapid pace. Nowadays there are a plethora of specialist fraud investigation organisations who can trace sophisticated fraud either through cracking rogue software, identifying IT-based fraud activities or where they can use IT to trace the stolen assets. They tend to be particularly used by the larger and more commercial organisations that can afford to pay for a highly competent technical specialist team to trace their lost assets.

For many organisations, particularly in the public sector, there has been a decade of increasing difficulty in finding experienced, high-quality investigators unless you've home-grown them and they've learnt at the organisation. The trend had slightly reversed during the early part of the recession as organisations tightened their belts and in the initial flurry fraud investigators found themselves also on the scrapheap or the specialist fraud firms found they were running out of clients who could afford to pay their bills. As the recession has bottomed out, organisations have begun to realise that effective fraud investigation and recovery of fraudulently obtained assets has merit in their fight for survival and once again the best and most experienced investigators are in demand. So, where does that leave those that can't afford to pay for the best, public or private sector? Hopefully it leaves them turning to those of its own in-house staff who have the right mindset and/or the right skillset for the job—or indeed, whoever caught the boss's eye at the right moment to find that they are now conducting a fraud investigation! If you are one of those, then this book is here to help where it can.

Ultimately, I have to admit that effective fraud investigation cannot be taught from a book. You can read enough to cover the basics in a book like this or have specialised training on one of the more technical areas, such as forensic accounting or criminal evidence, gaining the weapons to use in the fight against fraud by those means. But all the book learning in the world won't help an individual on the ground when something breaks if either they haven't got the nous to realise what is going on or they simply have never come across that situation before and don't know how to put the theory into practice.

I was always a great believer in having technically and professionally qualified staff wherever possible but also recognised that a proper qualification, where one exists, is simply a building block. It doesn't make the individual proficient or competent, it simply guarantees that they have been properly trained, without which it is hard to perform effectively. Once the basic principles of fraud investigation are understood, the best way to develop your skills is to work with an experienced investigator, learning the craft in the field. The next best option, if that isn't possible, is to do as I did for much of my career, learning investigation by investigation on your own or in a small team where you are all developing your skills at the same time.

Sometimes serious errors can be made either by the investigator or others and yet the investigation can recover. Often, through no lack of skill on the investigator's part outside events can conspire to put them on the back foot. A line manager who through ignorance challenges a fraudster with insufficient evidence or charges after an innocent person like the proverbial bull in the china shop can throw an investigation off-course before it has begun. Even so, with luck and careful research such investigations may recover and get the right result. Sometimes the investigation can hit a wall of indifference and resistance and fail to break through, despite the skill of the investigator. On other occasions one mistake in a vital interview or one fact overlooked can doom an investigation (that otherwise might have succeeded) to failure and leave the investigator doubting their own abilities.

The key point is that fraud investigation inside an organisation isn't an exact science and the techniques cannot be applied either robotically or technically as a research scientist might approach a problem. They are crafted and honed through years of experience, both of life and one's fellow human beings, as well as an ability to realise the significance of disparate facts randomly presented in a sea of ordinary data and events. A certain type of mind has the propensity to succeed in fraud investigation where others, however intellectually clever—or cleverer—they may be, simply cannot see the same patterns or feel the inner sense tugging away that all is not well with the matter in front of them.

People can be trained to be investigators and they can be trained in the law and the techniques of gathering evidence and interviewing witnesses and suspects. These things can be learned but they may remain pedestrian in their art; solid enough to bring home straightforward cases of fraudulent activity but unable to see the broader picture or recognise larger or more complex frauds.

Many investigators by nature are obsessed with the minutiae of an investigation. As with auditing, an analytical mind is indeed one of the key ingredients essential for a good investigator and, in many respects, an approach that leaves no stone unturned and meticulously observes everything is a boon during a fraud inquiry. However, to be a truly successful frauditor you need two key additional ingredients. The first is the ability to think strategically as well as tactically (the qualities throughout history of a good general); the second is that extra ingredient that Napoleon always sought in his generals—luck.

How much luck comes about by having the right experience and the right mind is a moot point. I certainly found over the years that I seemed either to be in the right place or to pick on something to review at the right time and a fraud would fall out and reveal itself to me. If I could bottle how to do that and sell it I would. I simply don't know. This book is the next best attempt, setting out as much as I can on the knowledge and experience I've accumulated over 38 years as an auditor and investigator—a frauditor.

Most people of an analytical nature are not by nature as strategically minded as they might be and that is where many can come adrift in the more complex or significant investigations. Equally you can't teach people to know when something is wrong—they can only learn that from experience, both of the organisation in which they work and in understanding the behaviour of fellow human beings and recognising signs that have cropped up before when all has not been well in the organisation. The investigator's or indeed the auditor's nose comes from both sound training and practical experience, combined with an ability to recognise the wood for the trees and at the same time spot the one leaf or branch or tree that is out of place with the rest of the wood.

So, ultimately is fraud investigation art or science? Most of human activity is developed through scientific analysis and the world of fraud investigations is no exception. However, to my mind it will always have more of a flavour of art and craft rather than science. The science helps develop the techniques and analyse the evidence, but it is the application of experience and knowledge and the ability to think on one's feet that is the hallmark of an effective fraud investigator—and, of course, that vital ingredient of luck!

I hope that this book has inspired rather than demoralised and enthused rather than defused those who are just setting out on the fraud investigator's trail. Ultimately I thoroughly enjoyed every investigation I worked on, especially in the last 20 years of my career. There were always frustrating days and pressurised times, especially when I found anything that made top management uncomfortable, but ultimately nothing I can think of in the work environment is as satisfying as a fraud investigation that you have brought to a successful outcome, with the fraud stopped and any recoverable assets returned—and occasionally the cherry on top of the culprit getting a criminal record.

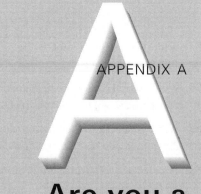

APPENDIX A

Are you a fraudfinder?

ANSWERS TO THE QUESTIONS IN CHAPTER 18

Fraud basics

Multiple choice scenarios

F1. I rate each £1 of income as equivalent to £5 of expenditure in terms of fraud risk. because

(c) With expenditure you know what you've spent, with income you don't know what you haven't received.

F2. When conducting a surprise cash-up it is important that you

(d) Do all of the above.

F3. Teeming and lading is a precursor to more extensive fraud. But how can you spot a teeming-and-ading fraud?

(d) By conducting a surprise cash-up.

F4. When might you want to apply Benford's Law?

(b) To find potentially fraudulent patterns in amounts of payments or receipts.

F5. Benford's Law only works for

(a) The first digit in any numerical value.

F6. Which one of the following statements is true?

(c) Fraud is easier to prove than corruption.

F7. Which one of the following statements is false?

(c) Bin cards are the most accurate and up-to-date record of stock in a store.

F8. Which of the following should arouse suspicion?

(f) All of (a) to (d).

F9. Why should you look closely at their expenses when trying to stop a fraudulent manager?

(d) Because they are likely to have defrauded their expenses and it is often the easier fraud to prove.

F10. Which of the following is—or isn't—a crime?

They are all a crime—even 'borrowing' the money overnight is theft.

(1 mark awarded for each correct answer—maximum for 'Basics' section is 15 marks)

Planning and managing investigations

P1. Which of the following individuals should run your investigation for you?

(e) None of the above.

P2. List three key players who should be present at the initial planning meeting prior to the start of the investigation *(1 mark for each correct player)*

Chief investigator/auditor, investigator, senior responsible officer (but not head of organisation), HR adviser, legal adviser (also source of allegation/information possibly).

P3. You should always begin an investigation with

(c) the end in mind.

P4. On which two of the following should the early effort of a fraud investigation concentrate its priorities?

(a) Stopping the fraud; and (c) Getting back the money lost to the fraud.

P5. Which one of the following is not a recommended 'end in mind'?

(d) Calling the police and waiting for the criminal investigation to start.

P6. What should you try to avoid at all costs late on a Friday afternoon?

(b) Interviewing a potential suspect.

P7. Expenses can be a short-cut route to

(a) A successful outcome in a fraud investigation.

P8. There are 10 basics of effective fraud investigation management. The first one is to select the right team for the investigation.
See 'Getting the basics right' in Chapter 4 (p. 72).

P8. If you are the senior investigator on the case you must ensure that
(a) All new evidence passes across your desk and you read it.

P9. The difference between intelligence and evidence is that
(a) There is no difference, it depends how you use the information (1 mark).
(d) Intelligence isn't part of your evidence but evidence can form part of your intelligence (2 marks).

P10. When should you administer a PACE caution?
(c) When interviewing a suspect after a police investigation has started.

P11. When gathering evidence you should gather it to the same standard as for a criminal case because
(c) It will be admissible if needed for a later criminal case.

P12. Which of the following statements are true and which are false?

(a)	To secure evidence properly it has to be in your own cabinet or cupboard	*False*
(b)	Original evidence is always best	*True*
(c)	Documents must be protected by placing in clear plastic wallets	*False*
(d)	Electronic images of hard drives are not acceptable as evidence	*False*
(e)	It is better to gather too much evidence rather than too little	*True*
(f)	An ESDA test checks for missing pages in documents	*False*
(g)	An ESDA test checks for indentations on the paper	*True*
(h)	An ESDA test identifies credit card abuses	*False*
(i)	Email traffic can only be used as evidence with the sender's permission	*False*

P13. Witness evidence is best gathered formally. Which of the following methods is acceptable (A) and which isn't? (N)

(a)	*Using a multi-deck tape machine and microphones*	A
(b)	*Using a digital recorder*	A
(c)	*Writing it out longhand with the witness*	A
(d)	*Taking it down over the telephone*	N
(e)	*Interviewing the witness on your own and secretly recording them*	N
(f)	*With a colleague taking notes*	A
(g)	*By writing to the witness and seeking a written signed reply*	A

P14. Who or what is a CHIS normally known as? What do the initials stand for?
An informant.
Covert Human Intelligence Source.

P15. What do the initials RIPA stand for? What bearing does RIPA have on use of a CHIS?

Regulation of Investigatory Powers Act 2000.
Sets out the rules for authorising and using a CHIS.

   (Total possible marks for 'Planning and managing' section = 50 marks)

Investigation techniques

It1. What is the primary function of an analyst?
To analyse data and present it in a more digestible form.

It2. Which of the following skills should an analyst be able to demonstrate?
(f)   All of the above.

It3. Give three advantages and three disadvantages for a spreadsheet as opposed to a database. Which is generally better to use for gathering and presenting financial evidence?
See Chapter 7.

It4. There are three commonly used data interrogation software tools. What are they and how do they differ, if at all?
IDEA and ACL largely identical, i2 different as it will map non-financial data and physical connections.

It5. Covert surveillance in the workplace can be risky and expensive, but can produce good visual and sound evidence of fraud and corruption. Which of the following statements about covert surveillance are true or false?

(a)   Covert surveillance at work is illegal if innocent staff are recorded   *False*
(b)   It is safer to use a hidden camera than use an undercover agent   *True*
(c)   It is legal to record someone travelling from their workplace up to the door of their home address without their knowledge   *False*
(d)   Bugging a telephone conversation between yourself and another party is a breach of the Human Rights Act and therefore illegal   *False*
(e)   Telephone bugging can only be done by the police and security services   *False*
(f)   Electronic sweeps will detect all planted bugs—provided that equipment is turned off before it is swept   *False*
(g)   Covert surveillance material can only be used for intelligence and not as evidence unless staff are warned in advance   *False*

It6. When interviewing a potential suspect what should you try never to do?
(c)   Ask a question that you don't know the answer to already.

It7. What does the mnemonic PEACE stand for and who normally uses it?

P reparation and planning
E ngage and explain
A ccount
C losure
E valuate

It is normally used by the police.

It8. There are two basic principles to all fraud-related interviews. What are they?

(1) Keep control of the structure of the interview.
(2) Relax the interviewee and gain their confidence.

It9. When is the one occasion when it is OK to abandon the second principle in order to achieve the first principle?

(b) When you are confronted by a hostile witness.

It10. What is transactional analysis a theory about?

(c) The games that people play and how to control or negate them.

It11. Which of the following should you know before interviewing a potential suspect?

(f) All of the above.

It12. See Chapter 9

It13. What must you begin a fact-finding interview with—and also any investigation.

The end in mind!

It14. What should you do if there is silence after a question in interview?

(d) Wait in silence for a while and see what happens.

It15. If a hostile witness or suspect has a colleague or representative with them

(a) Tell them they can't answer or interrupt—they are only there to observe proceedings.
(b) Stop them if they try to interrupt.

It16. Which three of the following should you do if you suspect that a witness has just lied to you?

(b) Explore their answer in more detail.
(c) Return to the question by as many different routes as you can.
(d) Challenge the veracity of their answer by body language as well as verbally.

It17. What should you do if a witness suddenly decides to confess to a fraud?

(c) Carry on, record the confession and get their signature to it.

It18. (a) What is the difference between attributes and variables sampling?

Attributes sampling measures characteristics in populations.
Variables sampling measures values in populations.

(b) What is a random interval sample and what risk does it run that a random sample doesn't?

It is taken at fixed intervals. It could hit an unusual bump in the population and distort the result.

It19. If you took a number of random samples from a large population of invoices which two of the following statements would be true?

(*a*) *They would have similar characteristics to the population that they've come from.*

(*b*) *They would be normally distributed around the mean value of the population.*

It20. Difference estimation is a variant of variables sampling that is particularly useful to

(*c*) *Work out the likely value of a fraud when there are at least 50 fraudulent transactions in the population.*

(*Maximum marks available in 'Investigation techniques' = 50*)

Fraud types

Ft1. Name three things that can be checked at Companies House about a contractor

See Chapter 11

Ft2. What is due diligence? When is the best time to conduct it?

Due diligence is a thorough examination of the current financial health and business capability of the contractor.
It is best conducted after short-listing but before award of contract.

Ft3. What is a Trojan fraudster?

An infiltrator into your organisation that intends financial harm!

Ft4. Why are low-value, high-volume frauds difficult to investigate?

Because inevitably there is a high volume of fraudulent invoices or claims to find and check—and because in criminal and civil law you still have to prove each individual item as a fraud.

Ft5. There are three broad groups of likely fraudsters for pay and pensions. One is the employees themselves. Who are the other two?

Payroll/HR staff, line managers.

Ft6. How does a ghost differ from an echo?

Ghosts are entirely bogus employees, echoes are details changed of past employees to make it seem that they are still employed.

Ft7. Name three tests that can be done on pay and pensions using the National Fraud Initiative (*1 mark for each*)

See List under NFI (Chapter 14, pp. 256–257).

Ft8. Why is proper, independent net-pay reconciliation important?

(c)   To identify and resolve discrepancies between cash and payroll totals.

Ft9. When reporting a discovered fraud to the staff in an organisation, what should you never under any circumstances explain?

(c)   The detail of how the fraud was committed.

Ft10. Why shouldn't you explain the answer at Ft9?

Because it may trigger a copycat fraud.

(The 'Fraud types' section is worth a maximum 15 marks)

Getting the right result

Gr1. What is twin-tracking?

Taking both a civil and a criminal action for the same fraudster—or taking court and disciplinary action for the same fraudster.

Gr2. When should you consider civil litigation?

(d)   When the cost of litigation is likely to be exceeded by the gain and the fraudster is known to have sufficient assets to pay.

Gr3. What is a freezing order?

A court order to freeze the bank accounts, other assets and financial transactions of an individual as a precursor to civil litigation.

Gr4. When are you most likely to be granted a freezing order?

(a)   When there is a significant risk that the fraudster will hide their ill-gotten gains. (Most judges are sympathetic to a freezing order when you are pursuing a fraudster as that fact in itself indicates that they may try to hide the money.)

Gr5. Which of the following statements are true or false?

(a)   Fraud is a crime in Scotland but not the rest of the UK   *False*
(b)   Fraud has only been identified as a crime in England and Wales since the 2006 Fraud Act became law   *True*
(c)   If you discover a fraud at work you have a legal duty to report it to the authorities *False*
(d)   If you discover a fraud at work you must immediately report it to the police *False*
(e)   If you discover a fraud at work you have a civic duty to report it to the authorities *True*
(f)   If you discover a fraud at work you may choose later to disclose it to the relevant authorities   *True*

Gr6. The three key parts of the Fraud Act are the offences of fraud by false representation, fraud by failing to disclose information and fraud by abuse of position. In all three cases the act by the fraudster must be dishonest. What 'either or' must the fraudster also have intended in order to commit the offence under each of these sections? *(2 marks if you get them both)*

(1)   Intend to make a gain or (2) cause a loss to another.

Gr7. Which is potentially the more serious offence? Why?

(a) Misconduct in public office. It can carry a life sentence.

Gr8. What is the difference between misfeasance and malfeasance?

Misfeasance is deliberately doing a wrong thing and malfeasance is deliberately doing a harmful thing. They can apply to civil and criminal law. Hence corporate card fraud, even by a public official, would be criminal misfeasance, but a public official deliberately abusing their powers to the detriment of others would be criminal malfeasance.

Gr9. What is the connection between the Data Protection Act and the Freedom of Information Act?

FOIA expands on DPA for public bodies.

Gr10. Which of the following statements are true or false?

(a)	The FOIA only applies to public bodies and their contractors	*True*
(b)	Investigations are exempt from the Data Protection Act	*False*
(c)	There is nothing in the DPA to prevent acquisition of personal data relevant to an investigation of fraud	*True*
(d)	Investigation reports are exempt under FOIA	*False*
(e)	Investigations into a crime are exempt from the requirements of FOIA	*True*
(f)	Exemptions under FOIA cannot be blanket	*True*
(g)	Individuals cannot make requests about themselves under either Act	*False*
(h)	Repeated FOIA requests can be refused as vexatious	*True*

Gr11. When running a parallel civil and criminal case, what should you never, ever rely on?

(b) Getting the criminal case home successfully.

Gr12. Is it allowable to use the same evidence in both criminal and civil courts for the same fraud case?

Yes, but sometimes it is more practical to keep separate evidence.

Gr13. If planning a twin or triple-track action you should

(b) Start the fact-finding and kick off any disciplinary or civil action before the criminal case starts.

Gr14. What is the difference between disclosure and discovery?

Disclosure is civil or criminal case sharing of evidence that will be relied upon in court to make your case with the other party. Discovery is a legal process in civil courts to obtain a document or information believed to exist by one party that has not been given to it by the other party under disclosure.

(Total marks available for 'Getting the right result' = 27)

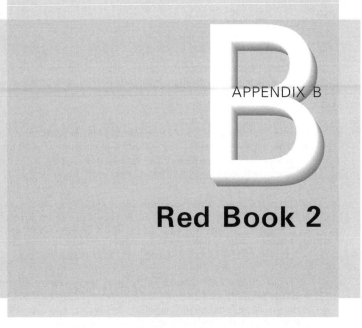

APPENDIX B

Red Book 2

CIPFA Better Governance Forum
Managing the risk of fraud
Actions to counter fraud and corruption

(reproduced by permission of CIPFA)

1.0 ADOPTING THE RIGHT STRATEGY

Key elements of a strategic approach

1.1 *Does the organisation have a counter fraud and corruption strategy that can be clearly linked to the organisation's overall strategic objectives?*
- A counter fraud and corruption strategic plan has been formulated.
- It contains actions to reach goals (desired end).
- The goals are aligned to the aims of the organisation.
- Do not isolate—counter fraud work is not the sole or main objective, not an end in itself.
- Heavy link to good overall governance.
- A strategic plan is essential in establishing an anti-fraud culture. Provides the opportunity to be explicit about the organisation's policy and to be championed by senior officers (e.g. Leader & Chief Executive).
- Advocates zero tolerance.

EXAMPLE
a. County Council Anti-Fraud & Corruption Strategy.
b. County Council Audit Accounts Committee consideration of: Fraud Strategy, Action Plan 2008–2011 and Briefing Paper.
c. County Council Anti-Fraud Strategy and Action Plan 2008–2011.

    d. Extract from County Council risk register (the risk being failure to identify & promote counter fraud) showing link to the organisational strategic objective.

1.2   *Is there a clear remit to reduce losses to fraud and corruption to an absolute minimum covering all areas of fraud and corruption affecting the organisation?*
- This aim—to reduce losses to fraud and corruption in all areas to an absolute minimum—is the policy of the organisation.
- Important message that there are not "safe" areas.

EXAMPLE
    a. County Council Anti-Fraud and Corruption Strategy.
    b. Borough Council Corporate Anti-Fraud & Corruption Strategy.
    c. Borough Council Corporate Anti-Fraud & Corruption Policy.
    d. NHS Framework for Countering Fraud.

1.3   *Are there effective links between 'policy' work (to develop an anti-fraud and corruption and 'zero tolerance' culture, create a strong deterrent effect and prevent fraud and corruption by designing and redesigning policies and systems) and 'operational' work (to detect and investigate fraud and corruption and seek to apply sanctions and recover losses where it is found)?*
- Good counter fraud measures and policy are mutually supportive. Review/introduce e.g. Fraud Response Plan Whistleblowing Code, Disciplinary Procedures, Financial Regulations, Police Referral, Recovery of Losses procedures.
- Build in and balance the risk of fraud against the need to deliver services. (Is there more risk/damage done to citizens/the public interest in ignoring the fraud risk?)
- As well as applying this to current activities, ensure proportionate counter fraud measures are applied to:
    —new systems/procedures
    —findings from fraud investigations (report changes needed).

EXAMPLE
    a. Fraud Review—Policy and Operational links, objectives/action areas, zero tolerance.
    b. County Council Fraud Awareness Leaflet—linking policy (organisational commitment to countering fraud) with operations (what to do when fraud suspected).
    c. County Council Confidential Reporting Policy—stating policy and connecting with operations.
    d. County Council Guidance for the Employment of External Workers—policies and actions.

1.4   *Is the full range of integrated action being taken forward or does the organisation 'pick and choose'?*
- Integrated action—all those at Point 4 of this *Red Book*.

EXAMPLE
    a. Fraud Review—Integrated Actions.
    b. CIPFA BGF Benchmarking.

1.5   Does the organisation focus on outcomes (i.e. reduced losses) and not just activity (i.e. the number of investigations, prosecutions, etc.)?
  ● Politicians/management make clear that reducing fraud is the key aim.
  ● Action should not take place just so that criticism of inaction can be avoided, but to achieve real, tangible results in terms of improved public confidence and reduced losses.
  EXAMPLE
  a. NHS—Counter Fraud Performance Report.
  b. Regulator focus on outcomes.

1.6   Has the strategy been directly agreed by those with political and executive authority for the organisation?
  ● Staff need to know there is buy-in from those in control and that it will be implemented. The governing body, citizen groups, staff groups like unions, partners. The AGS/SIC defines the organisation's commitment to countering fraud.
  EXAMPLE
  a. County Council letter to Members, staff and partners from Leader of the Council and Chief Executive.

▪ 2.0 ACCURATELY IDENTIFYING THE RISKS

Measuring fraud & corruption losses

2.1   Are fraud and corruption risks considered a part of the organisation's strategic risk management arrangements?
  ● Counter fraud action is risk based. Risk management arrangements consider fraud and corruption.
  EXAMPLE
  a. Standard for Risk Advisors.
  b. CIPFA BGF Fraud Risk Evaluation Diagnostic.
  c. County Council Fraud Risk Assessment.

2.2   Is the organisation seeking to identify accurately the nature and scale of losses to fraud and corruption?
  ● The organisation has adopted a definition of fraud and a method of quantification for known losses and losses prevented.
  ● There have been crucial fraud initiatives since publication of *Managing the Risk of Fraud—Actions to Counter Fraud and Corruption—Red Book 1*. The Fraud Review has taken place, the National Fraud Reporting Centre was established, the Fraud Act provides a legal criminal fraud definition, the National Fraud Strategic Authority was established, with a working group on fraud measurement.
  ● Measured counter "fraud" outcomes should not be restricted to only that prosecuted criminally (beyond reasonable doubt) and should include civil (balance of probabilities), disciplinary and administrative action.
  ● This guidance is not intended to restrict the scale of losses only to the amount of fraud detected.

- Measuring fraud is informative and important.
- Holistic actions to counter fraud should take place even where there is lack of current accurate fraud measurement.

EXAMPLE
a. Fraud Review—Research Methodologies Used to Measure Fraud
b. Assessing the Scale of the Threat—Estimates, Operational Research, Statistical Modelling, Sampling.

2.3 *Does the organisation use accurate estimates of losses to make informed judgements about levels of budgetary investment in work to counter fraud and corruption?*
- The application of resources is informed by fraud risk including financial loss and savings.
- Targeted and proportionate budgetary investment is prompted and justified through robust data in counter fraud reports.

EXAMPLE
a. Focusing Resources on the Most Effective Anti-Fraud Measures.

3.0 CREATING AND MAINTAINING A STRONG STRUCTURE

Having the necessary authority & support

3.1 *Do those tasked with countering fraud and corruption have the appropriate authority needed to pursue their remit effectively, linked to the organisation's counter fraud and corruption strategy?*
- The job of the counter fraud professional puts into action the counter fraud and corruption strategy and they are mutually supportive. Achieving the remit requires sufficient power and authority (for example, access to staff/documents/meetings/data/events). Specific liaison and meetings with key personnel—directors & managers.
- The organisation makes clear the provision of this authority in documents such as standing financial instructions/memoranda of understanding/partnership agreements.

EXAMPLE
a. London Borough Constitution.

3.2 *Is there strong political and executive support for work to counter fraud and corruption?*
- "Strong" means it is genuine—i.e. policy declaration of zero tolerance is a good start, but this is evidenced by actions such as public statements, involvement (e.g. in identifying risks) and provision of risk proportionate resource allocation.

EXAMPLE
a. City Council Political and Executive support.

3.3   *Is there a level of financial investment in work to counter fraud and corruption that is proportionate to the risk that has been identified?*
- Commitment to reduce fraud is demonstrated by the overall level of investment, the timescale, risk, results and the application of resources. Note: little investment is likely to result in little identified fraud. Often interpreted as good result.

EXAMPLE
a. NHS Counter Fraud Specialist work plan.
b. Council Audit Plan—with scope for proportionality (specific investigative contingency).

Specialist training and accreditation

3.4   *Are all those working to counter fraud and corruption professionally trained and accredited for their role?*
- Undertaking the right action and being effective through combination of relevant experience, accredited qualification and continuous professional development.

EXAMPLE
a. Links to counter fraud courses.

3.5   *Do those employees who are trained and accredited normally review their skills base and attend regular refresher courses to ensure they are abreast of new developments and legislation?*
- The organisation has a personal development process to help identify skill gaps and support continuous professional development.
- Individuals take steps to keep up to date.

EXAMPLE
a. The Excellent Internal Auditor.

3.6   *Are all those working to counter fraud and corruption undertaking this work in accordance with a clear ethical framework and standards of personal conduct?*
- The behaviour of counter fraud professionals is ethical. Activities are governed by a code of conduct/ethical framework.

EXAMPLE
a. NHS Professional and Ethical Approach.

Propriety checks

3.7   *Is an effective propriety checking process:*
    —implemented by appropriately trained staff?
    — in place that includes appropriate action where individuals fail the check?
- All applicants (including contractors, temporary staff, promotions) or jobs are "vetted" by trained staff and the outcome determines what actions are taken.
- Applicants authorise propriety checks.
- Potential checks include identity, qualifications, address, references, employment, data matching and criminal records.

EXAMPLE
a. Audio seminar—Pre employment screening: How to keep fraudsters off the payroll.
b. London Borough—Presentation on Vetting Approach.

3.8   *Does the organisation regularly review its propriety checking and are random checks carried out to ensure that it is implemented?*
   ● The organisation ensures that this employment screening process is robust. Initiatives may include reporting the results, periodic independent review, spot checks, liaison and agreement with stakeholders such as staff groups/agencies/professional bodies.
   EXAMPLE
   a. London Borough—Review.

Developing effective relationships with other organisations

3.9   *Are there framework agreements in place to work with other organisations and agencies?*
   ● Relationships are agreed. This is intended to clarify issues such as responsibilities/obligations, exchange of information, liaison/communication/meetings with key personnel. It can be accomplished through framework agreements, memoranda of understanding and service level agreements.
   EXAMPLE
   a. NHS and Local Authorities—Agreement.
   b. Crown Prosecution Service—Agreements.

3.10 *Are the framework agreements focused on the practicalities of common work?*
   ● The agreement concentrates on issues that support effective operational cooperation i.e. areas of mutual interest, viable and helpful arrangements to deliver work and not merely theoretical. Potentially such as joint planning and coordinated action.
   EXAMPLE
   a. NHS and Association of Chief Police Officers—Agreement.

3.11 *Are there regular meetings to implement and update these arrangements?*
   ● Arrangements are maintained and kept up to date and relevant. This may include inter-organisation meetings and joint review boards specified in MoU's as well as wider liaison/through groups such as the local regional fraud forum.
   EXAMPLE
   a. London Borough—Partnership meetings approach.

4.0 TAKING ACTION TO TACKLE THE PROBLEM

Taking the full range of actions and integrating different strands

4.1   *Is the organisation undertaking the full range of necessary action (see also 1.3 & 1.4)?*
   ● A holistic approach is used incorporating action on culture, deterrence, prevention, detection, investigation, sanction and redress.
   EXAMPLE—Fraud Review
   a. Deterrence.
   b. Prevention.

c. Detection.
d. Investigation.
e. Sanctions.
f. Redress.
g. Independent Review of Counter Fraud Arrangements.

Taking action to tackle the problem—culture

4.2   *Does the organisation have a clear programme of work attempting to create a real anti-fraud and corruption and zero tolerance culture (including strong arrangements to facilitate whistleblowing)?*
   • The strategy and work programme address the approach to culture and change. The strategy is publicised, promoted and commits to protecting those who report instances of misconduct. Actions may include face to face fraud awareness training/campaigns/presentations/hotlines/mailboxes, delivering a communications strategy and electronic/hard copy information/newsletters/surveys/producing documentation to contribute to induction packs/leaflets/posters.
   • The aim is to involve the honest majority in owning the approach and creating a supportive culture that counters fraud.
   EXAMPLE
   a. Audit Commission Changing Organisational Cultures Toolkit—link (also at 4.5 & 4.15).
   b. Audit Commission Changing Organisational Cultures—information.
   c. NHS—Counter Fraud and Royal College of Nursing Charter.
   d. London Borough Fraud Awareness Leaflet.
   e. London Borough Whistleblowing Leaflet.

4.3   *Are there clear goals for this work (to maximise the percentage of staff and public who recognise their responsibilities to protect the organisation and its resources)?*
   • Targets and timelines are established for work on culture.
   EXAMPLE
   a. Report—including culture target.
   b. Culture programme—including timelines.

4.4   *Is this programme of work being effectively implemented?*
   • Action is planned (for instance to present at all induction sessions), delivered and results are measured (for instance questionnaires/feedback).
   EXAMPLE
   a. Unitary Council Fraud awareness questionnaire.

4.5   *Are there arrangements in place to evaluate the extent to which a real anti-fraud and corruption culture exists or is developing throughout the organisation?*
   • Staff awareness is measured through questionnaires. The sources of fraud referrals are categorised and assessed for cultural implications. Other indicators are noted—these may include requests for the input/advice of counter fraud professionals and the degree of cooperation on counter fraud work.

EXAMPLE
a. Audit Commission Changing Organisational Cultures Toolkit—link (also at 4.2
   & 4.15).
b. Unitary Council Fraud survey.

4.6   *Are agreements in place with stakeholder representatives to work together to counter*
      fraud and corruption?
      • Agreements such as charters/protocols/partnership agreements with staff
        groups/professions/unions. Operational staff are involved in identifying fraud
        risk.

EXAMPLE
a. NHS—Counter Fraud and UNISON Charter.

4.7   *Have arrangements been made to ensure that stakeholder representatives benefit from*
      successful counter fraud and corruption work?
      • Stakeholders obtain a return on investment in terms of loss prevention and
        actual recoveries.
      • Feedback is provided so that remedial action can be taken and recovered losses
        are returned.
      • Financial recoveries and loss prevention goes to, or stays with, the stakeholder.

EXAMPLE
a. Police Authority Finance and Strategy Committee Report—Confiscation and
   cash seizure proceeds (also at 4.31, 4.33).

Taking action to tackle the problem—deterrence

4.8   *Does the organisation have a clear programme of work attempting to create a strong*
      deterrent effect?
      • A specific programme aimed at deterrence. Proactive work—communication,
        establishing agreements with stakeholders, induction, other events, training,
        creating disincentives such as sanctions and redress are all things that
        contribute to deterrence. Aimed at staff, service users, service providers,
        partners.

EXAMPLE
a. Council Audit Plan—including "Fraud Control Plan" specifying particular
   deterrence and prevention work.

4.9   *Does the organisation have a clear programme of work to publicise the:*
      —hostility of the honest majority to fraud and corruption;
      —effectiveness of preventative arrangements;
      —sophistication of arrangements to detect fraud and corruption;
      —professionalism of those investigating fraud and corruption and their ability to uncover
        evidence;
      —likelihood of proportionate sanctions being applied; and
      —likelihood of losses being recovered?
      • Internal and external publicity.
      • Forge relationship, take advice from, and involve the organisation's press
        officer.

- In-year annual reports, survey results, policies, plans, initiatives, pay-slip information, report case outcomes, emails.
- Press releases, newspaper/magazine articles, tv, radio, media briefings.
- To provide clear messages that the organisation is serious about countering fraud.
- Demonstrating the impact by highlighting successes.
- Making clear that potential fraudsters are up against active, dedicated professionals who have many advantages over them (such as the law, training, organisational support, access, data, resources).

EXAMPLE

a. NHS Counter Fraud work programme.

4.10 Has the organisation successfully publicised work in this area?
- Results—such as: hits on the intranet site, press releases leading to inclusion by the publication, distribution levels (e.g. local/national/international), appearance in electronic alerts, survey measurement of staff/public awareness, feedback.

EXAMPLE

a. Executive Agency publicity.
b. Institute of Counter Fraud Specialists Members Newsletter.
c. NHS—Internal Staff Newsletter.

4.11 Has the publicity been targeted at the areas of greatest fraud losses?
- The appropriate publicity initiatives/methods are consciously considered in plans, initiatives and specific cases. For example, publicity may be most suitable prior to a campaign, during an initiative, following the known outcome of a particular case, or all three. The intended result being to achieve the highest level of fraud deterrence impact by employing the most fitting approach to publicity.

EXAMPLE

a. City Council Publication.

Taking action to tackle the problem—prevention

4.12 Does the organisation seek to design fraud and corruption out of new policies and systems and to revise existing ones to remove apparent weaknesses?
- Fraud proof procedures/systems to avoid occurrence & re-occurrence of fraud. Protect ability to prosecute by demonstrating organisational effort to counter fraud. Involve and encourage staff to identify weaknesses. Link to and act on, the results of reviews.

EXAMPLE

a. London Borough—Operational managers' identification of fraud risks.

4.13 Do concluding reports on investigations include a specific section on identified policy and systems weaknesses that allowed the fraud and corruption to take place?
- Reports highlight weaknesses, agreement is reached to address and follow up takes place to confirm action.

EXAMPLE

a. CIPFA Technical Information Service extract.

4.14 *Is there a system for considering and prioritising action to remove these identified weaknesses?*
- A clear system is in place which grades system/procedure weaknesses and assigns responsibility for change implementation within a timescale.
- Counter fraud plans include post case follow up.
- Audit Committee reports/discussion/review/input/influence/monitoring/sign-off.

EXAMPLE

a. London Borough—Fraud weakness consideration and prioritising.

Taking action to tackle the problem—detection

4.15 *Are there effective "whistleblowing" arrangements in place?*
- A well publicised, user friendly and readily accessible policy and process is in place.
- Fraud suspicions are dealt with by counter fraud professionals.
- Internal and external hotline and ready access to counter fraud staff are in place.
- The sources and nature of the disclosures is monitored.

EXAMPLE

a. The Audit Commission Changing Organisational Cultures—link (also at 4.2 & 4.55).
b. Code of Practice—whistleblowing.

4.16 *Are analytical intelligence techniques used to identify potential fraud and corruption?*
- Data matching initiatives are carried out and acted upon—for instance the national fraud initiative. Variance analysis is undertaken across a range of activities. Unusual trends/anomalies indicating potential fraud are identified. Information from external sources is included.
- Counter fraud staff can build pictures of transactions/activity that indicate/provide evidence of fraud.

EXAMPLE

a. Audit Commission National Fraud Initiative.

4.17 *Are there effective arrangements for collating, sharing and analysing intelligence?*
- Data warehousing is used to collect and analyse data from a variety of sources.
- Counter fraud professionals are aware of the consequences of the Data Protection Act on data sharing and that the Information Commissioner supports the view that DPA is not in place for organisations or individuals to "hide behind".
- Memoranda of Understanding/Service Level Agreements are gateways for legal sharing of data between organisations.
- Connections are made between individual pieces of intelligence gathered.

EXAMPLE

a. Serious Crime Act 2007.

4.18 *Are there arrangements in place to ensure that suspected cases of fraud or corruption are reported promptly to the appropriate person for further investigation?*
- A Fraud Response Plan is followed in all cases of suspected fraud. There is a duty on all staff to report actual cases, or suspicions, of fraud.

- The organisation has a clear policy on the reporting of factual or suspected fraud/crimes/misconduct.
- Induction training, ongoing staff awareness training, staff employment contract requirement to adhere to above.
- Suspected cases are reported to and investigations are only undertaken by trained counter fraud professionals. Evidence is not compromised.

EXAMPLE
a. City Council Managers Guide—Don't Ignore Fraud.
b. City Council Managers Guide—Managing the Risk of Fraud.

4.19 *Are arrangements in place to ensure that identified potential cases are promptly and appropriately investigated?*
- All fraud referrals are risk assessed and timescales are agreed for the completion of all investigations, taking account of potential further loss of evidence and finance. Action is undertaken within Operational Manuals and Code of Conduct requirements.

EXAMPLE
a. City Council Fraud Response Procedure.

4.20 *Are proactive exercises undertaken in key areas of fraud risk or known systems weaknesses?*
- A proactive fraud plan is developed based upon an assessment of known fraud risks.
- Counter fraud resources are directed to areas with the greatest potential benefit.

EXAMPLE
a. Proactive exercise—press release.

Taking action to tackle the problem—investigation

4.21 *Is the organisation's investigation work effective?*
- An analysis is undertaken of investigations carried out, to assess the timeliness, outcomes, level of sanctions, prosecutions and amount of losses recovered. Continuous feedback is given to the client/stakeholder.
- Could include the measurement of the percentage of positive case outcomes, recoveries and loss prevention, number of cases triple-tracked''.

EXAMPLE
a. Borough Council Investigation.

4.22 *Is it carried out in accordance with clear guidance?*
- Clear operating procedures exist for counter fraud professionals undertaking their work.
- A quality assurance process is in place. Work is completed per any Operational Manuals and Codes of Conduct.

EXAMPLE
a. Investigation Management Checklist.

4.23   *Do those undertaking investigations have the necessary powers, both in law, where necessary, and within the organisation?*
- Financial Regulations clearly stipulate powers. Policies and procedures embed this into the organisation, and provide methods (i.e. PACE) and names of authorising officers (i.e. RIPA).
- Partnership Agreements give internal rights of investigation.
- See 3.1.

EXAMPLE
a. NHS Code of Practice for the use of powers.

4.24   *Are referrals handled and investigations undertaken in a timely manner?*
- All referrals are logged and the progress of those which are subsequently investigated, are regularly monitored. Measured against timescales/operational manuals and partnership agreements.

EXAMPLE
a. Timeliness of handling referrals and undertaking investigations—systems.
b. County Council Form to record telephone referrals.
c. County Council Form to record, determine and prompt action.

4.25   *Does the organisation have arrangements in place for assessing the effectiveness of investigations?*
- Client feedback is sought for each investigation carried out. Investigators are given feedback on their performance.
- Independent quality assurance of outcomes.

EXAMPLE
a. Government Department—Routine quality assurance.

Taking action to tackle the problem—sanctions

4.26   *Does the organisation have a clear and consistent policy on the application of sanctions where fraud or corruption is proven to be present?*
- The approach is that use of sanctions will always be considered and will be applied as appropriate to the case. The full range available will be considered and their application is discretionary as appropriate to individual cases. This policy is unambiguous, consistent and known to be a powerful weapon in the armoury of the counter fraud professional. It is the framework for sanctions that is clear and consistent, not that the same sanctions will always be applied.

EXAMPLE
a. Borough Council Prosecutions Policy.

4.27   *Are all possible sanctions—disciplinary/regulatory, civil and criminal—considered?*
- Policy is to investigate to criminal standard and to "triple track", including applying sanctions. Do not prejudge at the beginning whether the case is, for instance, only a disciplinary matter.

EXAMPLE
a. NHS—Parallel Sanctions (also at 4.32).

4.28 *Does the consideration of appropriate sanctions take place at the end of the investigation when all the evidence is available?*
- All the evidence is available at the end of an investigation enabling appropriate sanctions to be considered/re-considered (it may be necessary to have applied sanctions earlier for example to prevent continuing activity/civil freezing/criminal restraint orders). Be concerned about the sanctions, considering the whole range, i.e. do not limit, ensure full penalty/record; providing recompense and inability of fraudster to gain similar employment.

EXAMPLE
a. City Council Prosecutions Policy.

4.29 *Does the organisation monitor the extent to which the application of sanctions is successful?*
- Investigation outcomes are monitored regularly and compared to previous outcomes to ensure that sanctions are being consistently applied.
- Independent quality assurance of outcomes.

EXAMPLE
a. NHS Monitoring.

Taking action to tackle the problem—redress

4.30 *Does the organisation have a clear policy on the recovery of losses incurred to fraud and corruption?*
- The policy outlines the options for recovering losses, for instance debtor invoice, insurance, pension seizure, Proceeds of Crime (POCA) and the organisation encourages losses recovered to be returned to stakeholders.
- Clarity helps show fairness, limiting the risk of challenge & adverse publicity, encourages reporting of suspicions, deterrence and a counter fraud culture.

EXAMPLE
a. London Borough prosecutions, sanctions and redress policy.

4.31 *Is the organisation effective in recovering any losses incurred by fraud and corruption?*
- The progress of recovering losses is monitored for each case, and all options for recovery are considered.
- This is standard procedure.

EXAMPLE
a. Police Authority Finance and Strategy Committee Report—Confiscation and cash seizure proceeds (also at 4.7, 4.33).

4.32 *Does the organisation use the criminal and civil law to the full in recovering losses?*
- The options are considered and are not mutually exclusive, for instance POCA applications, debtor invoices raised and insurance claims made.

EXAMPLE
a. NHS—Parallel Sanctions (also at 4.27).

4.33 Does the organisation monitor proceedings for the recovery of losses?
- The progress of recovering losses is monitored for each case.

EXAMPLE
a. Police Authority Finance and Strategy Committee Report—Confiscation and cash seizure proceeds (also at 4.7, 4.31).

4.34 What is the organisation's successful recovery rate?
- Recovery rates are monitored. Options include year on year comparisons, benchmarking and percentage of cases with positive recovery outcomes.

EXAMPLE
a. NHS Recovery rate (also at 1.5).

5.0 DEFINING SUCCESS

Focusing on outcomes and not merely activity

5.1 Are there clear outcomes described for work to counter fraud and corruption?
- An assessment against *Red Book* standards is undertaken.
- Audit Commission Managing the Risk of Fraud assessment tool.
- CAA requirements.
- Indicators embedded.
- Increased awareness.
- Concentrate on real achievements—what the outcome is, the results of action taken, rather than merely activity. For instance, outcomes include awareness levels, reports of suspicions, sanctions applied, fraud levels, recoveries. Targets may be determined (e.g. for increased reporting of suspicions following an awareness campaign, sanctions applied and amount of losses recovered). The achievements against these targets, and the actions taken to minimize future cases of fraud, are contained in an annual fraud report to the executive. Counter fraud has input to the AGS/SIC. Monitoring reports focus on outcomes.
- Policy and partnership agreements outline expected outcomes.
- Intended achievements are set out in the annual plan.

EXAMPLE
a. Independent Report.
b. County Council Fraud Response Plan for Managers.
c. Borough Council Report availability.

5.2 Do the desired outcomes relate to the actual sums lost to and harm caused by fraud and corruption?
- Targets are related to financial savings/losses.
- Actual includes amounts at risk, potential, recurrent as well as proven fraud losses.

EXAMPLE
a. Council Policy—includes reporting of outcomes.

Fraud risk wheel (the 'wheel of misfortune')

The risk of fraud in the Met

(reproduced by permission of the Metropolitan Police Authority)

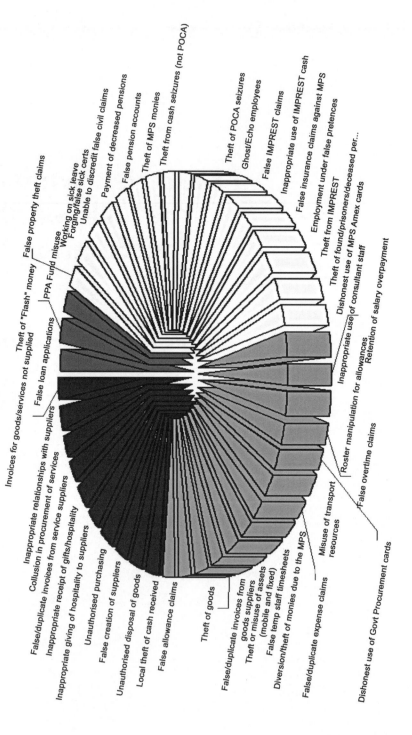

FRAUD RISK IDENTIFICATION

Audit Commission Toolkit

Changing organisational cultures

(reproduced by permission of the Audit Commission)

A robust ethical governance framework is fundamental to effective service provision and the proper stewardship of funds in public-sector organisations. Instilling a strong anti-fraud culture, combined with the highest standards of conduct and behaviour, is a key component of such an ethical governance framework. While strong systems, procedures and controls are important, they can be severely compromised if those responsible are not sufficiently committed to operating them effectively.

The *10th Report by the Committee on Standards in Public Life* stated:

> Embedding the right culture, as well as the right processes is the key to achieving long-lasting improvement in the governance of public services.
>
> We were particularly impressed with the innovative experience-based learning techniques pioneered by the Audit Commission which help organisations reach their own determination of their strengths and weaknesses and allow the solutions to come from within rather than imposed from outside. The tool (Changing Organisational Cultures) has the added benefit of allowing benchmarking against similar organisations and, if widely used, will provide useful aggregate data on ethical culture across the public sector.

Recommendation 35: The boards of all public bodies should commit themselves to the adoption and use of the Audit Commission's self-assessment tool, Changing Organisational Cultures, which is especially designed to help embed a good conduct culture.

The Audit Commission has developed a comprehensive Changing Organisational Cultures toolkit which can help organisations carry out self-assessments in order to identify risks and deliver facilitated workshops focused on improving the organisation's culture and arrangements. The toolkit provides an A to Z guide on the delivery of facilitated workshops. At its core is a self-assessment facility which

- ▪ is web-based and allows all staff in an organisation to be surveyed;

- ▪ provides access to a database of public-sector organisation in England and Wales; and

- ▪ can benchmark results against similar organisations or be used to measure improvement over time.

Audit Commission staff work with each individual organisation to tailor the workshops to meet their particular needs. The toolkit is available in CD-ROM format and delivered through a facilitated Audit Commission approach.

Summary of modules in the CIPFA Certificate in Investigative Practice

(reproduced by kind permission of CIPFA)

CIPFA CERTIFICATE IN INVESTIGATIVE PRACTICE QUALIFICATION IN COUNTER FRAUD

The training modules

Roles, Responsibilities and Ethics of Investigations *(1 day)*

DESCRIPTION OF TRAINING

This one-day module is designed to equip delegates with a broad overview of their role and responsibility in the context of investigations. The training will cover the full range of options available to an investigator to tackle fraud. The investigator will also consider the opportunities for carrying out a successful investigation within the necessary boundaries of objectivity, fairness and proportionality.

Law, Evidence, Procedure and Best Practice   *(2 days)*

DESCRIPTION OF TRAINING

This training develops the knowledge of law, evidence and procedures necessary for the investigator to carry out an effective and compliant investigation. The purpose of the unit is to give the candidate an ability to operate within a legal framework, and to carry out their work to Best Practice Standards. They will then gather evidence that is admissible in any subsequent court hearing and conduct an investigation that is compliant with the Human Rights Act and the Police and Criminal Evidence Act (PACE) and Codes. Delegates will analyse a case to determine what has to be proved and how to prove it. They will consider case studies tailored to their specific areas or work. This module will assist those who investigate to carry out both criminal or employment investigations.

Advanced Statement/Report Writing and Giving Evidence   *(2 days)*

DESCRIPTION OF TRAINING

This training develops the skills of writing evidence in statements, and giving oral evidence effectively. Delegates will analyse statements they have written in the workplace and practise writing statements. Delegates will develop and improve their written and oral evidence. Delegates will learn how to present themselves when giving evidence, what techniques lawyers use in cross examination, and how they can survive in the witness box. They will experience being cross-examined by a solicitor or barrister, and will receive feedback on evidence giving in the witness box as a witness of fact and experience how an investigation can be undermined as a result of poor investigation practices and procedures.

Investigative Interviewing including cognitive interviewing   *(3 days)*

DESCRIPTION OF TRAINING

This training develops skill in obtaining accurate, relevant and complete accounts from witnesses during an interview. Delegates will learn how to conduct interviews with their own witnesses and other types of interviewees (suspects and or employees) by applying the PEACE (planning, preparation, engage and explain, account, closure and evaluate) method. If conducting suspect interviews of employees they will also consider the Police and Criminal Evidence Act 1984 (PACE) and the Codes and the way in which the manner in which the interview is conducted may affect the admissibility of the evidence.

Questioning techniques will be dealt with and practised. Different types of interviewing techniques and interviews will be dealt with, for example interviewing witnesses who will be giving helpful evidence. Delegates will consider the duty of disclosure prior to interview. Delegates will conduct interviews in their public sector specific role-play. Delegates will be trained to an advanced level.

RIPA and DPA   (2 days)

DESCRIPTION OF TRAINING

This training will give non-lawyers an understanding of the legal regime imposed under RIPA (Regulation of Investigatory Powers Act) and DPA (Data Protection Act). The training will highlight the need for risk assessment in relation to carrying out of any interceptions/surveillance and the storing of recorded information. The distinction between directed and intrusive covert surveillance will be explored. The need for careful analysis of the purpose and outcomes of the surveillance is considered. The importance of having gathered sufficient evidence to justify interception or surveillance in relation to the monitoring and recording of email and phone calls will be considered. Candidates will consider their obligations under the DPA and the need to keep accurate records and know how requests for access to data can be dealt with, in the new world of Freedom of Information and data sharing.

Employment Investigations   (2 days)

DESCRIPTION OF TRAINING

This training is designed to give practical guidance on law, procedures, evidence and practices in relation to both employment law and internal investigations. The purpose of the training is to assist those candidates who carry out internal investigations, for their own or another organisation, to understand the legal framework to employment disputes. Candidates will consider the types of claims that may be made by an employee, including wrongful dismissal, redundancy, unfair dismissal, and sex, race and disability discrimination, dignity at Work, bullying and harassment.

Delegates will look at the terms of the contract (express and implied), constructive dismissal, conduct and capability dismissals. The reasonableness of the investigation as carried out by the employer in accordance with the Burchell test as reconfirmed in HSBC and Madden, will be considered in a practical case based context using an investigations checklist and case analysis. The relevant statutory grievance and disciplinary procedures will be examined and applied in the context of a case study.

Collecting Electronic/Digital Evidence *(2 days)*

DESCRIPTION OF TRAINING

The training introduces and develops legal knowledge and practical skills in relation to Computer Crime Investigations. Many organisations employ or designate investigators to carry out civil, criminal or regulatory investigations. These investigations may require the securing, seizing, handling and preservation of electronic/digital/computer based evidence.

Delegates learn best practice in dealing with all forms of electronic evidence. Delegates consider the legal aspects of collecting electronic evidence. To be admissible in a criminal trial, the evidence must be collected so that it does not infringe the relevant legislation including the Computer Misuse Act 1990, the Human Rights Act 1998, The Regulation of Investigatory Powers Act 2000, the Police Act 1997, the Police and Criminal Evidence Act 1984 (PACE) and the Codes under PACE.

The training gives a sound understanding of the ACPO (Association of Chief Police Officers) guidelines for dealing with Computer Based Evidence. Delegates learn how to plan and prepare for, and execute the collection of electronic evidence. Delegates consider how to ensure that continuity of evidence is preserved and the evidence obtained is reliable and credible. Practical exercises will demonstrate where and how vital electronic evidence can be obtained.

Formulae and a table to assist advanced techniques

Formulae and a table to aid scientific sampling of populations containing fraudulent transactions or items

(see Chapter 10 'Advanced techniques')

SAMPLE SIZE FORMULAE

Note: The attributes formulae given below, once built into a mathematical model, can be turned around to work out sample size for a given precision and level of confidence. Alternatively, once a sample size is selected, they will calculate the precision at any chosen confidence level and the confidence level at any chosen precision for the same sample size. If these formulae are built into a spreadsheet the user then can feed in two of the variables of precision, confidence and sample size to calculate the value of the missing element.

Put in the total number of items in the random sample, the confidence level that the sample is representative (either 90% or 95% recommended) and the formula will tell you how precise the results will be. If that isn't precise enough, lower your confidence level or increase the sample size. The error rate is the level of fraud or error found in the sample—or estimated in the population. If there is no basis for estimating the level of fraud, take a random sample of 50 items, which can then be added to your full sample, and use it to estimate the level of fraud for the population. Once you get the error rate (number of fraudulent items) of the full sample then use that error rate to recalculate the accuracy of your sample with these formulae.

Example		
Invoice population	= 10,000	= 10,000
Sample size	= 100	= 200
Confidence level	= 90%	= 90%
Number of sample items found to be fraudulent	= 5	= 10
Sample fraud/error rate	= 5%	= 5%
Precision calculation result: Precision is	±3.5%	±2.5%

In other words for a sample size of 100 items you can conclude that the likely level of fraud in the population of 10,000 items is 5% ± 3.5% (i.e., it lies between 150 and 850 fraudulent items but is most likely to be 500 fraudulent items). For a sample size of 200 items with the same level of fraud you can conclude that the level of fraud in the population is 5% ± 2.5% (i.e., it lies between 250 and 750 fraudulent items but is most likely to be 500 fraudulent items).

Note 2: For usage in fraud investigations I would recommend that the level of precision required should be between 2% and 5% and the level of confidence either 90% (use 1.64 in the formulae) or 95% (use 1.96 in the formulae). Don't try to be too precise or the required sample size will climb dramatically for these confidence levels. Sampling is for estimation purposes, to help make a judgement call about whether to pursue a fraud by a particular strategy or whether to conclude that the level of fraud is too low to justify an investigation.

Formula for determining the precision of a random sample taken from a population of under 5,000 items

Key

p = Precision percentage
n = Sample size
N = Population size

fe = Fraud/Error percentage found in sample
nfe = Percentage in sample with no fraud error
cl = Confidence level (1.64 for 90% confidence level, 1.96 for 95% confidence level)

$$p = cl\sqrt{\frac{(fe \times nfe)}{n}} \times \sqrt{(1 - n/N)}$$

This formula is designed to estimate the precision of an attributes sample for a population between 1,000 and 5,000 items. If the population is smaller than that you should have the resources to check the lot!

Formula for determining the precision of a random sample taken from a population of 5,000 or larger[1]

$$p = cl\sqrt{\frac{(fe \times nfe)}{n}}$$

This simpler formula is accurate for all large samples. If you want to work out a sample size or pre-determine the precision and find a sample size, simply square every item and follow the normal rules of algebra and you'll end up with a value for n.

Stop-or-go table for determining the likelihood of errors or frauds in a population of at least 2,000 items

The tables (overleaf) have been created from a formula from probability theory about the likelihood of a particular result in a given number of items of population. The formula was developed by two statisticians at my request when I used to teach the basics of audit sampling to students in the early 1980s. It is based on, but more accurate than, tables originally produced by the Lockheed Aircraft Corporation in the 1940s and subsequently reproduced by the Institute of Internal Auditors, Inc. in *Sampling Manual for Auditors*, 1967.[2]

How to use the stop-or-go table

As long as a random selection of an initial 30 items is made from a population of at least 2,000 items the table is accurate.[3] Where possible it is best to select 50 random items to start with. If no errors are found then there is a good probability that the population is fraud-free.

Stop-or-go sampling—table for populations of 2,000 or more with a sample size of 30

Percentage probability that fraudulent items in the population do not exceed:

No. of frauds	1%	2%	3%	4%	5%	6%	7%	8%	9%	10%
0			59.9	70.6	78.5	84.4	88.7	91.8	94.1	95.8
1							63.1	70.4	76.6	81.6
2										58.9

Note: Probabilities close to or below 50% have been excluded as they are too low to draw any inference.

Examples that can be read from the above table:

■ If 30 randomly selected items are not fraudulent there is an 89% probability that the level of fraud in the population is 7% or less.

■ If just one of the 30 randomly selected items is fraudulent there is only a 63% probability that the level of fraud is 7% or less.

Stop-or-go sampling—table for populations of 2,000 or more with a sample size of 50

Percentage probability that fraudulent items in the population do not exceed:

No. of frauds	1%	2%	3%	4%	5%	6%	7%	8%	9%	10%
0		63.6	78.2	87.0	92.3	95.5	97.3	98.5	99.1	99.5
1				60.0	72.1	81.0	87.4	91.7	94.7	96.6
2						58.4	68.9	77.4	84.0	88.8
3								57.5	67.0	75.0

Note: Probabilities close to or below 50% have been excluded as they are too low to draw any inference.

Examples that can be read from the above table:

■ If 50 randomly selected items are not fraudulent there is an 92% probability that the level of fraud in the population is 5% or less.

■ If just one of the 50 randomly selected items is fraudulent there is only a 72% probability that the level of fraud is 5% or less.

Stop-or-go sampling—table for populations of 2,000 or more with a sample size of 70

Percentage probability that fraudulent items in the population do not exceed:

No. of frauds	1%	2%	3%	4%	5%	6%	7%	8%	9%	10%
0		75.7	88.1	94.3	97.2	98.7	99.4	99.7	99.9	99.9
1			62.5	77.5	87.1	92.8	96.1	97.9	98.9	99.5
2					68.6	79.9	87.6	92.6	95.7	97.6
3						61.2	73.1	82.1	88.5	92.9
4								66.8	76.6	84.1
5									61.1	71.3

Note: Probabilities close to or below 50% have been excluded as they are too low to draw any inference.

Examples that can be read from the above table:

- If 70 randomly selected items are not fraudulent there is a 99% probability that the level of fraud in the population is 6% or less.
- If just one of the 70 randomly selected items is fraudulent there is still a good probability, 93%, that the level of fraud is 6% or less.
- If two of the randomly selected items are fraudulent there is only an 80% probability that the level of fraud is 6% or less.

Start by deciding what the acceptable level of fraud or error is going to be. If you are not going to accept any frauds in the population then don't use these tables! These tables allow for a level of fraud or error that is either an accepted risk or simply would be too small to be worth pursuing. For instance, a well-known retail chain used to allow for 3% pilferage of stock. If a 3% level of fraud is acceptable and you check 50 items in the sample and don't find any fraud, then look across the top of the chart to 3% and read the percentage underneath it against 0 errors. That tells you that there is a 78% chance the level of fraud/error in the population is indeed 3% or less.

If you need a better probability then you need to take a larger sample. Equally if an error or fraud is found in the sample of 50, then you need to take a further sample of 20 and if no further errors or frauds are found then read the probability table against the column for one error on the 70 sample size line. If that result is not clean enough sample a further 20 and so on.

The tables I've included cover samples of 30, 50 and 70. If you decide to pursue this for larger sample sizes and more accuracy then tables covering from 90 upwards can be created or found in more specialised audit-sampling books and statistical tables. But the tables on the previous spread are sufficient for a fraud-finder and are as far as I would want to go.

For example

Original random sample = 50

No errors or frauds are found. There is a 78% probability that the error/fraud rate is 3% or less.

Further random sample of 20 – total sample size now = 70

If no further errors are found, the probability that the error/fraud rate is 3% or below climbs to 88%.

If one fraud/error is found in the next 20 items the probability that the fraud/error rate is 3% or below drops to 62%.

This is a table to use when you want to eliminate a population from a fraud investigation. The moment several frauds are found in the sample the population cannot be declared clean and needs to be searched on a full sample basis or full review to establish the level of fraud.

Detecting abuse in credit card transactions

By Richard Kusnierz[1]

Managing Director, Investigative Data Mining Ltd.

AN INTRODUCTION TO DATA-MINING CONCEPTS

The analysis of information within an organisation and the comparison of data between different bodies may collectively be known as data mining or data matching. To successfully fight fraud in all of its many guises, be that of

- A single employee abusing their authority and making use of a loophole in the system, such as abusing the expenses system to falsify or inflate claims;
- Multiple employees colluding in an institutionalised 'perk';

---

[1] Richard Kusnierz has been investigating fraud using a variety of analytical techniques for over 19 years. In 1998 he founded Investigative Data Mining Limited (IDM), a specialist consultancy to focus on using data-mining techniques to prevent, detect and investigate fraud. In 1999 he co-founded IDM D.A.T.A. Solutions Limited (IDS) to provide innovative and cost-effective counter fraud data-mining solutions for both public-sector and private companies. Clients of IDM and IDS include the MoD's specialist Defence Fraud Analysis Unit and the Metropolitan Police Authority, where IDS worked closely with Peter Tickner and Internal Audit to refine and enhance the IDS Corporate Procurement Card Profiler (CPCP™).

- Collusion between employees and outsiders; or
- A deliberate attempt by organised crime to fund terrorist activities by money laundering;

requires an understanding of both the mechanisms of fraud and the potential of data mining. The aim of this appendix is to describe the potential for using data mining to detect and prevent fraud, with specific reference to abuses in expenses systems. Data-mining techniques may be used proactively to review a business process to identify anomalies, and reactively to assist in criminal or civil investigations.

PROACTIVE FRAUD DETECTION

Proactive fraud detection may be approached in two ways. The first is similar to a corporate health screen, where the organisation does not believe that there is a problem, but wants to make sure. The second is to ensure that there is a quantitative mechanism to implement some of the best practices of corporate governance. Recent reports have suggested that there should be regular reviews of the risks and exposures facing an organisation, and that these should be incorporated under the heading of 'Corporate Governance'. Data-mining techniques can be used to gauge fraud risks and exposures by applying quantitative routines to identify potential fraud. In both cases, the first step in conducting proactive data mining is to gather as much data as possible and to understand the key risks and exposures. Once these mechanisms are understood, it will be possible to develop theories and profiles for detecting patterns of fraud. The entire process is cyclic and may require more than one iteration, to ensure that all the variables have been included, and that the parameters have been set at realistic levels. Figure 1 explains this concept in more detail.

Stage 1 defines the area or business practice that is to be analysed or assessed, such as identifying potential credit card abuse, and outlines all the different types of risks and exposures that could occur. As such, this process will establish a number of theories or profiles that can used to test for fraud in a quantitative manner. Furthermore, this stage identifies all the different data sources available (both hardcopy and electronic) that are necessary for detecting fraud. It is simpler if the data is stored in a digital format; however, it is still possible, and usually very informative, to incorporate information from manual sources as well.

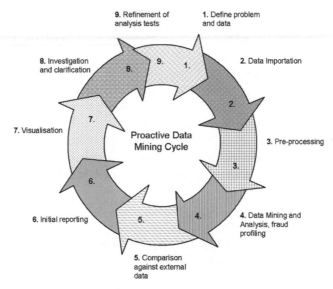

Figure 1. Corporate governance (© 2009 Investigative Data Mining Ltd).

Stages 2 and 3 deal with data importation and, depending on its format, this may include some form of pre-processing. It is not uncommon to have to review alternative sources of data or request a fresh download from the appropriate group.

Stage 4 comprises a high-level review of the gathered data against selected fraud profiles. It is at this stage that data-mining techniques allow the comparison of many different formats of information.

In Stage 5, data that is external to the organisation can be included into the proactive data-mining cycle. This process allows additional information to be introduced so that seemingly innocent relationships are compared against known suspect data. For example, post-September 11, the US Treasury compiled a list of organisations, countries and individuals that it believed to have links with terrorist or criminal activities. The Office of Foreign Assets Control uploaded to their Internet site a 'Specially Designated Nationals and Blocked Person' list, which can be downloaded and compared against an organisation's data. Other sites provide similar information such as the World Bank's list of disbarred companies. As such, data mining can be used to reveal unusual relationships that should be considered in the context of the organisation's overall business activities.

The remaining stages of the cycle involve validating the findings to exclude both 'false positive' and 'false negative' results, and refining the original fraud profiles. As part of the iterative nature of the cycle, additional data may be required that will result in a second or third iteration before any findings may be reported.

One area where many organisations, including government agencies, are greatly exposed is in the management of staff expenses. There are a number of different fraud profiles within such a system which lends itself to proactive data mining to detect such abuses.

The following example is based on the work which IDS did with a number of government agencies to refine its data-mining software tool—the CPCP^{TM}—to detect abuse by authorised employees in their credit card transactions.

KEY FAILINGS AND MISCONCEPTIONS IN EXPENSES MANAGEMENT

Most organisations recognise that the expenses system will be abused by their employees and adopt the pragmatic approach that provided the abuse is not excessive the organisation can live with such losses. The retail trade has a similar concept to shop lifting by customers and employees and these losses are quaintly referred to as 'shrinkage'. However, there is still a belief that expenses fraud is low level and manageable because

- ▦ Everyone does it;
- ▦ It doesn't harm the organisation as it is low level; and
- ▦ It is part of the culture and deemed as "custom and practice".

When it comes to the use of corporate credit cards there are a number of other key misconceptions which tend to increase the organisation's exposure to systematic fraud, basically these can be summarised as

- ▦ The card provider has sophisticated counter-fraud detection techniques and will protect us from fraud;
- ▦ Our managers check and validate each item on the expense claim and would question any transaction which looks odd; and
- ▦ All our staff are honest.

Sadly none of these assumptions are true and while card providers focus on external frauds such as 'cloning or skimming' and 'card not present' (CNP) frauds they leave it to the user organisations to detect internal frauds committed by the authorised user.

CORPORATE PROCUREMENT CARD PROFILER

The CPCP™ is a standalone software tool designed to provide its user with meaningful information to detect the possible sign of credit card abuse by authorised card holders. It has been designed by investigators for use by investigators and so does not require the user to be a data-mining analyst. The key features of such a system are

- Ease of data importation;
- Recognition that each user organisation is different and will require the software to cater for differences in departments and they way that they use credit cards;
- Variable risk weighting, as with differences between departments, some organisations will place a higher emphasis on certain styles of transactions which in their environment will indicate a clear breach of expense policy and potential fraud; and
- The consolidation of the test results and analysis to produce a simple "most likely offenders list".

This last item is an important concept as it dramatically reduces the time required to focus on those card holders and the transactions which appear to fraudulent. This reduces what is often referred to as 'information overload' which is a valid criticism of many data-mining tools that they produce too many false-positive results to be practically useful.

The key elements of credit card transactions for personal benefit can be broken down into the following basic categories:

- Transactions with merchants which are more likely to be of a personal nature (e.g., using the card to surf the net and log on to X- rated adult websites;
- Transactions with recognised and approved merchants, but which could be of personal benefit to the authorised card holder (e.g., purchases of stationery or printer consumables for use by a partner or child at home, or using the card to pay for the week's grocery shopping);

▪ Deliberate splitting of a single large purchase over several transactions to by-pass a card transaction limit, or

▪ Deliberately splitting the large transaction over two or more cards to disguise the transaction even more;

▪ Colluding with a line manager to make a transaction which provides a personal benefit to both with the line manager authorising the transaction; and

▪ Recognising that there is no comparison between the credit card system and a separate cash expenses system so that the dishonest employee may submit a single transaction through both systems and gain a double benefit.

The CPCP^{TM} is designed to recognise all of the above profiles by having a series of interlocking rule-based tests which incorporate a company's own expenses policies and allows for the creation of 'black lists' to identify inappropriate merchants either by the credit card industry's own Merchant Category Codes or a specific merchant name. Figure 2 diagrammatically represents the data-matching concept within credit card transactions.

Many data-mining applications suffer from the generation of false-positive results which can cause information overload. There are just too many results to be able to manage the problem, the CPCP^{TM} addresses this by assigning a risk score to each of the 10 key risk areas and all the automated routines it runs which results in a series of screens which highlight those card holders with transactions which match the risk profiles. Figure 3, which is based on sanitised, dummy data, illustrates the concept of the 'most likely offenders' summary.

The weighted risk score is based on user-defined parameters and can easily be re-run by altering the individual risk scores. This allows the investigator to customise the application for the specific circumstances of that organisation. Behind this screen for each of these card holders is a more detailed explanation of how the scores were made up. This is shown in Figure 4.

This 'drill down' facility enables the investigator to focus on material risk to the organisation so that time is not wasted in chasing down 'false positives'.

Example

A number of unusual transactions have been made by Mr D I Rector and Mr A N Other in connection with a marketing trip to Monaco. The cost of the yacht has been split over two cards and cash has been withdrawn.

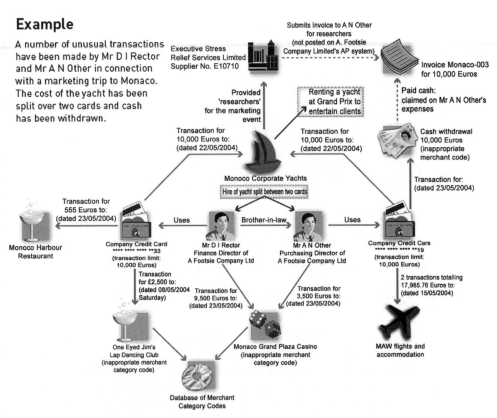

Figure 2. Identifying unusual credit card transactions (© IDM D.A.T.A. Solutions Ltd).

Figure 3. Card holder with the highest risk scores (© IDM D.A.T.A. Solutions Ltd).

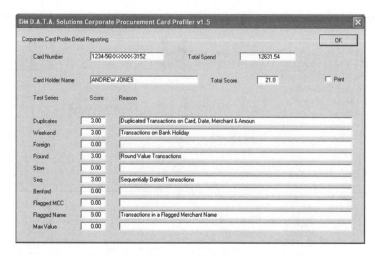

Figure 4. Details of individual scores (© IDM D.A.T.A. Solutions Ltd).

CONCLUSION

The CPCP^{TM} is an example of a specific counter-fraud data-mining application designed with a specific aim in mind and based on feedback from key client organisations. Many other systems and applications exist to assist both public and private-sector organisations be more proactive in the detection of fraud and to provide much needed independent control mechanisms.

APPENDIX H

Notes

Chapter 1

1. Prior to then all criminal definitions around fraud relied mainly on the Theft Acts 1968 and 1978, with additional help from either the Forgeries Act or for some commercial offences the Companies Acts.
2. Ken Gort, Assistant Director of Internal Audit (Forensic), Metropolitan Police Authority.
3. There is still, at the time of writing, no police performance target set by the government, Her Majesty's Inspectorate of Constabulary or the Audit Commission around fraud.
4. An imprest is a self-balancing float, where on proof of expenditure it is topped up to the original float value.

Chapter 2

1. George Polya (1887–1985), mathematician and scientist, author of the 1957 best seller *How to Solve It*.
2. Pyrrho of Elis (ca. 360 BC–ca. 270 BC), credited as the father of Pyrrhonism, the first sceptic movement, founded nearly two centuries after his death.
3. I have covered this type of fraudster, the 'Trojan', in more depth in Chapter 12.
4. This case became the subject of a documentary entitled *The Billion Dollar Bubble*. Even today, it is worth watching if you come across a copy of it.
5. Chapter 6 contains a case study around the use of analytical tools and other practical examples of both what can—and cannot—be done.
6. Williams removed the paragraph recommending checks and balances from the senior officer's note by cutting that part of the note off and pasting the final paragraph underneath the first part of the note, keeping the original and posting a seamless photocopy without the offending paragraph but with the senior officer's approval onto the official files.
7. We had to be absolutely sure that she had left the premises with the stolen cash to avoid

any element of doubt about her intentions, increasing the likelihood of a later successful criminal prosecution.
8. In the MPS, creditors are known as 'vendors' in the accounting system.

Chapter 3

1. Not usually best practice to involve the very top executive officer at this stage, in case matters come unstuck later and they need to have clear water between them and the investigation to enable the organisation to take any executive action deemed necessary.
2. Data mining is the process of analysing computer data to identify potentially fraudulent transactions or unauthorised activity in any computer or networked system.
3. For example, by putting any paperwork immediately into a locked cupboard or filing cabinet to which the only keys are kept securely by the line manager.
4. This will depend on the specific nature of such policies in your organisation—hence why HR advice is always needed before taking or planning to take such steps.

Chapter 4

1. From *On Strategy*, published 1871. General Colin Powell updated it with *No Battle Plan Survives Contact with the Enemy* after the Gulf War.
2. If there are of necessity a number of key documents then they should form a separate bundle, not attached to the report. Generally you will only need the full bundle at final report stage; it is sufficient to have the material that supports your initial conclusions at this stage.

Chapter 5

1. Sun Tzu, ca. 500 BC. Quote from *The Art of War*, Chapter XIII: *The Use of Intelligence and Spies*.
2. The police use a five-point scale, but this grid should be sufficient for most internal investigations.
3. The criminal courts have already ruled that Revenue and Customs investigators, OFT investigators and Federation Against Software Theft investigators are covered by the requirements of PACE when interviewing suspects, as well as some public authority officials.
4. *R v Welcher* [2007] EWCA Crim 480.
5. For example, by inappropriate threats, bullying or physical restraint.
6. Electro-static document analysis.
7. Helpfully the Office of Surveillance Commissioners provides guidance for local authorities on its website. The Home Office also has a Code of Practice on the use of covert surveillance by public bodies.
8. In civil cases this is also known as 'discovery' whereby either party may make enquiries to seek discovery of a document or electronic record that they have reason to believe exists.

Chapter 7

1. Provided by IDM D.A.T.A. Solutions Ltd. (see Appendix G).

Chapter 8

1. Regulation of Investigatory Powers Act 2000. See 'CHIS or informant: What are the differences—and the risks?' section on p. 102 and also the Office of Surveillance Commissioners website guidance for public authorities.
2. An organisation I know asked for a leak investigation as they were convinced that their offices had been bugged. It turned out that they were right, but the villains needn't have bothered. The organisation had a hearing loop from all meeting rooms and when it was switched on you just needed to sit outside in the street with the appropriate hearing aid and you could legitimately hear every detail of what was being discussed!

3. I have learnt over the years that very few individuals have the gift of being able to lie and match body language to spoken word. It is also alien to my nature to lie so I find it much more comfortable just to limit the truth when it proves necessary.

Chapter 9

1. *The Art of War*, Chapter III: *Attack by Stratagem.*
2. We used specialised three-deck interview tape-recorders throughout most of my time at the Met. It meant we could record three tapes simultaneously linked, giving one to the witness or suspect, putting one away with the case papers for any court production later and having one transcribed.
3. A little unfortunate as, although I did it as a 'comfort' reaction, it can also be a signal when done vigorously of disagreement with something that has been said!
4. *Games People Play*, written in 1964 by Eric Berne.

Chapter 10

1. William of Occam (or Ockham), a 14th-century monk who determined that in solving problems, the simplest and least complicated proof was likely to be best.
2. One of the earliest random number tables was drawn up by a scientist after the American Civil War. He went to a war cemetery and took the plot numbers against the name of the soldier buried in the plot. Since they died randomly they were not buried in any particular name or rank order.
3. This is potentially prone to any one-off oddity in population but you can solve this by dividing the sample in three, taking three random starts and adding on three intervals multiplied by a factor of three to end up with the same sample size. If one of the three doesn't give a similar result to the other two then the population isn't normal.

Chapter 11

1. The 'White Fleet' is all the non-operational vehicles supporting the RAF.
2. In police jargon a 'Gold Group' considers strategic issues and the way forward, sitting above the operational day-to-day business but bringing together all the heads of the businesses and operations affected by the matter in hand.

Chapter 12

1. In one of those oddities that can only occur under our wonderful constitution, Scotland Yard controls policing inside the Greater London boundary but neither it nor the Mayor of London have any responsibility for the old City of London, which has its own Lord Mayor and a separate, if somewhat smaller, police force.
2. To this day the Met is responsible for the investigation of the murder of any UK citizen outside the borders of the UK.
3. Companies must annually declare who their main directors, company secretary, etc. are and show the home addresses for each of these.

Chapter 13

1. The biggest users of linguists in the UK are the military, the Foreign Office, the police, the ports, the Border Agency and local government.
2. The reason why this is done is to ensure that the police have the power to search for evidence at the home of the suspect, as an arrest elsewhere would not confer that right.

Chapter 14

1. The account will always have a balance, as there are timing differences for staff on sick pay, accidental over-payments and under-payments being collected and in many organisations advances of pay for holiday or season ticket loans that will need to be adjusted to reconcile payroll to cash.

Chapter 15

1. Parts of the Theft Act that deal with fraud are still in force, particularly the Theft Act offence of 'false accounting' used to charge MPs in the expenses scandal.
2. For instance, they may intend to deceive someone who is in fact not deceived, or they may attempt to steal something that doesn't exist.
3. In civil contract law there is also nonfeasance (failure to provide a service). Misfeasance and malfeasance (but not nonfeasance) can also be applied to public officials and public bodies in a civil court case. All three are available for contractual disputes provided the matter in dispute is not already covered by contract law.

Chapter 16

1. A freezing order temporarily freezes the bank accounts and other assets of the fraudster so that they cannot access them or transact any other business with them (e.g., sell a property).
2. Whether you notify the civil courts at this stage will depend on legal advice about the best way forward for your circumstances—and a financial decision about the risks and benefits of the case.

Chapter 17

1. I have only selected a limited number of generic items to illustrate a flavour of what was found.

Chapter 19

1. Solon was an Athenian statesman and poet who reformed Greek politics. His quote was a sideswipe at corrupt politicians who thought themselves above the law. Somehow it seems as appropriate today as then.
2. National Fraud Authority, *Annual Fraud Indicator Report*, January 2010.
3. CIFAS was awarded Specified Anti-Fraud Organisation (SAFO) status by the Home Office, under Section 68 of the Serious Crime Act 2007 which came into force on 1 October 2008.

Chapter 20

1. The summary of each module's coverage for CIPFA's certificate is set out in Appendix E.
2. All police officers are classed as constables, sworn officers but not technically employees. As a result they had rights of tenure to whichever post they held.

Appendix F

1. Once the population is large enough the error correction factor is so tiny that there is no need to allow for population size in the formula.
2. At the time these tables were originally produced the entries were manually typeset. Our later table was automatically generated by computer from my colleagues' formulae and corrects typographical errors in the original tables.
3. If the population size is smaller the true probabilities gradually increase for each number. For example, at a sample size of 50 and no errors the probability of the error rate being below 1% is 39.5% for populations of 2,000 or more, but if the population is only 800 the probability increases to 40.5%.

Index